A Level Playing Field

A Level Playing Field

School Finance in the Northeast

Jane Fowler Morse

State University of New York Press

Published by
State University of New York Press, Albany

For information, address State University of New York Press,
194 Washington Avenue, Suite 305, Albany, NY 12210-2384

Production by Diane Ganeles
Marketing by Anne M. Valentine

Library of Congress Cataloging-in-Publication Data

Morse, Jane Fowler, 1940–
    A level playing field : school finance in the Northeast / Jane Flowler Morse.
        p. cm.
    Includes bibliographical references and index.
    ISBN-13: 978-0-7914-6931-6 (hardcover : alk. paper)
    ISBN-10: 0-7914-6931-X (hardcover : alk. paper)
    ISBN-13: 978-0-7914-6932-3 (pbk. : alk. paper)
    ISBN-10: 0-7914-6932-8 (pbk. : alk. paper)
    1. Public schools—Northeastern States—Finance. I. Title.

LB2825.M56 2007
379.1'10974—dc22

                                                        2005036303

10 9 8 7 6 5 4 3 2 1

I dedicate this book to my parents, Eleanor Woolley Fowler and Cedric Weeden Fowler, in grateful appreciation for instilling a sense of social justice in me as I grew up. Although they are long deceased, their deep concern for the welfare of working class people continues to inspire my work.

Contents

Tables

Preface

In 1968, I read Jonathan Kozol's book, *Death at an Early Age*. The descriptions of the harm done to children in school appalled me. They also rang a bell. In South Jersey in the late 1940s, I had seen my black friend, Frances, humiliated at school so much that one day she was driven to drink a bottle of ink in reply to our teacher's asking her, in annoyance, why she was so black. Frances was extremely talented. At ten she could split wood, wash clothes in a bucket, take care of her younger siblings, make Shirley Temple curls on her older sister, and slaughter, pluck, eviscerate, cut up, and cook a chicken on a woodstove. She worked picking crops in the fields in the summer to earn money for her family. It seemed to me that Frances (or Franny, as everyone except her teacher called her) could deal with everything, from her two-year-old brother Jimmy's tears over the refusal of the grocer to cut him a slice of baloney for a nickel, to the death of her father from exposure to agricultural chemicals. Frances knew how to survive. A grade behind me at Blue Anchor Grammar School, Franny disappeared from my sight after her freshman year in high school. After fifty years I still wonder, with admiration, love, and regret, what happened to her. Despite her incredible strength, Franny did not have much of a chance, but she was tough. I hope she survived, but I wish she had a chance to thrive. I also hope that no child will have to struggle to survive in the coming century. Unfortunately, this is not yet the case.

Kozol's book made me realize that I wanted to do something. In 1949 I could not help Franny, except by being her friend, but in the 1970s, mother of three young children, I could do something for children like her. I volunteered to tutor students at the local junior high my children would attend. My first student was a young black boy, Alex, who was about Franny's age when I had played with her in South Jersey, boiling over with hostility, struggling with learning disabilities and attention problems, but with a fine poetic and artistic streak. His teacher, Hilda Enoch, cared so deeply about each child that she wanted Alex to have the special attention he needed. After working with Hilda, I decided to become certified as a teacher so that I could do what she was doing. Years later, after teaching for more than a decade, I am a teacher of teachers.

The ideals of democracy—liberty and justice for all—require that there be a level playing field. To realize such an ideal, all children must receive a quality education. The dice cannot be loaded against some of them from the start. They must be equipped to participate fully, both as children and as adults, in the political, social, intellectual, artistic, and economic life of the community. For this reason, the United States had long proclaimed dedication to the ideal of free, tax-supported public education, offering equality of educational opportunity to all children regardless of their status. In 1647, the Massachusetts Bay Colony required towns of more than fifty households to establish public schools. In the 1830s, Horace Mann proclaimed a common education "the great equalizer," which would allow working-class children to escape the poverty of their parents. When the California Supreme Court ruled that the public school finance system of the state violated the equal protection clauses of both the constitution of California and the United States in *Serrano* v. *Priest* (1971), the justices quoted Horace Mann on education as a natural right.

> I believe in the existence of a great, immortal immutable principle of natural law, or natural ethics,—a principle antecedent to all human institutions, and incapable of being abrogated by any ordinance of man . . . , which proves *the absolute right* to an education of every human being that comes into the world, and which, of course, proves the correlative duty of every government to see that the means of that education are provided for all . . . (italics in original, reference omitted)[1]

Mann included girls and women, opening the door to higher education for women teachers in normal schools. In the heyday of the melting-pot metaphor, education was thought to serve as the vehicle of assimilation. In the 1920s and 1930s, George Counts and others thought that education could reconstruct society along more equitable lines. In the 1950s, James Conant pronounced that education should promote both social mobility and national security. In 1954, the historic Supreme Court case, *Brown* v. *Board of Education of Topeka*, declared unanimously, "separate schools are inherently unequal," mandating racial desegregation.[2] In the 1970s, the Pennsylvania Association for Retarded Children won a ruling against Pennsylvania, guaranteeing an appropriate education in the least restrictive environment for all handicapped children.[3]

Despite these ideals, reform of what essentially remains an unequal educational system has been painfully slow and difficult, with considerable backsliding after *Milliken* v. *Bradley* ruled mandatory busing unconstitutional in 1974. After years of desegregation plans, schools are resegregating. School finance, based largely on state aid and local property taxes, is grossly unequal, both within and among the states. Federal funding declines while unfunded federal mandates increase. Local control of schools remains an ideal, one which is, alas, believed to require local funding, although there is no particular reason that this must be the case. Poverty has increased steadily since 2002, especially for children under six, extreme poverty (half the poverty rate) is increasing, especially among black children, the income gap has widened, racial and economic isolation are up, and the official poverty line is so low that children falling just above, who desperately need social services, are denied them. The minimum wage is not livable, welfare has become workfare, and workfare often fails to provide child care. Many urban children are lead-poisoned, hungry, and without health care. Some are homeless. Equality of educational opportunity is an ideal without a reality. Yet public faith in the power of the educational system to remedy these wrongs remains strong.

In this book I argue that additional spending can produce better results for children who have not been accorded equitable school funding. I argue for equity rather than equality, since these children need more resources than their more fortunate peers to accomplish the same goals. Although there is no doubt that the money must be well spent, there is equally no doubt that money is required for children to receive a quality education. In fact, focusing on outcomes, as is now the mode of evaluation, instead of inputs, as researchers of the Coleman Report did in the 1950s, educators realize that disadvantaged children require substantially more resources. Rich people have never questioned the need for money for the education of their children, so it should be evident to them that there is also a need for adequate resources for poor children. Education policy makers know a great deal about what works, but politicians implement little of it. It is my hope that an examination of school funding will result in leveling the playing field for all children seeking an education as they struggle against the disadvantages that are not their doing and not under their, or their family's, control. The last line of Jonathan Kozol's *Savage Inequalities* has haunted me since its publication in 1991—"We soil them needlessly." It is time to stop.

The Organization of This Book

In chapter 1, I review issues and developments in school finance reform. In chapters 2, 3, and 4, I recount three recent attempts at school finance reform in New York, Ontario, and Vermont, where very different scenarios are playing out as I write. In chapters 5 and 6, I investigate the impacts of poverty and racism on children in school. In chapter 7, I address the question of justice asking, why is the political will to reform inequitable educational opportunities for children lacking? I conclude with some recommendations gleaned from the cases I have examined.

Acknowledgments

I would like to acknowledge the many people who assisted in my work, including my husband, Lars Mazzola, for his patience; my children Adina (who assisted with legal questions galore), Lonny, and Caleb Morse, for their inspiration; my colleagues, especially Sue Books, of SUNY at New Paltz; Rebecca Lewis of SUNY Geneseo for copyediting; my secretary, Dawn Rowe; my work-study, Christen Sullivan; and many students who inspired me to do this work, especially Bryce Ludlow, Sarah Ortner, Lisa Patanjo, and Julie Stone, who responded to my call in 1999 for students interested in studying inequitable school finance with youthful energy and enthusiasm.

Chapter 1

Education, Inequity, and the Level Playing Field

If all the rich and all of the church people should send their children to the public schools they would feel bound to concentrate their money on improving these schools until they met the highest ideals.

Susan B. Anthony, Letter to Dr. Sarah R. Dolley, 1900

The Need for Public Education

Political and social philosophers have long affirmed the need for education. In the *Republic*, Plato organizes his ideal state around an educational system. Aristotle's *Politics* proposes public education. Hellenistic, Roman, Medieval, Renaissance, and Baroque thinkers wrote about education. In the late seventeenth century, John Locke argued that the people have a right to overthrow a government that did not fulfill the purposes for which it was established—to protect natural rights to life, liberty, and property. In answer to the key question—"Who is to judge when the government needs to be replaced?" Locke replied, "The people shall judge."[1] For this, they must be educated. Because Locke's *Second Treatise on Government* provided the basis of the Bill of Rights, it has played a large role in education law.

In *Some Thoughts Concerning Education*,[2] Locke set forth the implications of his empiricist epistemology for education. He advised parents of the class of gentlemen to educate their children at home. Although Locke did not include girls in his plan, he illustrates the educational value of absorbing games and actual activities from his observations of girls playing jacks and learning to speak French from their maids. Locke believed that both boys and girls could learn. Scorning instruction in classical languages,

1

Locke derided forcing children to write essays in Latin on topics beyond their childish understanding. He proposed the astonishing ideas that children should study English and modern languages, have recess, read illustrated storybooks written at their level of understanding, play with educational games and toys, and even learn to dance.

A hundred years after Locke, Mary Wollstonecraft wrote an impassioned appeal that women be accorded an education in *A Vindication of the Rights of Women.*[3] She thought that cultivating reason was the avenue to virtue. She disagreed with Locke on home schooling, which isolated upper-class children, although she, too, disliked the boarding schools. Ahead of her time by more than a century, Wollstonecraft recommended establishing tax-supported, coeducational neighborhood day schools, attended by children of all social classes. She envisioned children of all levels in society learning and playing together without detrimental, false distinctions based on class, wealth, and gender. She wanted teachers to use the Socratic method; she thought children should be allowed to play; and, like Locke, she was aware of developmentally appropriate practice and age-appropriate educational materials. For this, Horace Walpole called her "a hyena in petticoats."[4] Her foresight was remarkable.

The question of who should provide schools and for what purposes was still unresolved in mid-nineteenth-century Britain. In *On Liberty*, John Stuart Mill advised that the government provide schooling, but only when parents were delinquent in doing so.[5] He feared too much uniformity if state schools became the norm. Although this is a step beyond Locke, it is a long way from establishing a right to an equal, public education. Wollstonecraft's proposal for public, tax-supported, comprehensive day schools fifty years before was more progressive than Mill's. In Mill's view, public schools represented a threat to individuality, a notion perhaps worth reconsidering in this time of standards and standardized testing.

In the colonies destined to become the United States, if parents wanted a school, they hired a teacher. Or, a teacher could set up shop, collecting fees. The Old Deluder Law of 1647 in the Massachusetts Bay Colony required towns of more than fifty households to establish a school so that children might resist the snares of that Old Deluder, Satan, by being able to read the Bible. During the colonial period schooling varied widely. After unification under the United States Constitution, the United States did not establish a national system of education. The Constitution does not contain an education clause, although it does have clauses useful in education finance litigation, which guarantee rights to life, liberty, property, and the pursuit of happiness (variously phrased) in the establishment clause, the equal protection clause, and the due process clause.[6] However, the tenth amendment reserves all powers not delegated to the federal government to the states, including education. This stopped the

Supreme Court from regulating funding, but not from mandating desegregation and special education, nor the Congress from passing the No Child Left Behind Act. In turn, states delegated education to local school districts, which they created for that purpose. Because of this history, it is commonly held in the United States that education is a local affair, subject to local control, although there are exceptions.[7]

In the 1830s, Secretary of the Massachusetts Board of Education Horace Mann conceived the Common School Movement, publicizing his ideas in *The Common School Journal*. Proclaiming education "the great equalizer," he believed that access to quality education would benefit not only the children of poor people, but also the nation, eliminating social unrest caused by the great divide between rich and poor. Mann thought this would be achieved by "common schools," which the state, not the town, supported and regulated. He wanted to minimize religious differences by limiting religion in public schools to the "common elements" of Christianity. This move offended Catholics, since the common elements were undeniably Protestant, prompting the development of a system of private Catholic schools that remains in place today. In becoming "common schools," public schools reduced their emphasis on religion, but did not eliminate it altogether. This remained unchanged until *Engel* v. *Vitale* (1959)[8] in New York barred school prayer under the establishment clause of the first amendment. The Constitutional commitment to separation of church and state implicit in the first amendment influenced education, but not until the second half of the twentieth century, and not without continuing opposition from the religious right.

With the spread of the Common School Movement beyond Massachusetts, education became the responsibility of states, rather than localities. Most state constitutions delegated their responsibility, including much of the funding, to local school districts, which they designated for that purpose.[9] This idea of local control created the inequitable school funding that persists at the beginning of the twenty-first century. In the second half of the twentieth century, states gradually assumed more control than localities over many aspects of schooling—regulating teacher education and certification, passing compulsory attendance laws, mandating curricula and testing, and, in the final decades of the twentieth century, adopting standards and high-stakes testing. States also gradually assumed a larger state share of funding, although this proportion is far from uniform. With the No Child Left Behind Act of 2001 (NCLB), the federal government assumed a larger role in regulation, imposing more federal testing, additional qualifications for teachers, and financial consequences for so-called failing schools, although without sufficient funding to cover the costs of these mandates. Federal funding has shrunk in the past several decades from highs of 7 percent to 9 percent to lows of 4 percent to 5 percent, a figure that varies widely by district and program.

Despite the lack of an education clause in the Constitution, in 1954 the United States Supreme Court held that segregated schools violated the Fourteenth Amendment's equal protection clause. In *Brown* v. *Board of Education of Topeka* (1954), all nine Supreme Court justices agreed:

> Today, education is perhaps the most important function of state and local governments. Compulsory school attendance laws and the great expenditures for education both demonstrate our recognition of the importance of education to our democratic society. It is required in the performance of our most basic public responsibilities, even service in the armed forces. It is the very foundation of good citizenship. Today it is a principal instrument in awakening the child to cultural values, in preparing him for later professional training, and in helping him to adjust normally to his environment. In these days, it is doubtful that any child may reasonably be expected to succeed in life if he is denied the opportunity of an education. Such an opportunity, where the state has undertaken to provide it, is a right which must be made available to all on equal terms.[10]

The justices made it clear in their conclusion that this ruling was made under the Fourteenth Amendment, guaranteeing equal protection of the laws, including state laws, to all citizens of the United States, not under the due process elements of the Fifth and Fourteenth amendments. The *Brown* court concluded:

> . . . in the field of public education the doctrine of "separate but equal" has no place. Separate educational facilities are inherently unequal. Therefore, we hold that the plaintiffs and others similarly situated for whom the actions have been brought are, by reason of the segregation complained of, deprived of the equal protection of the laws guaranteed by the Fourteenth Amendment. This disposition makes unnecessary any discussion whether such segregation also violates the Due Process Clause of the Fourteenth Amendment.[11]

Despite their care to avoid the due process clause in *Brown*, the court issued a much-overlooked ruling, *Bolling* v. *Sharpe* (1954),[12] on the same day, which applied the due process clause to school desegregation. *Bolling* fell under Supreme Court jurisdiction since it was brought in the District of Columbia. Chief Justice Warren argued in *Bolling* that "the 'equal protection of the laws' is a more explicit safeguard of prohibited unfairness than 'due process of law,' and, therefore, we do not imply that the two are always interchangeable phrases."

But he added, "Discrimination may be so unjustifiable as to be violative of due process."[13] Consequently, the court ruled that black school children in the District of Columbia could not be racially segregated in the public schools simply because the Fourteenth Amendment only applied to states. In Warren's words:

> . . . it would be unthinkable that the same Constitution would impose a lesser duty on the Federal Government. We hold that racial segregation in the public schools of the District of Columbia is a denial of the due process of law guaranteed by the Fifth Amendment to the Constitution.[14]

In *Goss* v. *Lopez* (1975)[15] the court ruled that students could not be suspended without due process (a hearing), because education is a "property" protected by the Fifth Amendment.[16] Nevertheless, the due process clause has not been used in school finance litigation. *Goss* is consistent with *Bolling*, but the court's 1973 ruling in *San Antonio Independent School District et al.*, v. *Demetrio Rodriguez, et al.*,[17] holding that education is not a fundamental right under the Constitution is clearly inconsistent with both.

Early School Finance Litigation

Brown seemed to early school finance litigators to be good precedent for equal protection of the laws in education finance, since equal protection was guaranteed in desegregation cases. In the first wave of finance cases, *Serrano* v. *Priest* was based on the equal protection clauses of both the United States Constitution and the California Constitution.[18] The California Supreme Court ruled for the plaintiffs in 1971, overturning an earlier dismissal of the charges. The court declared:

> We are called upon to determine whether the California public school financing system, with its substantial dependence on local property taxes and resultant wide disparities in school revenue, violates the equal protection clause of the Fourteenth Amendment. We have determined that this funding scheme invidiously discriminates against the poor because it makes the quality of a child's education a function of the wealth of his parents and neighbors. Recognizing as we must that the right to an education in our public schools is a fundamental interest which cannot be conditioned on wealth, we can discern no compelling state purpose necessitating the present method of financing. We have concluded, therefore, that such a system cannot withstand constitutional challenge and must fall before the equal protection clause.[19]

The court remanded the case to the trial court, having decided that there was sufficient cause for action. The trial commenced in 1972 and was decided in favor of the plaintiffs in 1974. The court determined that the California school finance system did not violate the Fourteenth Amendment of the federal constitution, but did violate the state constitution. This decision was appealed, and the state supreme court upheld the ruling under the state's equal protection clause in 1977. The intervening years brought the *Rodriguez* case to the Supreme Court, which forced lawyers in *Serrano* to drop the federal violation. *Rodriguez* has had a tremendous impact on school finance litigation.

In 1973, when the Supreme Court of the United States chose to overrule the Texas courts in *Rodriguez*, not only were they inequitably funded, the Texas schools involved were also segregated. Admitting that there were "substantial disparities"[20] established in the case, the court was unwilling to mandate a federal remedy for fear that this would involve the court in further decisions for which they felt local policy makers should be responsible. This fateful five-to-four decision declared that education was not a "fundamental right"[21] under the United States constitution (despite the earlier declaration in *Brown*), nor were poor children a "suspect class"[22] as black children were in *Brown*. Consequently, the court applied rational basis scrutiny, rather than the strict scrutiny required when a constitutional right is invoked. Under rational basis scrutiny, the state need only claim that there is some rational basis for its action. Texas claimed local control of the schools as its rational basis. Although Marshall's dissent rejected local control as a rational basis for inequitable funding, nevertheless, the controversial five-to-four decision stands as precedent. Marshall called "local control," proffered as "an excuse" for "grossly inequitable funding," a "sham."[23] He pointed out that there is no necessary connection between state-supplied funding and local control. Indeed, he remarked that local control was a "cruel irony" for poor districts, which had to tax at high rates to provide the bare minimum. Such districts could not choose to provide an excellent education.[24] Marshall also held that the clearly disparate impact of inequitable school funding violated the Civil Rights Act of 1964.

> In my view, then, it is inequality—not some notion of gross inadequacy—of educational opportunity that raises a question of denial of equal protection of the laws. I find any other approach to the issue unintelligible, and without directing principle. Here, appellees have made a substantial showing of wide variations in educational funding and the resulting educational opportunity afforded to the school children of Texas. This discrimination is, in large measure, attributable to significant disparities in the taxable wealth of local Texas school districts. This is a sufficient showing to raise a substantial question of discriminatory state action in violation of the Equal Protection Clause.[25]

Despite Marshall's opposition, the majority ruled against any federal action in school funding. The decision in *Rodriguez* drove school funding cases into state courts. Although state courts are free to apply intermediate or strict scrutiny, they often choose rational basis scrutiny following *Rodriguez,* despite the fact that many state constitutions have education clauses that allow education to be construed as a fundamental right.

In 1984, parents and districts in Texas brought another case against school funding, under the Texas constitution, *Edgewood* v. *Kirby*.[26] The trial court ruled the Texas funding formula unconstitutional, but this ruling was overturned on appeal in 1988 in a two-to-one decision based on the Supreme Court ruling that education was not a fundamental right in *Rodriguez.* However, the Texas Supreme Court ruled unanimously that the funding formula was unconstitutional under the Texas constitution, returning to the trial court's ruling.[27] Then the battle between the courts and the legislature began. The situation was complicated by a provision in the Texas constitution forbidding the establishment of a statewide property tax. The plan the legislature first proposed was challenged by the plaintiff school districts and ruled unconstitutional. The second plan was challenged by wealthy districts, which would lose money, and was also ruled unconstitutional. By 1993, the legislature passed a plan providing five options for recalcitrant districts to share their wealth, which the court accepted in 1995, after more challenges, although the judge added that it needed more work and periodic updating.[28] This took place twenty-three years after the United States Supreme Court decision in *Rodriguez* in 1973, and twenty-six years after the original filing of *Rodriguez* in 1969.

Two weeks after the *Rodriguez* decision, the New Jersey Supreme Court issued the first ruling that declared inequitable school funding unconstitutional under the New Jersey Constitution, in *Robinson* v. *Cahill* (1973).[29] The court declared a violation of the state education clause, which mandated that a "thorough and efficient" education be provided the children of New Jersey. *Robinson* v. *Cahill* was followed by a long series of failed policies, more rulings, more failed policies, and more rulings before the Supreme Court judged that the solution was constitutional. The same thing happened in New York, California, and other states. Solutions often took more than thirty years to implement, cases followed cases in succession, and, in many states, there is still egregious inequality. Since *Rodriguez* had ruled out appeal to the federal constitution, subsequent cases cited state education clauses, marking a change in strategy and making a nationwide, uniform solution to the problem of inequitable school funding impossible.

Although *Brown I* laid the groundwork for federal enforcement of equal educational opportunity in integrated schools in 1954, the decision was not construed in later cases to include equitable funding. In fact, some states in the years before *Brown I* attempted to equalize funding for segregated schools, in an effort to avoid desegregation by complying with *Plessy* v. *Ferguson's*[30] "separate but equal" formulation. Neither did *Brown I* make clear that *de facto* segregated schools (located in the north) were un-constitutional, nor that inequitably funded schools were unconstitutional. Ordered to integrate "with all deliberate speed" in *Brown II* (1955),[31] states stalled on enforcing the decision. Some southern states even closed their public schools, shifting education to the private sector to avoid inte-gration. Efforts to enforce *Brown* have been hampered by court rulings in the last half of the twentieth century that effectively overruled *Brown*. De-segregation would have required hard work over the long term to remedy a complex series of factors. Where desegregation had at least begun, mostly in the South, it has recently been undone. Schools are resegregat-ing. In the *de facto* segregated schools in the North, schools were never de-segregated.[32] In the 1970s, regressive rulings interfered with what progress had been made. The *Milliken* v. *Bradley* (1974)[33] decision in De-troit removed one of the most readily available remedies: busing children between districts. In *Milliken II*,[34] the following year, the court ordered re-medial programs for the segregated Detroit Metro district. *Milliken II* dis-regarded the unanimous *Brown* judgment, "Separate educational facilities are inherently unequal."[35] Nor were the remedial programs effective. Re-districting might have offered a solution, but the suburban districts op-posed it effectively on the grounds that they were not involved in the harm, so they should not be involved in the remedy. By the late 1970s, it appeared that *de facto* segregation was almost impossible to eliminate, be-cause the court ruled out mandatory busing. In an all-black district like Detroit Metro, there were few other strategies.

Before 1989, school finance battles had gone through two stages in strategy: *Serrano* sought equality of inputs; the New Jersey cases sought eq-uity of inputs. The Kentucky case, *Rose* v. *Council for Better Education* (1989), marked the beginning of a third strategy, one that focused on the adequacy of the education supplied.[36] The Kentucky Supreme Court, upholding the trial court, mandated that the entire state's educational system be revamped. The justices did not hesitate to set a template, al-though they explicitly declared the implementation of the reform to be "the sole responsibility of the General Assembly." The template proved, in time, to be the most far-reaching of those proposed by state courts and became a model for other, although often less ambitious, templates. It included seven points as follows:

> (i)   sufficient oral and written communication skills to enable students to function in a complex and rapidly changing civilization;

(ii)   sufficient knowledge of economic, social, and political sys-
         tems to enable the student to make informed choices;
(iii)   sufficient understanding of governmental processes to en-
         able the student to understand the issues that affect his or
         her community, state, and nation;
(iv)   sufficient self-knowledge and knowledge of his or her mental
         and physical wellness;
(v)   sufficient grounding in the arts; to enable each student to
         appreciate his or her cultural and historical heritage;
(vi)   sufficient training or preparation for advanced training in ei-
         ther academic or vocational fields so as to enable each child
         to choose and pursue life work intelligently;
(vii)   sufficient levels of academic or vocational skills to enable
         public school students to compete favorably with their
         counterparts in surrounding states, in academics or in the
         job market.[37]

The Kentucky Supreme Court stated that these seven characteristics were
"*minimum* goals" (emphasis in original) and defined "efficient" schools as
"free" schools "available to all" and "substantially uniform throughout
the state," which provided "equal educational opportunities to all Kentucky children, regardless of place of residence or economic circumstances."[38] The formulation made it clear that a mere "minimally
adequate" education, such as the earlier New York cases stated, is not sufficient. Interestingly, the Kentucky case involved largely rural white children, although children of color in urban areas also benefited. Many
later adequacy cases, notably the *Paynter* and *Campaign for Fiscal Equity*
cases in Rochester and New York City, involved mostly urban children of
color and did not fare as well as the Kentucky case.

 Paynter v. *State* and *Campaign for Fiscal Equity* in New York contained
an element of equity of outcomes, although it was not quite the same as
the Kentucky concept of adequacy. Earlier New York decisions had specified the level of adequacy to be "minimally adequate," enough to provide only the "sound basic education" stated in the state's education
clause. In each case, the children concerned were largely children of
color. Recently, the desegregation elements of school funding cases have
been abandoned, as in *United States* v. *Yonkers*,[39] in which children in segregated schools were accorded funding for remedial programs. This
strategy is more reminiscent of *Plessy* v. *Ferguson's* "separate but equal"
than *Brown's* "separate is inherently unequal." The idea implies equity because children who are "difficult to educate" need more resources. Although it might be preferable not to classify children as "difficult to
educate," (which allows people to ignore root causes of the difficulty, like

poverty and racism, by blaming the victim), it is true that children who have fewer resources in their homes and communities need more in their schools. Many of these children live in poverty, are urban, recent immigrants, or members of various minority groups. In enormous districts like New York City, it is difficult to see how desegregation of the schools can be accomplished without addressing the root causes of segregation in the society. How this strategy will play out remains to be seen, although it was successful in New York's final decision in *Campaign for Fiscal Equity* v. *State.* Success still requires legislation that works to remedy the situation, and after that, research on effective ways to use the additional funding. In *Payner* v. *State,*[40] which failed at the Court of Appeals, a solution to either segregation or an inadequate education is not even in the offing.

Resegregation, Doubtful Remedies, and Other Problems

During much of the twentieth century, schools in many urban areas were inadequate. Often segregated by race and class, they rarely enjoyed equal funding, let alone equitable funding affording poor children an equal educational opportunity.[41] This situation persists in many places. In *Board of Education of Oklahoma City Public Schools* v. *Dowell* (1991), the Supreme Court ruled that a school district need be declared "unitary," that is, desegregated, only once, after which it was released from court supervision.[42] In practical terms, this meant that districts were free to resegregate, which happened in Oklahoma City by 1996, three years later.[43] In *Missouri* v. *Jenkins* (1995)[44] the United States Supreme Court ruled out using statewide taxes to create "desegregative attractiveness" to lure white students from the suburbs to magnet schools in inner cities. In consequence of these rulings, resegregation emerged in the 1990s, mostly in urban schools, more in the North than the South.[45] In *Sheff* v. *O'Neill* (1996),[46] the state of Connecticut ruled that the hypersegregation and economic isolation of school children in Hartford violated the state's equal protection and desegregation clauses. Alas, without busing or redistricting, remedies are hard to find.[47] Dennis Parker reported in 1999 that the panel appointed by the governor to make recommendations on how to implement this ruling issued a report that addressed the main problem (racial and economic isolation) in only one of its four recommendations. According to Parker, the panel suggested remedies that had already proved "ineffectual" and "lacked enforceable goals and timetables."[48] The Harvard Civil Rights Project reported in 2003 that Connecticut is still one of the states in which the percentage of black exposure to whites is lowest.[49]

De facto segregation is maintained, in part, because Title VIII of the 1964 Civil Rights Act, containing the fair housing law, has not been enforced. Redrawing district lines to desegregate neighborhood schools is rare.[50] Nor have all hypersegregation cases been decided in favor of the plaintiffs. In New York, several cases on behalf of children attending segregated urban schools have failed or been dismissed. Plaintiffs in New York's *Paynter* cases complained that the racial and economic isolation caused by the concentration of low-income housing in the city of Rochester resulted in the "wholesale academic failure" of city school children. These charges were dismissed in two stages, the trial court dismissing some, the Appellate Division the remainder. On June 26, 2003, on final appeal, the Court of Appeals upheld the dismissal of charges in *Paynter*, despite Judge George Bundy Smith's stinging dissent. Smith reviewed the history of New York's commitment to educating all children, including those born into poverty, reviewed cases in which other states declared education a fundamental right under education clauses similar to New York's, and placed blame on the state for intentionally creating the racial and economic isolation of schools in the Rochester City School District.[51] *Paynter* showed the Rochester City Schools violate *Brown*, but remedies for desegregation are difficult to obtain in the current political climate. The judges dismissed the charges because the funding is not inequitable, just inadequate. It doesn't compensate for segregation, which is illegal.

School choice has received attention as a remedy for schools that are "failing" according to standards set by NCLB. Charters, vouchers, and magnet schools could provide ways for parents to improve their children's education now, rather than waiting twenty or thirty years for courts and legislatures to solve the problem. Unfortunately, there are serious drawbacks to all three plans. Vouchers redirect public school money to private schools, many of them religious. If not means-tested, vouchers provide a subsidy to parents wealthy enough to send their children to private schools. They often are insufficient to cover the entire cost of a private education, which includes additional costs like uniforms, books, and transportation.[52] Charter schools appeal to parents who are knowledgeable about education, can provide transportation, and have time to devote to volunteering. But charter schools have yet to prove that they increase achievement or produce a "ripple effect" of improvement in public schools.[53] All three modes of "choice" are selective (unless run by lotteries) or may be exclusive on some grounds. They may have racial quotas; they may exclude children with disabilities; they may require parents to volunteer. They may exclude children whose grades are not good, or children requiring special education, or children who need transportation. Resources for children left behind in the unimproved neighborhood schools are diminished by "choice" plans. Furthermore, there are not enough "choice" schools to go around. NCLB, intended to provide an exit option for parents whose children are in "failing" schools, in 2003 spawned lawsuits contesting lax enforcement in New York.[54] Low participation in remedies results from lack of information, lack of places to transfer children, or unwillingness on the part of parents or children to transfer far from home.[55] Tutoring services, for which school districts have to pay, are inadequate or unavailable. All "choice" options leave the so-called "neighborhood" schools unimproved, and with less funding to remediate their problems. Furthermore, punitive removal of funding as a "punishment" for failing schools makes no sense. Research suggests that "choice" programs will result in more social stratification, not less.[56]

Education, once considered the leveling device for poor people, varies in quality. Wealthy and middle-class white people have long insisted that their children receive a well-funded, quality education. Poor, minority, immigrant, urban, rural, and working-class children have faced inequitable, discriminatory schooling for centuries. In the twentieth century, a host of deliberate public policies such as redlining areas in order to deny mortgages or loans, refusing to sell housing in the suburbs to blacks, location of freeways that divide poor neighborhoods while providing easy access to the suburbs for middle-class whites, lack of enforcement of building safety codes, urban pollution, an unsafe environment, racial and economic isolation, and welfare "reform" have contributed to what has become a crisis.[57] Social services such as paid maternity leave, health care, day care, nutrition programs, and state-supported early childhood education programs, which could improve the lives of the increasing number of children living in poverty, are lacking. Many other industrialized countries offer such services. Fair housing laws, once prominent in political debate, have receded into the background. Even wealthy suburban neighborhoods are rarely mixed. According to Henry Louis Gates Jr., in the 2004 PBS documentary, *America Beyond The Color Line,* upper class black neighborhoods exist, but they are "self-segregated."[58] More commonly, as blacks from the city move to the suburbs, neighborhoods "tip" because of white flight. What began as desegregation becomes resegregation, but in the suburbs. Inner cities have become hypersegregated, the gap between rich and poor has grown wider, child poverty has increased while the poverty level set by the federal government is absurdly low, at $14,494 for a family of a parent and two children.[59] The federal minimum wage of $5.15 per hour has not been raised since September 1, 1997; the formula dates from 1955. This is not a livable wage. Even New York's slated increase in the minimum wage to $7.15 an hour in 2007 is scarcely livable, although it is better. Many working Americans are now referred to as "the working poor," at 185 percent to 200 percent of the poverty level. Workers' productivity in the United

States has been increasing, but not their pay. As productivity goes up, so does unemployment. As unemployment goes up, those remaining employed must often accept wage cuts, longer hours, and more work to keep their jobs. In 2004, legislation threatened overtime pay; meanwhile, part-time employees at Wal-mart are forced to work off the clock but receive no benefits. The working poor get poorer and work longer hours to keep their precarious jobs, and so it goes.

In the meantime, so-called welfare reform has affected many poor families, taking mothers away from their small children without supplying adequate, affordable day care or training for jobs other than menial minimum-wage jobs.[60] In some cases, the "reforms" have deprived mothers of a chance to finish their college degrees or seek training for better jobs.[61] On the other side, people on workfare can't make a living, nor can they lose their jobs without losing their benefits. However, the pool of low-skilled, service jobs is shrinking.[62] A third-world population is emerging within an affluent first-world country, which does not bode well for democracy. The impact of poverty on children is tremendous, as I shall document in chapter 5. Racism, which also abounds, is equally detrimental, as I shall document in chapter 6. Children do not choose the socioeconomic conditions of their existence, but they are treated as if they were somehow culpable. Schooling, which could address some of these disparities, fails do to so. The school-to-prison pipeline is the result.

Lacking: The Political Will to Reform School Finance Reform

The political will to remedy social injustice seems to be lacking, although people express outrage at the status quo. Part of this is the lack of will to fix inequitable school funding. The courts have failed to enforce equal educational opportunity under the equal protection clause, following *Brown*, or under the due process clause, following *Bolling* v. *Sharpe*. Many factors contribute to the lack of political will. The main argument of the defendants in the *Rodriguez* case stemmed from a common belief that local control, needed to maintain local interest and support of schools, depends on local financing, although there is no necessary connection. Local financing has, in turn, traditionally depended on local property taxes, but the tax districts, whether school districts, counties, or towns, have widely varying resources. Tax burden varies inversely in proportion to the wealth of the district; poorer districts must set higher rates to provide even minimal services. State aid supposedly evens out the inequities, but this rarely works, since the aid formulae must be decided in legislatures where powerful, suburban constituencies rule. Where the state's share of the budget is high, the funding is more equitable. The average state share is around 50 percent. Even if states manage to fund schools equitably (and some do), inequities among the states would remain. A child's educational opportunities should no more depend on place of residence than on gender, racial or ethnic identity, socioeconomic status, immigrant status, language, handicapping conditions, or other accidental factors.

In addition to the issues of local control and property taxes, inertia, precedent, and tradition contribute to the difficulty of obtaining school finance reform. Most people are conservative by nature and like to do things as they have done them in the past. Many thinkers in the classical liberal tradition propose that people are naturally inclined to be self-interested, although others propose that perhaps they could be educated to seek the common good, or at least to be ethical in seeking their own self-interest. According to the classical liberal tradition, in addition to being self-interested, people form political factions to pursue special interests. The tax revolt in California following *Serrano* resulted in capping increases in property taxes. Proposition 13 revealed taxpayers thinking primarily of their own pocketbooks, not the common good. Now, more than twenty-five years later, California's once highly ranked schools are among the lowest. In *The Federalist Papers*, Number 10, Madison argued in the early 1790s that the new constitution will "break and control the violence of faction,"[63] but will not be able to change the factional nature of human beings themselves:

> As long as the reason of man continues fallible, and he is at liberty to exercise it, different opinions will be formed. As long as the connection subsists between his reason and his self-love, his opinions and his passions will have a reciprocal influence on each other and the former will be objects to which the latter will attach themselves. (*Federalist Papers*, 78)

According to Madison, diversity of faculties produces a differential in the ability to acquire property, which inevitably leads to diversity of interests because some people will be rich (presumably the intelligent people) and others poor (presumably the unintelligent people). From this arises the misconception that poor people are poor because they are not intelligent enough to be rich. In this conception, their poverty, since it arises from their own nature, is irremediable. Madison concluded that factions cannot be avoided, only mitigated: "The latent causes of faction are thus sown in the nature of man; and we see them everywhere brought into different degree of activity, according to the different circumstances of civil society" (79). The "greater variety of parties" under the new constitution, he believed, would provide security for minority rights against "local prejudices" and "schemes of injustice" (84) because permanent factions contrary to the public good will be less likely to form in such a large group (77–78).

Unfortunately, history has proved Madison wrong. It is now apparent that "intelligence," including that tested by pencil and paper tests, can be taught. As evidence, test scores of United States citizens in general have been rising while gaps between minority groups formerly thought to be inferior by nature and privileged white students supposed to be superior are shrinking.[64] Nor are the fluid, shifting groups that Madison envisioned characteristic of politics in the United States today. Contrary to Madison's view, the two-party system is entrenched in custom; many people even believe that it is enshrined in the Constitution. Unfortunately, the right of minorities to an equitable education has become more difficult to protect, despite *Brown*, since the *Rodriguez* court refused to accord education constitutional protection as a fundamental right. Jurists, scholars, and legal writers have suggested that an implicit right to an education could be construed as supporting explicit rights granted in the constitution, such as the right to participate in the political process, the right to due process, or the right to equal protection of the laws. The right to vote in state elections is not explicitly granted, but has been supported in federal decisions concerning voting rights and reapportionment cases in state elections.[65] Other implicit rights include the right to procreate (or not), the right to travel, the right to desegregated schools and housing, and more. The courts could have chosen to protect the right to an education similarly, and could still define and protect the right to a "minimally adequate" education without overturning *Rodriguez's* "absolute deprivation."[66]

Education is often thought to be a conservative venture, in the traditional sense defined by Edmund Burke in his *Reflections on the French Revolution*. Burke maintains that political institutions evolve gradually through experience. Gradual change makes much more sense to him than Thomas Paine's call for a revolution every generation if necessary. In Burke's view, "A spirit of innovation is generally the result of a selfish temper, and confined views."[67] People who attempt it are "confounded by the complication of distempered passions, their reason is disturbed; their views become vast and perplexed; to others inexplicable; to themselves uncertain" (194). Simply put, Burke warns against rocking the boat. Many educators have long seen their function as reproduction of cultural knowledge and values, rather than transformation. Perhaps because of this idea, education has changed little during the second half of the twentieth century. Many administrators are concerned with budgets and bond issues, hiring, school-community relations, buildings, and capital outlay, not innovative pedagogy or critical literacy, certainly not challenging the political and social status quo by promoting social justice. Instead, their goal is static—to produce a few "meritocratic" leaders and a large, docile workforce. Their epistemology focuses on re-productive knowledge.

For decades the organization of schooling has remained much the same, for the most part, in spite of some advances.[68] Funding has under-gone little real reform. Legislatures sometimes cooperate with court man-dates, but often they do not. State constitutions contain some form of education clause, classified into four categories from weak to strong,[69] and often an equal protection clause as well, yet some states with weak clauses take strong action; others with strong clauses resist reform.[70] Since state legislatures rarely take up the banner of school finance reform of their own volition, plaintiffs have turned to the courts for redress. This raises ar-guments about separation of powers and judicial activism. Some state courts are reluctant to step into the arena of school funding policy on the grounds that this is the responsibility of the legislature.[71] Others are less re-luctant.[72] The question becomes, what level of educational opportunity—minimally adequate, excellent, or something in between—should be provided to the children of a state? Should public schooling provide an equal, equitable, or differentiated opportunity? The goals of schooling de-termine what constitutes a quality education, an adequate education, or even a minimally adequate education. Some courts are willing to set a tem-plate for education, be it excellent, adequate, or minimal.[73] Others are not.[74] Some templates are more ambitious than others.[75] The questions of judicial activism and efficacy may prevent courts from setting a template ei-ther out of respect for separation of powers or fear that if they do, the leg-islature may refuse to act on it.

Another issue that retards reform is the cost of education and the apparent inefficiency of money spent under some circumstances. A critic of the equity movement, Eric Hanushek claims that "throwing money at the schools" has not increased test scores, so it must be ineffective.[76] The loaded language of this claim appeals to critics of the schools, property tax resisters, and opponents of what is regarded as excessive government intervention. But Hanushek's view assumes that test scores provide reli-able and valid evidence of effective schools. This is not always the case.[77] Hanushek also neglects to take into account increased expenditures on special education. He does not correct for inflation. Nor does he con-sider the impact of money removed from schools by magnets, vouchers, and charters. Richard Rothstein points out that spending on special ed-ucation accounts for much of the increase.[78] In addition, Hanushek's data does not follow a cohort of students longitudinally, but compares students in different grade levels over short periods of time. The prob-lem with this strategy is that the effects of educational spending are cumulative. Children do not recover from lack of resources in a year.

Furthermore, even if educators agreed that tests are reliable and valid, it matters how scores are analyzed and interpreted. It also matters whether the content of tests reflects what children are learning. It is easier to test trivial "factoids" than important skills, attitudes, and processes of constructing knowledge.

In addition, there are other goals of education beyond test scores. They may be personal, such as parental and student satisfaction, personal development, happiness, or obtaining meaningful employment. They consist of acquiring kinds of knowledge, skills, and dispositions that are not on the tests—how to do science, as opposed to memorizing what is considered "normal" science at the time,[79] how to read and write for information and appreciation, how to think mathematically, how to interact productively and pleasantly with others, how to recognize and utilize personal strengths. These goals are not necessarily connected to test scores. Even if we adopt some rather unlovely goals that have been proposed, such as training an efficient workforce, acquiring military and technological superiority, or having a competitive economy, these are not necessarily advanced by improving test scores. The only goal that would be unequivocally confirmed by test scores is the goal of exceeding the test scores of other districts or countries. This goal also fails to address the reliability and validity of the tests, as well as the educational value of the material tested.

When the scores are disaggregated by poverty (of the children and of the district), they show clearly that money does matter in education. Many districts in the United States have not collected data that can be disaggregated to yield this information. A benefit of NCLB may be the requirement that test scores be disaggregated by race and ethnicity, but only if the data is used to provide resources where they are needed. Bruce Biddle used data sets from the Second International Mathematics Study (SIMS), Third International Mathematics and Science Study (TIMSS), and the National Assessment of Educational Progress (NAEP), in combination with figures on funding from *Education Week's* Quality Counts issues, to show that United States scores from advantaged districts are highly competitive with other nations. Indeed, advantaged United States students score below only Japan and Singapore on SIMS and TIMSS.

Unfortunately, the same is not true for disadvantaged districts, whose scores are comparable to those of Nigeria and Swaziland. Not only are there individual differences in scores between advantaged and disadvantaged children, but there are huge differences between states that spend more and states that spend less on education, as well as states where child poverty is high and those where it is low. Biddle found that school funding and child poverty together account for 55 percent of variances in state scores.[80] Hanushek and others apply the business model to education—schools must be cost-effective, the bottom line is all that matters, and educated children are products to benefit the economy. But somehow these critics manage to ignore the human wastefulness of not allowing children sufficient resources to maximize their potential.

Accomplishing Goals Requires Resources

As educational reform proceeds, it is certainly desirable to think about the goals of education. If John Dewey is right in his proposition that practice informs theory, then reforms have to be honed through practice. Reflection on what the goals of education might be, as well as how educators plan to reach them, is in order; but the value of any proposed reforms might not materialize immediately. Children's learning advances longitudinally. If we could teach them everything in one year, school would be much simpler and cheaper. In addition, many goals of schooling are not academic, but have to do with developing skills, dispositions, socialization, character, and so forth, along with knowledge. In focusing on test scores, conservatives ignore goals that are not testable in this way, many of which can and must be cultivated in schools.

Using test scores as the primary indication of success invites inappropriate, invidious comparisons among children and among schools, following a model of competition. An ideal society does not consist of individuals competing against each other to engross the most resources for themselves, either locally or globally. As Dewey says, people should want for every child what all parents want for their own children.[81] His definition of society supports a cooperative model. "Society is a number of people held together because they are working along common lines, in a common spirit, and with reference to common aims." Consequently, school should be a "miniature community, an embryonic society," which aims at developing a "spirit of social cooperation and community life" (302–303). Inequitable funding is incompatible with the very aim of education, just as is competitive testing aimed at rank-ordering children, rather than diagnosing their educational needs. To achieve a just society, we must value justice over expediency in our arrangements for school finance. Surely most people want to live in a community of well-educated, civil, cultured, skillful, and happy people who have a disposition to contribute to the common good, rather than in a divided, cut-throat world of haves and have-nots. Democracy does not flourish where some people have the power to advance their own self-interest and others do not.

A full list of goals for a quality education might include:

1. civility, politeness, taking turns, sharing, interpersonal relations, citizenship; the feeling that "what I do matters"; a disposition to be politically thoughtful, open-minded, and active; an understanding of others as individuals possessing equal human dignity; a disposition to respect the rights of others and to be proactive on others' behalf, and related social skills;

2. a disposition to be thoughtfully introspective, to develop a realistic understanding of one's self, the potentialities one possesses, and how to develop them; dispositions of attentiveness, open-mindedness, and responsiveness; an understanding of how one's life circumstances have contributed to or detracted from one's accomplishments; a positive attitude toward oneself and others; a disposition to care for and about others;

3. knowledge of one's own history and that of others; an understanding that historical accounts of events vary according to the life experiences and outlooks of different peoples; an awareness and acceptance of the cultural diversity of the world; knowledge of alternative versions of history, including social history, women's history, histories of the enslavement and liberation, working-class history, histories of imperialism, histories of religions and cultures, and related matters;

4. knowledge of reading, skills of comprehension, and critical assessment of print, nonprint, and electronic media used for pleasure and information; reading and speaking knowledge of at least one language other than one's own and familiarity with the culture of the people speaking that language;

5. knowledge of mathematics and the role that mathematics plays in human life; an ability to solve problems mathematically, an awareness of the relationships and patterns of numbers and their explanatory and descriptive power; knowledge of the history of mathematics;

6. knowledge of the natural sciences and the role of public policy in protecting the environment; knowledge of the hard sciences and their uses in human life; an understanding of the importance of scientific knowledge in human life and an appreciation of the history of science, including an assessment of how scientific knowledge is advanced and an understanding of the contributions of many diverse scientists;

7. knowledge of politics and economics sufficient to understand and assess the impact of public policies on human beings and to inform participation in public life; sufficient knowledge of economics to make wise and ethical decisions regarding the use of personal and public funds; a commitment to social justice

and the common good by promoting the economic well-being
of all denizens of the earth;

8. physical fitness, a disposition to participate in lifetime sports and
    physical activities; knowledge of nutrition, exercise, and health
    sufficient to promote the well-being of oneself and others;

9. knowledge of the fine arts for appreciation and production; par-
    ticipation in art for pleasure and expression; knowledge of the
    practical arts that allow people's lives to be more comfortable,
    safe, convenient, and aesthetically pleasing, such as rewiring ap-
    pliances, basic carpentry, roofing, guttering, interior decorating,
    child care, management of personal finances, cooking, sewing,
    gardening.[82]

In short, ideally, children should be cooperative, sympathetic, informed,
critically literate, pleasant, artistic, ethical, employable, productive, civil,
social, familial, healthy, and happy. Such an expansive list of goals will
cost more to accomplish than a "minimally adequate" education aiming
at eighth grade proficiency. It might also seem to be subjective, but it is
all too easy to forget that human beings decide what to include and what
to exclude on the tests. They make up the questions, decide how to score
the answers, and set the passing level on tests. Tests are not as objective
as they appear.

Until choices are made concerning goals, issues like the thorough-
ness, efficiency, and soundness of education, cannot be assessed. How
much a society is willing to pay for education limits such choices. In the
early nineteenth century, a fourth-grade education was an accomplishment; later, eighth grade. During the twentieth century, high school became common. By the end of the twentieth century, some form of higher
education—vocational training or college, and some graduate or professional school—became the norm for many. A standard of basic literacy
and numeracy would not be particularly hard or expensive to accomplish.[83] But surely citizens of a democracy want a standard higher than
this in a complex world where children have, on the whole, less adult supervision, and must make, as adults, more decisions requiring critical
thinking skills and knowledge of complex technological, social, political,
scientific, and economic issues. This means more public expense. Other
demands for public resources raise the question of priorities. Conservatives assume that test scores provide an accurate measure of success, but
test scores are enhanced by items that cost money: smaller classes, qualified teachers, a longer school year, individual attention, after-school
care, nutrition and health programs. Such policies may contribute to better test scores, but they are also valuable for more than test scores. A

model of education that is stingy with resources, crowds classrooms, and pays small salaries will not attract the best people to the teaching profession or keep them there. Neither will the concept of offering an education that is only minimally adequate.[84] Differences over efficiency in spending money on education arise from competing claims about the goals of education, the means of achieving them, and the proper measure to assess progress toward them. Although these are issues on which reasonable people may differ, there is a double standard. No one questions whether an expensive education is better for the children of the wealthy. Only where the poor are concerned is the value of additional funding questioned.

In school funding, equity is important. Equity means that children who need more services, get more resources. As the situation stands now, they often get fewer, not more. Equality of educational spending does not account for differences in need, costs, composition of the student body, and so forth. In California's early school finance litigation, equality was the goal. Voters responded by leveling down; that is, lowering expenditures everywhere. Twenty-five years later, California schools had plummeted in national rankings.[85] Equality alone doesn't produce positive results; funding also needs to be adequate. Disparate need makes equal funding inadequate. The goals of education, quality of education, accessibility of education, equity and adequacy of funding, although difficult matters to decide, determine the quality of life in a society. The recent shift in school finance litigation to an emphasis on outcomes, rather than inputs, may help. On the other hand, in *Powell* v. *Ridge*,[86] Philadelphia's school finance case, charges were dismissed at the trial court, appealed to the United States Third Circuit Court of Appeals, which reinstated the charges, then remanded from the Supreme Court to the United States District Court, which declared that disparate need does not equal disparate impact in the terms of civil rights litigation. The decision ruled out questioning the adequacy of outcomes.

In *Sandoval* v. *Hagan*,[87] a key decision on the issue of challenging discrimination under the Civil Rights Act of 1964, the trial court upheld the plaintiffs' claim that Alabama discriminated against Spanish speakers by requiring drivers' tests to be given in English, pursuant to an "English only" constitutional amendment passed in 1990. The Eleventh United States Circuit Court upheld this decision in 1999, entering a permanent injunction against "English only" drivers' tests.[88] Unfortunately, in 2001, the United States Supreme Court overturned both previous decisions, ruling that there is no private right to sue for disparate impact violations of Title 601 of the Civil Rights Act in *Alexander* v. *Sandoval*.[89] This ruling has already proved an obstacle to school finance reform, and will continue to be so.

A common method of attempting to achieve equity is to weight the per pupil expenditures so that children who are more expensive to educate get additional resources. This is already the case in special education, but can also be done for children who speak languages other than English, for minority children, and for poor children. The standards movement has introduced the idea that children ought to be able to meet the standards set by a state through the educational system established by that same state. If children are not meeting standards, the argument goes, more instructional resources of the kind needed to enable them to reach the standards must be provided, if standards are to be meaningful. Otherwise, standards will serve to widen the gap in privilege between wealthy and middle-class white children and poor, minority, and immigrant children. In *Brown* the Justices called for "an opportunity [for education] on equal terms."[90] In *Equality of Educational Opportunity*, often referred to as The Coleman Report, James Coleman was charged with determining whether schools offered "equal educational opportunity," following the language of the Civil Rights Act of 1964. The word "opportunity" is problematic. How can it be ascertained that schools have presented an equal opportunity when a group of students are unable to perform proficiently on any measure? And how is that opportunity to be measured, if not by outputs? Coleman, in measuring inputs, concluded that inputs don't matter much, especially for white children. He failed to emphasize the positive impact of additional resources for black children contained in his data. In New York's second round of cases in *Campaign for Fiscal Equity*, lawyers for the state argued that the state had provided the opportunity for a "sound, basic education," but the children failed to take advantage of it. Whether this happened because they are poor, or don't speak English, or for some other reason, the state's position was that it cannot be faulted.[91] Fortunately for the children of New York City, this decision was overturned by a 2003 ruling, which declared that students have a constitutional right to "a meaningful high school education."[92] In 2002, Michael Heise predicted that the connection of standards to funding will became the issue in the new wave of adequacy cases.[93] However, in the 2003 Court of Appeals ruling in *Campaign for Fiscal Equity* in New York, the Court of Appeals took pains to avoid naming the Regents Learning Standards as the measure of a "sound basic education."

Americans believe in a level playing field, but balk at making school funding both equitable and adequate enough to accomplish this. If gaps in disaggregated test scores[94] are taken to indicate that poor and minority children need more resources for an adequate education, NCLB will prove beneficial, but not if such gaps are taken to mean that money spent on these children is wasted. There is no doubt that more research needs to be done on how to use money well in schools.[95] Too often, reform consists of doing more of what was not working in the first place. Neither does instituting more testing constitute a reform. It is expensive and does not result in innovative pedagogy, an improved curriculum, or smaller classes, which are known to improve educational results. Testing spends precious resources on things that do not improve learning and focuses on test preparation instead of constructivist pedagogy. Punitive measures like those in the NCLB degrade the quality of education poor children receive by removing funding from the public schools that serve the neediest children.[96] The National Education Association and school districts in three states (Michigan, Texas, and Vermont) sued in April, 2005 because the mandates of the No Child Left Behind Act (NCLB) imposed additional costs on the schools which were not funded by the federal government. The legislation itself prohibits unfunded mandates. This case was dismissed on November 23, 2005 in the United States District Court for the Eastern District of Michigan, Third Division on the grounds that the statute "cannot reasonably be interpreted to prohibit Congress itself from offering federal funds on the condition that States and school districts comply with the many statutory requirements [of NCLB]. . ."[97]

Another group of issues revolves around the proportion of state aid, the tax effort, and tax rates of localities, also called tax burden. The more the state contributes, the better the chance of equity, if state aid is targeted to needy districts. The proportion of state aid to local costs varies widely. In most states, tax rates are far from uniform. The concept of tax effort—how much a community is willing to tax itself for the support of education—must include consideration of a community's assessed property evaluation. State aid, which is supposed to remedy deficiencies created by unequal tax bases, often fails to work. In 1923, the Educational Finance Inquiry Commission investigating school finance in New York observed, "Even though no material change is made in the amount of state support, *the present system of apportioning state aid among the localities has no valid excuse for continued existence*" (italics mine).[98]

As documented in the *Rodriguez* and *Edgewood* cases in Texas, the *Brigham* and *Stowe* cases in Vermont, the New York cases, and many more, including the landmark *Serrano* cases in California, property-poor districts have to pay taxes at a much higher rate than property-rich districts to maintain even minimal facilities. Certain basic costs are unavoidable. Schools must have four walls, a roof, plumbing, furniture, books, and teachers. Poor districts often make a much greater tax effort than wealthy districts. In 1970, Coons, Clune, and Sugarman proposed a "power equalizing" plan in *Private Wealth and Public Education*. Their idea was that districts making the same tax effort ought to be guaranteed the same per pupil expenditure through state aid.[99] Although this would be more fair than high tax rates, which yield less in poor districts while wealthy districts have plenty of revenue at a lower rate, the plan would nevertheless allow children to be deprived of adequate facilities whenever voters were unwilling (or unable) to raise taxes.

Efficiency is often an issue in state constitutional education clauses. Generally in the 1950s and 1960s in the United States, districts were consolidated in the name of efficiency. In Ontario, school funding changed under Premier Mike Harris in 1996. Boards (as they are called in Ontario) were "amalgamated" as a money-saving device, their number reduced from 129 to 72. This type of "efficiency" does not represent educational improvement. Despite the temptation to think so, productivity measures in schools are unlike those in business. Should efficient schools be the cheapest, educate the most people in the shortest time, produce the highest scores, be the most inclusive, send the most students to college, or be educationally the most sound? If school finance reform is undertaken to cut taxes, "efficient" is likely to mean cheap, rather than educationally sound. Unfortunately, the business model often prevails, but schools are basically unlike businesses. Schools provide a social service to citizens and the country as a whole, rather than a sell a product to a customer. Students are not products; nor should public schools be profit-driven. The bottom line is not money but well-educated citizens. Of course schools should use their resources wisely and be sure their methods of educating obtain results. Resources for public schools are not unlimited, but they ought to be sufficient.

In addition to efficiency, adequacy is also an important consideration in school funding. Many recent school finance cases are moving toward an adequacy argument, based on either adequacy of resources (inputs) or adequacy of achievement (outcomes), but, again, the question is, adequate for what? As part of the Ontario reforms in 1996, centralized tax collection deprived boards of the right to tax. When the government demanded balanced budgets from the boards, but did not grant adequate funds, boards were forced to cut programs. By late summer of 2002, some boards refused to submit a balanced budget in the face of continuing inadequate funding.[100] These boards were taken over by the provincial government.[101] Premier Eves ultimately was voted out of office, in part over this issue. In New York City, Mayor Bloomberg won a decades-long battle to control the city's single district in the same summer.[102] Likewise, in Rochester, the mayor became responsible for the city schools. That these takeovers will prove to be more "efficient" seems doubtful. Decentralization usually promotes efficiency better than centralizing the power in one person's hands, especially if that person is only remotely connected with the situation. The problem of size is also germane. Smaller school districts were consolidated, while many city districts, which need to be divided, remain huge. Identifying efficiency with economies of scale is likely to lend credence to the idea that bigger is better. However, these enormous, bureaucratic structures are much more likely to be subject to graft and corruption than smaller units.

The latest trend in school finance litigation in the United States examines the adequacy of the education children are receiving. Unfortunately, this may be construed as either the educational opportunity to which the children supposedly have access (inputs) or the performance of children on various measures (outcomes). The real question is the relation between the inputs and the outcomes; that is, the causal link between spending and progress toward identified goals. In 1995, the Court of Appeals demanded that *Campaign for Fiscal Equity (CFE)* establish a "causal link" between the lack of money and low achievement in New York City schools. In 2003, the favorable Court of Appeals ruling acknowledged that *Campaign for Fiscal Equity* lawyers had done so.[103] Blaming children for not taking advantage of the opportunities supposedly offered to them, as the Appellate Division did, is all too easy. If standards are "merely aspirational" as the defendants in *CFE* claimed, then there is no need to ensure that children have what they need to reach the standards.[104] This vitiates the standards movement as a strategy of reform. The usefulness of the adequacy argument in school finance will also depend on what is defined as "adequate," or, alas, in some states, "minimally adequate." In New York, plaintiffs in the *Paynter* and *CFE* cases claim that the education children are receiving in Rochester and New York City is inadequate because the children do not meet the New York standards as indicated by state-mandated testing. Plaintiffs in *CFE* tied the inadequacy to the smaller share of state aid New York City receives, as well as to municipal overburden and the additional expense of educating poor, minority, and immigrant children. New York City schools enroll more than 80 percent of the state's minority students. Evidence of the inadequacy at the trial court ranged from inputs, the poor condition and capacity of facilities, to outcomes, the poor performance of city school children on state examinations. This case ultimately prevailed in New York's highest court.

In the *Paynter* v. *State* case in Rochester, plaintiffs alleged that racial and economic isolation of children in the Rochester City School District resulting from state and federal policies was responsible for poor performance. Deliberate public policies regarding housing and school-attendance zones concentrate the children of the poor in Rochester schools. This case ultimately failed in the state's highest court, ironically on the same day that *CFE* succeeded. Both cases argued that the conditions found in city schools violate the implementing regulations of the Civil

Rights Act of 1964. But in both cases, civil rights claims, which could have had national significance, were dismissed on the grounds that there is no private right to sue under the Civil Rights Act in *Alexander* v. *Sandoval*. In the previous cases, *Sandoval* v. *Hagan*, in 1998 and 1999,[105] charges of discrimination under the implementing regulations of the Civil Rights Act allowed the private right to sue state regulatory agencies on the basis of disparate impact, but the Supreme Court overturned these in *Alexander* v. *Sandoval* in 2001. The question of intentional discrimination versus disparate impact discrimination also bears on school finance litigation. Under Section 601 of the Civil Rights Act of 1964, proof of intent to discriminate is required, which comes from precedent and the law's origin in outlawing *de jure* rather than *de facto* segregation. Before *Sandoval*, Section 602, establishing the right to make implementing regulations in states and agencies to enforce Section 601, allowed disparate impact claims in which intentionality did not need to be demonstrated. The highest court in New York has refused to rule in favor of these claims in school finance. Such a ruling could have changed the direction of school finance reform.

In Vermont, both the legal process and the legislative process of reforming school finance took place in record time, following a 1997 Vermont Supreme Court ruling in *Amanda Brigham* v. *State of Vermont* that the state's finance scheme violated the state constitution.[106] Both the plaintiffs and the defendants did not like the ruling issued by the trial court, which gave something to both sides, but not completely what either side wanted. When they both appealed, the Supreme Court took the case and ruled the school finance system unconstitutional without an evidentiary record such as was developed in New York.[107] Vermont was among the states with the widest disparities at the time. The legislature enacted comprehensive school finance reform within a few months. Act 60, although not uncontroversial, retained the local control that independent Vermonters demand. The legislation made the property tax rate uniform statewide, collected it statewide, and disbursed it according to a foundation formula that raised expenditures in poor districts but substantially lowered those in rich districts. Act 60 allowed districts to raise money over the foundation grant through locally approved additional taxes, but forced them to share the extra funds with property-poor localities. The result was not absolute equality, but had an equalizing effect. Vermont's plan was phased in over a four-year period starting in 1998. The achievement gap between the scores of children in property-poor districts and property-rich districts began to narrow by 2000, with additional gains reported in 2001 and 2002.[108] In 2003, the legislature abandoned the sharing pool, raised the flat-rate state contribution, and financed the increase by instituting a statewide sales tax.[109] Once again, property-rich districts can levy additional taxes if the voters are willing, but now they keep the proceeds. The new law, Act 68, contains a guaranteed yield provision, but this neglects the reality that poor districts may be unable to raise local tax rates.

Why is School Finance Reform so Difficult?

Many policies contribute to the intractability of school finance reform. The *Rodriguez* case might have facilitated school finance reform by declaring inequitable funding unconstitutional under the United States constitution. When that failed to happen, state courts had to address the question individually, which cannot solve the problem of inequitable school funding nationwide. Furthermore, school finance reform is a complex and contentious issue, involving the courts, the legislative and executive branches of government, local government, and many individual and institutional stakeholders. Property taxes, which traditionally provide the bulk of local funding for schools, are unpopular, to say the least. Although they appear to place the heaviest responsibility on property owners, they do not distribute the tax burden fairly when districts have very different tax bases. Poor people pay a greater percentage of their wealth to maintain schools than rich people. When tax revolts are directed against property taxes, tax reform decreases the money available for public education. If legislators are unwilling to pass school finance reform legislation, which it is their responsibility to do, citizens call upon the courts to decide whether the present method of funding is constitutional. Since state education clauses, equal protection clauses, desegregation clauses, and civil rights protections differ widely, such state decisions do not solve the national problem.

When courts step into the breach, separation of powers complicates things further. There often is a lack of political will to reform even after the court has ordered it. Courts hesitate to set a template for constitutional legislation, even though a general template outlining what legislation is constitutional is within their power and would further the process. The question of judicial efficacy comes into play when legislatures refuse to pass legislation that can be judged constitutional. If courts mandate reform that does not become law, will the courts appear to be feeble? If the political will for reform is lacking, it is unlikely that judicially mandated reform will accomplish the job, at least not without a protracted battle between the courts and the legislatures. There are other avenues to assure an equal educational opportunity for all children. Increasing the state share diminishes the importance of the local tax base. Some states are moving in this direction. Targeting state aid to address imbalances is another strategy. Unfortunately, state legislators often represent the needs of their particular constituency, rather than the whole, a condition that is deeply embedded in the political traditions of the United States. Increasing the state share while decreasing reliance on local taxes can equalize the tax burden, which lies heaviest on poor localities. Some states pay for this increased state share by sales taxes, but these are unreliable in times of economic downturn. Sales taxes are regressive, especially if necessary items like food are included. The complexities and the possibilities are vast, but school finance can be made fair if the desire to do so exists.

Many social ills such as lack of health insurance, lack of state subsidized day care, a low minimum wage, poverty, and persistent racism create conditions that affect children's performance in school. Environmental racism creates the unhealthful conditions for many of our children who live in poverty. Researchers are beginning to make the connection between lead poisoning, asthma, and other health problems created by an impoverished working class, lack of social services, and "failing" schools.[110] Inequitable funding of neighborhood schools may be linked to the widening gap between rich and poor, racial prejudice, and housing that is still segregated despite the Fair Housing Law. But inequitable school funding also contributes to these things continuing. Can schools fix inequities resulting from public policies that they did not make?[111] Maybe not entirely, but they can certainly equip future citizens who have the knowledge, skills, and dispositions needed to do so.

Justices of the United States Supreme Court declared unanimously in *Brown* that segregated schools are "inherently unequal." In New York, Justice DeGrasse opened his 2001 opinion in *Campaign for Fiscal Equity I* by quoting *Brown*. Judge Judith Kaye, in the 2003 Court of Appeals decision in *CFE* declaring the school funding formulae unconstitutional in New York, opened her opinion with the statement, "We begin with a unanimous recognition of the importance of education in our democracy." The 1954 *Brown* decision still appeals to the values of Americans today: all children deserve an equal educational opportunity. The question often, all too often, comes back to desegregation. If *Brown* had been enforced, children might now be provided with the equal educational opportunity that fairness demands and democracy requires. The nine judges of the *Brown* court set a mark Americans have yet to achieve.

The remainder of this book addresses these problems through a case study of New York, Vermont, and Ontario, three adjacent places that are working out the knotty problems of public school finance in strikingly different ways. In New York, legal attempts at reform started in the 1970s, but culminated with the ruling that allowed *Campaign for Fiscal Equity* to go to trial in 1995. In Vermont, the *Brigham* case took place in 1996. In Ontario, the Harris government also initiated reform in 1996. On the face of it, political, economic, and demographic factors are similar in the three places. All three are Northeastern; partly industrialized, partly rural; within larger, democratic federations; with local control over schools organized into districts. Problems were similar. All exhibited inequitable school funding based on local property taxes, which yielded inadequate funds in urban areas where municipal overburden obtained and in rural areas with low property valuations. In all three localities, the divisive nature of public debate over educational funding interfered with reasonable reform in equity of funding. Despite these similar conditions, problems were addressed quite differently, with different results. New York's judicially originated reforms dragged out over thirty years (and still counting); Vermont's were addressed in record time after the court decision, but now may be eroding; Ontario's proceeded from the executive branch as a tax-cutting, cost-saving reform, accompanied by much more centralized control over education, directed by a conservative agenda. At the same time, the three cases showed larger thematic strands, which can be found in school finance reform in most places. Policies such as standardized curriculum and testing, resistance to redistricting or consolidation, and various modes of tax reform, which shifted the school tax burdens to other segments of the population or attempted to cut costs in various ways, were present in all three localities. I offer my analysis of the three very different scenarios of school finance reform in hope that it will contribute to the understanding of the need for equitable funding of public education nationwide, and indeed, ultimately on a global scale.

Chapter 2

The Search for a Legal Solution
in New York

The legislature shall provide for the maintenance and support of a system of free common schools, wherein all the children of this state may be educated.

The New York State Constitution, Article XI, Section 1 (1894)

The History of School Finance in New York

New York has a long history of support for public education. Somehow, somewhere, the state lost the political will to provide both adequate and equitable funding for the common schools mandated by the 1894 constitution. By 1923, a state-appointed commission recommended sweeping changes that were never implemented. In the 1970s and 1980s, a series of protracted court battles ended in defeat for reformers. After a favorable ruling in 2003 in *Campaign for Fiscal Equity* v. *State*,[1] the legislature refused to act on a court order to correct inequities, obtained after six trials. Even this case contains language that allows the legislature to limit the remedy to New York City alone, although the ruling asserts that students in New York State have a constitutional right to a meaningful high school education. In *Stone ex rel. Paynter* v. *New York*,[2] the city of Rochester, faced with what the court admits to be "widespread academic failure," was denied a court-ordered remedy on the same day, by the same court, from which New York City received a favorable ruling. Nor have the cases based on civil rights prevailed. Such a series of defeats and denials is not uncommon. This chapter will examine the history of the issue in New York in hope of revealing some of the causes for the lack of political will to fix inequitable school funding.

The state established an education system in 1795 and set up a trust fund to pay salaries of elementary teachers in 1812. By 1849 the state share of education costs was 52 percent. In 1900, the state created two categories of districts—those possessing more than $40,000 in assessed property valuation per pupil and those possessing less than $40,000; the latter received a higher allotment of state aid. By the 1920s the Cole-Rice Law guaranteed a minimum per-pupil expenditure to all districts making a minimum tax effort.[3] However, in 1923, members of a task force, the Educational Finance Inquiry Commission, concluded, after a two-year study, that "Even though no material change is made in the amount of state support, the present system of apportioning state aid among the localities has *no valid excuse for continued existence*" (italics mine).[4] The report suggested reforming personal, property, and business taxes, reassessing property and redistricting to accomplish more equity, and setting a statewide tax rate based on what would "provide the richest district with all it needs" (Strayer and Haig, 171, 158–159, 166). The richest districts would then raise all their own revenue, while the state made up for deficiencies in other districts, which would tax at the same rate (175). Given the "vacillation to be found in recent history of school legislation in the state of New York," the Commission raised the question of whether "the machinery of representation has been operating efficiently" (177).

By the 1950s, more problems surfaced. According to Austin D. Swanson, New York schools had suffered a serious decline caused, at least in part, by retrenchment in funding.[5] After legislative action failed to meet increasing costs for three successive years,[6] the New York State Educational Conference Board recommended a commitment by the state to an adjustable funding formula "to [meet] changing socioeconomic conditions."[7] Studies of the New York State Educational Conference Board addressed topics that foreshadowed problems that New York State still faces: variations in the local tax base,[8] municipal overburden,[9] and disadvantages for small and rural schools.[10] The group published "A Proposed Plan for Distribution of State Aid for Education in New York,"[11] dubbed the "shared-cost formula." This plan proposed a flat grant of 25 percent for all districts, followed by a percentage of state funding, which would vary with the wealth of the district of up to 90 percent for poor districts, with a projected phase-in over five years.[12] The proposal addressed the problem of the differential tax efforts that districts had to make under the old formula to meet the required local share of $600 per-pupil expenditure.[13] As reported in "Checkerboard II: An Analysis of Tax Effort, Equalization, and Extraordinary Needs Aid" in 2001, "the tax aid program, from its beginning, has had some inconsistent effects, but the recent experience has been disastrous."[14]

In 1962, New York State adopted the "percentage equalizing formula" proposed by the Diefendorf Committee, in which the average district gets 50 percent; the district with twice the average wealth, 25 percent; and the district with half the average wealth, 75 percent (Berke et al., *Politicians*, 5). In 1956, under Governor Dewey, New York State expanded aid for special education as well (5). In 1974, the Fleischman Commission's proposal for compensatory aid for districts with low-achieving students was enacted, but never implemented (5). The history of New York's school funding is mixed; there was concern, but not enough action to create equitable funding. (See Appendix 2.1 for the full text of the education clause in the New York State Constitution; see Appendix 2.2 for a chart of the cases in New York's school funding litigation.)

While this discussion of reform was going on in New York, proponents of equitable school funding nationwide began to resort to the courts, attacking inequitable school funding under the education clauses of states' constitutions, sometimes combined with other clauses. The story of the court battle in New York is long and complex, with little to no reform, despite egregious inequities. In 1995 H. Carl McCall, state comptroller, reported inequities ranging from $11,000 per-pupil expenditure in the highest wealth decile of school districts to $5,000 in the lowest wealth decile.[15] In keeping with trends in school finance litigation, the initial court cases were equity cases, based on unequal inputs. In *Levittown Union Free School District* v. *Nyquist*,[16] plaintiffs pointed to a huge discrepancy in funding for schools in property-rich areas and those in property-poor areas. Successful at the trial court, the inequity was not enough for the upper courts. In the final appeal, the Court of Appeals demanded a clear connection between lack of funding and denial of a "sound basic education," the formulation of the *Levittown* court following the education clause of the New York State Constitution. Given that the education clause does not specify that the education offered should have an equity component, the *Levittown* court decided that education did not merit equal protection analysis, over the dissent of Judge Fuchsberg:

> In any meaningful ordering of priorities, it is in the impact education makes on the minds, characters and capabilities of our young citizens that we must find the answer to many seemingly insoluble societal problems. In the long run, nothing may be more important—and therefore more fundamental—to the future of our country. Can it be gainsaid that, without education there is no exit from the ghetto, no solution to unemployment, no cutting down on crime, no dissipation of intergroup tension, no mastery of the age of the computer? Horace Mann put it pragmatically that education is not only "the great equalizer of men," but, by alleviating poverty and its societal costs,

more than pays for itself. So, too, only this past week, the Supreme
Court of the United States reminded us that it had recognized the
public school "as the primary vehicle for transmitting the values on
which our society rests." (Quoting *Plyler* v. *Doe*, 457 U.S. 202) [17]

The United States Supreme Court, however, turned down an appeal in
Levittown "for want of a substantial federal question."[18] In doing so, the
court denied any federal civil rights protection on the question of inequity on school funding to the children of New York. *Levittown* was followed by another equity case, which also failed in the courts.

Another legal approach taken in New York was to attack inequitable school funding as a violation of the federal Civil Rights Act of
1964, sometimes accompanied by a violation of equal protection clauses
of the federal and/or state constitution, rather than the education
clause. Four earlier New York cases also charged civil rights violations,
following *Brown*. Civil rights claims in school funding cases were made
even more difficult after the United States Supreme Court's five-to-four
decision in *Alexander* v. *Sandoval* in 2001.[19] This case established, against
precedent, that there is no private right to sue for disparate impact civil
rights violations under Section 602 of the Civil Rights Act of 1964. Section 601 states, as Justice Stevens points out in his dissent to *Sandoval*, a
broad principle, "No person in the United States shall, on ground of
race, color, or national origin, be excluded from participation in, or denied the benefits of, or be subjected to discrimination under any program or activity receiving federal financial assistance."[20] Section 601 thus
contains the "rights creating language." The court has agreed "that regulations applying Section 601's ban on *intentional* discrimination are covered by the cause of action to enforce that section" (*285) (italics mine).
The dispute arises over Section 602, which permits various agencies to
create implementing regulations for the enforcement of Section 601.
Under those regulations, the Department of Justice allows a showing of
disparate impact to prove a violation. But the court ruled in *Sandoval* that
there is no "rights creating language" in 602, hence no private right to
sue under 602. The majority of the Court argued that Section 602 does
not address either the regulated agency, or the persons discriminated
against, but only the regulatory agency (*289). To account for previous
rulings based on disparate impact claims, the Court stated, "We must assume for purposes of deciding this case that regulations promulgated
under Section 602 of Title VI may validly proscribe activities that have a
disparate impact on racial groups, even though such activities [disparate
impact activities] are permissible under Section 601" (*282). No disparate impact cases could have succeeded under this interpretation;
however, disparate impact regulations have been upheld since *Bakke*.[21]

Section 601 does not address how its antidiscrimination mandate will be enforced, for which purpose Congress added Section 602. With the interpretation of 601 as requiring intentional discrimination, and the interpretation of 602 as not permitting private suits, it is unclear how any individual or group could sue for violation of their civil rights unless they could prove intent. The majority in *Sandoval* decided that the text of the law alone established congressional intent, without reference to congressional discussions concerning its passage, which is contrary to usual practice in interpreting laws and the Constitution.[22] Consequently they did not refer to congressional debates on the law, which might well have established congressional intent to prevent disparate impact regulations. The regulatory agency, which is doing the discriminating, is unlikely to change without a court challenge. Justice Stevens' dissent disagreed sharply with the majority opinion. First, he pointed out that the decision is "unfounded in our precedent" (Stevens dissenting in *Sandoval*, *294). Second, he questioned the complicated relationship between Section 601 and Section 602 construed by the majority. According to Stevens, Section 601 sets forth a broad principle that "no person in the United States shall be discriminated against . . . on the grounds of race, color, or national origin" (*303). Section 602 provides remedies by directing federal agencies to issue "broad, prophylactic regulations" to "effectuate" Section 601's principle of nondiscrimination (*305). Stevens did not see any precedent in law or legislation to "bifurcate" remedies under Title VI into two separate categories [for intentional and disparate impact offenses] (*304). Indeed, Stevens remarked, "Regulations prohibiting policies that have a disparate impact are not necessarily aimed only—or even primarily—at intentional discrimination. Many policies whose very intent is to discriminate are framed in a race-neutral manner" (note 13). Stevens is right—in many cases, the intent was well disguised. Apparently neutral policies can have a disparate impact. Regardless, *Sandoval* quashed federal disparate impact claims in school-funding litigation.

After *Levittown*, its companion, and the civil rights cases, some of which were brought concurrently, did not obtain favorable rulings in the state upper courts, the strategy of school finance litigation changed from making equity claims to making adequacy claims, sometimes combined with civil rights claims. *Campaign for Fiscal Equity* and *Paynter* both included a civil rights portion, which went unrecognized by the courts. The 1995 ruling by New York's highest court, the Court of Appeals allowed *Campaign for Fiscal Equity* v. *State*[23] to go to trial. According to the *Levittown* court, "a sound basic education" consisted of "minimally adequate" facilities, instrumentalities of learning, and teachers, which the Court of Appeals retained. Both adequacy and civil rights tactics were adopted in *CFE II*. At the trial court, Justice LeLand DeGrasse ruled in favor of the plaintiffs in 2001; he was overruled in 2002 by the Appellate Division, and that ruling was overruled in 2003 by the Court of Appeals. However, *Paynter*, which alleged inadequate outcomes rather than inadequate inputs, failed in the same court on the same day. Before DeGrasse's ruling, repeated attempts to equalize school funding in New York met with legal and legislative rebuffs for thirty years, culminating in a crisis, to which I turn in the next section.

The Crisis in New York

In 2002, almost thirty years after *Levittown* and eight cases later, Judge Peter Tom, in *Campaign for Fiscal Equity IIb* at the Appellate level, wrote separately in his concurrence to emphasize his alarm at the state of affairs in education in New York. As he put it, "a nascent educational crisis has been growing over the years, with roots decades deep, but with consequences that are taking on a new urgency."[24] Indicative of the crisis for Judge Tom was that 30 percent of high school students in New York City fail to graduate. Although Judge Tom's alarm was justified, the crisis has wider proportions than the high school graduation rate in New York City. Nevertheless, Judge Tom concurred in the majority opinion at the Appellate Division, ruling the New York funding formulae constitutional.

According to a study conducted by the Economic Policy Institute, New York has widest gap in income between rich and poor in the nation.[25] Disaggregating 2001–2002 test data for elementary and middle school students by race and ethnicity revealed a wide racial gap in test scores across New York, with some of the widest gaps in New York City.[26] These gaps remain in 2003.[27] New York's schools are among the most segregated in the nation[28] and Long Island's schools are now the most segregated suburban schools.[29] According to *Education Week's* Quality Counts issues, New York was among the six states that had the most inequitable school funding in 2000, the second most inequitable in 2001, the fourteenth in 2002,[30] but back to twelfth in 2003. This represents a D+ rating, a small improvement on 2000's rating of F. In *Education Week's* Quality Counts issue of 2003, an article focusing on teacher qualifications found that

> In New York State, an analysis of data from 1984–85 through 1999–2000 found that fewer than half the teachers in some high-poverty, high-minority schools were fully certified in all the courses they taught. Low-income, low-achieving, and nonwhite students also were more likely to have teachers who lacked prior teaching experience, had failed a teacher-licensing exam on the first try, or had attended less selective colleges as undergraduates.[31]

Likewise, *The Funding Gap*, a study first conducted by the Education Trust in August 2002[32] and repeated in 2004 and 2005, revealed that a gap of $2,280 existed between the lowest and highest poverty districts and a similar gap of $1,965 existed between districts with the lowest and highest minority.[33] Adjusted for low-income students this increases to $2,930 and $2,419.[34] "Schools [in New York] teaching the poorest students receive $2,152 per student less from state and local government sources than schools with the fewest needy students." These gaps remained substantially unchanged during the period 2002–2005.[35] The connection with achievement is elusive since many factors can influence educational outcomes, but "students in six of the biggest and most diverse United States cities are well behind the national average in reading and writing" despite some recent gains.[36] Disturbingly, according to the 2002 edition of *The Funding Gap*, white pupils in urban schools account for much of the improvement; black and Hispanic children, isolated from their white peers in segregated schools with fewer resources, account for much of the difference between urban and suburban scores. In 2005, New York failed to make progress despite the favorable court ruling in *Campaign for Fiscal Equity*.

The income gap nationwide has increased over the past twenty years, despite a brief respite during Clinton's second term in office.[37] According to 2001 census figures reported in fall 2002, "poverty in the nation is up to 11.7% after nearly a decade of decline, while median household income fell 2.2%, the first statistically significant decline in a decade." In 2003, the median income did not change, but poverty rose again, to an average of 12.5 percent.[38] Child poverty is even higher. According to Columbia University's National Center for Children in Poverty (NCCP), 17 percent of children live in poverty, and 38 percent of children are low income. For children under six, the figure increases to 36 percent in poverty. These figures were averaged over the years 2001, 2002, and 2003.[39] Nationwide, poverty rates among black, Asian, and Hispanic young children, defined as those under six years of age, are even higher, hovering around 42–43 percent.[40] Nearly half of these live in "extreme poverty," defined as half the poverty level.[41] In predominantly minority cities, rates of extreme poverty for black and Hispanic children are high.[42] In New York, 18 percent of the black children in Rochester, 17 percent in New York City, and 20 percent in Buffalo live in extreme poverty, compared to 10.5 percent across the state.[43] Other cities show similar statistics. The nationwide percentage of children living in poverty and "near poverty" (at 185 percent of the poverty level) hovers around 43 percent, although the economic downturn starting in March 2001 increased the number of black children living in extreme poverty.[44] According to the National Center for Children in Poverty, figures published in July 2005 show 38 percent of children ages birth to eighteen live in low-income families, and the percentages increase to 42 percent and 43 percent for young children under six and under three.[45] Poverty is especially harmful to young children because of its negative impact on development. Malnutrition, lack of medical care, exposure to lead poisoning, and many other hazards harm young children permanently. Combined with poor education, unemployment or low-paid jobs, and sometimes prison, poverty wrecks lives.

According to the Personal Responsibility and Work Opportunity Reconciliation Act (PRWORA) of 1996,[46] recipients of public assistance must work for their benefits, including students eligible for college and mothers of young children. New York requires thirty-five hours per week, more than the statute's minimum,[47] which President Bush has proposed raising to forty hours.[48] Bush touted his plan for block grants to states as adding "flexibility," which meant that states could request a waiver to cut programs, although not to lower the work requirements.[49] The jobs provided are low-end, minimum-wage jobs requiring few skills and offering little opportunity for advancement; such jobs rarely lead to permanent, well-paid employment. Temporary Assistance to Needy Families (TANF) and its associated regulations are known to have a negative impact on vulnerable families.[50] The Senate proposed to correct some of these problems in October 2003, but reconciliation between the Senate and the House versions of the bill failed in spring 2004.[51] Since then, the program has been funded by short-term extensions through June 30, 2005. As this book goes to press, Senate Bill 667 and House Bill Resolution 240 remain to be reconciled. The President proposed a budget by which 100,000 children per year will lose child care under TANF legislation. This will deprive at least 300,000 children of decent day care while their parents fulfill TANF work requirements by 2009.[52] The enacted program diverts money from child care to state public education facilities.[53] Although the policy might be beneficial to state-funded early childhood programs, not all states have such, some children are excluded under current proposals, and child-care monies were inadequate from the start. As work requirements increase, it becomes more difficult for parents of young children to train for meaningful, sustainable employment.[54] Children's ability to learn is connected with their nutrition, health, supervision, and surroundings. If these remain substandard, children will be hurt in the name of "welfare reform." Welfare rolls have been cut in half since 1996, with a corresponding rise in poverty and extreme poverty. Inequitable school funding exacerbates problems of young children. Many children in the United States children are at risk of not achieving their potential. In New York, where the poverty level is higher than the national poverty level for children, and increasing faster, many more are in danger.

School Finance Reform Litigation in New York

Despite its long history of dedication to education, the record of New York's school finance litigation from 1973 to 2002 was dismal. The first full-fledged funding case arose in 1973 as an equity case under the New York Constitution and the United States Constitution—*Levittown Union Free School District, et al.,* v. *Nyquist, Commissioner of Education, et al.*[55] Plaintiffs charged that gross disparities in school funding were unconstitutional on equal protection grounds and under New York's education clause. The clause provides that the state supply a "sound basic education" to all its children. *Levittown* was upheld at the trial and appellate level.[56] When the state appealed in 1982, the Court of Appeals, New York's highest court, ruled in favor of the state in *Levittown,* taking the position that, although the plaintiffs demonstrated wide disparities in funding, they did not make a causal connection between inequitable funding and the state's constitutional mandate to provide a "sound basic education."[57] The Court of Appeals cited *Rodriguez* in choosing rational basis scrutiny. Likewise, it denied that education is a fundamental right, noting, in a curiously obtuse comparison, that the state constitution also provides for the maintenance of canals.[58] The opinion cited the lone dissenter at the Appellate Division, Judge Hopkins, who claimed that it is beyond the power of the courts to fix municipal overburden (*42). However, the Court of Appeals did admit that ". . . we would be reluctant to override these decisions [state funding decisions] by mandating an even higher priority for education *in the absence of gross and glaring inadequacy*—something not shown to exist in consequence of the present school financing system" (italics mine) (*48). The trial established a 46:1 disparity in taxable property per district and a 9:1 disparity in school funding. The court concluded that the plaintiffs in *Levittown* had not established that the education received by children in poorly funded districts was inadequate, given that the constitution specified only a "sound basic education" for all children. No reforms ensued. The United States Supreme Court refused to hear the case.

Reform Educational Financing Inequities Today v. *Cuomo* (*REFIT*) was brought in 1992. The plaintiffs were property-poor school districts, who could not compete with their wealthier neighbors in financing schools. Judge Robert Roberto, Jr. dismissed the charges, based on the *Levittown* ruling ten years earlier. His dismissal was appealed to the Appellate Division, Second Department.[59] The Appellate Court also relied on the preceding *Levittown* cases, citing the Court of Appeals decision:

> Interpreting the term education, as we do, to connote a sound basic
> education, we have no difficulty in determining that the constitu-
> tional requirement is being met in this state, in which it is said with-

out contradiction that the average per pupil expenditure exceeds
that in all other states but two. There can be no dispute that New
York has long been regarded as a leader in free public education.
(*REFIT*, Appellate Division at *488)

The court neglected to notice that the *average* spending in New York was
not at issue.

In the appeal, plaintiffs claimed that the disparities had become
"gross and glaring" enough since the *Levittown* ruling to reopen the constitutional issue. Michael Rebell among others, who became the lead
lawyer in *Campaign for Fiscal Equity*, filed a brief as *amicus curiae*. The *amici
curiae* claimed that a "sound basic education" was not provided in the
property-poor districts, but the judges ruled that the *amici* "have no status to raise issues or cite alleged errors which were never raised or cited
by the plaintiffs" (*490). The Appellate Division upheld the lower court
decision with what they hoped was finality, declaring "We modify the
judgment appealed from to declare that the New York State's scheme for
financing its public elementary and secondary schools is constitutional"
(*490). The ruling declared that the causal link between funding disparities and educational inadequacy had not been established.

This decision was in turn appealed to the Court of Appeals.[60] The
plaintiffs made four claims. First, the inequities had worsened since *Levittown*, which did not require proof that the students were deprived of some
undefined "minimum" level of education. Second, the demonstrated
worsening of circumstances since 1982 was sufficient grounds to declare
the funding unconstitutional. Third, if *Levittown* is now read to require
proof of denial of some unspecified minimum of education, then it
should be modified or overruled. Fourth, should the school-funding
scheme somehow be deemed constitutional under the education article,
then it should be deemed unconstitutional under the equal protection
clause (*REFIT*, *283–285). The court decided that the constitution "does
not mandate that all educational facilities and services should be substantially the same throughout the state" (*283). The court went further, stating, "Even a claim of extreme disparity cannot demonstrate the 'gross and
glaring inadequacy' that we referred to in *Levittown*" (*284). Under this
interpretation, it is hard to imagine what the judges in *Levittown* could
have intended by their reservation. This pronouncement comes close to
stating that any disparity would not be adequate grounds for a suit. The
judges chose to follow the level of scrutiny in *Rodriguez*, despite the fact
that the state constitution, unlike the federal constitution, contains an education clause; instead, the judges held that inequitable funding was supported by rational basis scrutiny on grounds of local control (*285). With
this ruling, funding challenges based on the New York education and
equal protection clauses seemed to be defeated, unless a causal link

between disparities in funding that exceeded "extreme" and lack of a "minimally adequate," "sound basic education" could be demonstrated. Nonetheless, the ruling ended with a statement that apparently left room for a new case, declaring:

> Finally, rather than affirm the Appellate Division's broad and definitive declaration of the constitutionality of the State educational financing system, we modify to declare that the school financing scheme of the State of New York *has not been shown in this case to be unconstitutional.* (italics mine) (*284)

Meanwhile, in 1994, New York City had sued the state for underfunding city schools in *City* v. *State.* At the same time, a companion case, *Campaign for Fiscal Equity* v. *State,*[61] made its first appearance with similar charges. In their first round of trials, *City* v. *State* was joined with *Campaign for Fiscal Equity.* In *City* v. *State,* New York City officials sued the state for allocating less state aid to the city than to suburban districts. New York City is considered an "average wealth district" for purposes of state funding, without consideration for municipal overburden and the needs of the largely minority, impoverished, and immigrant children who attend its public schools. Justice Leland DeGrasse presided over these combined cases. As DeGrasse summarized them, both cases alleged violation of the Education Article, Article XI, Section 1, of the New York Constitution. Second, they both alleged violations of the equal protection clause of New York Constitution and the Fourteenth Amendment of the United States Constitution. Third for *City* and fourth for *CFE,* they both alleged violation of the Civil Rights Act of 1964 and its implementing regulations. The third cause of action for *CFE* was a violation of the New York's constitutional clause forbidding discrimination by race, color, creed, and religion (*496). The clause, Article I, Section 11, reads, "No person shall, because of race, color, creed, or religion, be subjected to any discrimination in his civil rights by any other person, or by any firm, corporation, or institution, or by the state or any agency or subdivision of the state." *CFE* lawyers, deliberately echoing the language of *Nyquist,* claimed that funding in New York City contained "gross and glaring" inadequacies, which caused the education of city school children to fall "below the Statewide minimum standard of educational quality and quantity fixed by the Board of Regents" (references omitted, *CFE/City* v. *State* at *497, citing *Board of Education, Levittown Union Free School Dist.* v. *Nyquist*). *REFIT* failed because it did not make the claim that the education received was inadequate. *Levittown* had ruled that "gross and glaring disparities" might be cause for reopening the question of adequacy, should the causal link between funding disparities and inadequacy be proven. On this reasoning, Justice DeGrasse ruled that *CFE's* claim was viable. He also ruled that *CFE* plaintiffs had the "capacity" [standing] to sue, which the city lacked. *CFE* had successfully combined adequacy and civil rights strategies.

In *City* v. *State,* DeGrasse ruled that the city must establish an exception to the rule that a city (or a city school board) being the creation of the state, can sue the state.[62] In his view, the city failed to establish any such claim. Second, the constitutionality of inequitable school funding had been established by *Levittown.* Third, the city had not established that it had a "proprietary interest" in the money collected to be disbursed by the state as state aid. DeGrasse dismissed part of the allegation that the school funding scheme violated the federal and state civil rights clauses because discriminatory intent had not been alleged. But he upheld the alleged violation of 34 CFR 100.3, a New York regulation from the Department of Housing, Education, and Welfare, which forbids discrimination in programs receiving federal assistance pursuant to Sections 601 and 602 of the Civil Rights Act. This regulation only required a showing of discriminatory effect, not intent to discriminate. DeGrasse's reasoning hinged on the "allegation that a substantial number of students were being deprived of meaningful education on grounds of race, color, or national origin."[63] DeGrasse also made a move that became extremely important—he equated lack of a sound basic education with the failure of students to meet the Regent's minimum standards, following the language in *Nyquist.* DeGrasse stated, "this court equates the provision of a sound basic education within the contemplation of *Levittown (supra)* with adherence to minimum educational standards approved by the Board of Regents" (*499).

Both sides of the cases cross-appealed DeGrasse's ruling to the Appellate Division in *CFE/City* v. *State.*[64] At the Appellate Division, the remaining allegation in *City* v. *State* was dismissed, as were all charges in *CFE,* in a unanimous decision by a four-judge panel. The curt opinion by Judge Wallach relied on his interpretation of Executive Law Section 291 (2), "which guarantees equal *opportunity* to education as a civil right" [emphasis added]. His ruling—"The statute *merely* assures every student an '*opportunity* to obtain education.' There is nothing in the funding allocation scheme which discriminates against any of the individual plaintiffs and thus deprives them of such educational *opportunity*" (*City* v. *State,* Appellate Division, at *276, italics mine). This interpretation was repudiated soundly in the Court of Appeals ruling in *CFE IIc* in 2003.

Again both cases were appealed, this time separately, to the Court of Appeals in 1995. Dismissal of charges in *City* v. *State* was upheld, but *Campaign for Fiscal Equity* was allowed to go forward.[65] *CFE IIa* would come to trial in 1999. The appeal of *City* v. *State* was overruled despite an apparent contradiction with one of the exceptions, that a city may sue a state if the state requires it to do something unconstitutional. The problem was that the constitutional standard of a "sound basic education" had not yet been defined as being beyond "merely an opportunity" for a "minimally adequate" education. As the judges stated in *CFE Ic* in 1995, they had not yet defined the meaning of a sound basic education, which would be "premature" before the evidentiary record was established. That was to become the trial court's task in *CFE IIa* (*318). In *City* v. *State* at the Court of Appeals, Judge Howard A. Levine, with three others concurring, ruled that the city had not identified any "prohibition" that the state forced it to violate.[66] Lack of money does not fit that category because it is not, strictly speaking, a "prohibition," even though it hindered the city's ability to carry out the state's constitutional mandate. The judges seemed not to regard "discrimination on the basis of race or color" as a constitutional prohibition (*295). Levine concluded, "The lack of capacity to sue is a necessary outgrowth of separation of powers doctrine: it expresses the extreme reluctance of courts to intrude in the political relationships between the Legislature, the State, and its government subdivisions" (*295–296). Judge Ciparick dissented vociferously to the majority ruling in *City* v. *State*, declaring, "When these local entities are unable to fulfill their constitutional and statutory obligations because of the State's failure to carry out its own constitutional obligations, a substantive right to sue has been and must continue to be recognized" (*300). She connected the right to sue with the importance of local control, citing both *Levittown's* and *Rodriguez's* use of local control as the rational basis for inequitable school funding (*301 and 303–304). Ciparick also supported New York City's standing to sue, reasoning that "if the system [of school funding] is constitutionally infirm . . . the city is obviously affected . . . [and] saddled with an increased financial burden . . . [from which]" "the right [to sue in order to protect the city's rights and interests] must be inferred" (*305–306). However, the decision was four-to-two to dismiss all charges, with Judge Kaye taking no part. It must have given Judge Ciparick a great deal of satisfaction to write the opposing majority decision in *CFE* in 1995, by which *CFE* was allowed to go forward. But, in the meantime, three more civil rights cases took place.

In 1998, the African American Legal Defense Fund (AALDF), the legal branch of the National Association for the Advancement of Colored People (NAACP), brought a school-funding suit in the United States District Court in *African American Legal Defense Fund on behalf of (named) students of the New York City Public School System and their parents* v. *New York State Department of Education, Pataki, et al.*[67] This group pursued their case on behalf of all New York schoolchildren, whereas Campaign for Fiscal Equity's case, then in preparation, involved only New York City schoolchildren. Plaintiffs charged that the school-funding scheme in

New York violated the education article and the equal protection clause of the New York Constitution, the equal protection clause of the Fourteenth Amendment to the United States Constitution, and Section 601 of Title VI of the Civil Rights Act of 1964, codified at 42 U.S.C. Section 2000d, and its implementing regulations. They also alleged a violation of the federal Voting Rights Act of 1968, since city school board members were appointed, not elected, whereas other state school board members were elected.

Judge Robert Owen dismissed all charges at the trial court. The case claimed the funding formula violated the civil rights of city schoolchildren, because "74% of the entire State's minority public school population attends city schools and [constitute] 81% of the City's public school enrollment, compared to 17% outside the city."[68] Based on 1992–1993 figures, plaintiffs stated that city schoolchildren received an average of $3,000 per student in state aid, compared to $3,400 statewide. Plaintiffs alleged that this provided "less of an opportunity to meet the State's minimum educational standards than their non-minority peers receive" (*334). On the charges against the state, Owen cited the Eleventh Amendment to the United States Constitution, granting what is called "sovereign immunity" to the states. The amendment reads, "The judicial power of the United States shall not be construed to extend to any suit in law or equity, commenced or prosecuted against one of the United States by Citizens of another state, or by Citizens of Subjects of any foreign state" (*334). In an 1890 case, *Hans* v. *Louisiana*, the United States Supreme Court construed the amendment to include actions against a state by its own citizens.[69] The only exceptions granted were if Congress had abrogated sovereign immunity by a "clear and unequivocal statement" or in cases where the state official is accused of violating the United States Constitution or federal law. Despite the fact that a Title VI claim makes this allegation, Judge Owen declared, on precedent, that actions of a state official who has violated state law are not justiciable in federal court. He ignored the complication that Title VI and its implementing regulations are not state laws, although state laws may be required to implement Title VI in states. This ruling effectively removed the charges under the New York constitution and laws from federal jurisdiction.

Owen also held that there is no suspect class nor any fundamental right to education, applying only rational basis review following *Rodriguez,* despite the fact that New York has the education clause that the federal constitution lacks, as well as an equal protection clause and a civil rights regulation forbidding discrimination (34 C.F.R. 100.3 (b) (2)), cited by Judge McKenna in *Caesar* v. *Pataki.* Neither did Owen examine the "rational" basis for a law (the funding formulae) that states its purpose to be "equalizing" and then proceeds to do the opposite. He dismissed the federal equal protection claims, because no fundamental right was violated.[70] Furthermore, Owen dismissed the plaintiffs' claim that the method of counting the number of pupils creates a substantially worse disparity in funding than is apparent from official figures.

Average daily attendance is used to calculate the number of pupils for purposes of allocating state aid, but city children have a worse attendance record for a number of reasons, including lack of child care for younger siblings, ill health, poor nutrition, parental poverty, and other factors beyond their control. A primary factor may well be the poor quality of the schools that are thus deprived of funding, creating a vicious circle.[71] The completion rate in New York City's lower-tier schools is indisputably dismal. Owen claimed that the state's interest in encouraging attendance is legitimate; hence, there is a rational basis for the rule.[72] He ignored abundant evidence that the strategy is ineffective, to say the least.

Owen also disposed of the plaintiffs' challenge to the "hold-harmless" provisions in the state funding formula. These rules prevent any district from receiving less aid than the three previous years averaged in programs to which the provision applies. Owen claimed that it legitimately protects districts against property valuation fluctuations, thus allowing them to honor long-term commitments (*337). But the problem is, if a district received more in the past, it receives the same amount; the tyranny of the percentage prevails. Poor districts never catch up. In effect, the hold-harmless provisions guaranteed that the more money districts had, the more they got. For Owen, hold-harmless provisions also passed rational basis scrutiny.

Finally, Owen took up the Title VI claim (this case took place before *Sandoval*). He claimed "to prevail under Title VI, a plaintiff must make a showing of discriminatory intent" (*337). Plaintiffs argued that discriminatory intent could be proved as follows. Defendants knew that the funding formula created "blatant inequities" and admitted to knowing that it needed reform, as shown by legislative discussions and the reports of many commissions, yet failed to enact changes. Officials knew that the scheme was unfair, and knew the consequences of that unfairness, so they must have known that it was discriminatory. Owen, once again, found grounds to dismiss. In his view "discriminatory purpose . . . implies that the decision maker, in this case a state legislature, selected or reaffirmed a particular course of action at least in part because of, not merely in spite of, its adverse effects upon an identifiable group" (*337). Under this view, discriminatory legislation and regulations could scarcely be disturbed, if the makers were careful with their language. Owen likewise dismissed the voting rights claim, arguing that it cannot apply to appointed officials unless it can be shown that the decision to appoint them was altered with intent to discriminate, which the plaintiffs did not establish.

Another civil rights suit, *Caesar* v. *Pataki*,[73] was brought in United States District Court in 2000 on behalf of children who attend "failing schools" outside New York City,[74] where suburban segregation is on the increase as city dwellers move to certain suburbs, causing increasingly segregated suburban schools.[75] In a challenge to dismiss made before *Sandoval*, the case survived. The ruling held that there was a private right to sue under Title VI and that the plaintiffs had made an adequate case that there might be a violation. The lawyers began to prepare for trial. However, after *Sandoval*, the plaintiffs changed their plea to a violation of 42 U.S.C. Section 1983, which reads,

> Every person who, under color of any statute, ordinance, regulation, custom, or usage, of any state or territory, subjects or causes to be subjected any citizen of the United States or other person within jurisdiction thereof to the deprivation of any rights, privileges, or immunities secured by the Constitution and laws, shall be liable to the party injured in an action at law, suit in equity, or other proper proceeding for redress.[76]

Nevertheless, Judge Lawrence M. McKenna dismissed the case in 2002 on grounds similar to *Sandoval*. McKenna cited precedent for the interpretation that Section 1983, like Section 602, does not create "substantive rights" but merely a "procedure for enforcing them."[77] In doing so, he cited two exceptions. One is "where Congress foreclosed such enforcement [as a suit under Section 1983] of the statute in the enactment itself." The indicator of this would be an implicit remedial scheme in the statute. The other exception is "where the statute did not create enforceable rights, privileges, and immunities within the meaning of Section 1983" (*4–5). Neither applied, in his opinion.

McKenna also noted that the Supreme Court established a three-part test for determining whether a plaintiff has the right to sue for a violation of civil rights in *Wilder* v. *Virginia Hospital Association* (1990). The test holds that "the plaintiff must show that the statute is (1) 'intended to benefit' the plaintiff seeking to enforce it, (2) is 'mandatory rather than hortatory,' and (3) is not so 'vague and amorphous' as to be 'beyond the competency of the judiciary to enforce'" (*4, citing *Wilder*). The third criterion is so subjective that it might even be called vague and amorphous itself. The case certainly satisfied the first two. Not applying these in any definitive way, McKenna claimed that "the ultimate question . . . becomes whether Congress intended to preclude Section 1983 suits when it enacted the relevant federal statute" (*4). So, the question became even more convoluted. Can plaintiffs sue under Section 1983 for enforcement of a disparate impact regulation promulgated by New York's Department of Housing, Education, and Welfare, pursuant to Section 602, which created a procedure to enforce Section 601 of Title VI of the Civil Rights Act? New York's regulation forbids

> ... criteria or methods of administration which have the effect of subjecting individuals to discrimination because of their race, color, or national origin, or have the effect of defeating or substantially impairing accomplishment of the objectives of the program as respects individuals of a particular race, color, or national origin. (*Caesar* v. *Pataki* at *7, citing 34 C.F.R. Section 100.3b2)

Realizing that there is precedent for both a narrow approach to construing Section 1983 (in which the statute itself must define the right) and a broad one (in which the implementing regulation may also define the right), McKenna chose the narrow interpretation, ruling that "this court cannot conclude that Congress intended to create a right for the plaintiffs to enforce the disparate impact regulation in this case through a Section 1983 claim . . ." citing *Graus* v. *Kaladjian*[78] as precedent. *Graus* held that ". . . if Congress intended that only certain specific statutory provisions give rise to private enforcement under Section 1983, it cannot have intended that private actions be predicated on administrative regulations not closely connected to these statutory sources of private power" (*542). He also followed *Graus* in ruling that to do to otherwise would be to violate separation of powers. Section 1983 cases could conceivably come before the Supreme Court in the future, but it seems unlikely, given the impact of the rulings in *Graus* and *Sandoval* on New York school-funding cases. It is unclear how a challenge could be raised other than by Congress clearly declaring its intent in an amendment to the law. Although the intent is clearer in Title IX, forbidding discrimination on the basis of sex, McKenna did not use that as precedent for interpreting Title VI. The New York Civil Liberties Union announced plans to appeal the ruling in *Caesar* v. *Pataki* in 2003,[79] which have not yet materialized as of this writing.

Yet another civil rights case, *New York Civil Liberties Union* v. *State of New York,* failed at the trial court in 2002.[80] Plaintiffs, the New York Civil Liberties Union (NYCLU) on behalf of all schoolchildren attending New York State public schools, charged that officials knew the state owed children a "sound basic education," yet took "insufficient steps to remedy numerous deficiencies in schools throughout the state" and that the commissioner failed to take sufficient steps to institute reforms or, alternatively, close Schools Under Registration Review (SURR) as is required by state law. Supreme Court Justice Teresi ruled that the NYCLU "had failed to allege that state policies were responsible for the deficiencies" in the schools.[81] He also allowed that officials have "discretionary judgment" to decide to place the "worst" schools under registration review, not all those that might be "failing."[82] Justice Teresi remarked that *Campaign for Fiscal Equity* was bringing a similar suit on behalf of children similarly situated in New York City, as if he expected that suit to cover this case. Following the Appellate Division decision in *CFE IIb* on June 15, 2002, Justice Teresi based his July 11, 2002, opinion largely on the Appellate Division's refusal to uphold the trial court decision in *CFE IIa*. The state threatened to vacate the case, based on the subsequent decisions in *Sandoval*.[83] In the meantime, the Appellate Division's decision in *CFE IIb* was overruled by the Court of Appeals in 2003, making Justice Teresi's reliance on it inappropriate. Subsequently, however, the Court of Appeals declared their intention that the *CFE* remedy need apply to New York City alone, even as they reinstated DeGrasse's earlier ruling.[84] Despite this, there was a popular movement to expand the reach of the case.[85] The Appellate Division, Third Department turned down NYCLU's appeal of the dismissal of charges in *NYCLU* v. *State* on Jan. 29, 2004.[86] The ruling claimed NYCLU failed to charge "widespread systemic failure" in the twenty-seven upstate schools in the case, which left only the claim that the Commissioner had failed to place these schools under registration review. The court declared that it is up to the discretion of the Commissioner how many schools should be so designated. The regulation says only that the "worst" schools shall be placed under registration review. This decision was upheld by the Court of Appeals on February 15, 2005, and a motion to reargue denied in May.[87]

In Yonkers, a 1980s desegregation suit connected with New York schools, was settled out of court on January 8, 2002, under terms that appeared less than favorable to the minority children involved. This suit ended the role of a federal monitor in the case, promised extra money from the state to remedy the effects of segregation, but failed to address the segregation itself. According to the *New York Times*, the programs mandated will only be in effect though the school year 2002–2003.[88] The portion of the case concerning segregated housing was not included in the settlement. Unfortunately, desegregation cases became hard to pursue after the regressive court rulings in *Milliken* v. *Bradley, Board of Education of Oklahoma City Public Schools* v. *Dowell,* and *Freeman* v. *Pitts,* discussed in chapter 1. The Yonkers situation is a case in point. The NAACP's pronouncement in the early desegregation battles that "green follows white" is still true; it may also be true that "action follows white."

While these cases were progressing through the courts, lawyers were preparing to establish the causal connection between poor funding and low achievement in New York City in the second round of *CFE*. In seeking this, lawyers combined a federal civil rights claim and a claim of inadequacy in educational attainment resulting from lower state expenditures. Ultimately, the claims of educational inadequacy and inequality in funding survived. In 1995, the Court of Appeals, with Judge Ciparick writing the opinion, had overruled the two previous dismissals of *Campaign for Fiscal Equity* with this declaration.

> Thirteen years after we decided *Board of Educ., Levittown Union Free School Dist.* v. *Nyquist* (57 NY2d 27) (hereinafter *Levittown)*, we are again faced with a challenge to the constitutionality of New York State's public school financing system. We are called upon to decide whether plaintiffs' (*Campaign for Fiscal Equity et al.*) complaint pleads viable causes of action under the Education Article of the State Constitution, the Equal Protection Clauses of the State and Federal Constitutions, and Title VI of the Civil Rights Act of 1964 and its implementing regulations.
>
> Judges Titone, Bellacosa, Smith and I conclude that the non-school board plaintiffs plead a sustainable claim under the Education Article. Judge Levine concurs in a separate opinion. The Court is unanimous that, as to the nonschool board plaintiffs, a valid cause of action has been pleaded under Title VI's implementing regulations. The remainder of this complaint should be dismissed. (Footnote omitted)[89]

Her reasoning echoing her dissent in *City* v. *State,* Judge Ciparick argued that the charges in *CFE* were not similar to those in *Levittown,* contrary to the Appellate Division's finding. *Levittown* never alleged that the education children received was inadequate, just that it was inequitably funded. *CFE* did exactly what the *Levittown* court asked—made the connection between insufficient spending and a sound basic education. *Levittown* set up some parameters governing what is to be considered a "sound basic education," while claiming that their statements were not a template. These were useful in the second round of *CFE* cases. Basing their decision on the 1894 New York Constitutional Convention debates, which mainly sought to replace a hodgepodge of academies, religious schools, and village schools with something more uniform, the *Levittown* judges described the state's constitutional obligation as "minimal":

> Children should have access to minimally adequate instrumentalities of learning such as desks, chairs, pencils, and reasonably current textbooks. Children are also entitled to minimally adequate teaching of reasonably up-to-date basic curricula such as reading, writing, mathematics, science, and social studies, by sufficient personnel adequately trained to teach those subject areas. (*CFE Ic at* *317)

The court put its concept of the minimum requirement succinctly:

> The trial court will have to evaluate whether the children in plaintiffs' districts are in fact being provided with the opportunity to

acquire the basic literacy, calculating, and verbal skills necessary to
enable them to function as civic participants capable of voting and
serving on a jury. (*317)

Judges cautioned against using the Regents Learning Standards alone as
a measure of constitutionality, because some of the standards are beyond
minimal adequacy, and some are even aspirational. They also advised
using standardized test scores with caution, stating, "performance levels
on such tests are helpful but should also be used cautiously as there are a
myriad of factors which have a causal bearing on test results" (*317). The
court, agreeing unanimously that Campaign for Fiscal Equity had standing to sue and valid causes of action under the state constitution, declared that the plaintiffs ought to have a chance to present the facts at a
trial. Two justices, Ciparick and Smith, would have sustained the cause of
action under the federal constitution as well. Staffers for Campaign for
Fiscal Equity began gathering evidence.

By 1999, the group was ready to challenge the state's school funding system once again. *Campaign for Fiscal Equity, Inc., et al.* v. *The State of
New York, et al. (CFE IIa)*[90] established a massive evidentiary record concerning the conditions in public schools of New York City. According to
the Campaign for Fiscal Equity organization, the case included 72 witnesses and 4,300 exhibits. The conditions surveyed included facilities,
such as buildings, laboratories, and libraries; qualifications of teachers,
such as certification, including teaching in the area of certification, passing the New York State mandated tests, and quality of undergraduate institutions attended by teachers; instrumentalities of learning such as
computers, textbooks, quality and quantity of library books, and curricula; outcomes of learning such as completion rates, proficiency levels,
and results on state-normed tests. Witnesses included experts, students
and staff of the New York City schools, state officials, and many more. Although *CFE* lawyers included state tests in their evidence, they did not
rely solely on these measures, as cautioned in *Levittown*. They also challenged the defendants' reliance on nationally normed tests and Regents
Competency Exams. The former do not compare the performance of
city students to New York students statewide; the latter were scheduled to
be phased out in 2003.

The plaintiffs developed policy statements that made it clear that
they considered a "sound basic education" to consist of a quality high
school education. In 2002, seniors were required to pass four regent's
exams to graduate, in 2003, five. In 2004, the regents planned to raise
the passing grade from 55 percent to 65 percent, but they extended the
55 percent in October 2003.[91] For providing measurable objectives to
No Child Left Behind (NCLB) to report Adequate Yearly Progress, New

York has determined that by spring 2014, 100 percent of students will score at or above 55 percent on regent's examinations, or not less than 65 percent on Regent's Competency Examinations, which had been phased out by the Board of Regents.[92] There have also been problems with the quality of the tests. In 2002, the practice of "editing" literary passages on the English exam came to light and Commissioner Mills was criticized roundly. In 2003, only 37 percent of students statewide passed the Regent's Math A Exam, required for graduation. After a tremendous public outcry about the unfairness of the exam, Mills discounted it, allowing thousands of seniors to graduate. But they will receive a certificate rather than a diploma, and juniors who failed must take the exam again.

CFE IIa also addressed the high dropout rate as part of the claim that the education in the city was inadequate. Judge Tom considered a 30 percent dropout rate a crisis, but the real figure is probably much higher. Thirty percent is an average of all schools in New York City. In addition, dropout rates are notoriously undercounted.[93] According to the *New York Daily News*, in 2003 the four-year graduation rate in New York City was 50 percent, down from 51 percent in 2002. A "completion rate" in New York is calculated including students who obtain a GED and students who take longer than four years to graduate. Nor does this tell the whole story. In the bottom ten schools in New York City, the four-year graduation rate ranged from 28.2 percent to 14.8 percent in 2003. Official figures on post-secondary plans of graduating seniors in the state as a whole look better, although still not very good. More than 80 percent of white and Asian, and a little less than 70 percent of black and Hispanic high school graduates statewide over the past decade (1990–1991 to 2000–2001) planned to attend some kind of "postsecondary education."[94] Whether their plans materialize is another matter.

Furthermore, calculating dropout figures for a low-performing school, in a class of a hundred aspiring ninth graders, even if seventy graduate, and 70 percent of those plan to go on to postsecondary education, even if all who plan to continue succeed, that is forty-nine students.[95] But if 50 percent graduate, and 70 percent of those plan to continue, that is twenty-five students. At the lowest performing high school in the city, 14.8 percent graduate.[95] At this rate, fewer than four will continue. Besides being statewide, the 70 percent figure tallies self-reported plans, which are not necessarily realized. Furthermore, calculations do not include students who drop out before showing up for their ninth-grade year. In addition, the 2003 graduation requirement of passing five regent's exams cuts more deeply into the graduation rates of students who have disadvantages and disabilities of various kinds. The new requirements make no adjustments for these students.

In their position paper, "Definition of a Sound Basic Education," Campaign for Fiscal Equity listed "essential resources" required to assist students to graduate from high school. Echoing *Levittown*, the group included teachers and personnel with appropriate skills; small classes; sufficient and up-to-date curricula, books, libraries, technology, and laboratories; appropriate support services for students who are at risk of academic failure; and adequate physical facilities in good repair. Researchers added requirements to create "a climate conducive to teaching and learning," including effective school leadership, professional development for teachers and staff, a safe, orderly, and respectful environment, good communication with parents/guardians and the community, and a range of extracurricular activities.[97]

Plaintiffs in *CFE IIa* adopted the Regents Learning Standards as indicative of a sound basic education, because these standards are required for high school graduation. But they included other outcomes as well. DeGrasse followed the *Levittown* court's caution concerning use of the standards carefully

> because many . . . exceed notions of a minimally adequate or sound basic education—some are also aspirational—prudence should govern [their] utilization . . . as benchmarks . . . noncompliance with one or more of the Regents' . . . standards may not, standing alone, establish a violation of the Education Article.[98]

Consequently, DeGrasse examined both inputs and outputs over "multiple years" (*24). Educational improvement takes more than a single year, so cohorts must be studied longitudinally.

Among inputs, DeGrasse found teachers' qualifications lacking (*25). Many do not teach in their area of certification. Special education has a very high rate of uncertified teachers (*27), which reveals the assumption that these children, most of them damaged by poverty, poor nutrition, lack of health care, and lead poisoning are ineducable. The passing rates on teachers' examinations in the city were abysmal; teachers in the most needy areas were the weakest and the least experienced. DeGrasse characterized the loss of experienced teachers to the suburbs as a "brain drain" and held that professional development opportunities were "inadequate" (*28). Although DeGrasse judged the curriculum to be "reasonably up-to-date," he noted that delivery was "hampered" by other deficiencies. For instance, arts and physical education classes, acknowledged as helpful to retain students in school were "defunded" and their spaces used for regular classes (*37–38).

DeGrasse noted other deficient inputs, including physical facilities (*43, *45–49), where overcrowding and lack of healthful and safe conditions presented serious problems (*50). Citing the Tennessee STAR program about the benefits of small classes, DeGrasse noted that large class sizes hamper educational opportunities for city schoolchildren. To compound the overcrowding, too little space is allotted per child in the formula to calculate capacity (*52). DeGrasse also held that, "While the present textbook allocation is adequate, it cannot remedy the negative effects of past shortages. Moreover, there is no structural funding mechanism that gives any assurance that the recent spike in textbook funding will continue" (*57). This same funding must also cover "consumables." DeGrasse judged the allocation of $41 (as of 1999–2000) per pupil "insufficient" (*57). In addition, "antiquated wiring" prevented computers from being installed in many schools; much of the existing technology was out-of-date. Although a survey showed one computer for every ten students, according to one expert, " 20,000 of the total of 109,341 computers in New York City public schools were essentially obsolete and that an additional number of aged '486s' and Apple computers were too weak to power recent operating platforms, Internet, or CD-ROM applications" (*60).

Among outputs, DeGrasse examined the ratio of so-called local (non-Regents) diplomas, GEDs, and Regents diplomas. Local diplomas were being phased out, replaced by Regents diplomas based on passing five regent's exams. He found:

> . . . of 100 ninth graders, 30% drop out, 10% get GEDs, that leaves 60%. . . . Historically, of the approximately 60% of ninth graders who ultimately received a Regents or local diploma, the vast majority received a local diploma. In recent years, less than 12% of all ninth graders have eventually received a Regents diploma. (*63)

Evidence also showed:

> In reading tests given in 1998–1999, 21.3% of City fourth graders scored in level one, the lowest level, while only 5.8% of fourth grade students in the rest of the State scored in level one. In the same year 17% of eighth graders scored in level one for reading, compared with 5% in the rest of the State. Similar results were recorded for math tests with City's eighth graders performing particularly poorly. On none of the tests did more than half of the City's students score in levels three and four, the higher levels that demonstrate that students are on track to meet the Regents' standards. (*66)

In the city, reading and math scores from 2001, as reported by the Manhattan Institute, lagged behind statewide scores by 10 percent or more; only 44 percent of blacks and 39 percent of Hispanics graduated in four years; SAT scores were 35 percent to 50 percent lower on each section of the test for city students, only 37 percent of whom take the test; and so forth.[99] No one disputes that the statistics are dismal. But the analysis of the cause differs. The conservative Manhattan Institute supports privatization of failing public schools.[100] Researchers in the Institute do not question whether the children of the wealthy and powerful need expensive resources—AP courses, Olympic-size swimming pools, and beautiful buildings. Other researchers conclude that inadequate spending on the public schools is the cause of poor performance, proof of which *CFE* lawyers sought to provide. DeGrasse noted:

> The establishment of such a causal link might appear to be fairly straightforward. If it can be shown that increased funding can provide New York City with better teachers, better school buildings, and better instrumentalities of learning, then it would appear that a causal link has been established between the current funding system and the poor performance of the City's public schools. (*68)

CFE lawyers succeeded in making the elusive causal link between deficient inputs and the poor outcomes of education in New York City, as demanded by the Court of Appeals in 1995. They showed that inputs were deficient and outputs were deficient. This was enough for Justice DeGrasse. Because poverty, racism, an unhealthful environment, malnutrition, and illness cloud the issue, the problem is not simple. But depriving these children of educational resources makes no sense whatsoever. It compounds their difficulties.

The court in *CFE IIa* rejected evidence compiled by defense witnesses, Dr. Hanushek and Dr. Armor, purportedly showing that there was no correlation between spending and test scores. Dr. Hanushek's evidence was not based on longitudinal measurements of a single cohort, but on studies of different cohorts in a single year; consequently, it did not show the impact of spending on a cohort through time. Dr. Armor's evidence

> . . . was skewed by his decision to "level the playing field" by adjusting test scores to account for socioeconomic characteristics of at-risk students . . . [which] rests on the premise that was not established at trial: that at-risk students' educational potential is immutably shaped by their backgrounds. (*72)

Armor's assumptions reflected the now discredited claim of the Coleman Report that the education of black students was influenced by quality of peers, background, and neighborhood factors more than by school spending. Dr. Armor's evidence, like Coleman's before him, also failed to link funding to the performance of individual students. DeGrasse wrote:

Dr. Armor's analyses of resources failed to track the effect of resources provided to individual students. For example, dollars spent on a reading recovery program in a given school would be attributed to a school's budget, but very few students would actually receive that benefit. (*72)

Justice DeGrasse rejected the claim that the state's policy of counting average daily attendance rather than enrollment for purposes of distributing state aid encouraged schools to improve attendance;

New York City, with its high percentage of at-risk students, has a lower average attendance rate than most districts in the rest of the State. Lower attendance rates do not reduce New York City's obligations, however. The City is still required to provide space and staff to serve all enrolled pupils. This is a source of disparate impact. The State's choice to base school funding on districts' average attendance is unnecessarily punitive. It creates a perverse direction of State aid by directing aid away from districts with large numbers of at-risk students. (*112)

As directed by the Court of Appeals in *CFE Ic*, DeGrasse "fleshed out" the meaning of a "sound basic education."[101]

Productive citizenship means more than just being qualified to vote and serve as a juror, but to do so capably and knowledgeably. It connotes civic engagement. An engaged, capable voter needs the intellectual tools to evaluate complex issues, such as campaign finance reform, tax policy, and global warming, to name only a few. . . . Productive citizenship implies engagement and contribution in the economy as well as in public life. . . . This court finds this duty [to give students the foundational skills they need to obtain productive employment or pursue higher education] inherent in the Court of Appeal's admonition that students must be prepared to become productive citizens. (*25–27)

After a seven-month trial, on January 10, 2001, DeGrasse found the school funding formula unconstitutional because it failed to supply New York City's school children with a "sound basic education" as required. He also supported the plaintiffs' allegations of civil rights violations:

New York State has over the course of many years consistently violated the Education Article of the NY Constitution by failing to provide the opportunity for a sound basic education to New York City public school students. In addition, the State's public school financing system has also had an unjustified disparate impact on minority students in violation of Federal law. (*113)

While deferring to the legislature, the governor, the State Education Department, and the regents to remedy the situation, DeGrasse directed the state to take corrective action, after determining the actual costs of a sound basic education in different areas of the state, a procedure called "costing out." While declining to follow Kentucky's ambitious template in *Rose*, DeGrasse listed seven points to be considered in a remedy, based on *Levittown's* directions and testimony in *CFE IIa*.

(i)   Sufficient numbers of qualified teachers, principals and other personnel.
(ii) Appropriate class sizes.
(iii) Adequate and accessible school buildings with sufficient space to ensure appropriate class size and implementation of a sound curriculum.
(iv) Sufficient and up-to-date books, supplies, libraries, educational technology and laboratories.
(v)   Suitable curricula, including an expanded platform of programs to help at-risk students by giving them "more time on task."
(vi) Adequate resources for students with extraordinary needs.
(vii) A safe orderly environment. (*115)

Finally, DeGrasse gave the state two deadlines—report back by June 15 on progress toward a solution of inequitable school funding and have reforms in place by September. In October 2005, the Legislature had yet to devise statewide reform.

Instead of implementing Justice DeGrasse's ruling, the state chose to appeal. The initial trial had lasted more than a year. It took Governor Pataki a scant month to announce his decision to appeal. A year later, on June 8, 2002, the Appellate Court, First Division, overruled Justice DeGrasse on both the law and the facts in a four-to-one decision.[102] The court denied both state constitutional and federal civil rights violations. The plaintiffs changed their civil rights claim to a Section 1983 claim that the funding scheme violated the implementing regulations of the Civil Rights Act, after *Sandoval* (*19–20). The Appellate Division rejected this argument, also refusing to acknowledge a causal link between low spending, poverty, and minority status and the quality of the education that a child receives in New York City, stating, "Even if we were to assume that the schools in the City do not provide a sound basic education, plaintiffs failed to prove that deficiencies in the City's school system are caused by the State's funding system" (*16). The judges even suggested that remedying "inappropriate placement" in special education could save the city $1 billion (*6). Other state courts where inequitable funding has been ruled unconstitutional under state constitutions did not question the causal link. Minnesota judges argued in *Van Dusartz v. Hatfield* (1977) that

> When the correlation between expenditure per pupil and the quality of education may be open to argument, the court must assume here that it is high. To do otherwise would be to hold that in those wealthy districts where the per-pupil expenditure is higher . . . the school boards are merely wasting the taxpayer's money.[103]

Instead, the New York Appellate Division held that

> The 'sound basic education' standard enunciated by the Court of Appeals in 1985 (86 NY2d 307) requires the State to provide a minimally adequate educational *opportunity*, but not, as the [trial] court held, to guarantee some higher, largely unspecified level of education, as laudable as that goal might be. Since the court, after a trial of the issues, applied an improper standard, we reverse. (*CFE IIb* *3)

This ruling effectively accused Judge DeGrasse of judicial activism for issuing his seven-point template for a constitutional education in New York. In so doing, the panel ruled that a "minimally adequate" education consisting of basic skills in reading, writing, and calculating "imparted between the eighth or ninth grade" fulfills the state's constitutional mandate for a "sound, basic education" (*9). The panel members held that the state only owes children an "opportunity" for a sound basic education; presumably, if students fail to take advantage of it, that is their problem. In the words of the court,

> It bears contemplation that the State's obligation is to provide children with the *opportunity* to obtain the fundamental skills comprising a sound basic education. That not all students actually achieve that level of education does not necessarily indicate a failure of the State to meet its constitutional obligations. (*9)

The court's interpretation of the constitutional mandate reveals a degree of arrogance that is surprising. As the court put it, "the ability to 'function productively' should be interpreted as the ability to get a job, and support oneself, and thereby not be a charge on the public fisc [sic]." This, they reasoned, would allow students "to obtain employment and to competently discharge [their] civic responsibilities." The majority argued that many new jobs are low-level, low-paid jobs, which someone must do (*8). That someone, according to their logic, is the poor and minority children of New York City and other urban areas in the state. The majority refused DeGrasse's argument that workers could not make a living on the minimum wage because "no evidence to that effect was given at the trial."[104] It doesn't take much insight to see that an education imparting only this level of functioning diminishes the life chances of those receiving it. In fact, the decision appears to release New York districts from an obligation to provide any high school education whatsoever. To blame public schoolchildren of New York City because they don't take advantage of the glorious opportunity offered them seems callous at best; at worst, it is both criminal and overtly racist.

In overturning DeGrasses's decision, the Appellate Division focused on inputs, rather than both inputs and outputs as the trial court had done. Persuaded by the state's lawyers that many of the Regents Learning Standards are merely aspirational, the court refused to recognize that these aspirational standards had indeed become the basis for high school graduation, which is a minimum standard for education in the twenty-first century. The judges accepted results of the phased-out Regents Competency Tests as proof of minimally adequate success instead. The position seems inconsistent with their insistence on separation of powers, since Commissioner Mills and the Board of Regents have adamantly refused to back down from the regents requirement, despite the many demonstrated difficulties with tying graduation to high-stakes testing. The court was satisfied that teacher's qualifications would improve as the new rule that all teachers must be certified went into effect in June 2003. (Predictably, that was postponed in New York City and other areas.)[105] In addition, the court blamed collective bargaining agreements for the lack of experienced teachers, because teachers with seniority are allowed to transfer (*18). It did not seem to occur to the court that, if the conditions were improved, experienced teachers might choose to stay. The court suggested that running schools year-round could eliminate overcrowding, stretching the existing buildings to cover the predicted increase in school population (*11). In so far as the court was concerned, the defendants' testimony that immediately hazardous conditions had been fixed since the trial was "indication of progress" (*10). On top of that, the court opined that obsolete computers could be used for "introductory classes" (*11), that out-of-date library books were "classics" (*12), and that the lack of money for the city's schools was at least partly due to over-referral of students to special education. The court claimed that "the savings created by returning improperly referred students to the general school population (where the cost is 50% to 75% less per student than special education) would amount to hundreds of millions of dollars, if not $1 billion . . ." (*17). The court also suggested that the city was responsible for the deficiencies, not the state.

Public outrage at the decision was immediate, universal, and scathing. H. Carl McCall called it "outrageous." Michael Rebell called it "callous" and "shocking."[106] The *New York Times* said it was "wrong-headed" and quoted Justice David Saxe's dissent that, "in essence the court was blaming the victim."[107] One reporter added, "I believe the judges, none of whom is Hispanic or black, would have handed down a different decision if the majority of the students in the New York City schools were white."[108] *Newsday* called it "disturbing." *City Beat* said that the "stunning" decision "defies logic." To the mayor, it was "deeply disappointing"; to the chancellor, then Harold Levy, "immoral." Levy added that, in effect, the decision condemned New York City schoolchildren to "become menial laborers."[109] After reaching an impasse in seeking an agreement with Governor Pataki, Campaign for Fiscal Equity announced its intention to appeal. The group filed a brief on January 8, 2003, asking for a June decision.[110]

At the same time as *CFE* was wending its way through the courts, a case in Rochester, New York, made another civil rights claim. *Amber Paynter et al., on Behalf of Themselves and All Others Similarly Situated*, v. *State of New York, et al.*[111] was brought in 1998, then challenged by defendants on the grounds that the suburban school districts were not included among the defendants. Judge Robert J. Lunn of the Supreme Court in Monroe County held that they could be joined later, at the remedial phase of the trial, should the plaintiffs prevail on the merits. The Appellate Division overturned this ruling in March 2000, requiring that the complaint be amended to include the suburban school districts as defendants, because they must participate in the remedy.[112] This the plaintiffs did, perhaps with some misgivings, because they specifically stated that they did not allege any wrongdoing by the suburban districts. The complaint, now amended to include the suburban districts, was decided in New York's Supreme Court by Judge John Ark on November 14, 2000.[113] The court promptly dismissed the charges against the suburban districts. The court also dismissed charges against Rochester City School District (RCSD) because of the ruling in *Milliken* v. *Bradley* that "no interdistrict remedy" can be forced upon districts (*230–231). The group bringing the suit, the Greater Rochester Area Coalition for Education (GRACE), did not allege that funding was inequitable, but that the education received by the children was inadequate. The schools were failing "on virtually every measure of educational outcomes" (*229). The plaintiffs' exclusive focus on outcomes proved fatal; citing *REFIT* and *Levittown*, the court ruled that "poor academic outcomes alone are insufficient to establish a claim under the Education Article" (*231). This ruling effectively dismissed evidence of massive academic failure.

Allegations of state and federal civil rights violations in the case were left. *Paynter* had alleged that racial and economic isolation in the hypersegregated and economically isolated RCSD had resulted in the "wholesale academic failure" of its schoolchildren (*228). The Appellate Division appeared not to question the link between racial and economic isolation and poor outcomes. In the first place, the state prevented location of low-income housing in suburban neighborhoods unless they consented. In the second place, the state required that city school districts be coterminous with city boundaries. Finally, children were required to attend schools in their neighborhood of residence. These regulations concentrated low-income, mostly minority children in city schools. The segregation in RCSD was (and remains) intense, creating a school population 90 percent poor and 80 percent black and Hispanic, as compared to other districts in Monroe County at 16 percent poor and 9 percent black and Hispanic (*229). The suit charged that this violated the state equal protection clause, and constituted intentional discrimination under Title VI, Section 601 of the Civil Rights Act of 1964 and disparate impact discrimination under the implementing regulations, 42 U.S.C. Section 2000d.[114] The court dismissed both equal protection charges, citing *Rodriguez* and *Levittown* in concluding that education is not a fundamental right (*234–235).

Warning that legislative actions "carry a strong presumption of constitutionality," and that "Title VI claims require proof of discriminatory intent" to succeed, the court left the Title VI charges intact (*237). Judge Ark ruled, "the plaintiffs may proceed to establish their claim that the repeal of the authority . . . to construct low-income housing without the approval of the municipalities was racially motivated and had a discriminatory intent" (*237). Once intent was established, then the defendant must prove "whether the practice is nevertheless sufficiently justified" (*237). The court decided, "the plaintiffs have presumptively established that the combined effect [of the two regulations] is sufficient to warrant refusing to dismiss the charge" (*237–238). Before the outcome of *Alexander* v. *Sandoval*[115] at the Supreme Court, Judge Ark allowed the plaintiffs to proceed. Acknowledging that low-income housing had "been shifted from the suburbs to the city,"[116] and that segregation has grown worse in New York since 1964, the court discussed possible remedies. Reviewing the problems, described as "unlimited needs . . . [to be satisfied by] limited resources" (*238), the impossibility of a court-ordered interdistrict remedy, and the failure of voluntary transfer programs that further isolated the most needy children in the city schools, Ark recommended that both parties seek a "composite remedy" (*239). Alluding to *Brown*, Judge Ark held that "the RCSD is separate but apparently not equal." Calling the plaintiff's case "compelling," he lamented that "the courts were not competent to resolve these most difficult education issues" (*239). Thus, Ark recommended to both parties to "consider committing their resources to the fashioning and application of remedies"

(*239). It was clear, however, that the defendants had not been interested in remedies for years.

The state appealed for dismissal of the remaining charge,[117] while the plaintiffs challenged the dismissal of the other charges. The Appellate Division upheld the previous dismissals, and sided with the state on the civil rights claim, ruling that the plaintiffs failed to state a viable cause of action. It decided that the education clause of the New York Constitution could not be challenged. It "constitutionalized" the system of schools in the state and the complaint, if acted upon, would undermine that system. On the civil rights claims, the court wrote:

> We reject plaintiffs' contention that 34 CFR 100.3 (b) (2) applies to section 3 of chapter 446 of the Laws of 1973. Section 3 restricts the authority of the Urban Development Corporation to build low-cost housing in the suburbs without local approval. Thus, it is not a "criterion or method of administration" used by the State with respect to the delivery of educational services. (34 CFR 100.3[b] [2])
>
> We further reject plaintiffs' contention that Education Law § 3202 has a racially disparate impact in violation of 34 CFR 100.3 (b) (2). Education Law § 3202 establishes the framework for resident-based public education in this State. Even assuming, arguendo, that the provisions of Education Law § 3202 have a racially disparate impact, we conclude that they do not violate 34 CFR 100.3 (b) (2) if they are uniformly applied because the "State . . . has a substantial interest in imposing bona fide residence requirements to maintain the quality of local public schools." Because plaintiffs fail to allege that Education Law § 3202 is not being uniformly applied, they have failed to allege a viable claim under 34 CFR 100.3 (b) (2). (*103, references omitted)

The rule did not create either intentional or disparate impact discrimination, so it did not violate Title VI or Section 1983 of the Civil Rights Act.[118] Interestingly, Justice LeLand DeGrasse ruled in favor of a similar civil rights claim two weeks later in *Campaign for Fiscal Equity* in January 2001. The difference, according to the Court of Appeals, is that the *CFE* case charged inadequacy of funding, which the *Paynter* case did not.

Judge Samuel L. Green, dissenting in part and concurring in part, agreed that the charges against the suburban school districts were properly dismissed. But he emphatically disagreed with the dismissal of the civil rights charges. He held that "wholesale academic failure" in itself was enough to charge that the state was not doing its job—offering all children the opportunity of a sound basic education. In *Paynter*, he stated, plaintiffs are "alleging that they are deprived of this constitutional right [to a sound basic education] as a result of causes unrelated to funding"

(*106). Green held that the state was responsible. He pointed out that the majority inappropriately concluded that "there will be myriad reasons for academic failure that are beyond the control of the State" before the plaintiffs have had an opportunity to make their case (*107). He also held that the majority's attempt to define a sound basic education is "premature," given that no evidentiary record has been established yet. This ruling preceded DeGrasse's decision in *CFE IIa*, which did establish an evidentiary record, by two weeks. Green's voice was not heeded, however. Now it was the plaintiffs' turn to appeal. At this point, the United States Supreme Court ruling in *Sandoval* took its toll on *Paynter*.

Both *CFE IIc*[119] and *Paynter*[120] were decided by New York's Court of Appeals in June 2003. Fortunately for New York City's schoolchildren, the Court of Appeals overturned the Appellate Division's decision in *CFE IIb*, remanding the case to DeGrasse's supervision with orders to the state do the costing-out study DeGrasse requested and reform the school-funding formula to eliminate the shortage in New York City by July 2004. Chief Judge Judith Kaye opened her opinion saying, "We begin with a unanimous recognition of the importance of education in our democracy" (*CFE IIc* *1–2). Affirming the duty of "this court" to adjudicate the nature of the state's obligation, Kaye accepted the template that Justice DeGrasse had developed. If New York had adopted the Appellate Division's decision, it would have condemned many of the city's poor and minority children to inhabit its jails, be on its welfare rolls, or join the swelling number of the homeless. Instead, the Court of Appeals wrote,

> In *CFE*, [*CFE Ic*] we equated a sound basic education with basic literary, calculating, and verbal skills to enable children to eventually function as civic participants capable of voting and sitting on a jury. We thus indicated that a sound basic education conveys not merely skills but skills fashioned to meet a practical goal: meaningful civic participation in contemporary society. (*11)

The judges agreed that more than an eighth grade education is required. They accepted the validity of New York Regents Learning Standards, but also acknowledged that many exceed the minimum requirement. According to the court, "To enshrine the Learning Standards would be to cede to a state agency the power to define a constitutional right" (*12). The plaintiffs did not request that this be done, but instead contended "children are entitled to a meaningful high school education" (*12). Most importantly, the court ruled that students in New York have a right to a meaningful high school education, arguing as follows:

> The Appellate Division concluded that "there was no evidence quantifying how many drop-outs fail to obtain a sound basic education"

(295 A.D.2d at 15). That conclusion follows from the Appellate Division's premise that a sound basic education is imparted by eighth or ninth grade. A sound basic education, however, means a meaningful high school education. Under that standard, it may, as a practical matter, be presumed that a dropout has not received a sound basic education. In any event the evidence was unrebutted that dropouts typically are not prepared for productive citizenship, as the trial court concluded. The Appellate Division would have required a precise quantitative division between those dropouts who somehow are adequately [*915] prepared and those who are not, but such a requirement is nowhere to be found in *CFE*. (*914–915)

The court decided that trial court's interpretation of a sound basic education prevailed over the Appellate Division's interpretation. The case was remanded to Justice DeGrasse's supervision, with a deadline of July 4, 2004, for a new funding formula to be in place.

When the legislature failed to meet that deadline, DeGrasse appointed a three-man panel to serve as special referees, William C. Thompson and E. Leo Milonas, retired Appellate Division justices, and John D. Feerick, former dean of the Fordham Law School. The panel recommended adding $5.6 billion to New York City schools over four years, a capital improvement plan of $9.18 billion over five years, and continued study of the school-funding formulae.[121] DeGrasse accepted the plan as constitutional in February 2005. Pataki opposed the recommendation, appealing DeGrasse's acceptance. In summer 2005, the legislature adjourned again without having revised the funding formulae, despite the introduction of a bill by Assemblyman Steven Sanders, crafted along the same lines as a bill proposed by Campaign for Fiscal Equity (CFE).[122] Instead of action, a bill creating yet another commission to study the situation languished in the education committee in July 2005.[123]

Unfortunately for Rochester's schoolchildren, the same Court of Appeals upheld the dismissal of all charges in *Paynter* on the same day. In both cases, the federal civil rights violations were denied. In *Paynter*, the claim under the state's equal protection and education clauses were also denied. Appellate Court and Court of Appeals judges refused to allow a trial to examine the question of racial and economic isolation, refused to determine that it was intentional, and refused to allow a disparate impact claim to stand, under Section 601 or Section 1983. The federal ruling in *Alexander* v. *Sandoval* had intervened.[124] *Sandoval* leaves little redress for individuals who have been harmed by discrimination. Apparently only state agencies may sue, which amounts to putting the fox in charge of the hencoop.

In *CFE IIc*, Judge Smith wrote separately, urging that the civil rights claims be reinstated. While the rest of the Court of Appeals agreed that the remedy could be restricted to New York City,[125] Smith's broader view would have included Rochester's children.

> I conclude that (a) the Regents Learning Standards provide students with the minimum skills required by a sound basic education, (b) the remedy should be Statewide in scope and (c) should include the reformulation of the present formula for allocating state funds. All the children of New York are constitutionally entitled to the opportunity of a high school education—up to the twelfth grade—that imparts the skills necessary to sustain competitive employment within the market of high school graduates, acquire higher education, and serve capably on a jury and vote.[126]

Judge Smith contrasted the word "may" in the clause, allowing the state to establish prisons with the word "shall" in the clause, commanding the state to establish schools. He disagreed vehemently with the state's claim that preparation for low-paid jobs meets the state's constitutional obligation to prepare "productive citizens."

> The record establishes what would strike many as an obvious truth: A high school education is today as indispensable as a primary education was in 1894. Children in the twenty-first century need the opportunity for more than a ninth grade education to be productive citizens. Back in the nineteenth century, a high school education was not needed to obtain a good job. Now, a high school education is a prerequisite to most good jobs. Those who lack a high school education and have obtained good jobs have done so in spite of, not because of, the lack of a high school education. While it may be true that there will always be menial low-skills jobs, and thus a need for people to fill them, it should not be the purpose of the public schools to prepare students for those jobs, which are limited in number and dwindling. (*64, references omitted)

Smith recounted the history of education in New York in detail to point out that the standard has constantly risen to meet the needs of the times. Judge Smith pointed to the interdependency of grade school, high school, and college. Even at the 1894 Constitutional Convention in New York, delegates stated, "higher education here, as in all other civilized countries, has been the chief factor in developing the elementary and secondary schools" (1894 NY Constitutional Convention, Doc. No. 62, p. 6) (*76). Smith also analyzed the current formulae used to determine state share, finding that, "Virtually every document in the record prepared by the Regents or the SED [State Education Department] dealing with funding has been critical of the formulas" (*91). Smith's conclusion:

> In place of the formulas, the Legislature should institute a scheme that: (1) Eliminates the current state formula for distributing aid to New York City; (2) Determines, to the extent possible, the actual costs of the resources needed to provide the opportunity for a sound basic education in all school districts in the State; (3) Ensures that at a minimum every school district has the necessary funds to provide an opportunity for a sound basic education to all of its students. While the foregoing may not guarantee that the opportunity of a basic education will be available to all the children in the State, they are necessary steps in that direction. In sum, I join the decision of the Chief Judge, but the Constitution requires the State to do even more than is stated to ensure a sound basic education for all students. (*98–99)

Alas, Rochester children's needs were ignored.

Lacking: The Political Will to Remedy Injustice in New York

The crisis in New York exemplifies much that makes reform of school funding in the United States difficult. These children did nothing to harm anyone, but they are being grievously harmed by the very state that depends on them as future citizens, family and community members, and workers. As things stand, if poorly educated, lower socioeconomic status students are lucky, they will become the working poor, barely able to support themselves, let alone a family, on two jobs at the minimum wage.[127] Even though the New York Legislature has opted to raise the minimum wage to $7.15 an hour by 2007,[128] it is nearly impossible to live on such a small wage without decent low-income public housing, health insurance, adequate nutrition for poor pregnant women and their children, state-subsidized day care, good public transportation, or equitably funded schools.[129] If the poor are not lucky, their children will be ill-educated, illiterate, unemployed, and perhaps in prison.

Since the rulings in *Milliken* v. *Bradley, Board of Education of Oklahoma City Public Schools* v. *Dowell,* and *Freeman* v. *Pitts,* easy remedies for segregation are hard to find. Of course, bold remedies do exist, such as redistricting, building mixed neighborhoods in both cities and suburbs, or using a system to mix school attendance zones, like that in Charlotte-Mecklenburg in the 1970s, which assigned all children from a predominately white and a predominantly black district to attend primary schools in one district and intermediate schools in the other. It remains to be seen what remedy can be found to ameliorate the effects of racial segregation and economic isolation in Rochester and many other cities. It is a good sign that the judges used outcomes language as the marker of success in their definition of a sound basic education. It certainly seems reasonable to claim that a child would have to graduate in order to receive "a meaningful high school education." Moreover, a constitutional right cannot be enforced in only one part of the state; lack of a state solution is sure to spawn more lawsuits.

Two different scenarios for reform of school funding in two regions adjacent to New York provide insight into school-funding reform. In Vermont, the judicial and legislative reforms went smoothly and quickly, but public reaction against having to share money raised for schools simmered for years and boiled over in 2003 when the legislature substituted a sales tax for the sharing pool. In Ontario, executive reform, undertaken to cut property taxes, was both high-handed and harmful. Ontario Boards were forced to amalgamate into unwieldy units. They lost their autonomy, their right to tax, and their control of curriculum. Years of inadequate funding snowballed, costing the premier an election in October 2003. I turn to these cases next, to see what we can learn from them.

Chapter 3

Sharing in Vermont

To keep a democracy competitive and thriving, students must be afforded equal access to all that our educational system has to offer. In the funding of what our Constitution places at the core of a successful democracy, the children of Vermont are entitled to a reasonably equal share.

Amanda Brigham v. *State of Vermont,* 1997

Gross and Glaring Inequity in Vermont

Vermont is generally known as a progressive state, yet, historically, it has spent considerably less money per pupil for education than many other states, including its neighbor, New York. Vermont also had the widest inequalities reported by the National Center for Education Statistics (NCES) in 1998.[1] In 1996, Carol Brigham, Amanda Brigham's mother, sued the state for its unequal funding of education in *Amanda Brigham* v. *State.*[2] The case quickly advanced to the state's Supreme Court, which ruled the funding formula unconstitutional in 1997. Act 60, reforming the state's funding was in place in record time, for the 1998 school year. Act 60 allowed towns to raise extra funds over the state allotment, but required them to share the extra funds with property-poor districts according to a recapture plan. In May 2003, the Vermont legislature revised Act 60 with Act 68, which eliminated the sharing pool in the school year 2004–2005. Apparently, the sharing pool provision of Act 60 was too contentious to last. In exchange for the elimination of the sharing pool, Vermont now pays a higher state share in the form of a larger flat grant regardless of the wealth of the district. In 2004–2005, under the new legislation, Vermont planned to spend a flat rate of a little more than $6,000 per pupil. Although the new state share is an improvement over earlier figures, nevertheless, the new amount is low compared to

New York's average per-pupil expenditure of more than $9,000. However, New York's figure is an average; some districts spend more, while others less, which will remain the case until the New York legislature acts on the Court of Appeals' decision in *Campaign for Fiscal Equity*.

The National Center for Education Statistics reported in 1996 (based on 1991–1992 figures) that districts in Vermont at the fifth percentile of revenues had total actual revenues per pupil of $5,382, whereas in the ninety-fifth percentile, revenues per pupil were $11,290. Large differences remained even when the indices were adjusted for cost and need. The adjusted total revenues per pupil were $4,546 in low-wealth districts at the fifth percentile, while revenues per pupil stood at $9,735 in high-wealth districts at the ninety-fifth percentile.[3] Vermont also had one of the widest differentials in per-pupil spending among its towns, which correspond to districts in other states.[4] Vermont ranked in the highest quartile in disparity among districts in both actual revenues and cost- and need-adjusted revenues. Only a handful of states joined Vermont at that rate of disparity—Illinois, Missouri, New Hampshire, and Ohio.[5] Sharing the honors with New Hampshire, New York, Missouri, Montana, Nebraska, Ohio, and Illinois, Vermont measured in the lowest quartile on all five measures of inequity used in the report.[6] By 1998 these disparities had increased. Based on 1998 figures published in *Education Week* in 2000, researchers Bruce Biddle and David Berliner reported that Vermont was a "winner" in the "inequity derby" with disparities of an average of $15,186 per pupil in the ninety-fifth percentile of per-pupil spending to $6,442 in the fifth percentile.[7] The reforms of 1998 aimed to reduce such disparities.

The political economy of Vermont is, in part, the source of the difficulty. Property-rich ski towns (called "gold towns" and "sending towns" under Act 60), with expensive resorts and vacation homes had higher taxable assets than the property-poor rural towns (called "receiving towns"). Consequently, poor towns had to levy taxes at higher rates in order to fund even the basic minimum in school services.[8] The gold towns, on the other hand, could raise enough for a quality education at a lower tax rate. According to William Mathis, the *Brigham* case began when Carol Brigham, Amanda's mother, who was also a member of the school board, noticed, "The town of Whiting has limited property wealth and has always had a difficult time funding their school. Standing in the playground, you can easily see the Killington ski resort which spent 25 percent more per pupil at a tax rate one-fourth of that in Whiting."[9] Vermont's small state share, varying between 20 percent and 35 percent, bore some of the responsibility for the inequality of funding as well. Another component of school funding in Vermont was the passion of Vermonters for local control. Town meetings, at which school budgets are debated and approved, are the norm under a much more direct form of democracy than exists in most states.[10]

The plaintiffs in *Brigham* v. *State* brought their suit under a variety of distinct but overlapping charges, as explained by the Supreme Court in *Brigham's* Procedural History.

> (1) two students . . . claimed that the State's method of financing public education deprived them of their right under the Vermont and federal constitutions to the same educational opportunities as students who reside in wealthier school districts; (2) several property owners from "property poor" school districts . . . claimed that the current school financing scheme compels them to contribute more than their just proportion of money to fund education, in violation of these constitutions; and (3) two school districts . . . claimed that the current financing scheme deprives them of the ability to raise sufficient money to provide their students with educational opportunities equal to those afforded students in wealthier school districts, and compels them to impose disproportionate tax rates in violation of the United States and Vermont Constitutions.[11]

At the trial in Lamoille Superior Court, Judge John J. Meeker dismissed the federal violations on the grounds that there was no federal right to an education. Because the Vermont constitution stipulates that "every member of society is 'bound to contribute his [sic] proportion towards the expense [of education] . . .'," Judge Meeker upheld the second and third claims under the state constitution.[12] Both parties were dissatisfied with the ruling, which contained something for both sides, but pleased neither. They asked the appeals court for a summary judgment to dismiss. This motion was denied and appealed to the Supreme Court. In an unusual move, the Vermont Supreme Court bypassed the appellate court to rule in favor of the plaintiffs in *Brigham* v. *State*. As the judges explained in the procedural history of *Brigham*, "The parties moved jointly for permission to appeal the judgment except for that portion disposing of plaintiffs' federal equal protection claims. The [appellate] court denied the motion. The parties thereupon renewed their motion with this Court, and we granted the motion" (*Brigham*, *252). The Supreme Court then proceeded to rule on the case. As the judges reasoned, "Where a party appeals a ruling, but devotes such scant attention to it that the appellate court would be forced to undertake a search for error because it was not adequately briefed or supported by arguments, the [appellate] court will decline to rule on the issue" (*248). The court's opening statement declared,

> In this appeal, we decide that the current system for funding public education in Vermont, with its substantial dependence on local

property taxes and resultant wide disparities in revenues available to
local school districts, deprives children of an equal educational opportunity in violation of the Vermont Constitution. In reaching this
conclusion, we acknowledge the conscientious and ongoing efforts of
the Legislature to achieve equity in educational financing and intend
no intrusion upon its prerogatives to define a system consistent with
constitutional requirements. In this context, the Court's duty today is
solely to define the impact of the State Constitution on educational
funding, not to fashion and impose a solution. The remedy at this
juncture properly lies with the Legislature. (*249)

The court's ruling was far-flung. Claiming that "the facts were not
in dispute," the court cited evidence supporting the plaintiffs' claims of
inequities from the Governor's Blue Ribbon Commission on Educational
and Municipal Financing Reform: Final Report and Recommendations
of 1993 and similar earlier efforts to reform Vermont's recognized disparities (*253). The opinion stated,

> The trial court noted the State had "conceded that the present fund-
> ing scheme denies children residing in comparatively property-poor
> school districts the same 'educational opportunities' that are avail-
> able to students residing in wealthier districts.' The State has not
> only failed to challenge this finding, it affirmatively relies on it to
> demonstrate that . . . no genuine issue of material fact remains to be
> resolved at trial. (*254)

Noting a close connection between education and virtue reflected in the
joining of the education and virtue clauses in Vermont's 1786 constitution (*262), the court established to its satisfaction that education was
considered important in Vermont's unique legislative and political history. The opinion also stated that other state cases did not constitute
compelling precedents for Vermont, since each state differs in its constitution, history, and legislation, although the judges did note that the current trend was to hold education to be a fundamental right in the states
(*259). Repudiating the idea that rational basis scrutiny was required
and local control would trump other claims after the precedent in the
federal case, *Board of Education of San Antonio* v. *Rodriguez,* the court denied that *Rodriguez* applied to Vermont. The judges even called local control in the property-poor districts of Vermont "a cruel illusion," echoing
the language of Marshall's dissent in *Rodriguez* (*266). Avoiding choosing
strict scrutiny outright, the court declared the current system of school
funding unconstitutional under any level of scrutiny.

> Whether we apply the "strict scrutiny" test urged by plaintiffs, the
> "rational standard" advocated by the State, or some intermediate

level of review, the conclusion remains the same; in Vermont the right to education is so integral to our constitutional form of government, and its guarantees of political and civil rights, that any statutory framework that infringes upon the equal enjoyment of that right bears a commensurate heavy burden of justification. (*256)

The weight of their argument fell on Vermont's Common Benefits Clause, whereby "distinctions will be found unconstitutional only if similar persons are treated differently on 'wholly arbitrary and capricious grounds'" (*268). The judges held this to be coextensive with the equivalent guarantee in the United States Constitution [the Equal Protection Clause] (*266). Furthermore, the court reasoned,

> . . . we are simply unable to fathom a legitimate governmental purpose to justify the gross inequities in educational opportunities evident from the record. The distribution of a resource as precious as educational opportunity may not have as its determining force the mere fortuity of a child's residence. It requires no particular constitutional expertise to recognize the capriciousness of such a system. (*265)

The judges compiled a historical record of Vermont's dedication to education, while also holding that Vermont schoolchildren in the twentieth century should not be held back by "eighteenth-century standards" (*268). The court did not order that absolute equality be established in school funding, but ordered that the legislature devise a plan for funding Vermont's schools, which would ensure "a reasonably equal share" to its poorer districts (*267).

In 1997, Peter Teachout, a Vermont Law School professor, attacked this decision, on the basis that it constituted a threat to local control. The Vermont judges had specifically rejected the local-control argument, holding that there is no *prime facie* reason why statewide funding has to obliterate local control. The judges, with eminent common sense, declared that "regardless of how the state finances public education, it may still leave the basic decision-making power with the districts."[13] Teachout also attacked the Vermont Supreme Court for putting "itself above the normal process of the law."[14] The court had anticipated this attack, stating that there was no dispute about the facts of the case; therefore, an evidentiary record like DeGrasse's in New York was not needed. Matters not briefed sufficiently before the trial court could, legally, be decided on appeal by the Supreme Court. Teachout accused the judges of patching *Brigham* together from other state court decisions, rather than basing it on evidence, despite the fact that the decision provided references to evidence of inequality compiled during formal inquiries by Vermont government officials. The judges had stated that they relied solely on the history of Vermont's education clause. The national consensus was also clear on the enormity of the inequities in Vermont, as demonstrated in National Center for Education Statistics (NCES) figures. Teachout also noted that *Brigham* was not opposed to unequal spending *per se*, but unequal spending based solely on where children happen to live (29). However, the funding system that created the enormous inequity in Vermont was based on where children happened to live. Not without some problems, Act 60 and the sharing pool came into existence as an experiment in retaining local control while introducing some equity into Vermont's school funding.

The Rise and Fall of Act 60

A few months after Vermont's Supreme Court declared the state's system of financing schools to be unconstitutional in *Brigham* v. *State*, the legislature passed the Equal Educational Opportunity Act (EEOA), also known as Act 60, reforming school finance, which was phased in over four years (1998–2001). The legislation evoked immediate controversy because of the recapture provision that wealthy towns would have to share any extra tax money collected for their schools with poor towns. Thus began a political battle of six years' duration. There was also a legal challenge to Act 60, which was squelched in short order by an adamant Vermont Supreme Court.

Vermont's Act 60 equalized property taxes by implementing a uniform tax rate while at the same time allowing local decision-making if a community wanted to spend more than the state-set tax rate would provide. However, money raised above the state rate had to be shared, so that each community would have an "equalized tax yield." Act 60 implemented statewide property taxes at $1.10 per $100,000 of assessed property valuation while decreasing commercial and industrial taxes,[15] increasing the state share of school finance,[16] and adding taxes on gasoline, hotel rooms, restaurant meals, and corporate income to pay for the increase.[17] Act 60 was also income-sensitive, limiting property taxes on lower-income households by a "prebate" issued to those with two acres or less. The qualifying income was raised in succeeding years to include more people and the minimum acreage requirement dropped for householders with one residence. To make it less painful for the "giving" towns, the act was phased in over four years. As the court pointed out in the case challenging Act 60, *Stowe Citizens for Responsible Government* v. *State of Vermont*, during the first year of implementation, Stowe's tax rate would only increase to $1.00 and Stowe would keep up to 73 percent of its extra taxes.[18] Before Act 60, Stowe citizens were then paying a property tax rate of $0.71 and spending more than $2,000 per pupil more than the state average. Poor communities were paying higher tax rates, while raising less money for their schools.

According to Act 60 supporter William Mathis, in 1997 people opposing Act 60 "caravanned" from one municipality to another where their behavior "bordered on uncivil."[19] However, according to Act 60 opponents, the act is "leftist" or even "Marxist."[20] Some went further. One prominent opponent, author John Irving, declared that he did not want his children subjected to "trailer court envy," implying that low-income students would somehow mistreat them in public schools. Irving started a private school, funded by his personal wealth, donations, and tuition.[21] Many towns "levied" so-called voluntary taxes in the form of private contributions. The Freeman Foundation of Stowe further undermined Act 60 by offering matching grants to towns raising funds privately. Such privately raised funds were not subject to the sharing pool.

Despite bitter opposition, Act 60 was effective in achieving three goals: 1) tax burden equity or "equalized yield;" 2) a reduction of the achievement gap between students who attend rich and poor schools; and 3) "a reasonably equal share" of revenues. According to Lorna Jimerson, of the Rural School and Community Trust, in 1998, a year after implementation of Act 60, a difference in per-pupil spending of 37 percent was reduced to 13 percent.[22] Despite the apparent fairness of equalizing educational resources available to children, resistance continued, organized around the recapture provisions. Officially called the equalized yield provisions, proponents dubbed this part of Act 60 "the sharing pool," while opponents called it "the shark pool." Ironically, the sharing pool, intended to mollify independent Vermonters by leaving some taxing authority in the hands of towns, became one of the main bones of contention. Since school taxes were set statewide, on the one hand, tax rates in wealthy towns rose substantially, while state revenue for schools shrank in these towns, since all towns received the same per-pupil allotment from the state under Act 60. On the other hand, taxes in poor towns went down, while revenues available for schools rose, even without the supplemental state aid from the sharing pool. Before Act 60, according to William Mathis, average town tax burdens varied from 0.1 percent to 8.2 percent of assessed property evaluation. After Act 60, tax burdens ranged from 2 percent to 4 percent.[23] Needless to say, the voters in wealthy towns were not pleased. However, the federal range ratio (which does not include the top 5 percent and the bottom 5 percent, to account for "abnormal" circumstances) went down from 271 percent to 107 percent by 2000.[24] The federal range ratio shows the disparity between schools in the top ninety-fifth percentile and those in the bottom fifth percentile, excluding "outliers." This means that before Act 60, schools in the top quintile in Vermont spent 271 percent more per pupil than schools in the bottom quintile. After Act 60 the disparity shrank to 107 percent, still a substantial difference among Vermont's districts. Under pressure from opponents of Act 60, the state share decreased in subsequent revisions of the law, from 84 percent in 1999 to 60 percent in 2001.[25] This did not bode well for equity, which is better where the state share is larger. Vermont towns were driven to depend on the sharing pool rather than a larger state share, which introduced an element of uncertainty into school finance for the receiving towns, although providing needed funds. A larger state share ultimately proved to be the solution to this problem, although the larger share gave the state more power over funding in the towns, which backfired in 2005.

In 1998, citizens opposed to Act 60 filed suit. In *Anderson v. State of Vermont*,[26] the Supreme Court refused to overturn the appeals court's decision overruling the plaintiffs' claim that Act 60 also violated the state's education clause for lack of a justiciable controversy.[27] The court dismissed two similar cases. Following these failed cases, citizens of Stowe, a wealthy town, brought a suit charging that Act 60 was unconstitutional because it violated the state's "delegation of powers" clause. The court reiterated its *Anderson* ruling in *Stowe Citizens for Responsible Government* v. *State of Vermont* in 1999. The plaintiffs, a nonprofit corporation consisting of Stowe taxpayers and parents, argued that Act 60 illegally delegated the state's obligation to provide sufficiency of school funding to local citizens of wealthy communities. The *Stowe* plaintiffs argued that the Constitution of Vermont forbids the legislature from delegating its authority, and that Act 60 violated this clause. However, the court relied on precedent in *Village of Waterbury* v. *Melendy* (1937) and *State* v. *Auclair* (1938), stating, "This doctrine is not violated when the Legislature vests municipalities 'with certain powers of legislation as to matters of purely local concern.'" The court added, "Nor is the doctrine violated when the Legislature gives the municipal corporations the authority or discretion merely to execute, rather than to make the laws" (*Stowe*, *560). On the other hand, the court declared that the doctrine is violated whenever the charge is "so vague and uncertain that, in exercising its discretion, the municipality must, in effect, make the laws" (*560). The Supreme Court, it appears, was aware of the irony of the charge. Judges prefaced their decision by saying, "Plaintiffs' attempt to cloak its argument under the legal mantle of the delegation doctrine does not withstand scrutiny" (*560). Before Act 60, Stowe citizens would hardly have sued the state for providing insufficient and grossly unequal school funding because of the policy of local control. The court declared that

> [s]tripped of its delegation-doctrine vestment, plaintiffs' argument is that because Act 60's equalized yield provision depends on voters in

> property-wealthy districts to provide additional funds for education
> beyond the basic state grant, it fails to satisfy the State's constitu-
> tional obligation as established in *Brigham*. (*562)

This amounts to the same argument the court declined to hear in the appeal of *Anderson*; furthermore, it does not take into account the provisions of Act 60 established to mitigate differences due to economies of
scale, differences in costs, and other factors. Act 60 is not "vague" at all,
but quite specific in its provisions. These two cases ended the legal challenge to Act 60, but the political battle continued.

Following implementation of Act 60 in 1998, taxpayers in the gold
towns sought ways to circumvent the law by raising money outside of the
regular taxing authority through voluntary levies that would be donated
to the town's schools by foundations created specifically to avoid partici-
pating in the sharing pool. Money donated privately did not have to be
shared. This strategy created dissension in many Vermont towns, where
citizens were being coerced into "voluntarily" paying an extra school tax
levied by a committee for the foundation.[28] Unless every citizen contributes, some will pay more while others benefit without contributing. In
addition, some towns initially withheld their sharing pool funds from the
state.[29] In the long run, however, these towns were forced into compliance. Raising additional money for the schools by "enforced contributions" caused the so-called receiving towns to lose sharing pool funds to
which they might otherwise have had access. This strategy was successful
at first. From 1998 to 2001, the Freeman Foundation of Stowe, Vermont,
a philanthropy with varied interests, offered to match funds raised privately by towns under its program, the Vermont Education Initiative.[30] If
sufficient money were raised by their foundation, schools in gold towns
could achieve their previous level of spending at less cost, even though
they would still have to pay the new statewide tax rate, which was higher
for them because their tax rate had been lower before Act 60. In 1999,
the Freeman Foundation contributed $5.5 million in first-round grants
alone. A few wealthy owners of vacation homes responded by contributing the amount they were expected to pay to private foundations to the
sharing pool instead.[31] Other towns decided against withholding funds
on the grounds that it was illegal, but stated their continued opposition
to the pool.[32]

Controversy over the Freeman Foundation grants erupted in early
1999, when it became apparent to legislators that the grants could cause
significant amounts of money to be lost to the sharing pool. Lieutenant
Governor Douglas Racine criticized the Freeman Foundation for "its role
in helping wealthy communities subvert the effects of Act 60." Governor
Howard Dean responded to his lieutenant governor by defending the

Freeman Foundation. His position: "If the money weakens Act 60, it's Act 60's fault, not the Freeman Foundation's fault." Dean accused Racine of being a "whiner" who was "misguided."[33] Bill Talbot, chief financial officer for the Vermont Department of Education, also criticized the program as an effort to undermine Act 60 by reducing the money available to the state to fund education.[34] In a move that highlighted the problem of bias in private giving, the Freeman Foundation tied grants for forest preservation, a cause that the foundation also supports, to participation in the Vermont Coalition of Municipalities, a group of about fifty towns that opposed Act 60.[35] This made Freeman Foundation lawyer Thomas Amidon's claim that the foundation "takes no position on any piece of legislation" less than credible.[36] Even though the state must fund schools under the constitution, the infusion of large amounts of private money make equity difficult to attain. In addition, a private foundation ought not to decide who gets money for public schools and who does not. Although the Freeman Foundation announced a decision not to continue funding matching grants after 2001,[37] it was apparently reconsidering in late 2000, perhaps in an effort to influence the state legislature to revise or replace Act 60.[38] However, the *Burlington Free Press* announced that the Freeman Foundation decided to stop providing the matching grants program in December 2000.[39] In all, the Foundation spent $20 million. Despite considerable pressures, both legal and extralegal, the Vermont legislature adjourned without changing the basic mechanism of the sharing pool of Act 60 from 1999 to 2002.

Opponents of Act 60 proposed an alternative funding scheme entitled Education Revenue Sharing (ERS) in 1999, the year after Act 60 went into effect. ERS, according to Jeffery Pascoe, an outspoken opponent of Act 60, would eliminate the statewide property tax, returning taxing authority to the towns. Towns would have to pay their own transportation, special education, and construction costs. Pascoe claimed, "this would free up millions in state funds that currently flow to towns regardless of their need."[40] How this would benefit property-poor towns is unclear; the plan did not include targeting the newfound money to their needs, nor did it solve the previous problem of tax-burden inequity. Pascoe merely claimed that the money saved by the state could then be added to money derived from ". . . federal aid, income and other taxes, and the lottery."[41] Most education finance analysts leave federal aid out of the equity equation, because it is intended to supplement resources for needy children, not replace other funds. Lotteries, which prey on the hopes of the poor, are a poor choice for education fundraising, with high overhead and low yields. Lotteries are a curious way of redistributing wealth, which affirms that unearned money is nevertheless a mark of status in the United States.

Economist J. Peter Gratiot, also an opponent of Act 60, formulated ERS, claiming that it would be more effective in equalizing revenues. In "Factors Controlling Foundation Spending in Vermont," Gratiot examined eight factors to explain the variations in spending in Vermont through a series of regression analyses. He claimed the Vermont Supreme Court exaggerated per-pupil spending differences in the *Brigham* decision.[42] According to Gratiot's analysis, property wealth is of less importance than local tax burden.[43] Gratiot's conclusion that the tax rate is the only variable directly under local control remained the case under Act 60; in addition, Act 60 achieved tax-burden equity, unless the voters were willing to pay a higher rate and share their proceeds, which placed a natural limit on resulting inequities. However, Gratiot used the order of variables in his analysis to argue that school finance reform in general has focused on the wrong variable—district property wealth per pupil. He claims that the other factors are "managed within a district . . . [to] control resident tax burden at an acceptable level," which "ensure[s] logical spending decisions."[44] "Logical" seems to mean "affordable" in Gratiot's lexicon. This argument ignores the need for both spending equity and tax-burden equity. Towns without a large tax base cannot "control resident tax burden within acceptable limits," as Gratiot suggested, and still raise sufficient money for the schools. However, Gratiot proposed adjusting the tax burden to have the same yield for the same tax effort, very much as Coons, Clune, and Sugarman suggested in *Private Wealth and Public Education* in 1970.[45] In that case, under the old system of setting tax rates, poor towns would receive a much higher yield than their richer counterparts whose tax rates were much lower. This seems as controversial as Act 60, maybe more so, although it could be argued that property-rich towns always had the option to raise their tax rates to receive a higher yield. If they did so, the inequities would resume, since property-poor towns do not have that option. In addition, state-equalizing aid rarely, if ever, results in equity. In practice, state-aid grants are not often distributed either according to tax effort or need. Instead, in Texas, New Jersey, Massachusetts, New York, Kansas, and elsewhere, the greater political clout of some districts (wealthy districts, or suburban districts, or even rural districts, as was the case in Kansas) negates the possibility of using state-aid grants to create equity, without additional reforms that target funds specifically to needy populations, disallow local tax cuts in response to increased state aid, and cap extra expenditures for wealthy districts. Although Gratiot's plan might have been feasible, it aimed at equity correlated to tax effort. Towns could still choose to make a low-tax effort, if they were satisfied with poorly funded schools. However, the reality was that poor towns had to make a greater tax effort to maintain a lower level of spending under

Vermont's old plan. The same is true in many states with inequitable funding. The property-rich towns in the Vermont Coalition of Municipalities supported Gratiot's plan. Both Gratiot and his wife, Daphne Gratiot, contributed articles opposing Act 60 to the Web site, *Act 60, What You Should Know.*[46]

In May 2003, the Vermont legislature succumbed to pressure to eliminate the sharing pool. The Democratic governor, Howard Dean was replaced by Republican Jim Douglas, who openly opposed Act 60. Dean, initially a supporter of Act 60, became disillusioned by 1999, concluding that the sharing pool did not work well. The sharing pool, an uncertain source of funds for poor towns at best, was also undermined by Freeman Foundation grants. Despite this, poor towns benefited from Act 60, which equalized tax burden and increased their share of school funding dramatically. Dean would naturally resist blaming the Vermont philanthropy, which funded many beneficial projects in Vermont such as local libraries, forestry, and schools. Douglas beat his opponent, Racine, who continued to support Act 60, in the election for governor of Vermont by a small margin, Douglas getting 45 percent of the vote to Racine's 42 percent. Douglas took office in 2002.[47] In his January 2003 budget address, he highlighted the state's financial distress.

> If we continue to spend at the current rate, a deficit of $30 million will fall upon us in the coming fiscal year. A deficit this large would delay economic recovery and threaten future prosperity. So my budget limits General Fund spending growth to only 1 percent, for a total of $893.8 million. When special funds, the transportation fund, and the education fund are combined, spending increases are limited to 1.7 percent, or a total of $2.3 billion. (Office of the Governor Web site, np)

Douglas added that he based his budget on five principles, including maintaining ". . . [Vermont's] commitment to the neediest Vermonters," while not dipping "even further into the pockets of struggling taxpayers" and "sharing sacrifice . . . broadly so that no one is asked to carry an undue burden." Douglas claimed "the most direct route back to prosperity is to invest in Vermonters' education, skills and aspirations" and promised to "[hold] harmless the state's commitment to the education fund." How these conflicting aims could be accomplished simultaneously is not clear. Douglas proposed transferring money from the general fund, generating new money through participation in a multistate lottery, and "capping the Act 60 property tax assistance at $2,500. . . ." [which came out of the pocket of the less-wealthy householders qualifying for "prebates" under Act 60]. Douglas also promised tax relief by returning "overcharges" of $16.5 million, meanwhile praising the legislature for "searching for a fair way to reform our system of funding education" for the past five years. This, of course, represents his opposition to Act 60, which the legislature had watered down considerably. Douglas declared, "There are no easy answers and we must work together to find a more permanent solution to this dilemma [of how to equalize school funding]."[48] However, tax relief dominated his plans. He claimed to have offered what he reported as 20 percent to 30 percent in property tax relief to Vermonters.

Although many Democrats in the legislature continued their support for Act 60, it was changed substantially.[49] The new legislation, an Act Relating to Education Funding,[50] passed both Houses in late May 2003, and was signed into law by the governor as Act 68. The legislation still based education funding on the statewide property tax, which was raised, initially, then lowered by the new governor. Act 68 also maintained some of the income sensitivity of Act 60 and some "guaranteed yield"–type provisions that would help guarantee some funding stability. The category of homestead was expanded to include the entire parcel on which the residence stands, unlike Act 60's 2-acre limit. The bill provided for inflation adjustments to the base rate of $6,800 each year. A "prebate" was built in for families with incomes below $47,000. By raising the tax rates for homeowners and businesses, the state raised the foundation grant from $5,800 in 2000 to $6,800, to go into effect by 2005. To raise the extra money needed for the increase in the flat-rate per pupil, Act 68 split the Grand List so that homeowners pay $1.10 while businesses and vacation homeowners pay $1.59 per assessed evaluation in property taxes. The increase was also be supported by a 1 percent increase in the sales tax, already at 6 percent, a tax on beer and soda, and other miscellaneous taxes. Act 68 abandoned the sharing pool, and will allow property-rich towns to raise taxes and keep the proceeds, up to 125 percent of the state allotment. Districts may choose to spend more than the $6,800 state flat grant at $1.10, but voters will have to approve tax hikes. An element of the sharing pool remains in that towns spending more than 125 percent of the state rate will be penalized for every dollar spent over the limit to minimize high spending. The new law went into effect July 1, 2004, for fiscal year 2005.

As of summer 2005, the new bill, Act 68, has yet to prove that it can maintain or produce more equity in spending than Act 60. There seem to be few mechanisms to avoid previous pitfalls, which resulted in the great disparities Vermont displayed before Act 60. The state share is dependent on the legislature's yearly vote; the property tax may indeed increase; sales taxes are regressive, taxing the poor a much larger percentage of their income than the rich; and provisions to prevent towns from raising their taxes are fairly weak. In addition, flat grants paid regardless of need do not lead to equity. One saving grace of the new legislation is a greater degree of certainty in school budgeting in comparison to the old method of the sharing pool, although the greater degree of control by the governor and the legislature raised the hackles of several towns in March 2005. Proposals to use the school funding appropriations to pay for a new computer system for the State Department of Education and for special education for prisoners in Vermont have elicited a resolution from the town of Grafton opposing the measures as contrary to the intent of the original law. Thirty-six members of the Vermont Coalition of Municipalities, a group once opposed to Act 60, signed the resolution.[51] Another is that the statewide uniform property tax rate remained in place, although it was lowered by Governor Douglas, fulfilling his campaign promise to lower property taxes. In February 2004, an amendment to Act 68 took five cents off the base for both residential and nonresidential taxes. The amendment set tax rates at $1.05 for residential or homestead property and $1.54 for nonresidential property, to go into effect in 2005.[52] The additional loss will have to be made up somehow. As in other states struggling with equity problems, targeted state aid will have to make up the difference between what property-poor and property-rich towns can raise. If Vermont school children are to receive "a reasonably equal share" as commanded by the State Supreme Court in *Brigham*, the state must keep the state share high and increase it to account for inflation and increases in enrollment.

An inflation adjustment alone may not suffice to keep spending at the present level. Official inflation rates are often underestimated. In addition, if enrollment declines, public schools suffer. Vermont is promoting the charter school movement, which could affect enrollment, already declining slightly. Dependency on yearly legislative votes for school funding creates uncertainty, limits stability, and hampers the ability of schools to plan their budgets before dire needs arise. In Kentucky, one of the more successful states in reforming school finance litigation, the same coalition of districts that brought *Rose* brought a new suit against the state over inadequacy of funding in September 2003. According to Greg Kocher of the *Lexington Herald-Leader*, Representative Sanders, of Franklin, Kentucky, said that "elementary and secondary education have been receiving a smaller percentage of the state's General Fund because of unavoidable spending increases for prisons and Medicaid."[53] Unfortunately, state priorities shift, sometimes unpredictably, often to the detriment of school funding. In good economic times, legislatures can keep pace; in bad times, schools suffer. Unfortunately, it seems to be difficult for legislators and voters to realize that spending on education is much more humane and beneficial to the community in the long run than spending on prisons for people who were not well-educated in the first place, for whom there is little work, and who require state support because they cannot support themselves. Overall, however, Act 68 represents an advance over the situation in Vermont prior to *Brigham.*

Did Act 60 Work?

According to a study conducted by Lorna Jimerson of the Rural School and Community Trust, Vermont's Act 60 was successful in achieving its goals in the first three years after implementation (1998–2001). According to Jimerson, the three goals of Act 60 were to achieve in equity in resources for students; second, to create tax-burden equity; and third, to narrow the gaps in academic achievement among children.[54] Jimerson argued that equity in all three areas showed significant gains. Equalized property value per pupil (in districts grouped in quintiles) narrowed a difference of $2,110 (from a range of from $5,654 to $7,764) in 1998 to a difference of $1,223 (from a range of $6,502–$7,725) in 2001, a reduction of $887 per-pupil expenditure. This is represents a substantial improvement (Jimerson, 6). Tax burden became more equal, although it still varied according to local choices (9), and the gap between academic achievement of students in low-spending districts and high-spending districts narrowed (11–12).[55]

The Vermont Department of Education (DOE) confirmed Jimerson's assessment in *The Equal Educational Opportunity Act: Measuring Equity,* April 17, 2001, although the Vermont DOE was more cautious in its claims. "In terms of financial equity, the EEOA [Equal Educational Opportunity Act, or, Act 60] has achieved the intended effect. Education tax rates are now uniformly tied to local per pupil spending levels across the state. This is a significant achievement."[56] The report states that "it is too early to draw definitive conclusions about the relationship between spending, school quality standards, and student performance," since the appropriate assessments are not yet fully in place; nor was there data on the full implementation of Act 60, since it had only completed the phase-in during the 2000–2001 school year. Nevertheless, the DOE noted that there was some evidence that Act 60 was achieving its goals in 2001. First, per-pupil spending gaps were narrowing. Second, districts that had historically spent less were increasing spending at a greater rate than districts that had historically spent more. Finally, performance gaps among different student groups (e.g., gender, socioeconomic background) appear not to exist in a small number of schools (Wolk, 1–2). In the 2001 report, the Vermont DOE cautioned that data would have to be collected by schools rather than districts to establish the connection between spending and student performance. Researchers reported that all districts had increased spending under Act 60. In addition, "giving towns," which did not benefit financially under

Act 60, have not suffered declines in student performance, while "receiving towns," which did, have seen improvement. Although "at all grade levels and areas of assessment, on average, high-poverty students score lower than those who are not in poverty" (2), the report shows that "overall performance tends to be on the rise" (15). Although "gaps in reading and writing remained the same or became smaller, while gaps in mathematics generally increased" (16), the report points out that it is difficult to attribute either of these changes to Act 60. Educational performance is better assessed over a longer period of time.

In March 2002, Jimerson reported again on Act 60 in *"Still 'A Reasonably Equal Share': Update on Educational Equity on Vermont: Year 2001–2002.*[57] The report found that "before Act 60 (FY 98), property-rich towns spent an average of 37 percent more, or $2,100, per pupil, compared to the poorest towns. In FY 2002, this spending gap was less than 13 percent, with the per-pupil disparity diminished to $900." Jimerson also noted that tax-burden equity had increased (indeed, it had switched) because "the poorest households paid less than two percent for school taxes (1.8 percent), while the wealthiest households paid 2.3 percent" (Jimerson, summary). Although academic achievement inequities still existed, the gap was reduced further, while all children continued to make progress in achievement. In her conclusion, Jimerson assessed the results.

> Given these positive findings, it seems wise to continue to financially and politically support the critical aspects of Act 60 that have been effective in improving equity. Though the tax impact for some Vermonters has been burdensome, the impact for students—*all* students—has been positive. The path to equal educational opportunity is rough and full of potholes and landmines. However, given the results of this analysis, we believe that Vermont is maintaining its bearing and pursuing the right direction in the way it funds its schools. (Jimerson, conclusion, np)

Vermont policy analysts were pleased to see Vermont's success, which confirmed that school finance could move toward both adequacy and equity. In *Rural Policy Matters*, Rachel Thompkins reported that "Act 60 is fulfilling the mandates of the Supreme Court decision and the goals of the legislation. . . . And local control has not been diminished."[58]

Jimerson also concluded in 2002 that Act 60 had achieved its goals.

> "(1) Significant progress has been made in reducing the spending gap between wealthy and poor towns. (2) The tax burden for school taxes is far more equitable. (3) The achievement gap between children residing in wealthy towns and those in poorer towns has continued to decrease for the second consecutive year.[59]

As the Vermont DOE pointed out in 2001, conclusions about improvement in achievement in Vermont were premature. The appropriate data had not been collected; figures for actual expenditures per pupil by school (expended in areas related to achievement, which would exclude, for instance, debt service) and achievement data for those same pupils are not available.[60] Vermont was in the process of reforming data collection and analysis to ascertain the effect of Act 60 more precisely, avoiding potential confounders in the analysis. However, in 2001, the DOE corroborated the initial Jimerson report with evidence that the achievement of children at Vermont's poor schools had improved.[61] The DOE report recognized that school spending matters, although the quality of the programs is also a factor, citing recent research to this effect, which contradicts Eric Hanushek and others who deny a link between spending and academic achievement.[62] Nor did Act 60 fully equalize school spending in Vermont. In 2002, the Vermont Department of Education publication, "FY 2002 Spending per pupil per school type," still showed wide disparities remaining in all twelve categories of school types. Towns that operated public K–12 schools ranged from $12,668.79 spent per equalized pupil in Craftsbury to $7,483.42 in Burlington. Towns that operated an elementary school and belonged to a union high school ranged from $12,805.72 spent in Windham to $7,010.21 in Lowell. In 2003, figures in the same categories ranged from $14,260.51 in Whitingham to $7,884.00 in Burlington, for towns that operated a K–12 system. In towns that belonged to a union high school, spending ranged from $13,270.48 in Windham to $7,324.33 in Woolford. These schools are mostly in the range of large (up to 1,000 pupils) to medium (up to 500 pupils).[63] Small schools generally spent less, although not without exceptions.

The final data collected on the success of Act 60 will cover only six years of implementation. It will be interesting to see if the achievement gap continues to decline, or widens once again under the new legislation, Act 68. As some commentators believe, Act 60 was undermined and diluted by private funding, so perhaps the new legislation will establish at least an equivalent amount of equity. This equity will depend partly on a continued legislative commitment to sufficient school funding. Five years after implementation of Act 68 in 2004–2005, the state can begin to assess the effects of the new legislation. In addition, the instability factor will be likely to distort measurements of the effects of Act 68. For instance, the legislature already reduced the new tax rates even before the law went into effect. If the legislature does not vote sufficient raises in the flat grant to keep up with inflation and increased enrollment, as happened in Ontario, the school children in Vermont will again suffer insufficient funding. Unfortunately, Vermont's grand experiment in combining equity and adequacy with local control ended precipitously before its worth could be firmly established. I hope commentators who laud the new plan are right, but I have my doubts.

What Next in Vermont?

At the inception of Act 60 in 1998, Bill Mathis suggested that the future of Act 60 depended on whether the legislature and the public would follow through with support, whether the Department of Education would be able to deliver on the promises of Act 60, and whether assessments would show that Act 60 achieved its goal of a better education for all of Vermont's children.[64] The crucial point turned on the first question: whether the public, the legislature, and the executive would continue to support the contentious sharing pool. The answer to this, unfortunately, was negative. The new Republican governor, Jim Douglas, put pressure on the legislators to abandon the sharing pool, which they did.[65] Opponents of Act 60 blamed past support on a "gang of ten," which they claimed somehow overcame the majority, forcing renewal of the sharing pool for four years.[66] The new legislation will face its own tests; it remains to be seen if the spending gap continues to decline. The gap was substantial in 2003, despite considerable improvement. Whether this was due to changes in Act 60, the matching funds of the Freeman Foundation, or other causes is not likely to be determined. Although the Freeman Foundation discontinued matching grants in school year 2001–2002 and the "voluntary" contributions slowed without them, much damage was done to the implementation of Act 60.

In 2005, compensations for losses to poor districts from the sharing pool came from the higher flat grant per pupil of $6,800.[67] As Act 60 was amended, the state share shrank slightly.[68] The new legislation will need to prevent this. The state must maintain its share. As the population increases and costs increase, the formula will need to be updated. Economic hard times will be dangerous for the children of Vermont. State appropriations for education are notoriously susceptible to fluctuations in the economy, the government's ideology, and other factors. Even if the state share remains constant, the new legislation substituted money derived from an increase in an already high sales tax,[69] a new telephone tax, and other taxes on non-necessary consumables.[70] These taxes are subject to economic downturns. The rise in the sales tax will probably reduce spending in Vermont (a small state), especially along the borders with New Hampshire, which already has lower sales taxes. In addition, sales taxes are regressive. One critic estimated that wealthy citizens would be spending 1 percent more of their income, whereas poor would be spending more than 7 percent more of their income on the 1 percent increase in sales tax.[71]

Schools in democracies have traditionally been funded according to the ability of citizens to pay. Property tax at least reflects the relative wealth of the property owners, however disliked or onerous it may be. Sales tax, unless it is limited to luxury items, does not. It is a hallmark of a democratically organized society that all children have access to a publicly supported education. If their wealth indicates a benefit, the wealthy benefit the most from the organization of such a society. Therefore, they benefit from educating poor children. As wealth becomes more concentrated and the income gap grows wider, the poor will spend an ever higher share of their income and the wealthy an ever smaller share on education. When productivity goes up while jobs disappear, fewer people are doing more work. With unemployment increasing in a climate of supposed economic recovery in late 2003, one must wonder, who will be able to buy the goods being manufactured? It is more likely that "a minimally adequate education" will be maintained (or slowly degraded) than that an excellent one will be built over time. The proposed increase in the flat rate for the school year 2004–2005 appears generous, but the new law also has to compensate for losses from the sharing pool. Both the public and the government that the public elects will have to have confidence that school expenditures are worth the high cost of an excellent education. This was also true under Act 60, but there was evidence that the achievement gap was decreasing. It is hard to assess whether public confidence will be maintained sufficiently to continue supplying adequate funding. If the new plan continues to close the gaps, perhaps it will prove to be an improvement over Act 60. But Act 60 contained an "equalized yield" provision in the mechanism of the sharing pool that seemed more likely actually to equalize yields than will penalties for spending above the limit of 125 percent.

Proceeds from taxes above the statewide rate are distributed on the basis of local tax effort. If tax effort is a function of the wealth of the community (which it was not under the old system of support for schools), presumably wealthy communities can afford to bear more of the tax burden. However, before Act 60, Stowe, Vermont, was paying seventy-one cents per $100 in property taxes, compared to a statewide average of $1.33.[72] If poor districts cannot afford the tax rates set by wealthy districts, or the state share does not keep up with inflation, children in poor districts will have fewer resources once again.

School bond issues are not overwhelming popular. They may pass in enlightened communities with young families, but they are notorious for failing elsewhere. Citizens of the United States seem to be very docile about paying their income taxes, but not their property taxes. In addition, many corporations pay much less than they should in property taxes, due to tax breaks and incentives offered by communities who want industries to locate in their area. If income taxes supported schools and property taxes were used for military equipment, there might be more protests against extravagance in military expenditures and fewer objections to educational expenditures. The phrase "tax revolt" most often means a revolt against property taxes. Upon signing the new bill, the governor of Vermont, Jim Douglas, expressed his satisfaction that property taxes will be reduced by 20 percent in 2005.[73] In addition, many corporations also find loopholes large enough to avoid paying any taxes at all.[74] But it would seem that they, too, benefit from an educated workforce and the orderly society that results; consequently, they should contribute their fair share to education.

Although there are some mitigating factors in Vermont's new plan, nothing protects the children against town voters who refuse to approve additional taxes. Nothing prevents wealthy towns from raising their school expenditures, at least to 125 percent, while poor towns face the same constraint they always had—their poverty. The equalized yield provision may well allow wealthy towns to benefit from raising their taxes, while leaving poor towns out. However, New York's Campaign for Fiscal Equity Web site hailed the plan as a success, calling it a "'win-win' measure." According to CFE's "Access" Web site, "Vermont's success in producing a bipartisan funding bill that avoids geographic divisiveness and remains uncompromising in its commitment to adequate resources and educational standards provides a valuable example for New York."[75] The Rural School and Community Trust also praised the new legislation, claiming, "Grass roots efforts and sustained support for equity helped make it impossible to roll back the benefits of equal educational opportunity for most Vermonters."[76]

However, problems have surfaced already. In his 2006 budget, Governor Douglas proposed spending $776,000 on special education of prisoners up to age twenty-four and $280,000 on a new computer system for the Department of Education. The justifications are fairly straightforward—towns would have had to pay those special education costs if the prisoners had not been imprisoned and the computer system will benefit all school districts, eventually. But the fact remains that the governor and the legislature have control of the budgets, not the towns. These costs had not previously been deducted from the general budget for schools. Twenty-five members of the Vermont Coalition of Municipalities, led by the town of Grafton, have signed a resolution condemning the proposal.[77] In addition, new taxes have been onerous on the ski towns. Killington and several other towns near New Hampshire have been threatening to secede. The legislature is studying ways to control what are characterized as "out of control" and "spiraling" real estate values. The Senate Ways and Means Committee proposed repealing the statewide property tax in 2007, while setting up panel to explore ways other than property taxes to fund education. The House voted against repealing the statewide property tax.[78] The House now has introduced a new bill to come under consideration in fall 2005 to reform property evaluation and review appraisals in hopes of achieving a unitary system of appraisal. This bill passed a second reading in the House on February 8, 2006 but had not advanced in the Senate as of this writing (Vermont Bill Tracking # H.0001).[79]

Some questions, originally raised by Bill Mathis in response to Act 60, remain. Will the Vermont Department of Education be able to provide adequate resources to continue the progress that Vermont children have made over the past five years? Will the DOE design and implement assessments, with results disaggregated by socioeconomic status and school, rather than just by district, which will be capable of showing whether children of poverty are not being left behind? Will they measure the impact of resources on children's success accurately and persuasively? Will teachers lose autonomy in the classroom as a result of mandated testing, as happened in New York and Ontario as the result of a move to lower property taxes, an avowed aim of Governor Racine? This kind of control has long been the case in New York, even without tax equity. Teachers in New York City are reported to be leaving "by the droves," including 29 percent of the new teachers.[80] Ontario's teachers, who have the right to strike, have expressed their displeasure at new regulations through this method. New York's teachers, forbidden to strike by the Taylor Law, may resort to leaving the profession or the state. Neither of these methods are good solutions. Teacher autonomy is important to attract and keep the best people in the profession.

Educational researchers still need to establish the link between spending and achievement beyond question, in Vermont as well as elsewhere. The legacy of the Coleman Report, belief that additional funding doesn't make any difference, is still with us. In order to establish the link, any increased money that comes to education must be spent on educational strategies and resources that work. Teachers must use a methodology and subject matter that succeeds with disadvantaged children. Schools of teacher education must teach critical pedagogy, update materials from a multicultural and postcolonial standpoint, and rebel against standardized tests that dictate a test-prep curriculum. These are difficult tasks. It appears to me that Vermont's reforms toward equity and adequacy while maintaining local control, may be in jeopardy, despite the more optimistic views of others. I hope the others are right.

In the meantime, in another scenario playing out in Ontario, a conservative government promising to cut taxes created an enormous education bureaucracy. The Harris government, elected in 1996, equalized expenditures, but failed to provide adequate funding, as I fear will happen in Vermont under Act 68. In Ontario, it took five years for the funding to prove insufficient. There were no provisions for updating the benchmarks based on 1996 costs. Once this happened, the conservative government lost power over the issue. As in New York, the government commissioned a study of the adequacy of its school funding. As with New York's Zarb Commission, the government found itself upstaged. The Rozanski Report recommended more increases in education spending than Premier Eves was willing to make. His refusal to follow his own commission's advice cost him the election. I turn to this sequence of events next.

Chapter 4

Executive Reform in Ontario

The chief immediate direction of social effort should be towards the attempt to give to every human being in childhood adequate food, clothing, education, and an opportunity in life. This will prove to be the beginning of many things.

Stephen Butler Leacock, Canadian economist
Unsolved Riddles of Social Justice, 1920

The Background of School Finance Reform in Ontario

School finance reform in Ontario from the late the 1990s to early 2004 differed from that in New York and Vermont. In Ontario, reform, driven by a conservative government, originated in the executive branch. "Student-Focused Funding" came to the province with the election of Premier Mike Harris in 1995. Elected by a substantial majority, Harris had promised to reduce the cost and complexity of government, reduce the provincial deficit, and cut taxes in what he called the "common sense revolution." As part of his tax-cutting program, Harris proposed reorganizing school funding to make it more equitable while saving the province money. Ironically, when Harris announced his resignation six years later, he left an enormous deficit and a huge education bureaucracy. Common sense seemed to have flown out the window. Chronic underfunding of schools had accumulated, causing a revolt by three major urban boards that forced the province to take over their administration and cut many programs. This, among other events and incidents of mismanagement, cost Harris his popularity and eventually cost his successor, Premier Ernie Eves, his post, after only one year in office, 2002–2003. Liberal Dalton McGuinty, who replaced Eves, was elected in October 2003. Improving school funding was among his campaign promises.

89

Reform in Ontario also bore some similarities to that in Vermont and New York. Clearly, school finance reform in all three places was contentious. The stated aims were similar, particularly equity, adequacy, transparency, flexibility, and local control. Economy, or efficiency, was an aim as well. The problem in all three places is perennial and widespread: not enough money for education in the face of rising costs and shrinking budgets. But in Ontario, the motive was a campaign promise to cut taxes. Equity was the vehicle to make the cuts palatable. The aim in New York and Vermont was equity itself, where the assumption has been that it would cost the government more money, not less. The battles were over how much more the government can afford. In Ontario, the battles were over how the government could deliver on promises to cut taxes and consequently how little the government could pay for education and stay in power. Despite differences, however, the similarities make the scenario of executive reform in Ontario useful to school finance reformers in the United States. Reformers in Ontario might also find New York and Vermont's experiences informative.

Before examining the executive reforms in Ontario, a brief review of education in Ontario for readers from the United States is in order.[1] Canada has thirteen systems of education in ten provinces and three territories. As in the United States, there is no provision for education in the federal constitution. A Council of Ministers of Education Canada meets at least twice annually to discuss policies concerning education, but it has no powers, which are reserved for the provinces. It appears that there is even less federal intervention in Canada than in the United States. In Ontario, four coterminous boards can exist in any area, public and separate (which is the term for the constitutionally protected, publicly funded Catholic schools), French and English, throughout the province. English-language boards predominate, almost equally divided between public and separate, with substantially fewer French-language boards. Since the French-language boards have fewer pupils, they are spread over larger territories. To attend separate schools, students have to produce a baptismal certificate. Only Francophone Section 93 rightsholders are allowed to attend French-language schools.

Unlike in the United States, Catholic schools in Canada are state funded, due to the 1867 agreement with the French promising no interference with Catholic institutions and French culture. This was bolstered by the 1975 Charter of Rights and Freedoms, which allowed tuition payments to Catholic schools to be considered a charitable donation for tax purposes, provided that the cost can be attributed to religious education and the school is registered as a charitable institution.[2] Schools had to determine what proportion of their costs went to secular education, for which they received provincial support. In 1982, funding for Catholic education expanded to include high schools. Under the New Democratic Party in 1990, funding for separate schools increased again. Under the Progressive Conservative Party Premier Mike Harris, Catholic boards were fully funded by the government for the first time. This raised a controversy because the private schools of other religions did not receive funding. Challenged in *Waldman* v. *Canada* in 1999, the only state funding for these schools is a small tax credit for parents paying tuition. There are also exclusive private preparatory schools that charge tuition and are supported by endowments, as in the United States. Because of the four coterminous boards, many services are duplicated, such as buildings and facilities, transportation, and administrative costs. Taxpayers may "dedicate" their taxes to the school of their choice, although this no longer makes any difference with the equalizing formulae in place. Under the Harris government's plan, separate schools receive the same funding as public and no longer have to depend on a weaker tax base. Needless to say, separate schools gained in the Harris reforms, while public schools lost. Taxes were not increased to provide the additional amount that went to separate schools.

Historically, Canadian schools have been funded differentially within and among the provinces, as in the United States, with differences based on the local property values and local ratepayers' willingness to accept the tax rates set by the school boards.[3] Reforms in the 1980s resulted in substantially equitable systems within provinces, according to Stephen B. Lawton.[4] In part, this was due to a higher provincial share of school funding than states were likely to pay in the United States. Adequacy of funding is another issue, however. According to the Ontario Secondary School Teachers Federation, Canadian funding is much lower than funding in the United States.[5] Given disparities both within and among provinces, as well as generally lower per-pupil expenditures, Canadian school funding suffers from deficiencies similar to those in property-poor districts in the United States. Although expenditures are lower, on average, than in the United States, some of the low-spending states are on a par with some Canadian provinces. The problem of inadequacy of funding plagues Canadian school finance, as in urban and poor areas of the United States. Executive reforms in Ontario aimed at cutting taxes by streamlining and targeting money to "inside-the-classroom" expenditures while decreasing school spending overall, reducing a system of education in Ontario that was once considered excellent to something considerably less than that.

Opposition to the Harris Reforms

The Harris reforms (which were continued under Harris' successor, Premier Ernie Eves) included many strategies. Perhaps the most contentious was the forced amalgamation of school boards (equivalent to school districts in the United States), reducing the number from 129 to 72. School districts in the United States underwent a similar consolidation during the 1950s. To cut administrative costs, the number of trustees was reduced from 1,800 to 700 and trustees' salaries were limited to $5,000 a year, which effectively reduced trustees' positions to something closer to the unpaid school-board members in the United States. Trustees who administered the boards were paid full-time salaries before the Harris reforms. To take their place, the Harris government set up parent councils in each board to assist in making school decisions. Parent participation varied considerably. Trustees of the boards once set the local mill rate, negotiated with teachers, and controlled the building program; these were controlled by the province under the Harris reforms. Before the reforms, mill rates were not subject to popular vote as in the United States, but trustees who set high taxes might not be reelected. After the reforms, the government set the tax rate, collected the taxes, and established a uniform, weighted rate for per-pupil expenditures, which was increased by token amounts during the Harris and Eves years (1996–2003). In the process, it became difficult to ascertain whether the government was disbursing the total amount of residential and commercial and industrial taxes to the schools.[6] Changes in the residential property-tax structure favored businesses over homeowners; for instance, landlords were not taxed for empty units in rental buildings.

In addition to these changes, a new curriculum was designed and implemented by the ministry of education, adding levels each year, finishing in 2003. Material formerly studied in the fifth year of high school, the Ontario Academic Credit year (OAC), was integrated into the earlier grades, saving the cost of an entire year. Outcomes were tested province wide after the reforms, replacing teacher-planned district assessments, and supervised by the Educational Quality Assessment Office (EQAO). According to the Ministry of Education and Training, the last provincewide testing took place in 1967 or 1968. The Educational Improvement Commission (EIC) was charged with supervising implementation of the new policies at the elementary level. Both organizations were "arm's length" committees, not under the direct control of the ministry. The reforms also implemented a standardized report card provincewide. In addition, the government established a College of Teachers responsible for standards in teacher education and licensure, a function that formerly belonged to districts and the teachers' unions, according to George Martell.[7] When the OAC year was phased out in 2003, a double cohort graduated, creating pressure on colleges and universities, whose applications rose by 46.7 percent.[8] Apparently not much advance planning went into solving the double-cohort problem, because money was not allocated until 2002 to build new residences and increase faculty and staff at Ontario's universities and colleges. The bulge created by the double cohort will continue to affect colleges until 2007; universities will be affected for a longer period of time. As the double cohort passes through the system, the types of needs will change from needing more seats in freshman classes to needing more places in graduate programs. In the years leading up to 2003, students in the double cohort were concerned about reductions in their chances for a post-secondary education.

The Harris government dubbed their new funding formula "Student-Focused Funding." Ministry officials cited a 30 percent variance in expenditures under the system that was in place in 1995.[9] This was misleading because the Harris government never implemented the equalizing formula that the New Democratic Party (NDP) had prepared prior to the 1995 election that brought Harris to power. Stated aims of the new system included transparency, equity, and economy or efficiency in funding, to which is added accountability for the outcomes specified in the new curricula. The formula contained a foundation grant, which accounted for about 60 percent of the funding, and nine special-purpose grants designed to meet varying needs of the boards equitably.[10] They included 1) a special education grant; 2) a language grant; 3) a geographic grant and school authority grant; 4) a learning opportunities grant; 5) an adult education, continuing education, and summer school grant; 6) a teacher-compensation grant; 7) an early-learning grant; 8) a transportation grant; and 9) a school-board and governance grant.[11] Buildings and maintenance were funded under a separate pupil-accommodation grant. The Eves government added a small local priorities grant in 2002 to allow more flexibility in local spending and a declining enrollment grant to help boards with extra capacity adjust to the requirement that current seats be filled before any new schools could be built.[12] Although the rule about extra capacity may have sounded logical, school boards cannot control normal population shifts, which affect them substantially. Nor should children be bused long distances simply to fill older schools to capacity. This rule caused school closings, sale of school buildings, and even demolitions, to allow boards to build new capacity where it was needed.

The ministry, headed by Dave Johnson in 1997, claimed that the plan increased inside-the-classroom expenditures while decreasing outside-the-classroom expenditures. The idea was to improve student learning while saving money. The plan mandated maximum class size at twenty-five at the elementary level and twenty-two at the high school level. These goals were the same as those in the NDP plan, which was not implemented when the NDP lost the election.

Other stated goals included eliminating excess capacity, capping administrative costs, and protecting funding for special education.

The ministry planned to phase in the changes so that no board would lose more than 4 percent of its revenue per year; this period was completed in 2002. In addition, the teaching load at the secondary level increased from 6 out of 8 periods to 6.67 out of 8 periods, which was maintained subsequently. Teacher preparation time was not counted as an inside-the-classroom expenditure initially, although that subsequently changed.

In response to the implementation of Bill 160, the Harris education bill, Ontario teachers staged a massive two-week walkout in 1997. According to Gordon Nore, more than half of Ontarians supported the teachers. Nore, among others, recognized that Bill 160 "has nothing to do with education . . . but everything to do with creat[ing] an illusion that the [Tories] have balanced the books while cutting taxes 30 percent."[13] The strike by 126,000 teachers affected more than 2 million Ontario schoolchildren, closing virtually all the schools. It went largely unreported in the United States, and only escaped becoming a general strike when the unions came to agreement with the government. Teachers opposed Bill 160's transfer of power from the local boards to the ministry, their loss of autonomy in the classroom, loss of funding, and an increase in their workload with no corresponding increase in pay. However, the unions called off the strike after Harris turned down the concessions they offered in exchange for maintaining control of negotiations.[14] Some teachers were outraged and felt betrayed. Tory defenders of Bill 160 published an ad declaring that Ontario schools were "broken" and "needed to be fixed," while trying to mollify teachers by claiming that "that class sizes would go down, teachers would have more time with students, report cards would be easier to read, etc.," according to Nore. These arguments proved wrong, in time. The teachers, many of whom saw the bill as a money grab by the Tories, proved to be right in the end.

In 1998, Catholic schools challenged Bill 160's constitutionality in court on grounds that it illegally deprived Catholic districts of the right to tax. Public boards joined the suit. Both types of boards were deprived of the right to tax under Bill 160, but Catholic boards had better constitutional grounds on which to sue. Because Catholic boards are constitutionally protected to have the same rights and powers as public boards, attorneys for the public boards used the "mirror argument," which argues that public boards cannot be deprived of more rights than the Catholic boards, since Catholic boards are supposed to be mirror images of the publics. In July 1998, Mr. Justice Cumming of the Ontario Court (General Division) found for the Catholic Boards but against the publics. According to a summary of the proceedings on the Ontario Secondary School Teachers' Federation (OSSTF) Web site,

[Justice Cumming] declared Bill 160 to be unconstitutional, and of no force and effect, insofar as it removes from Roman Catholic school boards their Constitutional right to raise revenues through taxation. Justice Cumming found that unlike denominational school boards, public school boards do not possess rights under the Constitution of Canada, with the possible exception of the "right to exist." However, he noted that while Bill 160 did not violate any rights legally guaranteed to public school boards, it did introduce drastic changes to the financial structure of the educational system. In particular, Bill 160 established an unprecedented degree of centralization of command and control, stripping local boards of the power to raise revenues, and creating a "monolithic structure" which provoked "furious and searing criticism from a broadly based spectrum of interests."[15]

Although Justice Cumming found these furious and searing criticisms to have some validity, he did not, as the teachers had hoped, declare the entire bill unconstitutional.

This decision temporarily postponed threats of another strike in 1998. Many teachers, encouraged by Justice Cumming's decision, signed a two-year contract, as required by Bill 160. Their hope that this decision would not only be upheld on appeal, but also extended to the public boards, was dashed when it was overturned by a five-judge panel of the Canadian Supreme Court in November.[16] According to OSSTF, the Canadian Supreme Court agreed that "equality of educational opportunity" was constitutionally guaranteed, but, when the question arose as to who should be legally accountable for adequacy of funding—the trustees or the legislature, balked at adding adequacy to the requirement of equality. Although Justice Cumming felt that boards were in a better position to judge adequacy than the courts or the legislature, according to the Supreme Court, equality was all that mattered. The public boards had also argued that their right to tax to supplement funding above the provincial share was constitutional by custom. The reply was that if neither public nor Catholic boards had the right to tax, "equality" was implicit. This, to the Court, answered the "mirror argument," since everybody was in the same boat.

As these court cases were proceeding, the Ontario Secondary School Teachers Federation criticized the new funding plan. Their concerns included no money allocated for inflation (estimated at 4 percent) or enrollment growth (estimated at 4.2 percent); a one-time sum for new textbooks for the new curriculum of approximately $25 per child that was not enough; inadequate preparation for teachers who were implementing the changes; and no future commitment for textbooks, supplies, computers, technology, and professional development for implementation of the new curriculum as it progressed up the grades. In addition, the proposed savings on educational costs were not slated to be reinvested in education (for instance, the money saved by amalgamation of districts, reduction of administrative costs, or the abolition of grade thirteen); and new schools and capital expenditures went unfunded. There was inadequate funding for maintenance and restoration of older buildings and no appropriations for purchasing land, leaving boards dependent on developers to provide locations for new schools. Furthermore, previously negotiated teachers' salaries in amalgamated districts varied widely under the centralized system, causing dissatisfaction. But there was no money to equalize salaries.

The schools also complained about the lack of flexibility in the system of grants, which were tightly "enveloped" by the government, restricting boards' abilities to make choices in spending to satisfy local needs and priorities. Adult and vocational education programs were canceled, as well as local plans for junior kindergarten, additional special-education classes, and other special-needs programs such as school-based social workers and nurses in urban areas.[17] These concerns proved well founded in the aftermath of implementation. Expenses increased, enrollment increased, and enrollment shifts occurred while funding decreased and boards were forced to submit balanced budgets that slashed programs and services to compensate for the shrinking pool of money.

When I interviewed officials at the ministry in 2000, they described the grant categories as flexible, responsive to new needs and perceptions as they emerge, and subject to yearly debate and approval. They felt the plan also accomplished three goals: economy, equality, and transparency. They neglected to mention that there was no provision for updating the benchmarks to which the grants were pegged. The question of adequacy did not come up. However, the ministry acknowledged that parts of the formula were problematic; for instance, transportation grants were difficult to calculate.[18] Changes to the formulae since implementation seemed to the government to simply be adjustments needed when a new system is implemented. The teachers and trustees were not as satisfied.

Teachers' unions in Ontario actively opposed Bill 160. In 2000, an executive assistant of the Ontario Secondary School Teachers Federation (OSSTF), although describing the work of the ministry officials as sincere, nevertheless expressed many reservations about the education policies of the Harris government.[19] In contrast to the ministry's three aims of economy, equity, and transparency, the assistant's criteria for education funding were equity, adequacy, and democracy, by which he meant the participation of teachers in the decision-making, or teacher autonomy. Bill 160 was notably lacking in democracy. The bill declares that it supersedes all other legislation concerning education and forbids taking the government to court regarding any of its provisions (which was obviated by the suits in 1998).[20] Three new bills joined Bill 160 in 2000–2001. Bill 81 allowed the Minister of Education to collect personal information such as medical and psychiatric records, private correspondence, information about race, ethnicity, and marital status about any individual in the school system. Bill 74 gave the minister *carte blanche* to calculate class size any way she wished. It also allowed a teacher to be fired for refusing to "volunteer" for duties, a measure aimed at forcing teachers to participate in unpaid, extra curricular activities.[21] Bill 45 promised tax rebates for private school tuition, which were postponed following fiscal difficulties in 2002–2003. The system failed on the adequacy criterion, the democracy criterion, and the autonomy criterion, although it passed on the equity criterion for public and separate schools. However, equity without adequacy is a problem.

Teacher morale was low during the Harris campaign and still lower by 2000–2001. The Harris government ran "teacher-bashing" advertisements during two campaigns, whose effect was similar to the blame placed on teachers in the United States by the 1983 *A Nation at Risk* report, which also blamed students and their parents for the government's economic difficulties.[22] The OSSTF official cited an increase in long-term disability claims as evidence of increased stress and predicted massive retirements, which would exacerbate a looming teacher shortage. The ministry set the average salary at $50,000 (Canadian), which the OSSTF regarded as inadequate. Teachers had no increases in salaries from 1991 to 2000; then a 1.95 percent raise in 2001. Teachers were not compensated for the increased workload under the new plan, although they were forced to participate in extracurricular activities without pay. In summer 2002, Ontario again faced the prospect of widespread labor unrest over salaries; some boards granted increases of 2 percent by dipping into their reserves. This created a gap between what boards received from the province to pay salaries and what they actually paid in salaries. The benchmark for teacher salaries had not kept up with reality. Teachers in Toronto and other boards threatened to strike again in 2002. Premier Eves, Harris' replacement, countered by threatening to ban teacher strikes, an action that did not endear him to teachers, but might have appealed to voters.[23] Liberal Dalton McGuinty challenged Eves to call an election, which took place in October 2003, after McGuinty's second challenge. The OSSTF's prediction of teacher shortages was acknowledged by the ministry in March 2003, with a new campaign to recruit teachers.[24]

The new curriculum, which was fully implemented throughout the grades by 2002–2003, required new course preparation from every teacher at every level. An average of three days was budgeted for training in 1999–2000, in which as few as one teacher from a board might be responsible for relaying information to the others.[25] Furthermore, the new curriculum was sent to boards only a few days before implementation. The board officials complained that they had to select books without having seen either sample copies or the curriculum. Only one official at the four boards I visited in 2000 felt the process of curriculum development was reasonable. Others, however, claimed that the curriculum was developed hastily without enough input from teachers and lacked provision for remediation of students who failed the old curriculum but would have to repeat a year under the new.[26] Provincewide examinations came in the wake of the new curriculum. The externally imposed curriculum and examinations violated the OSSTF official's autonomy criterion.

On the equity criterion, the OSSTF official noted that the New Democratic Party (NDP) formula had been equitable, without the disadvantages of the Harris formula's inflexibility and lack of autonomy. Insufficiency was a problem under the previous administration, however. Bob Rae, the first premier from the NDP, was elected in 1990. School-funding reform was part of his party's platform. Rae was forced out of office after only one term, in part by the worst recession since the 1930s. Because of the recession, retrenchment in school funding became so bad that teachers were required to take "Rae days" with no work and no pay to save money. Under Rae, restructuring education finance had been the subject of a Fair Tax Commission study, which formulated a plan in 1993 that was never implemented. Likewise, a 1993 plan from the Royal Commission on Learning was not implemented, although it contained many ideas later used by the Harris government.[27] Funding for separate schools had also been included under the NDP government. When the Harris government took over in 1995, the OSSTF official commented that "they [the Harris government] wanted a new formula and they wanted it fast."[28] But the NDP had already worked out many of the features of the Harris plan, such as reducing the number of grants, amalgamating boards, and creating more equity for separate schools. Class sizes under the NDP plan had been the same as those in Bill 160, but without Bill 160's methods of fudging the figures. Harris' ministry of education did not acknowledge the debt to the NDP.

In many respects, the Harris plan was less progressive. Actual student-teacher ratios were larger under the new policy than they had been before, because every person who held a teaching certificate in a board, which included administrators, counselors, and consultants, counted as a teacher. In 1999–2000, special-education classes, which are small, were included in the calculation of class sizes, reducing apparent class size that year. In the regulations for 2000–2001, some noncredit classes were dropped from the calculation and special-education classes were no longer included in averages.[29] Also, boards were allowed to increase class sizes if they found it necessary. Changing the date on which enrollment counts are taken from September 30 to October 31 decreased enrollment figures, reducing the per-pupil allocation, especially in urban areas. In addition, the time a student must be enrolled to count as full time was increased from 151 to 210 minutes a day.[30] In reality, these changes increased class sizes as calculated under the old system, rather than reducing them as the ministry claimed.

Any fiscally responsible boards that had made budget cuts and delayed capital expenditures prior to 1995 were out of luck after 1996. Money for new construction and maintenance became scarce. On the other hand, boards that had large debts were in luck—these were assumed by the province. Other problems plagued the transition from the old system to the new. Since the formula was based on costs in 1996, many boards faced a shortage in subsequent years. Benchmark costs set in 1996 were not updated throughout the Harris and Eves regimes. Boards that had expensive special-education programs had to cut back; they no longer had the right to tax to support such options. One board official interviewed claimed that ways of counting special-education students the first year, which varied considerably from board to board, had a significant impact on funding during the second year. All four boards interviewed in 2000 complained about lack of adequate funds for special education. Although some problems have been addressed each year in the annual reports, the main complaints—enveloping the money too tightly, using outdated or inadequate benchmarks, inadequate funding for special education, and lack of flexibility in spending—remained.[31]

Lack of democracy in making local decisions on how to use the money was a complaint in the four boards I visited in January 2000. The funding formula did not allow money to be moved from inside-the-classroom to outside-the-classroom expenses. Although this seems like a good policy, problems arose in the definition of what counts as an inside-the-classroom expense; for instance, initially, preparation time for teachers was not included. In addition, there are other restrictions on how money is to be used. In 1999–2000, special-education grants covered only inside expenses, leaving no way to cover administrative costs, which are considerable in special education. This changed in the 2000–2001 plan, which states that special-education moneys will be provided "in one envelope."[32] Ontario schools used to offer three "streams" (tracks in the United States): basic, applied, and academic. The basic stream was eliminated under the new plan. In New York, the new ruling that all students will have to pass the Regents Examinations to graduate may have a similar effect: more inadequately prepared students entering the job market because of dropouts.[33] "Sweatering" or "enveloping" the special-purpose grants does not permit boards to move money around to meet local needs. All boards I visited felt this keenly. Although the use of parent councils as decision-making bodies in boards appears democratic, some boards lacked participation; parent councils cannot run schools on a daily basis. With the pay and numbers of trustees reduced substantially, boards reported covering this lack by creating new positions, such as assistant superintendents and various kinds of consultants, who were teachers moved to the central office for a period of time. Coincidentally, all certified staff members are counted in a board's student-to-teacher ratio, which created a ratio that appeared to lower class sizes while it actually increased them.

Another difficulty lay in evaluation. The ministry appointed an Educational Improvement Commission (EIC) to determine how effectively the reforms were being carried out in the newly amalgamated boards. The EIC had to visit and evaluate seventy-two boards in one year. The OSSTF contact calculated that they had a maximum of three days per board. Their reports on the Web were largely concerned with efficiency issues; the "best practice" sections dealt with cost-effective procedures such as purchasing cooperatives.[34] However, the impact on pedagogy is of primary concern to educators. For instance, it is clear in the United States that smaller schools are better pedagogically,[35] although less economical to operate. If the aim is economy, pedagogical best practices are likely to be ignored. In addition, teachers without the autonomy to make pedagogical and curricular decisions according to their professional judgment are less likely to function as well as they might in the profession.[36]

The pupil accommodation grant was also contentious. The Harris government aimed to eliminate "excess capacity" by not funding new pupil places if the board had any unused space, no matter what its location. However, population shifts in ways that are not controllable by school boards. As one board administrator explained, in a stable neighborhood, the school-age population blooms and then fades; children leave when they grow up while their parents stay. In the amalgamated boards, excess capacity in a fading population will have to be sold or dismantled, when it is too far to bus students and the unused space prevents funding for new construction elsewhere. Schools closings have resulted, which are always unpopular and often spell doom for the local economy. Many schools were designed to accommodate additions easily; however, subtracting excess additions later proved more troublesome and was clearly wasteful. The use of portables has been a solution that seems likely to continue, although it has many problems.

The Learning Opportunities Grant was designed to assist cities with the extra costs of immigrant and urban children; nevertheless, the metropolitan boards have lost considerable money under the new policies, since they used to be assessment-rich. According to the union official, when the NDP began cutting social services, schools hired psychologists, health-care workers, and social workers to provide services needed by children in urban areas. Many of these programs had to be abandoned. Cities in New York have long been trying to establish a claim to additional education funding to cover the combined costs of a population of children who are expensive to educate as well as the municipal overburden, which results from the need for other services, such as police, fire protection, garbage collection, and now "homeland security" in some cities. Although these claims have not been successful so far in the United States, the guarantee of a "meaningful high school education" in *Campaign for Fiscal Equity* may change that.[37] Ontario urban schools face a similar problem: municipal overburden and lack of necessary social services for children and families. In urban areas, chronic underfunding for these costs brought on a crisis in 2002–2003. Three urban boards refused to comply with the government's demand for a balanced budget based on inadequate funding, which would have forced them to cut services they regarded as essential. They refused to submit such a budget, forcing provincial takeover, which made it clear to voters by 2003 that the government, not the municipalities, was doing the cutting.

Other losses reported during my interviews with the boards included a loss of adult education, apprenticeship, and junior kindergarten programs, which boards could no longer afford (although the ministry supported an increase of $1 million for junior kindergarten in the 2000–2001 plan, this was a relatively small amount);[38] loss of experienced department heads and a shortage of principals; and a loss of teachers for extra duties like hall duty, lunch duty, and unpaid extracurricular activities. As columnist Michele Landsberg reported, the new Bill 74 "enshrine[d] in law the right to force teachers to work overtime . . . without choice . . . and without pay" and allows any teacher who "slow[ed] down or protest[ed]" to be declared "illegally on strike" and fired summarily.[39] I calculated an increase from $6,703 per pupil or $13.2 billion total dollars in 1999–2000 to $6,754 per pupil or $13.4 billion total dollars in 2000–2001 (in Canadian dollars), which amounts to an increase of about 0.99 percent.[40] From all this, it is clear that economy was the main aim of the Harris government, with transparency when politic and equity bought at the cost of adequacy. What the OSSTF official called democracy is not evident, because of loss of local control, flexibility, and teacher autonomy.

The funding formulae were adjusted in March 2000 for the 2000–2001 school year. Although some problems were addressed, many remained. The new formula included more special-education funding for students needing intensive support, but the regular per-pupil allotment remained as it was.[41] Some other programs appeared to add money, but closer examination revealed otherwise. For instance, new money for transportation grants was added in the form of interest-free loans to boards to invest in technology designed to achieve savings in transportation costs by consolidating routes. Boards were expected to use the savings to repay the loans. The ministry added $182 million to the teacher compensation grant, but mandated a teacher-advisor program for grades seven to twelve (funded at $64 million, which funds the program for grades seven to eleven and "allows the school boards to extend the program to grade twelve"). Extracurricular activities were not covered by the ministry's 2000–2001 definition of "co-instructional" time. Instead, Bill 74 subjected teachers to punishments if they did not participate. The revisions did not allow districts to include more than one teacher in a team-teaching situation or teachers who are not certified in the specific area of instruction in student-teacher ratios.[42] Other new funds covered grade ten textbooks (required for the new curriculum), remedial programs (required for the "slide back" effect of introducing the new curriculum), French language and English as a Second Language (ESL) programs, where definitions were adjusted to allow school boards to access additional money if they qualify. Funding was added to administration for principals in small and remote schools.

At the end of the document, the government revealed that $83 million of this was funded through a pension plan "holiday" resulting from a surplus in the Ontario Municipal Employees' Retirement System.[43] Of the $190 million growth announced by the government in March 2001,[44] $83 million came from the pension plan and $64 million was for a new program, a total of $147 million. This left only $43 million in new money, some of which covered new programs. Although the official Parents' Guide to Student-focused Funding for 2001–2002 claimed that the funding had increased by 7.7 percent while enrollment only increased by 4.2 percent, there was no adjustment for inflation.[45] New revisions were announced each year, with more minor changes, but the basic formula remained intact. The question of inadequacy continued to dog the ministry.

Funding of religious education was also contentious, adding to the inadequacy. Under the Harris-Eves reforms, separate schools were fully funded for the first time. However, little additional money was added to the pot. The funding of Catholic religious education was challenged in 1999 in *Waldman* v. *Canada*, which contended that funding Catholic religious schools and not other religious schools is contrary to the United Nations Universal Declaration of Human Rights, which Canada has signed.[46] The United Nations position is that signatories must either fund all religious schools equally, or none. The United Nations human rights committee summoned Canada's ambassador in 2000 to explain why Ontario doesn't fund all religious education. The ambassador claimed that the federal government has no power in the matter. The Ontario Ministry of Education initially took the position that it is unconstitutional for Ontario to cease funding Catholic schools, but it would be too great an expense to fund all religious schools.[47] Since the provincial share per pupil is $7,000 (Canadian), the government stood to gain by giving a tax credit of any lesser amount, while mollifying parents requesting support for private religious schools. Public schools, however, would lose $7,000 for every pupil who ceased attending, because their funding is based on attendance. The province would save $3,500 on every pupil who attended a private school under this plan. In June 2001, Parliament passed Bill 45, granting a tax credit of $3,500 (Canadian), to be phased in over a five-year period. During the first year of the phase-in, parents of students attending private schools received a tax credit of $700. In 2002–2003, the first phase of the tax credit, slated as 20 percent, was postponed for one year; the tax credit remained at $700 at the time of McGuinty's election.[48] In 2003, the Liberals released statistics showing that private school enrollment was up.[49] Critics contend that the tax credit is a subsidy for parents who already send their children to private schools, as vouchers are in the United States, especially if they are not means-tested. The policy has proved contentious, but the province later chose not to support separate schools for other religions beyond the $700 tax credit. Private schools are not required to follow the provincial curriculum, which has added to the contention, because public schools are subject to many regulations. The separate schools have to calculate what part of the education they offer is not religious for tax purposes, but the rules are loose.[50]

By 2002, funding had remained static for five years, with only minor increases and a 1.95 percent raise for teachers, with the exception of some one-time "fixes." By 2003, the funding system was clearly coming up short in almost all categories. The system for funding school places, the accommodation grant, was especially troublesome, resulting in school closings in one-school towns, long bus trips for pupils (especially in French-language boards), and deferred maintenance in boards with older schools. The allocation for maintenance at $5.20 per square foot was inadequate. The idea that boards should not be allowed to build new places as long as there was unused capacity anywhere in the district resulted in selling or even demolishing school buildings that were not located where they were needed. By March 2002, the date for releasing new government figures for the 2002–2003 school year, the situation approached a crisis for a number of reasons. First, the ministry had still not updated the cost benchmarks since 1996, the year they were set. Second, many districts had postponed construction or renovation projects due to the manner of funding capital improvements based on the computation of available floor space per student. Absurdly, having large hallways or

abundant closet space counted against schools. Third, the chronic underfunding accumulated. Although the ministry calculated the increase
for 2002 at $13.8 billion, up from $13.5 billion in 2001, a 2.8 percent increase, inflation increased by an estimated 4 percent and enrollment by
4 percent. The ministry claims that enrollment was projected to increase
by "less than 1 percent";[51] other sources disagreed. The "local priorities
grant," which Eves added to the foundation grant to provide more flexibility in spending, was quite small, $200 million. Rules about spending
money in envelopes relaxed somewhat, but money for special education,
capital improvements, and inside-the-classroom expenditures was still
protected. Boards are still responsible for obtaining land for new schools,
but are not provided with any funding for that purpose. The phase-in period over, metropolitan boards faced yet more cuts. Their refusal to submit the required balanced budgets with a yet smaller allotment of funds
precipitated a crisis. In response to this crisis, Eves appointed a commission to investigate the funding situation and make recommendations.
Facing an election, he had to take some action.

The Rozanski Report

Premier Eves created the Equality Education Task Force in May 2002,
headed by Guelph University president Mordecai Rozanski. As the phase-
in period of five years (1998–2003) drew to a close, a double cohort of
students graduated simultaneously from the old five-year Ontario Academic Credit (OAC) program and the new four-year program.[52] The public concern that there would not be enough university places for these
students came to a head.[53] The planning appears to have been dysfunctional, at best. At the same time, metropolitan districts were rebelling.
Things began to fall apart.

   The task force was asked to investigate six aspects of education
funding including 1) the effectiveness of the model for distributing the
money between different boards; 2) the structure of the cost benchmarks
established in 1996; 3) the degree of local-spending flexibility boards
need; 4) approaches to funding school maintenance, repairs, and reno-
vations; 5) the approach to funding special education; and 6) ways to
maximize the efficiency of funding for transportation while maintaining
appropriate services for the four types of boards and the students they
serve. The task force was also asked to consider the official, original principles of school funding reform, which were specified as: fairness, equity,
responsiveness to students' needs, and accountability. The charge also
included consideration of how to improve stability of funding. The task
force was required to respect the constitutional framework and to make
recommendations within the range of what was affordable.

Rozanski scrupulously observed these limits. The task force accepted the premises of the province's involvement—that the province is responsible for providing a "quality" education that permits "continuous improvement in learning." The group did not examine the issues of provincial control of curriculum and testing, adequacy of funding, or the massive new education bureaucracy created by the Harris reforms. As David Corson, of the Canadian Centre for Policy Alternatives, pointed out, the report assumed that the concept of the funding plan was sound at bottom. Rozanski did not challenge the curriculum, testing, or division of funds under the plan. Nor did he challenge the provincial taxing, assessment, or appropriation of commercial and industrial taxes. Corson believed that the reforms in curriculum moved Ontario away from a traditional, liberal arts orientation to a less rigorous curriculum designed to promote business interests and globalization. His claim was similar to the complaints of critical theorists in the United States. It also echoed Mark Van Doran's notion of the value of a liberal arts education for all, as opposed to James Conant's idea that a differentiated curriculum would be best at selecting the meritocracy destined to rule. According to Corson's analysis,

> When compulsory education was extended to the masses in the nineteenth century, school systems looked to the formal education already received by the leisured classes for suitable curriculum models. . . . Formal liberal education . . . is being replaced, in high-risk sites like Ontario, by policies mandating teaching and learning activities biased towards serving the utilitarian needs of a corporate and globalized marketplace. Preparation for the short-term needs of employers is rapidly replacing the conventional liberal preparation of initiating students into worthwhile forms of life. In effect, educational policy making in the province is increasingly biased towards preparing students to meet the needs of employers and business. Using what's good for business as its benchmark of human value, the Ontario government is routinely treating the province's student body unethically: It is not respecting them as persons because it is using them as a means to its own ideological ends.[54]

Claims like these, which went beyond the mandate, were not addressed. Nevertheless, the Rozanski report surprised critics of the Harris-Eves reforms. They expected a whitewash and they got an exposé.

Rozanski reaffirmed the charge of inadequacy forcefully. He concluded that the cost benchmarks set up in 1997, based on 1996 school expenditures and 1992 census data, were outdated. With only minor increases, funding had remained static with the exception of some one-time fixes or grants, such as loans for transportation software and grants for the textbooks required by the new curriculum. By 2003, the accumulated shortages had caused a great deal of discontent familiar to educators in the United States. Problems included inadequate raises, deferred maintenance, lack of professional development, and not enough books and supplies. Equality had been accomplished, but at the cost of adequacy.

Announcing that none of the witnesses called by his commission had attacked the concept of equity, Rozanski reported universal condemnation of the inadequacy of the funding. His report recommended a substantial infusion of money into the system over the next three years, accompanied by an updating of the benchmarks for costs on a yearly basis thereafter. The report's thirty-three recommendations included immediate funding for negotiated teachers' salaries, money needed for a backlog of special education services that had been approved but not delivered, and funding for urgent transportation needs. The first recommendation advised updating the benchmark costs and implementing the increases recommended in the report over a three-year period. Other recommendations advised "costing out procedures" very like those ordered in New York to be used in reallocating money among the grant categories. Deferred maintenance, school renewal costs, updates in technology, and a thorough review of the governance structure of schools were included. Rozanski estimated the cost of his recommendations at $1.769 billion over three years, not including salaries and benefits to be negotiated. The task force served a function very similar to the Zarb Commission appointed by Governor Pataki and Panel of Special Referees appointed by Justice DeGrasse to investigate conditions related to spending in New York City schools, but without the legal sanction that will be obtained if DeGrasse's acceptance of the Special Referees' report is upheld after all appeals are finished. Many recommendations were similar to those made by both commissions in New York.

With the issue of the Rozanski report in December 2002, it became clear that Premier Eves would have to implement some of the report's recommendations in his new budget proposals, due in March 2003. *Education Week* assessed the situation this way, "Some question Mr. Eves' motives. He was the finance minister in the former government that many critics blame for the steep education cuts. And an election will likely be called within a year."[55] Eves was anxious to avoid blame for the inadequacies of school funding. The title of the Rozanski report alone could not have been encouraging to his prospects—*Investing in Public Education: The Goal of Continuous Improvement in Student Learning and Achievement.*[56] Eves would have to respond to enough of the recommendations to satisfy the public, or risk losing the election. He went to work finding money to spend on education. The so-called Magna Budget of 2003 was the result. In his policies, however, Eves did not implement the first and most important of Rozanski's recommendations—to put in place a mechanism for regularly updating the cost benchmarks. He tried to focus the electorate's attention on a one-time infusion of cash instead. His actions gave too little and came too late. Hugh McKenzie, of the Canadian Centre for Policy Alternatives (CCPA), summed up the aftermath as "the consequence of twin political imperatives of tax cuts and a balanced budget."[57] Some areas of education benefited; special education received $250 million and $340 million (Canadian) was provided to cover outstanding contracts for teachers' salaries. But Liberal and NDP candidates had a field day with Eves on this issue. When the Eves government chose to implement some of the Rozanski report's recommendations with a one-time infusion of cash, rather than updating benchmarks as the report advised, Jim Bradley, a Member of Parliament from St. Catharine's, called the magna budget inadequate. At a press conference, he said, "It reminds me of someone who has broken all the windows in a building and comes in and says, 'I'm here to fix the windows.'"[58] Tax cuts and balanced budgets are rarely compatible, as the massive deficits of George W. Bush have shown in the United States. Like the Zarb Commission in New York, the Rozanski Commission recommended spending more money than the government was willing to spend.

Although Harris and Eves both claimed to have balanced the budget, they gave the people of Ontario a massive deficit instead. An analysis by Erik Peters, provincial auditor, in early November 2003, revealed the extent of the shortages—a deficit of $5.6 billion. Accounting irregularities allowed the Harris-Eves government to appear to achieve a balanced budget, but they did so by selling valuable provincial assets, for instance, Highway 407, which went for $1.88 billion. According to Hugh McKenzie, the Dominion Bond Rating Service discounted sales of assets when evaluating the worth of government bonds in April 2003,[59] because this influx of cash "does not reflect the Province's long term fiscal capacity."[60] McKenzie likened it to "selling the family silver to pay the rent" (2). He cited auditor Erik Peters' threat to withhold his approval of government accounts in 2000 by "includ[ing] a reservation in [his] auditor's report on the province's financial statements" as an "unprecedented" indication that Peters was well aware of the Harris-Eves government's fiscal malfeasance long before the 2002 audit revealed massive deficits (3).

The Metropolitan School Boards Revolt

In 1997, the Ontario Teachers Unions had called a massive strike to protest the changes to education mandated in Bill 160. However, teachers' unions called off the strike after two weeks and made substantial concessions to the government.[61] Some teachers felt betrayed. A general strike failed to materialize in their support. Afterward, the newly amalgamated school boards were fairly compliant early in the reform. However, after two years of underfunding, activists pursued and won seats on the school boards. Dissatisfaction mounted. After five years, boards were running out of reserves and falling further and further behind. Critics were calling the government plan the "defunding plan."[62] The charge of inadequacy refused to go away. Throughout 2001–2002, the Toronto, Hamilton-Wentworth, Ottawa-Carlton, and nine other boards struggled to formulate balanced budgets that they could countenance. The Ontario Ministry of Education and Training required boards to submit a balanced budget, using the amounts the new funding formulae allocated. Urban boards whose tax base was higher than suburban or rural boards prior to 1996 had continuously lost funding over the implementation period, but losses were cushioned by the five-year phase-in period, reserves, and grants for textbooks. Metropolitan boards had begun to resist as early as 1999–2000. In 2002, a rebellion coalesced around the three major urban boards willing to stick their necks out. They could refuse to submit a balanced budget, or fail to provide a decent education.[63] From May to August 2002, the government twice postponed the deadline to submit a balanced budget. In the end, following the lead of Ottawa-Carlton, the Toronto and Hamilton-Wentworth boards refused to submit balanced budgets for 2002–2003 as required by law. The cumulative inadequacy in funding proved to be the tipping point.

Teachers also contributed to public recognition of the inadequacy of funding. After striking in 1997, they struck again in 1998, although some of these "strikes" were lockouts. The new funding plan separated teachers and administrators into different unions, setting up a situation in which boards and teachers are adversaries, rather than colleagues, as before the Harris reforms. The Harris government introduced back-to-work legislation, which the Liberals and New Democrats opposed. The dispute this time was over extra workload requirements without extra pay. Boards scrambled to offer teachers a small raise, usually from reserves. In 2000, another strike loomed, this time over proposed regulation of "volunteer" hours, new definitions of instructional time, and competency exams. Some teachers were also angered by an increase of only 1.6 percent in the province's school budget.[64] In 2002, teachers unions warned of another strike in January 2003 if teachers did not receive substantial raises. By December, Premier Eves, facing an election, promised an injection of cash into the system in response to the Rozanski Commission's report criticizing the inadequacy of the funding. He also threatened to ban teachers' strikes. He advised boards to negotiate short term contracts to tide them over.

Boards had been solving budget problems by illegally using money from other funds to run essential services and give meager raises to teachers.[65] Their reserves running out, boards found themselves up against the wall. They decided to push back. Meeting in Hamilton at what came to be called "The Hamilton Summit" on July 18, 2002, parents, trustees, and school communities mounted what Mitchell Beer called "a wall of opposition."[66] Premier Eves responded by placing the three metropolitan boards under provincial control.[67] The appointment by the ministry of managers who would be responsible for cutting programs made it clear to constituents that the government itself was responsible for the inadequacies. The province now came under a furious attack for depriving communities of political representation, forcing them to accept school closings, defer maintenance, cancel special-education programs, and wipe out adult education.

Gail Stuart, the vice-chair of Our Schools, Our Communities, an Ottawa education advocacy group, summed up the situation at a hearing on education issues held in Ottawa on January 30, 2003, by the provincial Liberal opposition:

> Last year, given two conflicting mandates: (1) to pass a balanced budget while receiving highly inadequate funding to do so; and, (2) to meet the legal obligation of providing appropriate programs and services to meet students needs, our democratically-elected trustees chose to respect their legal and moral mandate to protect students and provide a quality education.[68]

Liz Sandals of the Ontario Public School Boards' Association commented, "School boards' question to the provincial government is rapidly becoming 'which law would you like us to break?'"[69]

After a short and disastrous period in office, during which he faced not only rebellious school boards, but also e. coli–contaminated water, the SARS outbreaks in Toronto, the United States–Canadian blackout of summer 2003, and fallout from the general economic downturn in the United States following the September 11 attacks on the World Trade Center in New York, Eves was forced to call an election. In 2002, Liberal Dalton McGuinty had criticized the Tory government for selling off assets to balance the budget. "The Harris-Eves government ripped off taxpayers when it gave away Highway 407 in a fire sale to raise money to get it through the last election," McGuinty said, "Now it looks like they are cooking up the same kind of deal for Hydro One—a short term fix to buy their way through an electricity mess that will only lead to even more price-gouging for hard-pressed Ontario consumers after the election."[70] In March 2003, the same month that school funding decisions are made in Ontario for the following year, McGuinty challenged Premier Eves to call an election, which he did. During the campaign, McGuinty also accused Eves of accumulating deficits of $2 million, reducing school funding, and privatizing hospitals. The campaign was heated, although close, according to Canadian sources, with Eves and McGuinty running neck-and-neck up to the end, while NDP candidate Howard Hampton interjected serious issues into the debate. Dalton McGuinty won, becoming premier in October 2003. As Eves pointed out in the debate, "the government will strike out in a new direction, if McGuinty is elected."[71] Apparently McGuinty was right—the majority of Ontarians judged Eves' leadership during a difficult period to be deficient. Andrea Baille of the Sun Media Corporation reported that, "The Liberals were elected in seventy-two ridings, the Conservatives in twenty-four and the NDP in seven." Baille assessed the result as, "a humiliating blow for Ernie Eves and his once unstoppable Tories." She noted, "For the first time in almost 70 years, a sitting Conservative premier in Ontario had lost an election outright."[72] Before the election, the Conservatives held fifty-six seats, the Liberals thirty-six, and the New Democrats nine. After the election, the Liberals held seventy-two seats, the Conservatives twenty-four, and the New Democrats seven. The New Democrat's party leader, Howard Hampton, who won in only seven ridings, criticized McGuinty's campaign promise of $1.6 billion more funding for the schools. During the campaign, NDP candidate Howard Hampton stated the case rather succinctly:

> Seven years ago, the Conservatives started a crisis in our schools—
> a crisis that has never ceased. Since 1995, the education of Ontario's
> children, and the lives of their parents, have been disrupted by Conservative mismanagement. Classrooms are overcrowded, textbooks
> too few, special education waiting lists too long. Support staff, the
> secretaries, janitors, librarians and guidance counselors have been
> decimated by Tory funding cuts. Early Years education, the most crucial and cost-effective way of preparing our children for a productive
> life, is a hollow promise. University tuition fees, and student debt,
> have soared.[73]

Furthermore, Hampton was derisive of McGuinty's proposed additional education funding, claiming that it did not provide an increase, because it was almost the same amount promised in the Conservative plan for increasing expenditures during 2003–2004.[74]

As he took office, McGuinty was saddled with a complex problem in school funding. Education was short substantial sums of money. At this writing, the McGuinty government appears to be taking the Rozanski report seriously, funding its recommendations, although not exactly to the letter of the report. In his election campaign, McGuinty promised to spend an additional $1.6 billion a year on education, cancel the private-school tax credit, increase the school-leaving age to eighteen, and impose a cap of twenty pupils on classes from junior kindergarten to grade three.[75] New Democrat Howard Hampton proposed affordable day care, more money for preschool, and better programs for language instruction, apprenticeship programs in the trades, adult education, and rollbacks in university tuition. Despite his more conservative program, McGuinty's progress as of this writing is encouraging. The ministry restored elected trustees of the three urban boards to power by February 18, 2004,[76] funded English-as-a-second-language and other literacy programs by an additional $112 million,[77] suspended a $55 million debt in the Toronto board 2002–2003, and formed an Education Partnership Table to discuss education issues with a wide array of stakeholders.[78] In the 2005 budget, McGuinty addressed other improvements, including making loans on which the province pays the interest available to boards for needed repairs, but 2 percent increases in teachers' salaries and 2 percent to cover rising costs is still not adequate.[79] Nevertheless, the new government appears to have good intentions.

In 1996, the Ontario Secondary School Teachers' Federation (OSSTF) commissioned an analysis of the original cost-of-education study done by Stephen Lawton for the ministry of education at the outset of the Harris reforms.[80] This costing-out study set the benchmarks in Ontario for the years of the Harris reforms. Flaws included using only two years of data, failing to weight teacher salaries, failing to account for immigration and poverty rates, using salary information for the decade 1983–1993 without accounting for the "Rae days" that diminished teachers' salaries, and comparing data that was not comparable across provinces. As events have played out since 1997, the OSSTF's criticisms of reductions in school funding were vindicated.

Another "Manufactured Crisis"

The original impetus to reform arising in the Harris years seemed to be forgotten—to pursue improvement in education, even if it was supposed to come by cutting taxes and blaming teachers for the failure of education, in a "manufactured crisis." As Berliner and Biddle showed in *The Manufactured Crisis,* the publication of *A Nation at Risk* did not document a crisis in United States education, it created one.[81] The strategy of Harris in 1995 was parallel to the conservatives' approach in the 1980s and 1990s in the United States—to curtail "run-away" funding, to blame local teachers, and to mandate curriculum and testing following a conservative agenda. Likewise, John Snobelen, Harris' first minister of education, boasted that he would create a "useful crisis" in education.[82] Scapegoating Ontario's teachers and schools aided Harris' election campaign, while getting the government off the hook for economic problems. Education in Ontario was not failing, nor were the teachers or the schools doing a bad job. Nor was the curriculum of low quality. Ontario's school system was widely recognized as exemplary. The fifth year of high school was unique in the Americas. As in the United States, the "reforms" resulting from the manufactured crisis were not necessarily beneficial, much like the questionable benefits of the standards and accountability movement that resulted from the publication of *A Nation at Risk*. Ironically, Harris' strategy resulted in an unparalleled bureaucratic control of education, contrary to stated conservative political ideals, just as Bush's reforms in the No Child Left Behind legislation. Fortunately, the states can refuse to comply, which some consider doing, since the costs of the program outweigh the federal funding that would be lost. In Ontario, rebellion by the urban boards was effective in drawing attention to the problem.

Instead of a court battle or a battle between the court and the legislature, the struggle for equitable and adequate school finance in Ontario was connected to the electoral politics of the executive branch. When Harris resigned his position in 2001 and Premier Eves, from the same party, was elected, Ontarians might have hoped for some reversal of the centralization and loss of control over education. Instead, Eves' provincial government took over the rebellious urban boards, parallel to the control Mayor Bloomberg and Mayor Johnson of New York City and Rochester were given over their respective city school districts, although on a smaller scale. According to one news source, student-focused funding was cut by $1,250 per pupil under Eves' government.[83]

Following the 1996 reforms, the problem in Ontario is no longer inequity of funding or an uneven tax burden, but inadequacy of funding. Equality is not enough. Equity is not enough, unless the equity is judged by adequacy of outcomes. Even that is not enough if the outcomes are deliberately set too low, as the Appellate Division decision in *CFE IIb* showed in New York, when judges pronounced an eighth- or ninth-grade education constitutionally adequate. Transparency, simplicity, equity, and flexibility of spending are clearly desirable goals. So is local control, as long as it is not used to justify inequitable spending. But Ontario's experience shows that these other goals must not be achieved at the cost of adequacy. During Ontario's experience with school-finance reform, other goals emerged, for instance, stable funding to facilitate planning for local priorities and local needs, money for maintenance and building, and money for urban areas faced with municipal overburden. Calculating the numbers of square feet per student, wherever such space is located—in hallways, closets, or neighborhoods full of retirees—is not practicable. Cheap buildings do not last, portables have many problems, and it is difficult to move excess capacity to where it is needed. The cost of providing "pupil accommodations" when and where they are needed simply must be accounted as one of the ordinary expenses of pubic schooling. Policies under the Harris and Eves governments have left a residue of deferred maintenance that will be hard to fix.

Ontario's experience raises the old question: Can local control be maintained in the face of centralized funding? It suggests that it is more difficult to maintain local control when the funding is centralized. Yet social justice depends on equity, just as a quality education depends on adequacy. The place of religion in the schools also vexed Ontarians. Should private religious schools receiving public money teach the same curriculum? Must a state either fund all private religious education, or none? In the United States, a firm principle of separation of church and state springing from the establishment clause in the First Amendment is thought to prevent unregulated private religious schools from siphoning off money from the public schools. But this principle is threatened by policies under the Bush administration. Vouchers, used in private religious schools, violate this principle; if the United States does not take care, public money will fund religious teachings. Charter schools also represent a threat to public education if they are exclusive, if they limit enrollment by artificial means, and if they do not serve children with exceptional needs. Even if charter schools do not do these things, they will siphon money from the public system, leaving neighborhood schools unimproved and further concentrating children by race, ethnicity, and poverty, as is happening in almost all major urban areas in the United States. Some proponents of private schools, especially religious private schools, do not wish to have any public funding precisely because of the possibility that it will come with strings attached. Others, however, are more confident that their sectarian elements will be preserved. The Bush administration's "faith-based" initiatives transfer funding from federal agencies to sectarian organizations with few protections against the money being used for indoctrination into dogmatic religious beliefs.

Although the Eves-Harris policies created massive deficits in Ontario, the federal government's deficits in the United States under George W. Bush are even greater. Tax cuts for the wealthy do not produce revenue to pay for public services required in a humane, democratic society. Although federal funds contribute little to education (about 4 percent), federal mandates for special education and the testing associated with No Child Left Behind (NCLB) are seriously underfunded. Although the conservatives in Ontario proposed using the news about deficits to cut more services, the Canadian Centre for Policy Alternatives advised McGuinty to change spending priorities and cancel tax cuts. As happened in the United States under George W. Bush, tax cuts benefiting mostly high-income taxpayers resulted in massive deficits, without any increase in the minimum wage, with substantial attempts to privatize government utilities and services, with increased user-fees and co-pays for public facilities, and at the expense of schoolchildren. As McKenzie remarked, "The notion that tax cuts increase revenue was a political invention of Ronald Reagan, and has since been totally discredited. There is no evidence in the data to support the claim."[84]

Lessons from Ontario

The states may well take heed of some of these lessons. First, transparency of funding formulae is a good idea. Transparency can be obtained by simplifying the categories and weighting systems. Often funding formulae are so complex that very few people understand how they work. In New York, allocations are subject to backroom deals in legislative chambers, which can be hidden from the public in the intricacies of the formulae. Ontario's categories are multiplying once again—simplicity and transparency need maintaining. But transparency should not trump substantive issues of funding.

Part of the difficulty is that the Ontario reforms were motivated by a desire to lower taxes rather than to improve schooling. In both Ontario and Vermont, where the property tax was also made statewide at a uniform tax rate, state curriculum, state testing, and state-mandated reporting have followed in the wake of state funding. These methods deprive teachers of autonomy, set external exams that are often inappropriate, and encourage reliance on standardized tests for assurance of success. Many (possibly) unintended consequences flow from these policies, such as increased dropouts, higher illiteracy, more prisoners, and high unemployment for the low-skilled workers educated in underfunded schools. But many states, especially New York, already have such state mandates (and more) without equity in funding or a uniform tax rate, resulting in inadequate funding in schools serving poor and minority children. The impact on these children is tremendous, since they emerge ill-equipped to make a decent living or participate in society as productive citizens.

Second, equality is a laudable goal, but equality without adequacy defeats its own purpose—improved education. Adequacy is the more important of the two, but it must be adequacy for everyone, not some chosen few. In the school funding reform movement in the United States, outcomes have become the measure of adequacy. Such adequacy implies equity of inputs, rather than equality. Children with more needs must have more resources to accomplish the same tasks. In the United States, adequacy depends on the state's commitment, on federal mandates and the associated federal aid or lack thereof, and now on the type of costing-out studies that are being done, such as those ordered by Justice LeLand DeGrasse in New York. One lesson from the Rozanski report is that cost benchmarks need to be updated yearly. Reliance on government for adequate funds can be troublesome. A remote governing body may not put the interests of children first. Sufficient funding has not been forthcoming in Ontario. I would not be surprised if Vermont found legislatures balking on appropriations in the future. In March 2002, directors of education across Ontario warned the Ministry of Education that they faced a massive shortfall from inadequate provincial funding that has "siphoned millions of dollars from education since 1995."[85] This indeed happened. In the United States, state legislatures are not usually forthcoming with substantial increases for education without much prodding.

A third lesson to be learned is that much damage can be done by too much standardized control over curriculum and testing. The staggering dropout rates in New York City, Philadelphia, Houston, Los Angeles, and other poor, urban areas demonstrate what happens to students whose needs are unmet by prescribed curriculum.[86] In all the states, districts are losing local control both because of the state standards movement and the imposition of new federal testing under NCLB. Districts are also losing funding. From 1991 to 2001 Buffalo Public Schools lost 7 percent enrollment, while other cities gained as much as 47 percent.[87] In Buffalo, in 2003 alone, the public schools lost 1,140 more students to charter schools; charter schools now cost the city's public school budget about $30 million a year.[88] The problem this causes is twofold—first it costs the public schools the per-pupil allotment for each student without commensurately cutting the expenses of the school, and second, it creates a two- (or three-) tiered system that leaves the most vulnerable children, the poorest, those whose parents are the least able to advocate for them, in unimproved "neighborhood schools." Charter schools and private schools "cream off" the students whose parents are able to seek the best for their own children, concentrating the others in schools untouched by reform and deprived of funding. Howard Dean advised states to refuse federal money with strings attached under the No Child Left Behind Act.[89] In May 2003, Vermont legislators passed a resolution condemning the federal regulations. *The Nation* reported that many states are dissatisfied with the requirements of NCLB. *The Nation* writer Peter Schrag reported,

> A gap of at least $6 billion annually between what Bush promised and Congress authorized under NCLB to pay for the mandated education programs—"highly qualified" teachers in every classroom by 2005–06, intensive reading programs for at-risk children and the required yearly progress in test scores. One researcher in Vermont calculated that it would take more than $84 billion to comply with NCLB annual progress requirements. Bush has proposed $1 billion.

> Every state, from New Hampshire to Washington, is feeling that
> pinch; New Hampshire's school administrators say that for every
> dollar the state gets from the Feds, it has to kick in $7 to meet the
> NCLB requirements.[90]

In 2005, Michigan sued the government over the additional costs accrued under NCLB in *Pontiac* v. *Spellings*; the case was dismissed in November, 2005, in the United States District Court.[91] In the meantime, Connecticut also brought a suit.[92] The law specifically states that the federal government may not "mandate a state or subdivision thereof to spend any funds or incur any costs not paid for under this act (Section 9527a)." The remedy requested is that the government not be allowed to withhold federal funding as punishment for noncompliance.

In many states, state standards and testing are imposing burdens on teachers, controlling the curriculum, limiting the autonomy of teachers, and (perhaps unintentionally) negatively affecting the education of children. Reforms in both Vermont and Ontario brought standardized testing and a mandated curriculum in their wake. New York already had these "accountability measures," as they are called, without any of the concomitant benefits of equity (or even equality) of resources. This mentality—that teachers are not professionals, but functionaries following the mandates of the state—goes back to Horace Mann and the feminization of teaching. The sanctity of "local control" in the United States is a sham, although this sanctity provided the rationale for the *Rodriguez* decision that local control provides a "rational basis" for grossly inequitable funding. As Marshall pointed out in his dissent to *Rodriguez*, "local control is a cruel illusion" for underfunded districts.[93] It takes money to introduce new programs, reduce class size, buy up-to-date textbooks, hire well-qualified teachers, sponsor genuine professional-development opportunities, and other items that districts could control if they had the resources. Obviously, money must be spent wisely and the results of reforms researched carefully. But without money, many necessary reforms are impossible. Tax reform, which sometimes results from taxpayer revolts, sometimes from tax reform initiated by the executive branch of government, and sometimes by legislatures strapped for cash during an economic downturn, can lead to inadequacy especially for urban, minority, and immigrant children and rural children living in poverty in impoverished districts.

Careful examination of school-funding reforms in New York, Vermont, and Ontario reveals a complex problem riddled with pitfalls and difficulties. Although the accomplishment of equitable school funding is far from easy, judges, legislators, administrators, teachers, school boards, parents, students, and citizens must accomplish the best education possible for all children if democracy is to thrive. Although difficult, an excellent education for each and every child is obtainable, just as social justice is obtainable, a nontoxic environment is obtainable, and world peace is obtainable. Other social factors also complicate the situation. Poverty and racism stand out in the United States as factors that inhibit the full development of children's potential. It is to these factors that I turn next. A commitment to "liberty and justice for all" makes it imperative to reduce or eliminate poverty and racism from the lives of children everywhere.

Chapter 5

The Impact of Poverty on Children's Performance in School

The law of human progress, what is it but the moral law? Just as social adjustments promote justice, just as they acknowledge the equality of right between man and man, just as they ensure to each the perfect liberty which is bounded only by the equal liberty of every other, must civilization advance. Just as they fail in this, must advancing civilization come to a halt and recede.

Chapter 24, Henry George
Progress and Poverty, 1879

Can Education Solve Social Ills? From Optimism to Pessimism in the Twentieth Century

Educators have long debated whether education can solve social ills. The argument still rages, although the nay-sayers seem to have won, for the time being. Perhaps an understanding of why this has happened will help to explain why reform seems so intractable, including equitable funding. A tendency to blame the public schools for a wide array of the nation's woes, from domestic to international problems, manifested itself in the publication of *A Nation at Risk* in 1983. This blame is misdirected. If reform has failed to address the root causes of children's lack of achievement, it may be because the goal of school has become improving the economy, or promoting national security, rather than benefiting the child. Alfred North Whitehead warned in 1917 against holding schools responsible to examinations set by outsiders.[1] The result is curriculum "a mile long and an inch deep." Those who emphasize testing, standards, and accountability neglect to take into account the social injustices that impede children's performance. Perhaps the yea-sayers who believe in

119

public education, noticing that social ills affect children's performance in school, can rally public opinion once again, as they did at the beginning of the twentieth century. These optimists believe in the potential of all children. They recognize that standardized tests do not represent children's accomplishments or their potential. Tests, even when they are reliable, valid, and fair, only represent the accomplishment of a specific task at a specific time—answering the particular questions on that test on that day. The No Child Left Behind Act of 2001 assumes that schools (and children) are failures when their test scores are low. However, this conclusion is a vast oversimplification. Lead poisoned or hungry children do not do well on tests, but the blame rests on a society that permits such conditions to persist. Educators agree that social ills interfere with children's performance in school.

Poverty, often coupled with minority status in the United States, is extremely harmful to children's life chances. Poverty entails a complex set of conditions harmful to children: inadequate medical attention to mother and child, poor nutrition, low birth weight, low-quality child care, health problems, and environmental hazards, to name a few. Equitable school funding could mitigate the effects of poverty on children. Unfortunately, such equity is rare. In addition to persistent poverty, racism also rears its ugly head. Low-income children living in deteriorating urban housing are more likely to be African-American, Hispanic, or immigrant children. The obstacles they face are far greater than those faced by white, middle-income-to-affluent children, as this chapter establishes. Historically, Americans have long believed in the power of education to eliminate poverty. The idea that all children, not just boys of European ancestry, deserve an equal educational opportunity gradually came to accompany this belief. Education broadened to include white girls, immigrant children, African-American children, working-class children, children with special needs, and children of poverty. Unfortunately, the ideal of an equal educational opportunity for all children has not yet been realized, despite many sincere efforts and a great deal of rhetoric. The question is, why? The first answer proposed by this book is inequitable school funding; the second, poverty, racism, and other social ills that persist. This chapter will discuss how these two factors converge.

In the Massachusetts Bay Colony, The "Old Deluder Law" established public schools so that children could learn to read the Bible. Horace Mann promoted his Common School Movement in the 1830s by appealing to parents with the idea their children would benefit economically. After the Civil War, African-Americans sought education to liberate themselves from dependence on their ex-owners through education. Despite their difference over the kind of education black children needed, both Booker T. Washington and W.E.B. Du Bois advocated educational opportunities for blacks. African-Americans have persisted in their quest for an education, although schools today are still suffering from racism. Jane Addams and other workers in the settlement house movement of the early twentieth century counted on the power of education to solve problems among the urban poor, particularly immigrants.

Addams felt that vocational guidance could solve social ills like child prostitution. She recommended, "vocational bureaus [be] properly connected with all the public schools" to give "a girl [sic] . . . an intelligent point of departure into her working life."[2] Addams' essay addressed the problem of "commercialized vice," a polite term for child prostitution, but her belief that education cures other social ills is evident in her work. The Vocational Guidance Movement sought to identify children's aptitudes to prepare them for their position in the working world. Helen Thompson Woolley's 1927 comparative study of working children and school children debunked the prevalent idea that going to work early benefited working-class children more than staying in school and contributed to passage of child labor laws in Ohio.[3] Woolley chastised the schools for not paying attention to the problem of early dropouts and suggested vocational education, which would allow children to participate in the entire manufacturing process perhaps even becoming capable of serving on "managing boards of the industry." She also notes that if they "share in the profits thereof" this would "increase [their] personal interest" and "result in more job satisfaction (Woolley, 747)." Woolley also called for shorter working hours to limit the time young people perform monotonous, repetitive work injurious to their health. Optimistically, she proposed that they be prepared in school for wise use of the resulting increase in leisure time, recommending cultivating both appreciation of the fine arts of music, literature, and drama, and practical skills that can increase their standard of living, such as sewing, cooking, and doing household repairs (747–748). She also saw the need for "specific training . . . of young people for home-making and parenthood," explicitly including boys (741).

Although Woolley recognized that her early work on psychometric testing was "a coarse and clumsy tool,"[4] nevertheless, she believed that such testing would eventually play a vital role in educational guidance. In hindsight, the tools have remained clumsy. The Vocational Guidance Movement, in which Woolley was active in the 1920s, with all its good intentions, promoted the tracking systems that many schools are now trying to dismantle. The underlying premise is similar to that in Plato's *Republic*: social classes are the result of inborn characteristics of people who need to be "trained" to fulfill their destined role in society well and happily. Unfortunately, there seems to be little acknowledgment in mainstream political thought, then or now, that perpetuating the class system is destructive of educational opportunities for children born into poverty.

In his 1958 book, *Education and Liberty*, Conant perceived the goal of education to be "national unity" rather than developing the potential of the individual or training children for the workforce.[5] Conant and others founded the Educational Testing Service to devise ways to identify bright students. He believed that social mobility, created by allowing the brightest students from the lower middle or working classes access to higher education, would make them useful to their country while keeping working-class people from contributing to labor unrest or criticizing the system (66). He himself was a student from the lower-middle class who made it into Harvard, later becoming its president. Promoting what he called the comprehensive high school—one attended by all social classes, although the courses within the school were tracked—Conant held that too many American students were attending four-year colleges. According to Conant, the system "works against the welfare of our industrialized society" by unnecessarily prolonging the education of students who do not have the aptitude for it (59).

Contrary to Conant's theory, the GI Bill of 1944 allowed access to higher education for nontraditional students who would otherwise have been considered unqualified. Although they probably would not have scored well on the Scholastic Aptitude Test, the veterans did well in school.[6] Following the launch of Sputnik in 1957, Admiral Hymen Rickover and others continued pressing a national goal for education, now reformulated as national security, rather than unity. They proposed that education was the catalyst for both the supremacy in military technology and the skill in foreign relations needed to create and maintain a balance of power in the favor of the United States. In response to Sputnik, the National Defense Education Act of 1958 (NDEA), focusing on mathematics, the sciences, and foreign languages considered essential for military supremacy and diplomacy, granted loans and fellowships to students to attend college. While the NDEA may have increased access to higher education for people who might not otherwise have been able to afford it, it also marked a shift in the goal of education from some benefit to the child, even if this was vocational preparation for low-level work, to national security. This shift marks the beginning of the pessimism about education's power to effect social change that culminated in *A Nation at Risk* in 1983. Making national security the goal of education obliterates the importance of the individual child and eliminates many other worthy aims, such as achieving a just and equitable society in which all citizens have the opportunity to participate fully. However, national security does not result from education unless education truly benefits children in a broad sense; real national security is a byproduct of a truly democratic society with good public policies.

Although access to education broadened throughout the first half of the twentieth century, it was rarely access to an education of equal quality. Following the Supreme Court's 1896 ruling, *Plessy v. Ferguson,* that "equal but separate accommodations for the white, and colored races" are constitutional, the "equal" part of the ruling has been ignored.[7] As 1954 approached, school officials in the South declared their intention of upgrading their segregated schools, but they did not actually do it. Civil rights leaders pushed for equal schools on the theory that states would have to desegregate, since having two equal school districts would be prohibitively expensive.[8] Instead, the historic 1954 *Brown I* decision declared separate schools inherently unequal, mandating desegregation. Despite the ruling, schools were still segregated a decade after *Brown I.* Unfortunately, the unanimous *Brown I* decision and its followup, *Brown II,* in 1955, lacked clear procedures and definite timetables. The phrase "with all deliberate speed" in *Brown II* was interpreted as permission to go slowly.[9] By 1964, the Supreme Court commented, "there had been entirely too much deliberation and not enough speed."[10] More effective desegregation policies were put in place when noncompliant schools were threatened with loss of federal funding following the Civil Rights Act of 1964. Since *Brown I* made *de jure* segregation illegal, desegregation took place mostly in the South, helped by key court decisions such as *Green*[11] and *Swann.*[12] In 1974, *Keyes v. School District #1*[13] spread the burden of desegregation to Northern states, if it could be demonstrated that the policies that resulted in *de facto* segregated schools could be shown to be intentional.[14] Later, unfortunately, a number of regressive Supreme Court decisions, *Milliken I* and *II, Freeman v. Pitts,*[15] *Board of Education v. Dowell,*[16] and *Jenkins,* allowed districts to back off from desegregation, causing rapid school resegregation nationwide. Orfield and his colleagues at the Harvard Civil Rights project have documented the erosion of the *Brown* decision that followed. This is certainly due, at least in part, to the appointments Nixon, Reagan, and the first Bush made to the Supreme Court.[17] The Warren Court's concern for equality of educational opportunity disappeared from public policy, although it surfaces in rhetoric at campaign time.

The Coleman Report also contributed to neglecting the need to desegregate public schools. In 1966, twelve years after the *Brown* decision and amid growing concern about poverty and crime in ghettoized inner cities, the federal government commissioned an unprecedented study to examine equality of educational opportunity, pursuant to the Civil Rights Act of 1964, Section 402. James Coleman and a team of researchers collected data from teachers and students of several thousand schools. The researchers expected to find evidence that school resources contributed significantly to student achievement, but instead concluded that the effect of expenditures on outcomes was minimal. They found that family background, education of parents, socioeconomic status, and the "educational aspirations and backgrounds of fellow students" explained the differences in educational outcomes, not the quality of education as measured by the educational resources available. The Coleman Report used educational resources as the measure of opportunity, rather than educational outcomes. The report states, "Attributes of other students account for far more variation in the achievement of minority group children than do any attributes of school facilities."[18] The argument took the form of a syllogism: (premise 1) "school to school variations on achievement, from whatever source (community differences, variations in the average home background of the student body, or variations in school factors), are much smaller than individual variations within the school, at all grade levels, for all racial and ethnic groups. This means that most of the variation in achievement could not possibly be accounted for by school differences" (2). If the variations "were largely a result of either school factors or community differences in support of school achievement, then the school-to-school differences would increase over the grades in school. . . . However, this is not the case . . ." (3). "A reasonable conclusion is, then, that our schools have great uniformity insofar as their effect on the learning of pupils is concerned. The data suggest that achievement of pupils is not highly related to variations in school quality" (296). The researchers concluded the same for the variations in teachers' qualifications, although they did admit that teacher quality makes more difference for black pupils than for white pupils, especially in the South (316–317). This evidence was played down, however, when the report came to be used four years later by the Nixon administration. The authors declare that ". . . variations in the facilities and curriculums of the schools account for very little variation in pupil achievement insofar as this is measured by standard tests" [I might add, by the particular tests that ETS constructed for the purpose]. Although the researchers admit that ". . . it is for the majority whites that the variations make the least difference; for minorities they make somewhat more difference."[19] However, in the final analysis, the report conveniently ignored this evidence. Coincidentally, the document also showed that schools were still deeply segregated four years after the Civil Rights Act and fourteen years after *Brown I.* This finding did not receive much attention at the time, perhaps because of a racism embedded so deeply that people did not notice statements addressing the needs of minority pupils. To justify their conclusion, the researchers simply decided that two attitudes held by pupils, self-concept and a sense of control of the environment "depend more on the home than the school" (Coleman Report, 22). This extraordinary assumption reveals a deep-seated prejudice against black families. Researchers concluded that the variable that shows the most significant correlation school achievement is "quality of peers" (23). Their conclusion is weak at best.

The Coleman Report contained many weaknesses besides poor logic. Although it surveyed many schools and populations, the data lacked a longitudinal component; it was like a snapshot, taken at a particular time. Other variables could well have been operative, variables that either were or were not included in the picture. Tangibles—laboratories, libraries, course offerings, class sizes, supplies—and things less tangible—teachers' attitudes toward students, teachers' preparation and experience, test bias, institutional racism, racism in the curriculum and materials, access to extracurricular activities, acceptance by other students, racial and economic isolation—make a complex mix of "school" factors that affect students' achievement in many ways. Only a few of these factors were examined; those that were, were not examined in their complex interrelationships. Tangibles like numbers of textbooks and number of years of teachers' experience are easy to count but may not hold much importance. Vocabulary tests (used as a measure of teachers' ability) and standardized tests are easy to grade, but may not be valid indicators of quality.

Another problem is that comparisons within a school involve a smaller norm group than comparisons among schools. A smaller group always shows more variability in results. This variation in reliability at the school level affects the validity of the conclusion. The same problem obtains in the No Child Left Behind Act. Small schools will be subject to wide variations in test results depending on the children who happen to be attending that year and how well that particular group is prepared. In a small group, several individuals can make a big difference statistically. The size of the group alone explains why differences in Coleman's data within schools were larger than differences among schools. In addition, the schools were clearly subject to racial and economic isolation, which, in a prejudiced environment, could easily cause loss of "a sense of control" for black pupils. Yet this connection was not examined. Aspects of the report could have been used to point out the ill effects of segregation, but were not. Although the researchers' wording in the report is tentative ("a reasonable conclusion is . . ." and "the data suggest"), the report was taken to present strong statistical evidence of the lack of impact of school resources on student achievement.

David Seeley, then Assistant U.S. Commissioner of Education for Equal Educational Opportunity, was originally assigned the task of conducting the national survey of educational opportunity mandated by Section 402 of the Civil Rights Act. However, according to Gerald Grant, Seeley's plans were deemed too small, and the assignment was given to

James Coleman.[20] However, Seeley remained on the advisory group to
review Coleman's plans and results. Initially "favorably impressed" with
the proposed methodology, Seeley began to have reservations by 1965, a
year into the project. In 1966, when the first draft came out for review,
Seeley dropped other responsibilities to draft his objections to what he
termed "a seriously deficient and dangerous" report. His assessment of
the situation, later posted on the Web, is worth quoting:

> In addition to . . . [the report's] implication that schools could do lit-
> tle to improve the achievement of minority children . . . I strongly
> objected to the report's lack of adequate data (and misleading data)
> on the continued existence of officially segregated schools, the lack
> of attention to "de facto" segregation (e.g. in the north), the lack of
> attention to "Mexican-Americans and Spanish-Americans" [who
> were arbitrarily classified as white], the lack of focus on inequalities
> of facilities (especially in the North!), unwarranted assumptions re-
> garding what might be causing what, a tendency to blame minority
> children for their negative characteristics instead of looking at "what
> kinds of inequalities of opportunity may be available in the school
> system that could be corrected."
>
> On the implication that "school characteristics have very little to
> do with pupil achievement," [the conclusion to the Coleman Re-
> port], my memos took two positions 1) that the data studied by the
> research team did not support this thesis ("I am reasonably sure that
> it is not true, and I am absolutely sure that it is not proven by the sur-
> vey") because, massive as the data were, they included virtually no
> data (mostly because little existed as the kind of statistical data used
> for this survey) on the factors that might most likely enable schools
> to succeed with poor and minority children, e.g., "teacher morale,"
> and "inappropriate training of teachers to deal with the problems
> confronting them," etc. 2) that the report's therefore unwarranted
> implication that schools cannot make a difference in children's
> learning is very harmful to the cause of school reform, especially for
> poor and minority children.[21]

At the time, little was done in response to Seeley's memos, except
some minor changes in the published report. Seeley notes, "much harm
was unintentionally done" by the report.[22] Seeley reports that Gerald
Grant in Teacher's College Record accused him of "illegitimate political
interference with social science."[23] According to Grant, the report initially received such a mixed response that three summaries were written.
The final one, which minimized the finding that school characteristics
had far less impact on learning and were far less unequal than suspected,
was chosen to represent the report, which was so bulky that few legislators actually read it.

Shortly after its release, the report was the subject of a seminar held at Harvard with the proceedings published in Moynihan and Mosteller, *On Equality of Educational Opportunity*. Despite its initial lukewarm reception, four years later the report gained influence for political reasons in the Nixon administration. The data were taken to justify less federal spending on compensatory programs. Curiously enough, the same administration opposed integration, which the Coleman Report clearly supported (Grant, 22–23). Coleman himself reanalyzed his data six years later using newer regression techniques to separate the effects of his chosen variables more clearly and found that the original report had overestimated the impact of family background and underestimated the effect of school characteristics (73). Gerald Grant also concluded in his article in *Teachers College Record* that the Coleman Report was misused.

> In some ways the pendulum has swung too far. Although one federal judge has dismissed the Coleman Report as "a single piece of much criticized sociological research," too much credibility may have been placed on the negative findings of both Coleman and derivative analyses such as Christopher Jencks' volume on Inequality. The Coleman and Jencks Reports have become the fundamentalist bibles of the Washington budget-cutters, and even a sophisticated magazine like the Atlantic will let stand such oversimplified interpretations of the Coleman Report that "schools make no difference; families make the difference." Schools do make enormous differences, of course, although social scientists may not be very adept at measuring those differences. What the Coleman Report shows is that existing schools are not equalizers of differences among social groups in school achievement. That says nothing about the differences that may result in a child's life because he goes to one school rather than another. In one school he may acquire a lifelong love of the violin and in another never even see a violin. (54)

More recently, Berliner and Biddle argued convincingly in *The Manufactured Crisis: Myths, Fraud, and the Attack on America's Public Schools* (1995) that the methodology of the report was flawed.[24] Biddle and Berliner give four very specific criticisms of Coleman's analysis. 1) The conclusion is based on only one of Coleman's four categories that might affect achievement (a) student's background, (b) characteristics of the student body, (c) characteristics of the teacher, and (d) school facilities and curriculum. The last was taken to indicate "school quality" by itself, but surely the third, and even the others should have been included. 2) Categories of analysis were chosen more for administrative convenience than for relevance. 3) The data was cross-sectional rather than longitudinal, i.e., the data was collected in one year. 4) The analysis was flawed, because, in the first step, the researchers estimated the effects of home background without any controls for other characteristics that might have affected performance. Those estimates were inflated because they included effects contributed by the other categories of analysis.

Coleman's conclusion that "a child's sense of control of his [sic] environment correlated strongly with his achievement"[25] has been examined more recently by Harold Berlak, in "Race and the Achievement Gap."[26] Studies reveal that many black and minority students see themselves as destined to fail no matter how well they do. As anthropologist Signithia Fordham reported in study of a Washington, DC high school, a young black man stated, "Well, we supposed to be stupid . . . we perform poorly in school 'cause we got it all thought up in our heads that we're supposed to be dumb so we might as well go ahead and be dumb" (Berlak, 11). In another study, Claude Steele of Stanford University gave the same difficult section of the Graduate Record Exam to two groups of African-American and white Stanford sophomores, telling one group that the test was a measure of ability, and the other that it was not. When the black students in the "ability" group did significantly less well than the white students, Steele attributed the difference to "stereotype vulnerability." Both African-American and white students in the other group did equally well (9). Berlak also reported a positive correlation between tracking and performance on tests, again, not hard to understand. He noted that the achievement gap is perpetuated by school policy—blacks are less likely to be in gifted and talented programs and more likely to be in special education programs (10). Stereotypes associated with these programs persist, even in the mind of the subject. Such stereotypes also undoubtedly affect teachers' interactions with children.

Another of Coleman's findings was that black children benefit more than white children from integration, although the factors of socioeconomic status and race seem to me to be conflated in the language of the report. As Grant reported, during the fierce battles over integration in the late 1960s and the 1970s, Congress did express some interest in the finding that "disadvantaged" children benefited more from associating with "those of a higher level" (i.e., white children) than from "school characteristics" (Grant, 36–37). Unfortunately, intense opposition to mandatory busing in the North led to the *Milliken I* decision, which blocked earlier decisions favorable to integration. *Milliken II* initiated remedial classes as remedy in lieu of desegregation, which smacks of *Plessy's* separate but equal. Ironically, schools in the south were more integrated than those in the north by 1971 (39). Nixon's "Southern strategy," designed to slow desegregation while shifting the blame to the courts, succeeded in delaying integration of Mississippi schools, which were facing a 1969 Justice Department deadline. Ehrlichman, Nixon's assistant on Domestic Affairs, enunciated the administration's opposition to using the schools to enforce "a purely social policy [integration]" (41). Coleman objected vociferously to no avail. All of this contributed to the resegregation that is underway today.

Although Coleman's methods and conclusions have been critiqued since,[27] the Coleman Report was immensely influential, contributing to the general public's belief that additional resources for schools do not make a difference in the achievement of students. This is absurd. Sensible people know that money for education must be spent wisely. However, the benefits of integration were ignored while the politically useful findings that the largely segregated schools were "equal" and that "school characteristics" had little impact on achievement were emphasized. This conclusion was part and parcel of the move from optimism that education could effect social change in the early twentieth century to pessimism in the later twentieth century. At the same time, people's belief that the purpose of education was primarily to benefit the child (even if only by preparing children for the work force) changed to the idea that education benefited the state, the economy, and the military. Conant formulated the purpose of schooling as quelling social unrest by allowing social mobility for intelligent but lower-class students; Rickover, as maintaining military supremacy. Such views may well encourage pessimism that schools will effect social change. However, there are too many factors that affect the political, military, and economic success of the state to automatically blame education for failures. It may be that schools don't function to benefit the child because they are not designed to do so. Instead, schools maintain the social status quo. This effect seems too efficient to be unintentional. But the myth is appealing and covers a less wholesome reality.

Unfortunately, the legacy of the Coleman Report still surfaces in the opinion that more spending will not solve the problems plaguing many of our inner city schools, which contributed to the reversal by the Appellate Division of *CFE* in New York in 2002. The judges' statement that somebody has to do the low-wage jobs in the new service economy implied that it is appropriate for the urban, poor, minority children in New York City to be destined for these jobs. This justified the court's conclusion that the state's constitution requires only an eighth- or ninth-grade education. The judges' assumption that the children and their culture are inferior lies at the root of the decision. While affirming that low-wage service workers can be "valuable, productive citizens," the judges refused to acknowledge DeGrasse's statement that these jobs do not pay a livable wage, claiming his "observation is unsupported by any statistics."[28] Fortunately, this opinion was overturned. But the reality is that black and minority children are still waiting for a solution to inequitable funding in New York.

The Impact of Child Poverty

President Lyndon Johnson introduced the War on Poverty in 1964 with the words, "Because it is right, because it is wise, and because, for the first time in our history, it is possible to conquer poverty, I submit, for the consideration of the Congress and the country, the Economic Opportunity Act of 1964."[29] Johnson's plan created the Office of Economic Opportunity, which directly addressed the problem of educational help for poor children and youth with Head Start, Job Corps, federal work-training and work-study programs, community involvement, and more. During the following two decades, the income gap narrowed,[30] children in the Head Start program showed benefits that persisted throughout school,[31] and more social safety nets were put in place for the very poor, such as food stamps and Aid to Families with Dependent Children (AFDC).[32] Many of these gains are threatened at the turn of the twenty-first century.[33] The so-called welfare reform of 1996 abolished AFDC and substituted Temporary Assistance to Needy Families (TANF), requiring recipients to work at menial jobs but providing neither job training nor adequate child care.[34] In 2003, the Bush administration proposed that the work requirements be increased to forty hours a week, while simultaneously freezing TANF funds at present levels and cutting funds for child care, which would affect 200,000 children by the administration's own estimate. The actual number of children affected was likely to be much higher, because costs rise due to inflation, the states' responsibility to provide jobs and child care increases as work requirements increase, and federal funding was slated for additional decreases in 2004.[35]

The president's plan remained stalled in Congress from 2002 to 2006. In 2003, the House complied with the president's requests, but the Senate passed a more moderate version. Seeking a compromise with the House version, the Senate Finance Committee increased work hours to thirty-four and maintained the current twelve-month limit on vocational education and the 30 percent cap on the number of recipients who can be in vocational education in a state at any given time. Senator Snowe of Maine added an amendment to permit 10 percent of a state's caseload to count post-secondary education as part of the workload. In 2004, Shawn Fremstad, of the Center on Budget and Policy Priorities, found that changes in TANF have not improved the status of TANF families. They are less likely to have jobs when they leave the system than prior TANF recipients, poverty rates are high and remain high, only half of the very poor families with children who are eligible for TANF receive it, and families with disabled members and immigrant families have suffered increased hardships with the changes.[36] The debate over reauthorization continued with no resolution until February 8, 2006, when the president signed the

Deficit Reduction Act of 2005, which finally reauthorized the TANF program. The new measure reinforces the work requirement by recalibrating the base year on which the 50% work requirement is calculated.[37] Voting against the bill in the House in October, 2005, Representative Raul M. Grijalva (Democrat, Arizona) commented, "I am shocked that the majority would pass such a stark and rigid measure. . . . [hurricane] Katrina has unearthed a systematic problem in our country: widespread and unresolved poverty. . . . This bill does little to address the needs of families which struggle under multiple barriers to sustainable employment."[38]

In addition to the effects of welfare "reform," poverty and unemployment have increased,[39] but the federal minimum wage of $5.15 an hour has not been raised since 1997.[40] The growing livable-wage movement reflects widespread concern by progressives about ever-widening economic inequities.[41] Welfare "reform" also cuts welfare rolls and disqualifies women who bear additional children while on welfare without even inquiring into the circumstances (while disallowing abortion). According to the Center for Law and Social Policy, "In 2001, about 20% of TANF funds that were transferred or spent were redirected toward child-care." At the same time, TANF caseloads were rising due to a failing economy. Allowing TANF funds to be transferred into child care will not solve the problems of needy families, many of whom will be excluded, especially when these funds are frozen.[42] Even though tax breaks for the wealthy failed to "trickle down" during the Reagan-Bush era, the second Bush administration follows the same strategy.[43] In addition, cutbacks in Medicaid have been coupled with rapidly rising medical costs.[44] The Economic Policy Institute's Jared Bernstein warned in 2001 that the "slowing economy may revive inequality."[45] This prediction has indeed proved true. In addition, public schools, always inequitably funded, are becoming increasingly resegregated. The government also consistently failed to enforce the Fair Housing Act,[46] despite the *Mt. Laurel* cases.[47] Problems include "redlining" in segregated districts where mortgages were more costly and less available,[48] discrimination in insurance,[49] urban "renewal" that displaces poor urban residents,[50] "steering" clients to same-race neighborhoods,[51] locating freeways in urban neighborhoods, which subsidizes white-flight while destroying inner city neighborhoods, and allowing the development of exclusive housing areas for the wealthy while refusing to locate subsidized, low-income housing in the suburbs. The hypersegregation and economic isolation of poor children in segregated urban schools in New York City, Philadelphia, Detroit, Newark, Hartford, Dallas, Los Angeles, and many other cities is the direct result of such deliberate public policies. The exodus of middle-class blacks from the inner cities further increased the economic and social isolation of those who were left behind.[52]

In 1968, President Johnson, alarmed by urban riots in Detroit, Los Angeles, Newark, and elsewhere, formed the Kerner Commission to investigate their causes. Expecting to find that "outside agitators" were responsible, evidence forced the Commission to conclude instead that discrimination, segregation, and continuing violence from whites were causing "our nation [to move] toward two societies, one black, one white, separate but unequal."[53] Presently we could add "two socioeconomic classes, one able to meet basic needs and the other not." The unfairness of the conditions most blacks encountered in the cities in the 1960s was obvious, highlighted by the civil rights movement, lack of enforcement of *Brown*, and rampant economic exploitation of black workers. The Kerner Report recommended a massive commitment "for specific, great, and sustained federal effort for new jobs, for improved education and training, for adequate housing, for livable income support, and for vigorous civil-rights enforcement."[54] However, support for antipoverty programs, among them Head Start, Job Corps, and Aid to Families with Dependent Children (AFDC), began declining after 1973, when a recession caused cuts in spending. The election of Richard Nixon also contributed substantially to the reversal of antipoverty programs.

In 1998, thirty years after the Kerner Commission, the staff of the Milton S. Eisenhower Foundation documented the failure of the government to sustain that commitment. Their report, *The Millennium Breach*, blames supply-side economics for the failed policies of the last two decades. Taxes for the poor increased while taxes for the rich decreased; the income gap widened; child poverty rose; deregulation resulted in corruption, as illustrated by the Savings and Loan bailout and other corporate scandals; enterprise zones failed to benefit the residents of designated inner city areas; prison building substituted for constructing affordable housing for the poor; and the incarceration rate rose. Jobs for low-skilled workers disappeared south of the border while poor and minority children were not prepared for skilled jobs by inequitably funded, increasingly segregated schools. Private charities and volunteerism were touted as better solutions to the problems of the poor than government spending, and welfare programs devolved onto the states, which are generally less able to fund them, especially in economic hard times when their own income is depleted but need for the programs increases. During the first years of the twenty-first century, states faced massive deficits, which will likely cause cuts in social services and education.

The Millennium Breach recommends a ten-point program, complete with illustrations of effective programs to replicate and plans to fund them. The plan includes 1) fully funding Head Start; 2) investing in developing safe havens for youth through adolescence; 3) reforming public schools (they suggest the Comer Plan); adding after-school programs; 4) creating a national nonprofit corporation to target urban federal job training to the truly disadvantaged and merging this with job creation and placement; 5) replacing the failed, supply-side Jobs Training Partnership Act (JTPA) with life-skills training to improve job retention (following the model developed by the Argus Learning for Living Community program); implementing "training-first" not "work-first" policies that prepare clients for jobs with a future; 6) creating a National Community Development Bank to support local economic development projects (the model is the South Shore Bank in Chicago); 7) investing in jobs in the public sector for graduates of the jobs program; 8) replicating effective desegregation programs in housing and schools, enhancing racial understanding, retaining affirmative action; 9) reversing the priorities in the War on Drugs from enforcement (then at 70 percent) to treatment (then at 30 percent) so that treatment becomes the focus; and 10) recognizing that federal funds are necessary to tackle these problems, but acknowledging the role played by local projects and matching funds, targeting the truly disadvantaged, and implementing programs locally, using tested strategies that work.[55]

Funding suggestions for programs that work include redirecting money from programs known to be ineffective (such as the JTPA, the DARE antidrug program, and prison building) into programs that work; reducing corporate "welfare" in the form of subsidies and tax breaks; closing tax loopholes and implementing progressive taxation; abandoning supply-side economics; redirecting money from defense spending to domestic spending; and focusing on preventive strategies (Head Start, health insurance) rather than more costly remedial measures after harm has been done (incarceration, emergency room medicine instead of regular doctor's visits, special education).[56]

Unfortunately, it is extremely unlikely that the political climate of Johnson's War on Poverty will return in the near future. The reasons are many. The poor, who are the most powerless, are often the first targets for budget cuts. In addition, the three conservative presidents, Nixon, Reagan, and George H. W. Bush, who followed Johnson, appointed Supreme Court justices whose outlook on social policy is much more conservative than that of the Warren Court. In 2000, the Eisenhower Foundation issued another report, *Locked in the Poorhouse: Cities, Race, and Poverty in the United States*, reiterating problems and solutions of *The Millennium Breach*. These problems are fairly universally acknowledged: declines in federal spending; more poor people; poverty more concentrated in the inner cities; a higher percentage of young children living in poverty; an increasing income gap; the decline of jobs in the inner city coupled with lack of transportation to the suburbs; an inadequate minimum wage; lack of child care; lack of medical insurance coupled with rising costs; more violence in ghetto neighborhoods; the failure of drug interdiction coupled with lack of treatment; gross disparities in arrest, sentencing, and incarceration rates for blacks and whites; the abandonment of *Brown*; plus, a general "poor bashing," which blames individuals for their poverty, a convenient strategy for avoiding formulating good social programs to remediate it. The writers of *Locked in the Poorhouse* also review positive progress made, such a affirmative action, which ". . . does not guarantee success, only an opportunity to compete."[57] However, overall these writers favor replicating models, often of private, nonprofit organizations, as recommended in *The Millennium Breach*. Some of these models are based on the classical liberal ideal of teaching individual responsibility so that clients can gain a position in the business world as it is currently organized. This approach fails to address the question of the changing economy in which downsizing, outsourcing, a low minimum wage, and no fringe benefits are treated as an economic necessity for corporations to remain viable. The hidden underside of the vaunted productivity of American workers is the rising unemployment that accompanies it. Fewer people are doing more work, which means there are more people without the means to support their families. In Europe, workers routinely get maternity leave, vacations, state-sponsored day care and medical care, decent pay, and even shorter workweeks to spread the work around. This is not true in the United States.

One reviewer of *Locked in the Poorhouse*, commented that although

> [a]nalysts with a liberal orientation will find it difficult to argue with much of the content of the book . . . one cannot help but get the impression that the authors are caught in a time warp. The type of massive redistribution proposed is simply not politically feasible now or in the foreseeable future given the growing similarity between the public policy orientation of Democrats and Republicans, and the absence of a social movement of the type existing in the '60s.[58]

The reviewer suggests that more emphasis needs to be given to the complexities of globalization, which is certainly true. Pauline Lipman has examined the connection of globalization to education reform under the second Bush administration. She notes, "the business rhetoric of efficiency and performance standards and the redefinition of education to serve the labor market has become the common vocabulary of educational policies across the U.S."[59] Canadian critics of Ontario's reform offer the same critique. The idea that the purpose of education is to benefit business is not new. Horace Mann recommended schooling for economic improvement of the lot of the poor, the vocational guidance movement focused on preparing children for work, and *A Nation at Risk* blamed education for economic stalemate. Nevertheless, the move to evaluate schooling on the business model has intensified with pressure to privatize through vouchers and charters, rigid standards, and increased testing. *The Millennium Breach* echoes this business rhetoric, although with a liberal slant. However, the business model is not the right model for education. In education, the bottom line does not determine success: the child is not a product, but a participant in a process of individual and social growth and development, and investments in education do not necessarily have a quantifiable return that is analogous to profits in business. For instance, much of the additional spending on education is going to special education, which is not designed to raise a school's test scores, although it certainly improves the quality of life of its recipients.[60]

Erosion of the gains made through Johnson's antipoverty programs is also documented by Collins, Hartman, and Sklar in "Divided Decade: Economic Disparity at the Century's Turn."[61] Workers are paid less in real dollars while corporate income soars to new highs, in spite of corporate officers' incompetent and often illegal behavior. Clinton's welfare reform proposals were never adopted, but replaced by the 1996 Personal Responsibility and Work Opportunity Reconciliation Act (PRWORA),[62] signed reluctantly by Clinton but more closely related to the poverty agenda of Gingrich's conservative Contract With America than Clinton's ideas, according to Sandefur, Martin, and Wells.[63] Evidence of this contention includes the change in antipoverty attitudes, which view only the elderly and disabled as in need of financial assistance, not able-bodied adults, who are required to work in return for temporary benefits under TANF, despite their lack of skills, the presence of young children in the home, and the lack of child care.[64]

In 1996, the Annual Report of Council of Economic Advisers under President Clinton changed Conant's formulation of the purpose of schooling from national security to the economic advancement of the nation. However, federal funding for education, always minimal, has been declining. Although Clinton acknowledged that the poor had been largely excluded from the prosperity of his early years in office, median family income rose and the poverty rate declined slightly in 1994.[65] Clinton's promise to initiate universal health care never came to fruition and has been submerged under the second Bush administration, which has made repeated requests for billions for the war in Iraq, while children living at the level of near poverty lack medical care.

Escalating medical costs are proving disastrous to the poor, who are increasingly forced to turn to emergency room care in lieu of any alternative. Under George W. Bush's first term, medical expenses continued to soar as funds for social programs were cut and family income fell.[66] The lack of single-payer prescription drug plans for the elderly prevents the federal government from having any leverage to bring down the cost of drugs.

The federal determination of the poverty level is out of touch with reality. Researchers at the Economic Policy Institute found that families at 200 percent of the official poverty line faced the same incidence of serious hardships as those with incomes at or below the poverty line.[67] New York, which has the widest gap between rich and poor,[68] also has severely racially segregated schools, including the highest suburban segregation (on Long Island),[69] and stands among the worst states for disparities in school spending.[70] These factors are not coincidental; they are connected.

Rebecca M. Blank analyzed the causes of persistent poverty and suggested policies to alleviate it in her 1997 book, *It Takes a Nation: A New Agenda for Fighting Poverty*. She disputed both the effectiveness and the humanity of the welfare "reforms" that took place under President Clinton. These reforms were exacerbated under Bush with rising work requirements and less access to child care. In Blank's opinion, the cash assistance offered by Aid to Families with Dependent Children (AFDC) was essential both for short-term needs and people who are unemployable due to disabilities. She attacked a number of "myths" about poverty, including that AFDC made women dependent on welfare, that "welfare moms" are unmarried, and that welfare encourages women to have additional children. Blank reported, "less than 20% of the poor live in families with never-married mothers."[71] It is not welfare recipients who commit welfare fraud, but fraudulent vendors who submit false documentation for medical procedures that were not performed or who traffic in food stamps. Few women are "continuously on welfare for long periods of time" (Blank, 13) despite the disincentives to work built into AFDC. Other myths Blank attacked are that poor families have no members who work; that the majority of poor are Latino or African-American; that the poor have large families, live in ghettos, and are essentially unlike the majority of Americans. In her estimation, Americans are all too ready to blame the poor for "behavioral" problems that result in their poverty, rather than understanding that deliberate public policies keep people poor (14). Fewer jobs for less-skilled workers, accompanied by a steady decline in their real wages, were largely responsible (52–53).[72] Globalization contributes by moving low-skilled work to other countries while technological changes decrease the need for low-skilled workers. These trends continue into the twenty-first century.

Contrary to the prevailing opinion that antipoverty programs did not work, Blank showed that well-designed antipoverty programs did work. The increasing prosperity of the 1960s benefited rich and poor alike. However, the prosperity of the 1990s and early years of the twentieth-first century left the poor out. The impact of George W. Bush's tax cuts will be felt for decades. Although it may seem fair to cut everyone's taxes by the same percentage, more money is refunded to the wealthy, while the poor receive little. Removing taxes on dividends benefits only people who own dividend-paying stocks. In the meantime, everyone's social security is taxed and everyone pays into social security. Public policies like these increase the income gap. Contrary to the Bush agenda, Blank recommended more federal involvement, rather than less, believing that the federal government is the proper vehicle for funding programs that apply to the population in general (228). The increase in antipoverty spending in the 1990s was due to the drastic increase in the cost of medical care, which Blank characterized as "out of control" (271–273). These increasing costs do not indicate a failed antipoverty program. Many federal antipoverty programs work, such as Social Security,[73] food stamps, and Medicaid. Blank proposes adding a child-support assurance program, by which the government would make up child-support payments that are not received by the care-giving parent, partly funded by attaching the wages of absent parents (269–270). Blank recommends increasing food stamps, a program that directly benefits children (253). She would revise AFDC to distinguish between families needing temporary assistance and those needing long-term assistance, and provide job training and placement for the former. Blank commended Head Start's model of federally funded but locally administered programs (231). Programs administered locally, although funded federally, are well run, in general. Small, targeted programs that address local issues can indeed be both funded and administered locally. The New Federalism,[74] in giving block grants to the states, moved the focus of the social safety net from general assistance to targeted assistance, which is usually implemented on a small scale and addresses very specific needs. According to Blank, the federal government is best suited to carry out large programs like food stamps or earned income tax credits, while the state may be the appropriate vehicle for smaller, targeted programs. Although there is certainly a role for private charities, Blank does not believe that they could replace governmental assistance.

Blank formulated five criteria for assessing the effectiveness of antipoverty programs: 1) the management criterion; 2) the sophistication criterion; 3) the linkage criterion; 4) the federalism criterion; and 5) the coordination criterion (239–249). In other words, Blank explains that programs should be well managed, should recognize and deal with a wide range of problems, should draw on the private and nonprofit sectors, should be designed to use the powers of the level of government that is best for that program, and should complement other programs and efforts that might be operating in the same neighborhood. She also understands the need for poverty programs to acknowledge the strong American insistence on the value of work; to provide incentives for responsible behavior within families and among individuals, particularly encouraging parents to support their children and young people to stay in school; and to be politically and administratively possible (252).

Although Blank offers no solutions for the problem of rising medical costs, she points out that they are largely responsible for the increase in government expenditure on "welfare." A single-payer health-care system would go far to manage rising medical costs, which are partly fueled by rising malpractice insurance rates. These are solvable problems. Neither does Blank mention equitably funded schools, but I am sure she would agree that this would help address poverty, which has a particularly severe impact on young children. Equitable funding for schools among the states would be best administered by the federal government, except for the unfortunate circumstance of the Supreme Court's refusal in *Rodriguez*. As it stands, funding can only be made equitable within states, and then, not all states have summoned the political will to do so. Blank emphasizes the role of education in helping teens develop job skills and obtain appropriate educational credentials (279–284). Surely funding schools equitably would help address the shockingly high dropout rate in poor, urban areas.[75] As Blank points out, "Money matters." However, effective programs may cost no more than ineffective programs. She estimates that her proposals will not cost substantially more than governments and agencies currently spend, and decries the "wishful thinking economics" of "those who support deep federal funding cuts . . . [and] seem to believe that the problem of poverty will go away if the United States just stops spending money on the poor" (268).

Blank's solutions cover many aspects of the complex problem of poverty, from behavioral causes, like the disincentive to work when workers lose benefits, to causes endemic to the system, like a minimum wage that is not livable. Her view is optimistic; she thinks many of the problems are solvable. Blank holds that a key strategy is raising the skill level of young adults. As she says, "If we can help only one group [in the present climate of retrenchment], surely our major focus must be on preventative programs aimed at teens and young adults" (279). Although the word "preventative" implies that people must be stopped from doing wrong things, rather than that misguided public policies should be changed, nevertheless, Blank recognizes the role public policy plays in maintaining or ameliorating poverty.

A 2001 report from the Economic Policy Institute (EPI), *Hardships in America: The Real Story of Working Families*, presents research showing that the methodology used to determine who is poor is seriously outdated. The federal government calculates the poverty line by multiplying the cost of the U.S. Department of Agriculture's "Thrifty Food Plan" for a given family size by three, based on research done in the late 1950s and early 1960s showing that poor families spent three times their food budget on overall expenses.[76] Although the rise in food costs is accounted for in the calculation, the proportion of other costs to food has changed drastically, especially medical care. Since poor working families are often not covered by health-care insurance, they either do without, pay exorbitant costs, or use the emergency room as their primary caregiver. Another cost that varies widely is housing, as does transportation, a problem for inner-city residents who could only find jobs in the suburbs as businesses moved out of the inner cities. Economists at the Economic Policy Institute researching *Hardships in America* devised more than 400 budgets based on realistic local costs for seven different types of families, rather than the single standard of the federal poverty guidelines. Using these measures, they found that "29 percent of families with one to two adults and two to three children under twelve . . . fall below basic family budget levels" (*Hardships*, 3). The basic budget levels were equal to approximately 200 percent of the poverty line as defined by the federal government, although in places where the cost of living is high, this can be as high as 300 percent. Because of these conditions, the unofficial poverty rate is even higher than the official poverty rate.

For children under six, the rate is yet higher. According to Columbia University's National Center for Children in Poverty (NCCP), "the number of poor children living in poverty grew from 3.4 million in 1972 to 6 million in 1992."[77] In the late 1990s, figures from the NCCP shows that almost one in four children in the United States (24.7 percent) lives in poverty, close to the 29 percent figure from the Economic Policy Institute at 200 percent of the poverty level.[78] With the addition of figures for "near poverty" (185 percent of the poverty line at the NCCP Web site), NCCP reports "10.3 million or 43% of young children [under six] are growing up in families living in poverty or near poverty."[79] In addition, a majority of these children live in families with one parent employed. The center's director, Jamie Hickner, deplored this situation:

> Young children have the highest poverty rate of any age group. There has been ample research that shows that poverty hurts young children the most. Poverty on children is devastating; it has an enormous impact on their psychological and physiological development. Childhood poverty has been very strongly correlated to high infant mortality, to the likelihood of experiencing violence during childhood and suffering from domestic violence, and to difficulties obtaining full-time employment. It is very depressing to think that this is well known and well documented, yet the problem still persists.[80]

The NCCP agrees with many of Blank's recommendations, listing strategies for mitigating poverty, including employment, earned income tax credits, financial work incentive programs, minimum wage standards, unemployment insurance, child-care subsidies, housing assistance, public health insurance, and food stamps.[81]

Since the poverty line is set too low,[82] many needy families are excluded from benefits like food stamps and Medicaid. Researchers for the Economic Policy Institute (EPI) report in *Hardships in America* that 87 percent of families living below the basic budgets correlates fairly well with a threshold 200 percent of the present poverty line (21–29). After figuring basic family budgets, researchers at EPI organized the conditions these families face into four broad categories: food, housing, health care, and child care (20). Within each category, they distinguished two levels of hardships—critical hardships and serious hardships. For critical hardships, the team focused on questions from two national surveys of families that revealed material deprivation; for serious hardships, they focused on hardships that revealed financial difficulties (20). For instance, food deprivation is a critical hardship, while food insecurity is a serious hardship (Table 6, 22–23). Data revealed that families at 200 percent of poverty experienced roughly the same number of hardships as families at the "official" poverty level. In other words, families at 200 percent of the poverty level were scarcely better off than those below them. The researchers concluded

> Hardships, both critical and serious, are more common among families living below 200% of the poverty threshold than among those above. We find that 29% of families below the poverty threshold and 25% of families between 100% and 200% of poverty experience critical hardships. The similarity of results for poor and near-poor families substantiates the family budget analysis. The family budgets reveal that the poverty threshold provides insufficient income for families to meet basic needs, since most budgets were approximately 200% of poverty. This is also the case for serious hardships. Families living above poverty but still below the average family budget level are unable to avoid hardships to the same extent as non-poor families. (29)

In addition, the report reveals that poverty is not limited to certain geographical regions or types of locations. Although one-third of families at or near poverty are urban, one-third are rural. On the other hand, only one-fifth are suburban. Disproportionately more African-American, Hispanic, and "other" families found it harder to meet expenses than white families, although white families represent the bulk of the poor and the near poor in absolute numbers. Young families are more vulnerable also; close to half of families headed by someone age thirty or younger fall below family basic budgets (13). This finding corroborates the NCCP's estimates of the large numbers of young children living in poverty. As the director of the NCCP commented in 1995, "Poor young children are not very visible to the rest of us. They live in isolated neighborhoods and are rarely noticed until they reach first grade and fail, become adolescents and get into trouble, or reach adulthood and can't find a job."[83] Since 1995 the situation has only worsened. According to the Bureau of Maternal and Child Health,

> In 2000, there were 11 million related children under 18 years of age living in families with income below the Federal poverty threshold (e.g., $17,603 for a family of four). Children living below the poverty level comprised 15.6 percent of all related children living in families. While 2000 brought the lowest childhood poverty rate since 1978, childhood poverty continues to exceed that of adults by 71 percent and the elderly by 58 percent. Poverty affects living conditions and access to health care and nutrition, all of which contribute to health status. Very young children and black and Hispanic children were particularly vulnerable. Related children under age 6 had a poverty rate of nearly 17 percent. A much higher proportion of black (30.4 percent) and Hispanic (27.3 percent) related children under age 18 were poor compared to related white children (12.3 percent).[84]

Steady rises in the poverty rate in the early twenty-first century are documented by the U.S. Census Bureau. While "real median household income remained unchanged between 2002 and 2003 at $43,318. . . . the nation's official poverty rate rose from 12.1 percent in 2002 to 12.5 percent in 2003." In addition, "the number of people without [health] coverage rose by 1.4 million to 45.0 million." The poverty rate for children increased disproportionately, from 16.7 percent in 2002 to 17.6 percent in 2003.[85]

The analysis in *Hardships in America* reveals the need for at least doubling the present poverty threshold. Resistance based on the widespread impulse to blame individuals for their state of impoverishment, is reflected in the title of the welfare reform act, the Personal Responsibility and Work Opportunity Reconciliation Act of 1996. Stemming from early political theory found in the Jeffersonian ideal of "rugged individualism" and the *Federalist Papers*, this belief was reinforced by the Coleman Report. Unfortunately, this impulse is misguided; poor people are often either trapped by a system that perpetuates their status or temporarily out of luck because of factors beyond their control, such as the illness or death of a family breadwinner or the loss of a job.

Lead Poisoning and Other Toxins

In addition to suffering from the impact of poverty in matters like nutrition and medical care, many poor children suffer from lead poisoning that reduces their IQ;[86] increases antisocial behavior, aggression,[87] and school failure; and is even correlated to tooth decay, retarded growth,[88] and delays in the development of puberty in girls.[89] Lead poisoning is directly connected to poverty, because many poor children live in deteriorating housing that contains lead hazards. The damage from lead is exacerbated by poor nutrition, from which many of these children also suffer.[90]

Lead poisoning is particularly pernicious because it harms young children's cognitive development permanently, which blocks the possibility for them to acquire the higher skills necessary for increased employment opportunities. According to the American Academy of Pediatricians, studies show that lead lowers IQ scores significantly even at fairly low concentrations.[91] At 20 micrograms per deciliter, severe effects are reported. More recently, additional research has shown lead causes deficits in attention/vigilance, aggression, somatic complaints, antisocial or delinquent behaviors, reduction in auditory threshold, abnormal postural balance, poor eye-hand coordination, longer reaction times, dental decay, and sleep disturbances.[92] Furthermore, evidence shows that lowering blood lead levels does not mitigate the impact of lead poisoning on cognition.[93] Lead is more easily removed from blood and soft tissue, but accumulates in bone, from which it leaches into the body slowly over many years, rendering the impact of chelation therapy temporary.[94] Paint companies agreed to a voluntary reduction of lead content in interior paint in 1955, but there is abundant evidence that they did not follow this.[95] Although lead paint for interior use has been banned since 1978, buildings built before then are likely to have lead paint hazards, especially if they are not properly maintained. Lead paint for exteriors is still legal. Lead could be safely removed from housing or encapsulated, if landlords were required to meet existing codes. The damaging effects of lead poisoning are concentrated in areas with higher lead exposure, very likely contributing to higher crime levels and lower achievement scores.[96]

With blood lead levels high among poor, inner-city children, it is reasonable to assume that lead poisoning contributes to higher crime levels. According to the Sentencing Project, the United States has the highest incarceration rate in the world, with the prison population increasing sixfold since 1970. Blacks and Hispanics are grotesquely disproportionately represented. Sixty-eight percent of the prison population consists of high school dropouts, 38 percent of whom were unemployed at the time of arrest, and 64 percent of whom had incomes less than $1,000 a month at the time of arrest.[97] In states where the law deprives felons of the vote, like New York, these facts represent a "disproportionate disenfranchisement of Black and Latino persons," which was the subject of *Hayden* v. *Pataki*, Civil Action No. 008586, dismissed in Federal District Court in 2004.[98] In this case, plaintiffs accused the State of New York of depriving their communities of potentially productive, participating citizens through felon disenfranchisement laws and restrictions on felons that remain in place after prisoners have completed their parole. According to the Community Service Society, "Approximately 80% of the New York State's prison population consists of Blacks and Latinos from the following New York City communities: East Harlem, Washington Heights, the Lower East Side, Hunts Point, Morrisania, Soundview, Central Brooklyn, East New York, Jamaica, and St. Albans."[99] This amounts to a tiny fraction of the state's regions. Drug laws and other public policies, including practices like racial profiling, lead to the incarceration of a disproportionately large number of black men. These figures are related to the increasing numbers of poor and near-poor who lack the basic necessities of food, safe housing, jobs at a livable wage, and sufficient health and child care in their communities. In consequence of felon disenfranchisement laws, these communities also lack a voice in government. Some of the laws are absurdly targeted at reducing ex-felons' opportunities for rehabilitation by denying them welfare benefits, not allowing them to occupy or even visit public housing, denying them financial aid for college, and denying them licenses to pursue careers in plumbing, barbering, or real estate.[100] Regulations like these are not productive of functional communities. When placed in the context of lead poisoning, such statistics are obscene.

According to the American Academy of Pediatricians,

> The percentage of US children 1 to 5 years of age with blood lead levels higher than 10 micrograms per deciliter has decreased from 88.2% to 4.4% [since the removal of lead from gasoline, food cans, and paint in 1978.] Of children 1 to 2 years of age, however, 5.9% had blood lead levels higher than 10 micrograms per deciliter, with the highest rates among African-American, low-income, or urban children. This means that an estimated 890,000 children in the United States have elevated blood lead levels higher than 10 micrograms per deciliter.[101]

In Chicago, "which has the highest number of children identified as lead-poisoned in any U.S. city," according to an article in the October 28, 2002 *Chicago Daily Law Bulletin*, 40 percent of the children tested (which was not all children) had toxic levels of lead in their blood.[102] Other cities report similarly high levels.[103] In 1991, U.S. Department of Health and Human Services lowered the level considered dangerous from 25 to 10 micrograms per deciliter.[104] This did not happen without opposition from the lead industry, which tried for three years to discredit the pioneering work of Dr. Herbert Needleman, whose research in Boston in the 1970s uncovered the connection between high lead levels in the baby teeth of children and lower IQ scores, poorer language function, and shorter attention spans.[105] Even in 1991, when *Essence Magazine* reported a staggering 55 percent of African-American children suffering from lead poisoning,[106] elements in the government fought lowering the standard.[107] There is increasing evidence that even lower levels do damage.[108] The American Academy of Pediatricians states that, "No threshold for the toxic effects of lead has been identified."[109] In addition, maternal lead exposure is now recognized to affect an unborn fetus. As reported in *Pediatrics* (July 2002), after accounting for all other factors known to affect the mental development of infants, lead levels in umbilical blood and the mother's trabecular bone were found to be inversely related to the Mental Development Index scores of the Bayley Scale.[110] Thus lead poisoning is passed from generation to generation.

Nor is lead poisoning limited to urban areas. Researchers found that significant numbers of two-year-old children in Vermont, a largely rural state, had toxic levels of lead in their blood. Children on Medicaid were more at risk than others.[111] In addition, children who live in communities contaminated with lead by industry are at high risk. The Doe Run lead smelting plant in Herculaneum, Missouri, contaminated the environment for years without warning residents of the danger to them and their children. Many were low-paid workers in the plant. Some children tested had blood lead levels as high as 44 micrograms per deciliter, more than four times the permissible level.[112] In Galena, Kansas, where lead mining has been going on for decades, the streams run clear—not a single living thing is in the water, no plants, no animals, no fish, no snails, no algae. Lead levels are too high for the streams to support life.[113] In Chelsea, Massachusetts, Dr. Matthew P. Dumont, a psychiatrist treating young children from poor families for behavioral disorders at a clinic, realized that they were not psychiatric cases, but were being poisoned by lead paint coming from the Mystic-Tobin bridge, which had been shedding lead chips and dust onto the houses and yards of poor people living under the bridge for decades. When he fought to have the bridge repaired, the government blasted the old lead paint off the bridge before repainting it, showering the neighborhood with yet more concentrated lead dust. Even so, they could not blast the area underneath the bridge, and so repainted that with lead paint. Dumont reported his utter frustration in getting the authorities to address a serious problem of their causing in a responsible way.[114]

Although federally assisted housing must meet a code established by the Department of Housing and Urban Development (HUD), enforcement is lax and cleanup expensive. According to a General Accounting Office report, HUD rules don't protect children from lead hazards. Housing receiving rental assistance must be inspected, but the visual inspections "did not effectively identify lead-based paint hazards."[115] Weinberg and Woltjen recommend removing hazards; coordinating the work of building inspectors and public health workers; sharing the resources of various agencies to address remedies; removing old windows, since they are the most likely source of contamination because of lead dust produced by raising and lowering them; educating contractors, parents, and landowners; and creating a register of safe housing so that prospective renters could be assured that lead contamination is not a risk. Despite its high cost, lead removal is better than trying to remediate the problems lead causes. Special education, school violence, incarceration for crime, and the human waste of permanent damage to children's cognitive abilities are more expensive in the long run.[116] The city of Rochester, New York, received a grant in 2003 for $2 million to fight lead poisoning. This grant "will help diminish the danger of lead poisoning in 420 houses and apartments."[117] Even noting that part of the money will go to educational endeavors, the cost for cleanup per unit is high. Furthermore, a study by Dr. Katrina Korfmacher comparing lead dust levels in treated and nontreated apartments showed that about one-third of the units "had similar lead dust levels" after lead hazard reduction treatments were done. In January 2006, Rochester's City Council passed a new law aimed at reducing the incidence of lead poisoning among the city's poorest children. The law, one of the stiffest in major cities, allows the city to inspect housing stock built before 1978 for lead hazards and requires landlords to make properties safe.[118] Korfmacher's study also revealed that "most post-treatment EBL units still remained well above EPA standards for lead in dust."[119] Some cities and states have brought suits against companies that produced lead paint in an attempt to recover the costs of cleanup. Milwaukee was among the first, suing in 1989. However, according to the Gannet News Service, companies succeeded in defeating more than forty lead-poisoning suits since 1989. A mistrial was declared in Rhode Island in October 2002, when a six-person jury could not agree.[120] In the second trial, *Rhode Island* v. *Lead Industries Association, Inc.*, the paint companies sought to have the judge, Michael Silverstein of Rhode Island Superior Court, recuse himself on the grounds that he owned a home built prior to 1978, but he refused. The second trial resulted in a decision for plaintiffs on February 22, 2006, in which Silverstein found the industry liable for clean-up damages but not punitive damages.[121] Unfortunately, lead-poisoning prevention programs are less visible than lead poisoning detection programs.

When children are diagnosed with lead poisoning, lead hazards are revealed. Children serve as "canaries in the coal mine," for other toxins, too, according to Dr. Sandra Steingraber, interviewed by Bill Moyers on PBS's news and issues program, *Now.* Most household chemicals have not been tested for their toxic effects on children.[122] According to Dr. Philip Landigan, also interviewed by Moyers, prior to 1996, when the Food Quality Protection Act was passed requiring stricter controls for the health effects of chemicals on children, regulations were based on the effects of chemicals on healthy young adults.[123] Children are much more vulnerable; they eat more per pound of body weight, they ingest poisons through normal hand-to-mouth activities, and they live closer to the ground. Although the use of household chemicals with unknown effects has exploded in the last quarter of the twentieth century, lead has been a known hazard for the entire century.[124] Unfortunately, the power of the lead industry effectively prevented regulation and fought liability for many years, although the outcome of the Rhode Island case may change that.

Caught up in federal politics, an advocate for stricter controls on lead poisoning, Dr. Bruce Lanphear, nominated by Clinton for a position on the health and human services committee that oversees lead poisoning in 2000, received notification in 2002 that his nomination was rejected by George W. Bush's administration. Dr. Lanphear, along with others who were rejected, has recommended that the lead level of 10 micrograms per deciliter be lowered. "Unless we lower it, we're not going to take action because there's no perceived threat to society," said Dr. Lanphear. "All the evidence coming out indicates that there's no discernible threshold [for a safe level of lead]; the effects below 10 are not subtle."[125] The committee was stacked with known pro-industry members instead.

Although prevention programs are rare, they are not unknown. Community-based solutions are more likely to work, as has been shown in a prevention program in North Philadelphia.[126] Some actions are relatively inexpensive, like washing hands, removing shoes or wiping feet when entering the house, house cleaning thoroughly to reduce lead dust, and proper nutrition. Unfortunately, these simple remedies are often out of reach of needy families, or unknown. Others are more costly, but federal grants are available for cleanup, education, and prevention campaigns. Even screening to find out where to target prevention efforts is costly. But the fact remains that lead poisoning is doing grave damage to many children, wasting their potential. This is entirely preventable, if only the society would make it a priority.

Other Health Hazards for Children of Color and Children Living in Poverty

There are so many health hazards for poor children and children of color, and so little treatment and prevention, that ex-public health nurse turned lawyer, Vernelia R. Randall, of the University of Dayton's Center for Education Law, labeled the health-care system (or nonsystem) "racist," calling for reparations for slavery to be dedicated to improving health care for minorities.[127] Centers for Disease Control listed health hazards for children in its 2000/2001 *Fact Book*, published in September 2000.[128] Many items affecting child health, where data disaggregated by race is available, are summarized in Table 5.1. Statistics where data is disaggregated by socioeconomic status are summarized in Table 5.2. Because the tables are collated from various sources, some figures might differ, depending on the

Table 5.1
Conditions Affecting Child Health By Race

Condition Affecting Child Health	Black	Hispanic	White
Children living in poverty by race	36.4%	33.6%	10% (larger number of actual children, however)
Child mortality rates ages 1–4	29.4 deaths per 100,000		18.2 deaths per 100,000
Infant mortality	13.6 per 1,000	5.8 per 1,000	6 per 1,000 (higher rate due to more multiple births)
Low birth-weight and very low birth-weight births	13.2%	6.4%	6.6% (higher rate reflects higher incidence of multiple births among white women)
No health insurance coverage	48.2%	47.3%	26.6%
Families living under the official poverty level (figures from U.S. Census 2001)	22.7%	21.4%	7.8%
National maternal death rate (1991–1997 CDC figures)	29.6 per 100,000 births	10.3 per 100,000 births	7.3 per 100,000 births
High school dropout rates (NCES figures, 1998)	12%	13%	3%
Teen pregnancy rate (decreasing) (1998 figures)	88.2 births per 1,000	93.6 births per 1,000	35.2 births per 1,000
New York City maternal death rate (Albert Einstein Medical Center study, 1994–1998)	29.6 per 100,000 births	14.4 per 100,000 births	7.1 per 100,000 births

Sources: Items 1–6, CDC Fact Book 2000/2001, http://www/cdc.gov/maso/factbook/ main.htm (accessed 1/15/03) 5–21; item 7, Leslie Casimir, "Maternal death rate for blacks troubles U.S.," *Seattle Times,* June 9, 2001, http://seattletimes.newsource.com (accessed 1/16/03); see also "Maternal Morality—United States 1982–1996," CDC, *MMWR Weekly,* 47(34) (September 4, 1998): 705–7, http://www.cdc.gov/epo/mmwr/preview/mmwrhtml/ 00054602.htm (accessed 1/13/03); items 8, NCES figures reported in CDC Fact Book, 2000/2001; item 9, CDC Fact Book, 2000–2001; item 10, Casimir, Maternal death rate.

Table 5.2
Conditions Affecting Child Health By Socioeconomic Status

Condition Affecting Child Health	Overall	Below the poverty level	Above the poverty level
High school dropout rate (closely connected to health)	4.8%	12.7% (low income)	3.8% (middle income) 2.7% (high income)
Children under 18 without health care coverage	14%	25% of children in families at 1–1.5% of the poverty level	6% of children at double the poverty level
Recent emergency room visits		Children under the poverty level were 50% more likely to have had a recent emergency-room visit	
Elevated blood lead levels (BLL)	4.4%	Can be as high as 40% in poor, urban populations or in contaminated areas	
Asthma (increasing)	62.0 per 1,000 (1996)	Disproportionately affects poor, urban children	
Obesity (increasing)		Disproportionately affects black girls	
Immunization rates (increasing)	CDC's program "Vaccines for Children" makes vaccines available for low-income and uninsured children	20% of two years olds, many of them poor, are lacking immunizations.	
Children living in poverty	16.3% of children under 18 (as compared to 11.7% people in poverty overall) (2001 figures)		

Sources: Item 1, National Center for Educational Statistics, Quick Tables, http://nces.ed. gov/quicktables/Detail.asp?Key=267 (accessed 1/20/03); items 2–6. CDC Fact Book 2000–2001; item 7, CDC Fact Book 2000–2001 and CDC Programs in Brief, "Vaccines for Children," http://www.cdc.gov/programs/immun9.ht (accessed 1/21/03); item 8, Holy Sklar, "Poverty up, income down, except for the top five percent" (Knight Ridder/Tribune News Service, Septembet 30, 2002) http://dsausa.org/lowage/lowwage.html (accessed 10/17/02).

might differ, depending on the source and format in which the figures are given. Nevertheless, they suffice to show in visual form the disadvantage of being a child of color or a child who lives in poverty in the United States. Other aspects of the health of children of color and children living in poverty, too many to report in detail, reflect the same pattern. In every case (with the exception of low birth weight, which is skewed by more multiple births to white women), the rate of incidence of hazards and health problems for black and Hispanic children is higher.

When statistics are disaggregated by socioeconomic status, the hazards for poor children are higher. This leads to persistence in health problems in a country that boasts of the excellence of its health care. For instance, the national maternal death rate in the United States has remained unchanged since 1982, despite a stated goal to lower it. In addition, African-American and Hispanic women are more likely to die in childbirth.[129] Although childhood lead poisoning declined dramatically after leaded gasoline, lead in tin cans, and leaded interior paint were banned in the 1970s, recently levels have declined only minimally, and remain high for poor children living in deteriorating housing or in mining towns,[130] despite a goal to eliminate childhood lead poisoning by 2010.[131] Unfortunately for the rural children affected, mining wastes are exempt from regulation under the Resource Conservation and Recovery Act.[132]

According to the Centers for Disease Control (CDC), less access to health care in general and prenatal care in particular causes discrepancies in health outcomes for people of color and minorities. The failure to enact universal health care illustrates the power of entrenched interests in the aptly named "health care industry." The United States is unusual among developed countries in lacking universal, single-payer health care; most of them have it. According to the World Health Organization, the global maternal death rate in the category of "more developed regions" (1995 figures) is 21 deaths per 100,000 births, although in northern and southern Europe, it is 12 deaths per 100,000 births.[133] However, the child mortality for African-Americans in the United States is 29.4 deaths per 100,000 births. In New York City, the rate of morbidity for both infant and mothers is the highest for Caribbean women, who are both black and immigrants.[134] In addition, poor nutrition contributes to ill health, especially in children. Blood lead levels are higher in children suffering from iron deficiency, for instance.[135] Asthma is another major problem which is on the increase, causing school absences, hospital visits, and death. It is known to be triggered by cockroach droppings, the presence of toxic chemicals, and air pollution, all of which exist in abundance in poor areas of cities.[136] According to the CDC, "Low-income populations, minorities, and children living in inner cities experience disproportionately higher morbidity and mortality due to asthma."[137] These figures lend support to Randall's contention that health care, or rather, the lack thereof, is racist.

Which Came First—The Impoverishment of Children or Their Lack of Achievement?

The conditions affecting the performance of children of color and children living in poverty are not the fault of the children and rarely of their families, but are blamed on these individuals nevertheless. A 1998 paper by scholars at the University of Wisconsin points out that one of the factors that limits success in conquering poverty is that poverty is regarded as a personal failure rather than a public health issue.[138] Moreover, poverty affects children's school performance. The lack of effective public policies to address poverty are either the result of governmental incompetence or they represent a "hidden" agenda to keep the poor and people of color in their place. In many cases, it is clear that deliberate public policies create and maintain poverty instead of ameliorating or eliminating it. Although many investigators are in accordance on the harms done, public policies that address these harms are relatively rare and often underfunded.

The sad part is that there are feasible solutions. They include increasing earned income tax credits; allowing sufficient cash assistance for needy families; implementing successful jobs placement and training programs; increasing the minimum wage; desegregating schools and neighborhoods; building sufficient low-income housing integrated into higher-income areas; enforcing the federal Fair Housing Act and HUD's building codes; eliminating childhood lead poisoning and other health problems associated with poverty; and providing state-subsidized, quality early childhood education programs and universal, single-payer health care coverage. These solutions are universally acknowledged to be effective by many investigators and public interest groups. In some cases, like the Fair Housing Act, there are laws on the books to be enforced. In other cases, like the minimum wage, changes in present laws are needed. In addition, equitable school funding could contribute significantly to alleviating the conditions that impede the school achievement of children of color and children living in poverty. In *Savage Inequalities,* Jonathan Kozol points out that equity is the appropriate concept, rather than equality.[139] Children harmed by poverty and other conditions beyond their control require more resources for their educational opportunities to be equivalent to those received by their more fortunate peers.

The idea that justice compensates for losses suffered by people at the hands of others has been around since Aristotle's time. In his *Politics,* distributive justice demands that resources be allocated fairly to those who need them and burdens be distributed fairly among those who can bear them. Unfortunately, the current move toward adequacy cases in school finance may work against poor children and children of color, especially if adequacy is defined as "minimally adequate," as it has been in New York. Despite national insistence that "no child [be] left behind" in the opening years of the twenty-first century,[140] the United States has yet to allocate even equal resources for education to accomplish this, let alone equitable resources. The argument that education will not benefit poor, urban, working-class children should have been put to rest long ago. The fact that 30 to 40 percent of poor, urban children are lead poisoned should refute the claims that their nature or culture makes it impossible for them to benefit from more than a minimal education. The environment can be made safe, healthy, and inviting. Schoolwork can be engaging. If children and schools are to be judged by achievement tests, the tests must be reliable and valid, the schools must be funded, and the children must be healthy, well-nourished, decently housed, and free of damaging toxins.

This chapter raises critical questions of the chicken-and-egg type: are children who live in poverty uneducable because they are poor, or are they poor because they and their parents are not educated? Are children of poverty uneducated because their neighborhoods are not wealthy enough to support high quality schools under the present school finance systems? Are they uneducable or just difficult to educate (which usually means expensive to educate)? Are children of poverty at such a disadvantage that they could not benefit even if offered comparable opportunities, or could education remediate these disadvantages? Surely children are educable, despite the disadvantages many of them face. Surely the goal of public education is to provide an opportunity for children to maximize their potential. Sound public policies of proven efficacy exist to solve many of the problems children of poverty may face. An equitable education is one among many solutions. People who object to equitable funding of the schools seem to think that money makes a difference for their children, but not for "those others." Theorists who conclude that children are at fault need do nothing. Theorists who conclude that children are harmed by poverty and inequitably funded schools must fight for reform.

Educators believe that education can remediate the disadvantages of children who live in poverty, based on both philosophical and humanitarian grounds, the practical work of social workers and reformers in the early twentieth century, and steady improvements in achievement largely ignored by the media and conservative school critics. Education can fix many, but not all, ills of society. Social, legal, political, environmental, and economic reforms must create a humane society in which every person has a chance to develop his or her potential to the fullest extent. Reforming inequitable education finance is a step toward solving a complex problem. In writing *Savage Inequalities,* Jonathan Kozol hoped that public outrage would stop the abuses of inequitable funding for schools, once people are aware of the damage such injustice causes. In *Amazing Grace*, he reveals the humanity of inner-city residents, who are damaged by poorly funded schools. But the moral outrage he hoped to arouse has not been forthcoming, at least not on a scale great enough to be effective. One reason for this lack of outrage might be racism, another, the invisible assumptions about the poor that Blank reveals as untrue, that the poor are people of color, immoral and lazy, and that their children are uneducable. The recent field of whiteness studies has begun to explore these hidden motives. I turn to this topic in chapter 6.

Chapter 6

The Impact of Racism on Children's Performance in School

Man is the only government-making animal in the world. His right to a participation in the production and operation of government is an inference from his nature, as direct and self-evident as is his right to acquire property or education.

Frederick Douglass
Address to Congress on Impartial Suffrage, January 1867

Racism, Hypersegregation, and Inadequacy in Education

In addition to poverty, segregation and racism take their toll on children's achievement in school. Children who are poor are clearly harmed by poverty, as chapter 5 documents. Often, poor children are also children of color, which results from the discrimination that deprives them and their parents of a good education, employment opportunities with decent pay, affordable housing, and many other social goods. Children of color suffer additional disadvantages. Their schools are less well funded, their scores are lower on standardized tests such as the National Assessment of Educational Progress (NAEP),[1] their unemployment rate is high,[2] they are incarcerated at a far greater rate than whites,[3] and more.[4] These differences are often blamed on genetic makeup, family background, neighborhood characteristics, or cultural deficiencies. However, the institutionalized racism of public policies is the real culprit. For instance, when controlled for socioeconomic class, the achievement gap melts away.[5] The analysis that the children or their parents are somehow at fault for the achievement gap provides a convenient way for policy makers to avoid responsibility for the harm that they do. Any discussion of equitable school funding would be incomplete without a discussion of racism.

153

Segregation harms children. Despite the unanimous decision of the Warren Court in *Brown I*, the problem of school segregation has proved resistant to change. The *Brown* court declared that separate facilities are "inherently unequal."[6] Accumulating evidence proves them right. Many of the current cases in school finance should have been desegregation cases, had not the Rehnquist Court effectively overruled *Brown* in subsequent decisions. Unfortunately, "green follows white," as the NAACP declared early in the desegregation battles. Segregated schools for children of color are still rarely as well equipped and staffed as segregated schools for white children. The Coleman Report systematically details the intense segregation of whites in the North and South (although making that point was not the intention of the report).[7] White children were rarely exposed to black children in the 1950s and 1960s. It comes as no surprise that the Coleman Report noted that black children benefit from going to school with white children, as long as there aren't too many of them.[8] The "tipping" of neighborhoods is still a serious problem, which causes desegregation to be cyclic rather than enduring. Tipping is the result of racism. This idea appears in the work of Christopher Jencks and Meredith Phillips, who note, "once black enrollment in a neighborhood school rises past something like 20%, white parents become reluctant to move into the neighborhood."[9] Well-documented by the Harvard Civil Rights Project, white children are once again becoming increasingly isolated and segregated in the late 1990s and early years of the twenty-first century.[10] This ill prepares them for the multicultural society in which they will live. Children who attend integrated schools understand and enjoy the benefits of diversity. It is an artifact of racism that all-white schools are rarely called segregated.

Since segregated schools are often inadequately financed, the fourth wave of school finance cases argued that the adequacy of educational outcomes was the proper measure. *Paynter* (2003), *CFE* (2003), and *Sheff* (1996) were cast as adequacy cases, because concepts of equal protection, equality, and equity did not work with the courts in the 1990s. The problem is that public policy-makers who are more concerned with lowering property taxes than with improving children's education define adequacy as minimal adequacy; it's less expensive. In New York, this happened in *Nyquist* (1982) and later in *CFE* at the Appellate Division (2002). In Ontario, where schools are more equitably funded, they are not adequately funded. In Vermont, poor children benefited from "a reasonably equal share,"[11] although, notably, they were often poor white children. However, I anticipate serious problems with determining what constitutes adequacy and calculating its cost through so-called "costing out" procedures.[12] Costing-out studies are liable to error and the benchmarked costs change. Two methods—assessing what it costs to educate the children in a school that is succeeding, under the assumption that this is the cost of a good education, and actually pricing the elements of a good education in an area—have potential problems. Since *Rose* v. *Council for Better Education* in 1989, cases have nevertheless turned to challenging state school finance schemes on grounds of the adequacy of the educational outcomes.

This raises the problem of how to measure adequacy of outcomes. Both the Coleman Report and the earlier waves of school finance cases measured inputs. Coleman defined these in a variety of ways, including the number (not the quality) of books in the library, the presence (but not the adequacy) of a science laboratory, the presence of a cafeteria (which is not directly linked to learning), scores on a single vocabulary test taken by teachers (but not their attitudes toward students), and so forth. The standards movement shifted the debate to outputs. Hence the adequacy debate arose. Children's achievement is the proper measure of adequacy, and outputs do depend on inputs at least to some degree, although the link may be difficult to determine. The *Brown* court's phrase "equal educational opportunity," from which the Coleman Report derived its mandate, was also unfortunate. Equality of opportunity can be interpreted in two ways, as equality (or equity or adequacy) of inputs or equality (or adequacy) of outputs. In *CFE IIb* (2002), the New York Appellate Division ruled that it is not the fault of the state that those ungrateful children in New York City failed to take advantage of the "opportunity" that the state provided.[13] The racism of their decision is evident; it was a classic case of blaming the victim. The same thing happened in Philadelphia, where the district court ruled that "disparate need" is not the same thing as "disparate impact," dismissing a Title VI claim in *Powell* v. *Ridge* in 1998.[14] The question of ends also recurs: it matters what people assume schooling is supposed to accomplish. Again, the New York Appellate Court, First Division decided that "minimally adequate" was constitutional, since it would prepare children to "vote and serve on a jury" as *Nyquist* (1982) had declared.[15] On the other hand, the *Rose* (1989) template, which DeGrasse's decision in *CFE* (2001) echoes, delineates the outcomes of a quality education.[16]

Ironically, in the land of freedom and equality, schools and neighborhoods are still largely segregated by race and socioeconomic status, especially in inner cities, although suburbs are also segregated. This results in what *Sheff* v. *O'Neill* (1996) called hypersegregation, and the *Paynter* cases in New York called racial and economic isolation. Even if "green did *not* follow white," substantially equal facilities would still be "inherently unequal" according to *Brown I* (1954) as long as they were segregated. Such isolation creates unequal educational opportunities for urban, mostly minority youth, many of whom live in poverty, by concentrating them in enclaves of despair.[17] Unfortunately, *Milliken II* (1977) set a precedent for substituting compensatory education for integration. This did not work in Detroit; it has not worked in Rochester; it has often not been implemented, as in Philadelphia. In addition, the Milliken funds schools receive for compensatory education are cut off when the districts are ruled unitary.[18] In addition, many rural children are also poor and isolated. Ohio is a good example. The achievement gap remains high and facilities are substandard to this day.

Under No Child Left Behind (NCLB), schools are labeled "failing," as if it were the fault of the school, the teachers, the children, or their parents. Holding "We can beat the test" pep rallies at elementary schools in Philadelphia, Virginia, and elsewhere implies that the children's lack of vigor causes their failure.[19] Americans are prone to blame the poor for their own troubles. But it is not the fault of the parents, the children, or the staff that schools are overcrowded, unsanitary, poorly equipped, with buildings literally falling down from lack of maintenance. It is the result of years of deliberate public policies. Schools are inequitably funded and the children who need the most resources get the fewest.[20] Inequitable funding results from too much reliance on local property taxes coupled with limiting attendance areas to homogeneous neighborhoods, creating economically and racially segregated schools. Based largely on local property taxes, funding for "failing" schools is often inadequate.

After the 1970s, school desegregation lost what little momentum it had, which was mostly in the South; resegregation has been advancing steadily, following a number of regressive decisions by the Supreme Court. Nixon's southern strategy contributed to this. The movement toward desegregation was effectively stymied by regressive Supreme Court decisions in the 1970s, such as *Serrano, Milliken I,* and *Rodriguez.* Early in the 1990s, the court continued to undermine both *Brown I and II* in *Dowell* (1991), *Freeman* (1992), and *Jenkins* (1995).[21] *De facto* segregation in the North was never addressed effectively, despite *Keyes* (1973) and state rulings such as *Serrano II* (1976) and the *Edgewood* (1989) decisions that overrode the Supreme Court's ruling in *Rodriguez* in Texas. Possible solutions to segregated neighborhood schools include redistricting so that urban and suburban districts are not divided, busing, enforcing the Fair Housing Act to create integrated housing, urban renewal (not the kind that displaces inner city residents), and subsidizing poor people's moving to integrated suburban housing as Chicago's Gautreaux Project did.[22] Developers should be required to include low and moderate income housing in developments, and not at a separate location, as happened after the Mt. Laurel cases in New Jersey.[23] In most places, solving problems by integrating neighborhoods lacks legal, financial, or political backing, or all three.

Charter schools and educational vouchers, which are supported by conservatives, may provide opportunities for children to leave "failing" schools, but they skim off the top students and leave those most in need of help concentrated in unimproved neighborhood schools.[24] Various modes of school choice remove funding from the neighborhood schools, which further degrades them. This will inevitably create a two- (or three-) tiered system, which is destructive of the children most in need, as shown in New York City.[25] In Hartford, despite the favorable ruling in *Sheff* v. *O'Neill*, schools remain hypersegregated. In Philadelphia, experiments with three new modes of school administration, including two for-profit companies and one planned by the Philadelphia school system, are substituting for integrated, equitably funded schools.[26] It is also evident that students in poorly funded, segregated schools do not do well on standardized tests.

One of the recommendations from the Center on Educational Policy's evaluation of the implications of the NCLB is that adequate funding must be provided to prepare students to "meet the standards."[27] This is all very well and good if the standards are appropriate and do not control the curriculum entirely; if materials are antiracist, culturally sensitive, and engaging; if the tests are not biased; if the children are accepted by their teachers and fellow students; and if there is support such as health insurance, housing, transportation, and so forth. Unfortunately, such comprehensive support is often lacking. Furthermore, funds that school districts must expend to meet the guidelines of NCLB are going to private corporations; according to Gerald W. Bracey, the main beneficiaries are associates of the Bush family.[28]

Whiteness Studies and the Assumption that "White" is Normal

The relatively new (and not uncontroversial) discipline of whiteness studies sheds light on the hidden racism of many institutions in the United States, including the lack of a political will to finance schools equitably. To be white is considered the norm by which all other things are measured; consequently many whites think that they don't have any "culture." The pressure to assimilate caused many immigrants to reject their roots; their ancestry was hidden from children, who were discouraged from learning their ancestors' language and customs.

Second- and third-generation immigrants often think of themselves as "whites." They can do this because they look white, or have become accepted as looking white. But, as David Roediger points out, immigrant groups have not always been considered "white." Discrimination against the Irish, for example, was rampant in New England until the mid-twentieth century. They were considered "black"[29] and referred to by the racial slur, "micks." Poles in the Chicago stockyards did not participate in race riots between blacks and whites, because they were neither white nor black;[30] they were Polacks. Italians in Hammonton, New Jersey, during my childhood were called "wops." Their "swarthy" skin was evidence of inferiority. Jews were slurred with "kikes."[31] Roediger explores how the concept of white supremacy was used to divide the labor movement, rendering both immigrant workers and "white trash" powerless. White workers were offered the consolation of "white supremacy," but did not receive higher wages or better working conditions.[32] On the contrary, bosses used the threat of replacing them with black workers (including immigrants considered "black") to break strikes. Many unions were racist, despite the existence of such nonracist unions as the International Workers of the World (IWW) and the Southern Tenant Farmers Union, which specifically outlawed discrimination.[33] Employers encouraged racism, because it afforded them the opportunity to pit workers against each other.

The roots of discrimination against immigrants are deep. Matthew Frye Jacobson reveals the instability of the concept of race in *Whiteness of a Different Color: European Immigrants and the Alchemy of Race.*[34] In 1790, the founding fathers limited immigration to "white persons." This category became too broad for the taste of Americans (who forgot that they once were immigrants) when Eastern Europeans, Irish, Germans, and many other groups who were not "Anglo-Saxon" began to dominate immigration. Frye recounts that they were described as "not white" because they were "unfit for self-government" whereas whites were fit for self-government (43–49). The "Anglo-Saxons" seem to have forgotten their own hybrid identity reflected in their very designation as Anglo-Saxon. Immigration quotas, devised in 1924 but deliberately based on the proportion of races in the 1890 census, effectively limited the "undesirable" categories of immigrants. Only later was the "Caucasian race" invented to be as inclusive as it is today, partly in response to fascism's deadly use of the idea of racial purity (96–99).

The discipline of whiteness studies explores the concept of whiteness, so that historians, policy makers, and pedagogues can evaluate its impact.[35] Joe Kinchloe, in his article, "The struggle to define and reinvent whiteness: A pedagogical analysis," admits that "scholars seem better equipped to explain white privilege than to define whiteness itself " but he proposes that whiteness is "intimately involved with issues of power and power differences between white and nonwhite, . . . cannot be separated from hegemony, . . . is profoundly influenced by demographic cycles, political realignments, and economic cycles, . . . [and has] material/economic implications [like] financial rewards [for white people] . . . [which constitute] unearned wages."[36] Jacobson adds that the conception of "whites" shifted in very specific ways, from the "free whites" of the eighteenth century and the "Anglo-Saxons" of the nineteenth century to the "Caucasians" of the twentieth century. By 1968, the Kerner Report reduced this to two categories in their declaration that the United States was becoming a divided society, one black, one white, the former composed of "have-nots" and the latter of "haves." This reduction marked the completion of the unification of "Europeans" or "Caucasians" into one "race." But, society was now bifurcated into blacks and whites; as Jacobson put it, "e pluribus duo."[37] Other racial and ethnic identities were ignored.

Scholars of whiteness note that the so-called family values endorsed in the rhetoric of conservatives these days are largely white, male, and middle-class values. Rebellion against them by white youth often takes the form of adopting black culture such as hip-hop, rap music, and styles of dress. Many of the middle-class values are materialistic and oriented toward maintaining male privilege. A high-paying job, marriage, a house in the suburbs, a housewife who stays home with the kids, and a two-car garage have become "the American Dream." In *Death of a Salesman*, Willie fails at his work, betrays his wife, and spoils his sons, but audiences still pity him, because his vision of the American dream has vanished. His house is surrounded by menacing city buildings, his job ruined by changes in the economy, and his beloved son, Biff, has become a sniveling liar. Because Willie is white, he is a victim. Despite his lack of insight into how he treats Biff and his blindness to his own faults, he is to be pitied. White men are supposed to have privileges, and Willie has been denied them. On the other hand, the narrator in Ralph Ellison's *Invisible Man* is not to be pitied. Being black, he did not lose privileges he had a right to expect. Since "family values" have been co-opted by conservative white males, Henry Giroux insists teachers owe it to their students to help them "reinvent whiteness." That disaffected white youth for whom these values have ceased to have any reality are perpetrators of school shootings reinforces Giroux's analysis.[38]

White resentment also fuels what is called "reverse racism," a phrase used to attack affirmative action policies, despite the fact that white people in the United States experience so much privilege on a daily basis that the comparison to real racism is insulting to people who experience it. The figures on infant mortality rates, school graduation rates, college attendance rates, salary differentials, and many statistics discussed in this book show unequivocally that blacks and other minorities suffer from discrimination. Although it is difficult to disassociate the effects of race and class, it is necessary to do so to gain insight into the causes of the failure of school children to become educated. George W. Bush's policy of opposing affirmative action was revealing. Fortunately, the Court chose to affirm the value of diversity in college and university admissions in *Grutter* v. *Bollinger*,[39] in which Sandra Day O'Connor's swing vote was enormously important. Although the court ruled in *Gratz* v. *Bollinger* that undergraduate programs at the University of Michigan cannot award "points" solely on the basis of race,[40] the decision makes it clear that there are constitutional admissions processes that support diversity. Had the Supreme Court ruled against the University of Michigan, many colleges would have been forced to abandon admissions policies that ensured some places for minority students, many of whom are less well prepared than their white counterparts, although that does not mean less intelligent, less creative, or less motivated to succeed. Diversity contributes to the educational experience, since it is from the cognitive dissonance aroused by hearing opinions and experiences different from their own that people learn. As the court stated in *Grutter*, "The Law School's educational judgment that such diversity is essential to its educational mission is one to which we defer. The Law School's assessment that diversity will, in fact, yield educational benefits is substantiated by respondents and their *amici*."[41]

Valerie Babb, in *Whiteness Visible: The Meaning of Whiteness in American Literature and Culture*, writes, "Certain periods in American cultural history best illuminate the development of an ideology of whiteness: in particular, the English settlement and colonial periods, the nineteenth century, and the beginning of the twentieth century."[42] I would extend that to the whole twentieth century. The overly broad term "Hispanic" came into existence when immigration from South and Central America increased significantly. The racial categories current now would have been totally unfamiliar in the nineteenth century; then the categories were "Celts," "Teutons," "Slavs," "Alpines," and "Mediterraneans." Through literature, Babb illustrates how the concept of race was socially constructed to maintain white hegemony in the face of immigration. Whites could not have held slaves had the slaves been considered human; Irish and Chinese people could not have been excluded from mainstream America had they been considered "white;" Jim Crow laws would not have been instituted had freed blacks been considered equals. Signs reading "No Irish need apply" or "Whites only" would not have been posted. In these cases, people's status determined their "racial" classification, not the other way around. In the twentieth century, the human genome project shows absolutely unequivocally that there is no biological basis for the concept of race,[43] yet institutional racism continues. This is abundantly evident in school-funding policies and many other contemporary situations.

The assumption that the white, middle-class, male "American Dream" is normal and everything else is deviant underlies many of the struggles to obtain what the Coleman era styled "an equal educational opportunity." The assumption becomes largely invisible, because it is unspoken. Families that don't conform to the norm are "dysfunctional." Single-parent homes are "broken." Children are "underprivileged," "minorities," "disadvantaged," "delinquents," or "culturally deprived," terms that often disguise the racial or ethnic basis for discrimination. People assume such children are black or recent immigrants, but they do not say so. They don't need to—"American" means a white person. Otherwise, the terms "African-American," "Hispanic-American," "Native-American," or any other distinguishing hyphenated designation would not be necessary. When law cases refer to schoolchildren in cities, they don't describe them as "black." They don't need to. It is assumed that poor children in the public schools of a city are black or immigrants. It is also assumed that "welfare mothers" are black or Hispanic, that poor people are black or Hispanic, and that black children or other "minorities" perform less well than whites because of their intrinsic characteristics. None of these assumptions are true. Some poor children are black or Hispanic, some women on welfare are black or Hispanic, but not all. The actual number of white women on welfare is larger. Poverty damages black children at a higher rate than white children because racism denied their parents a good education and a livable wage. However, poverty damages more white children in absolute numbers because there are more of them.

Understanding the invisibility of white privilege will shed some light on the success (or lack thereof) of school finance reform. The two school-funding cases that have achieved the most notable success involved mostly rural, white children in Kentucky and Vermont. In Ohio, Supreme Court judges in December 2002 ruled the funding system unconstitutional for the fourth time. Even though rural white children were involved, black children in Ohio's cities would benefit most from a solution. Because the court refused to establish any court oversight, no remedies exist. In Arkansas, the Supreme Court ruled on November 21, 2002, in *Lake View School District* v. *Huckabee* that the state's funding system violates the state constitution. This case involved rural white children. The Rural School and Community Trust (RSCT) recognized that the decision could also impact urban black children, if the state were to take the remedial action that RSCT recommends—dividing large city schools into smaller units.[44] However, this was not ordered by the court. The Tennessee Supreme Court overturned a trial court's 1991 decision for defendants in a challenge to *Tennessee Small School Systems* v. *McWherter II* in 1992.[45] This is the third time that the Tennessee Supreme Court has upheld its ruling in *McWherter I*.[46] At issue was the failure of the state's school funding plan, the Basic Education Plan (BEP) to supply equally qualified teachers to small, rural schools populated mostly by white children. In 1998, James E. Ryan reported, "the majority of successful challenges were brought by suburban or rural white districts, in states such as West Virginia, Wyoming, Connecticut, Arkansas, Kentucky, Montana, Tennessee, New Hampshire, Idaho, and Vermont."[47] Suburban or integrated districts fare reasonably well, but segregated districts have two problems: they either lose the case, or, if they win, there is a protracted court battle or no legislative remedy (or both). Ryan lists cases involving minority children that failed in the courts—the urban districts of New York (*CFE* finally succeeded but many others failed), Philadelphia, Baltimore, Milwaukee, East St. Louis (Illinois), Providence, and Riceland County, South Carolina. Hispanic and rural districts lost in Colorado, and a predominantly minority rural district lost in South Carolina. Up to 1999, Ryan computes figures for the wins and losses. Minority districts won only 25 percent of the challenges, while white districts won 73 percent, and coalitions of many districts, including white and suburban won 60 percent.[48] These figures tell a sad story of continuing racism.

After the early desegregation victories, *Brown I* and *II*, *Swann*, *Keyes*, and others, important cases that involved mostly black, urban children have failed, as *Milliken I and II*, which concerned black, urban children in Detroit or *Rodriguez*, which concerned Hispanic children in Texas. These two cases from the early 1970s marked a turn in the school desegregation and equitable school-funding movements of momentous proportions, *Milliken* ending practicable remedies for desegregation, *Rodriguez* ending hope for a federal remedy for admittedly egregiously inequitable funding. Would the Supreme Court would have refused to designate education a "fundamental right" and poor children a "suspect class" if white children had been receiving less money, in the "glaring inequities" in Texas? Later decisions, such as *Freeman, Dowell,* and *Jenkins* in the early 1990s, continued the process of dismantling desegregation. Cases that involved black or minority children often had a notorious history even when they were successful in the courts. In the *Robinson* v. *Cahill* (1972) and *Abbot* v. *Burke* (2005) cases in New Jersey, the New Jersey Supreme Court stood its ground for more than thirty years while the legislature enacted inadequate remedies, which the court then struck down. In Connecticut, there was a favorable ruling in *Horton* v. *Meskill*[49] in 1977, but remedies were not effective. The case had to be brought again in *Sheff* v. *O'Neill* in 1996. Again, there are few remedies, despite the desegregation and equal rights clauses in the Connecticut Constitution. Hypersegregated inner-city children were the plaintiffs in both these cases.

In February 2003, Michael Rebell, of Campaign for Fiscal Equity, expressed optimism that the tide had turned. Despite the downturn in the economy, Rebell noted that since September 11, 2001, plaintiffs have won five out of six cases in state supreme courts.[50] The problem will {be making sure that remedies are implemented. Ironically, Southern schools are more integrated than Northern schools at the present time, although resegregation is rapidly occurring in the South. The U.S. Department of Justice, Civil Rights Division, Education Section, proudly claimed that "[a]s a result of its compliance activities, the Section regularly achieves a number of consent decrees and favorable decisions that enhance desegregation in affected school districts."[51] However, settlements for additional money spent on remedial programs for segregated schools do not represent a victory for the ideal of integrated schools in integrated communities. School districts in Yonkers, St. Louis, and Alabama are being released from court orders to desegregate, citing recent settlements for remedial programs in lieu of desegregation. This marks a return to *Plessy's* "separate but equal" except for one thing—the schools are not equal.

Many of the failed school-funding cases examined in earlier chapters should have been desegregation cases. Discrimination stemmed from racial and economic hypersegregation in public schools due to the drawing of school district lines and segregated housing. New York cases of *Paynter, Campaign for Fiscal Equity, Caesar v. Pataki,* and *AALDF v. New York State Department of Education* are, at base, desegregation cases. *Sheff v. O'Neill* in Connecticut is a desegregation case. After *Milliken I* banned mandatory busing, *Milliken II* ordered compensatory programs for inner city Detroit schools, but these had little effect.

In the Coleman era, Coleman proposed compensatory programs that bused black children to white schools or a neutral place such as a playing field for joint activities, not necessarily academic.[52] Such plans allow segregated schools to continue. In Connecticut, *Sheff* v. *O'Neill* declared the hypersegregated schools of Hartford unconstitutional under the state constitution in 1996, but remedies are scarce, given that mandatory busing is not allowed, nor have district lines been redrawn or the housing integrated.

In the most recent development, plaintiffs and government education officials worked for six months to outline a plan. The goal is to integrate 30 percent of Hartford's school children into magnet or urban/suburban exchanges by 2007. These remedies are voluntary. Milo Sheff, now twenty-four, is "not optimistic" about the success of the plan.[53] He commented that earlier plans to integrate the schools had failed to materialize. Furthermore, if the poor performance of Hartford, New York City, Rochester, and other urban children is due to racial and economic isolation (as well as urban pollution, lead poisoning, lack of health care, poor nutrition, etc.), as it appears, magnet schools and urban/suburban exchanges will not provide a universal remedy. Many children will still be segregated in their home schools. The disadvantages of segregation may become even more evident to the children who travel to suburban schools

for sports events and the like. Hartford's plan proposes building expensive new magnet schools to attract white children into the city. (Surely
they can't be expected to go to school under the same conditions as Hartford city school children were and are.) Urban/suburban exchanges
often go one way, out to the suburbs, leaving city schools unimproved.
The Hartford plaintiffs had hoped for redistricting, but this did not happen. The state would rather pay exorbitant sums to keep district lines the
same. In most cases of voluntary (and even mandatory) busing, white children were not bused to black schools; the busing went the other way. But
some busing programs worked. Charlotte-Mecklenburg, the location of
the *Swann* decision, created reasonable plans for integrated schools.
Done under court order, the plan worked for many years. The court ruled
in 2001 that the district was no longer under court supervision.[54] Subsequently, the superintendent who shepherded the cities through the plan
successfully for many years resigned, and the two cities are resegregating.

After mandatory busing was ruled out, magnet schools, such as
those in Kansas City, Missouri, were designed to attract white children
from the surrounding suburban districts. Such magnet schools often
specify quotas of black children so as to reserve spaces for white children,
who, incidentally, already had access to quality schools in the suburbs.
Nor were all the schools improved. Nor were the black children excluded from the magnet schools admitted to quality suburban schools.
The plan flourished for a time, but again, funding was a problem. In
1995, the state's share of extra funding was successfully challenged in
Missouri v. *Jenkins*. Even if this program had been successful, black children were still disadvantaged by it. Because 50 percent of the students
benefiting were white, the legislature passed and funded the program.
Even so, magnet schools do not provide an equal educational opportunity for all children, unless all the schools become magnets and magnets
are not selective in admissions. Otherwise, the so-called "neighborhood
schools," those left out of the program, will have even less funding and
even more pupils who need special attention. The same arguments apply
to charter schools. Some successful magnets and charters admit students
by a lottery, which is nondiscriminatory, yet this still moves funding from
the "losers" to the "winners" of the lottery.

Unfortunately, education still reproduces the racial and social stratification that early reformers like Jane Addams hoped it would correct.
Statistics on the dropout rate, the incarceration rate, the achievement
gap, the growing wage gap, college attendance figures, and the like show
that white, affluent students are far better prepared, in general, than minority or poor children for success in adult life. The incarceration rate in
the United States topped 2 million at the end of 2001.[55] Many of these
prisoners are under age eighteen, roughly 70 percent are functionally

illiterate. Only about 51 percent have completed high school or its equivalent.[56] According to the Bureau of Justice Statistics, in the forty largest urban counties in 1998, approximately 7,135 juveniles were transferred to adult criminal court.[57] State laws determine the age at which offenders are tried in adult court. New York has the lowest age, set at fifteen. The juveniles tried in adult courts are more likely to be convicted of a felony than the adults (64 percent to 24 percent). Many of the prisoners come from highly dysfunctional inner-city schools.[58] Although powerful reforms took place in education during the twentieth century,[59] many schools are still failing to meet the needs of children. Prisons fail to educate juvenile offenders. Many urban schools prepare children for prison, not for college. High dropout rates contribute to this failure. The criminalization of misbehavior, which occurs when discipline is handed over to police stationed in schools, keeps the school-to-prison pipeline flowing.[60] Finally, neglected and abused children are more likely to engage in criminal behavior, both as juveniles and as adults.[61]

The United States does not spend as much on education as many industrialized nations. The difference is exacerbated by the fact that the United States spends more on special education and higher education, and less on early childhood education and regular public education than other countries. In response to the first President Bush's claim that the United States "lavishes unsurpassed resources on education," Edith Rasell and Lawrence Mishel show that the United States was third from the bottom in education spending for K–12 as a percentage of gross national product, in their 1990 report "Shortchanging Education: How United States Spending on Grades K–12 Lags Behind Other Industrial Nations." Education spending peaked in 1974, but has fallen since (Rasell and Michel, 8).[62] Furthermore, the United States lags behind almost all industrialized nations in the provision of early childhood education. In France, 100 percent of four years olds received early childhood education in 1985, but in the United States only 20 percent of those eligible for Head Start, which means 20 percent of the poorest children, received services in 1990 (2). In 1992, F. Howard Nelson, in "The Myth of High Public Spending on American Education" concluded,

> Considering all of the measures of education spending, the United States fails to spend lavishly on education in comparison to other countries. . . . Nations with an expensive but highly productive labor force and a higher standard of living, like the United States, must spend more per pupil just to stay even . . . nonprogressive sectors of the economy, such as education, should be expected to comprise a larger share of the economy in nations with the highest productivity levels and incomes. (cited in Rasell and Mishel, "conclusion," np)

Berliner and Biddle confirm this analysis in *The Manufactured Crisis.* At best, spending in the United States is average. Besides that, it is grossly inequitable. Although more total resources have been allocated to education in recent years, after accounting for inflation, most of this increase is directed to special education.[63] In addition, enrollments have increased, and schools are expected to enable all of their students to reach higher standards while providing more services, such as advanced classes, counseling, health education, afterschool programs, nutrition, and more.

Racism and Special Education

In 1972, *Pennsylvania Association for Retarded Children* v. *Pennsylvania* (*PARC*) extended special education to children with various disabilities. The claims of the plaintiffs in *PARC* were based on *Brown's* promise of "equal educational opportunity." The case was resolved in a pretrial consent decree, which stated that all mentally retarded children must receive a public education in the least restrictive environment appropriate to the child's capacity. Soon after, the same right was extended to children with other types of disabilities, but in 1973 the Supreme Court balked at extending the right to poor children in *Rodriguez.* In 1975, Public Law 94-142 mandated special education by law, guaranteeing an appropriate education in the least restrictive environment to all children. English Language Learners (ELLs) are another "protected" group, following *Lau* v. *Nichols* in 1974,[64] which mandated appropriate language instruction. ELLs, however, fared less well than special education students in the long run. Bilingual and English as a Second Language (ESL) programs are often subtractive, inadequate, or absent. "English only" rules in California, Arizona, and Florida have disadvantaged ELLs despite the *Lau* ruling. On the other hand, in Kansas, a favorable ruling against inequitable school funding in *Montoy* v. *State* was handed down on December 3, 2003.[65] Nevertheless, it took two years for the legislature to come up with a plan acceptable to the court.[66] The plaintiffs included ELL students.

Richard Rothstein of the Economic Policy Institute points out that the increase in educational spending that opponents characterize as a failure neglects to take into account the tremendous increase in special education spending. Expenditures on special education have increased astronomically, while spending on regular education has declined.[67] There is only so much money in the pot, and special education had a federal mandate that regular education lacks. Special education is also very expensive. The cost of special education alone should prompt public officials in the United States to be more vigorous in preventing childhood lead poisoning, even if they do not care about the human cost. Furthermore, many European nations spend much more on early childhood education, an inexpensive program known to be effective, than the United States. Special education, as laudable as it is, does not increase standardized test scores. Nor is the implementation of special education without controversy. Children's capacities are underestimated; labeling has a detrimental lifelong effect; special education students take less demanding courses; some special education induces a learned helplessness that comes from being guided through everything. These factors, plus discrimination in special education, work together to reduce opportunities available to children later in life. Special education must be well and carefully done, paying attention to the social problems and cultural differences that may underlie what well-meaning people identify as educational problems.

The Harvard Civil Rights Project documents "gross" discrimination in special education programs, in identification and placement, especially for mental retardation and emotional disturbance; in programming and quality of services; in disciplinary referrals; in geographical location (higher rates of identification in the South); and in higher rates of incarceration and lower rates of employment for blacks after leaving school. Poverty does not explain away these disparities, although there is no question that poverty undermines children's ability to perform in school. The gross racial disparities showing discrimination against blacks are found only in the categories of mental retardation and emotional disturbance, not specific learning disabilities or any medically diagnosed conditions.[68] In addition, many programs rely on IQ tests and/or achievement tests that may well be culturally or racially biased.

According to other sources, black children are two or three times more likely to be identified for special education,[69] less likely to be in gifted and talented programs,[70] and more likely to drop out.[71] Although conservatives may conclude that these results are the natural results of the children's individual characteristics, or even the inferiority of their culture or race, Tim Wise, relying on statistics from the National Center of Education Statistics (NCES), rejects such explanations, calling them "not-so-little white lies"—that black people do not value education, that black students do poorly on purpose to avoid "acting white," that black parents help their children with homework less and black students do less homework, that black parents read to their children less, that black children lack exposure to cultural resources such as museums and concerts, miss more school, and are less capable of taking advanced classes, and so forth.[72] As Wise pointed out,

> The entire history of African Americans has been one of constant struggle to obtain scholarly credentials: from learning to read English even when it was illegal to do so, to establishing their own colleges

and universities when white schools blocked their access, to setting up freedom schools in places like Mississippi, with the intention of providing the comprehensive learning opportunities that the state routinely denied to blacks.[73]

The higher dropout rate for blacks and other minorities may result from institutionalized racism as well. Black children are stereotyped as not very intelligent, as troublemakers, and as culturally "deprived." No wonder some are not motivated to stay in school. Their achievements are not accorded much importance, nor does school success improve their situation. As Rothstein and Carnoy point out, as the achievement gap narrows, the pay gap widens for minorities and low-wage workers.[74] If getting an education does not bring external rewards, dedicated people can persist, but many would become discouraged. Wise's conclusion—that "substantially unequal outcomes are the result of substantially unequal opportunities"[75]—makes more sense than to say "race" causes differential outcomes. We know that there is a racial gap. Another article slips into this tautology: The authors claim that

> [Our study] uses data from Louisiana's Graduation Exit Examination, an achievement test administered to all public high school students in the state. It finds that there is a substantial gap between the test scores of white and African American students, which exists even when we control for various indicators of students' involvement with school, family socioeconomic level, family structure, and school racial composition. . . . Notably, the gap is smallest in predominately white schools. The reason for this appears to be that African American students show the highest scores in predominantly white schools.[76]

Not surprisingly, these authors also find that race is the major factor in the achievement gap. They call for a return to an "assimilationist" education for minorities.[77] This misses the point that an assimilationist education (i.e., no black authors, no black history, no black cultural studies in the curriculum) may be responsible for the phenomenon in the first place. It makes more sense to investigate how racism impacts students' school performance, especially in the highly segregated Southern venue of Louisiana. Although most scholars agree that the achievement gap between blacks and whites is smaller when corrected for class, Vincent J. Roscigno agrees that race still accounts for the better part of this gap,[78] although he admits that socioeconomic status and other factors influence the gap in a smaller way. Despite Roscigno's careful regression analysis of potential factors influencing school performance, he starts by identifying as "critical" factors family background, including race, income, parent's education, family structure, and peer group influence (np). These he ties to characteristics of black families, which are more likely to have low income, lower parental educational attainment, and be headed by a single parent. Their children are also likely to attend segregated schools and live in an environment that does not promote self-esteem or an internal locus of control. Roscigno does recognize that "stratification practices within the school," such as teacher expectations and ability grouping, may well have consequences for "general and race-specific achievement patterns" (np), but he doesn't seem to connect this with the long-term consequences of systematic racial discrimination. In a careful review of the literature on the "test score gap," Ronald Ferguson finds that "teachers' perceptions, expectations, and behaviors probably do help sustain, and perhaps even expand, the Black-White test score gap."[79] It is my conclusion that racism, rather than race, is the critical factor that accounts for the achievement gap. The socioeconomic and educational status of black families is likely to be created by persistent racism over generations. Using the same source for his data as Wise, Roscigno draws the opposite conclusion. Researchers can find what they are looking for. Other results of racism include a higher dropout rate for minorities; higher unemployment, especially for black youth;[80] less authority at their jobs among black men;[81] lower income among black and Hispanic families[82]; medical and sociological factors mentioned in the previous chapter; and undoubtedly other factors as well.

Is it an Excellence Movement or Racism? Standards, Testing, and Dropouts

The "excellence movement" was born in response to *A Nation at Risk* (1983), which claimed that America's schools were failing to provide youth with an education sufficient to maintain the United States' economic and military superiority. The National Commission on Excellence in Education used exaggerated language to claim that the educational system was inadequate, without making reference to social and economic policies that damage poor and minority children, including inequitable school funding. The commission relied on solicited papers; four searches for exemplary programs, which elicited self-descriptions from 200 schools, school districts, colleges, and other programs; and anecdotal evidence from witnesses. The report, couched as an open letter to American citizens, was informal and did not cite evidence for many of its assertions. The inflammatory language of the introduction compared the entire system of public education in the United States to a hostile enemy attack.

> Our Nation is at risk. Our once unchallenged preeminence in industry, science, and technological innovation is being overtaken by competitors throughout the world . . . the educational foundations of our society are presently being eroded by a rising tide of mediocrity that threatens our very future as a Nation and a people . . . others are matching and surpassing our educational attainments.
>
> If an unfriendly foreign power had attempted to impose on America the mediocre educational performance that exists today, we might well have viewed it as an act of war. . . .
>
> If only to keep and improve on the slim competitive edge we still retain in world markets, we must dedicate ourselves to the reform of our educational system for the benefit of all—old and young alike, affluent and poor, majority and minority.[83]

Blaming the schools in general, and teachers, parents, and students in particular, the report declared that "asking schools to provide solutions to personal, social, and political problems that the home and other institutions either will not or cannot resolve" (Introduction) undermines the academic rigor of the curriculum and dilutes available educational resources with "undemanding and superfluous high school offerings" (Excellence in Education). The Commission claimed that watered-down curriculum and declining test scores diminish economic competitiveness, asserting as evidence "some of the best economists have shown in their research, that education is one of the chief engines of a society's material well-being" (Excellence in Education). The commission failed to mention that the acknowledged increase in enrollment also increases the number of test-takers, which accounts for declining scores. Nor does it mention that commercial tests are recalibrated every few years to make them harder as students and teachers accommodate to them, or tests are changed so that they do not provide reliable longitudinal comparisons. Furthermore, while asking readers not to scapegoat teachers, they do so themselves by describing teacher candidates as being at the bottom one-quarter of their high school and college classes and schools of education as not having high standards. The report also implicitly blames students and parents when it exhorts them to try harder and be more responsible (To the Student and To Parents). When students, persuaded that their failures are their fault, make efforts to improve, which do not work because their failures are not their fault, they become discouraged. They may even become cynical. Effort is not the remedy, any more than lack of effort is the cause. The commission made sweeping recommendations for more rigorous course content, better textbooks, improvement in the preparation of teachers, better leadership from "officials," and more financial support from "citizens." The value of these factors cannot be disputed, but the list omits the role of federal, state, and local government in crucial areas like funding for federal mandates like special education, desegregation, equitable school funding, up-to-date, engaging materials, and well-qualified teachers. Instead, the commission, in perhaps well-intended but misguided rhetoric, exhorts parents and students that, "America Can Do It." The burden seems to fall on the students themselves, who are assumed to be lacking in effort.

> You forfeit your chance for life at its fullest when you withhold your best effort in learning. When you give only the minimum to learning, you receive only the minimum in return. Even with your parents' best example and your teachers' best efforts, in the end it is your work that determines how much and how well you learn. When you work to your full capacity, you can hope to attain the knowledge and skills that will enable you to create your future and control your destiny. (To the Student)

Disadvantaged children and children who are subjected to discrimination know full well that their future is not unquestionably within their control.

The recommendations of the commission eventually resulted in the "standards movement," which swept elementary, secondary, and now post-secondary education in the last decade of the twentieth century and into the opening years of the twenty-first. The strategy chosen to raise the level of "excellence" became a bureaucratic, top-down imposition of state (and now federal) standards enforced by standardized tests, which ultimately drive the curriculum; often the state describes the curriculum in minute detail, as in the reforms in New York and Ontario I have described show clearly. This deprives teachers of autonomy and flexibility, locking them into preplanned lesson plans and "teacher proof" materials provided by the state or the district. Social and political conditions that affect children's performance in school were not reformed, alas. Imposing standards from above without providing the support needed to prepare children to meet them is not productive of a better education. In fact, the Harvard Civil Rights Project notes that "following the path of standards-based reform" results in more retention of ninth graders, which has been known for forty years to increase the dropout rate, not decrease it. Blacks and Hispanics are three times more likely to be retained.[84] Dropout rates are notoriously underestimated. Ninth graders who do not show up for high school are assumed to have moved; many are roaming the streets in search of meaningful work. Others are in prison, where they do not receive an education worthy of the name.

Bruce Biddle and David Berliner questioned the dismal picture presented in *A Nation at Risk*,[85] pointing out that its rhetoric was slanted. The claims that "student achievement had greatly declined" and a "massive crisis" was at hand, in which we would "lose our competitive edge in industry" have ideological roots—a desire for less government expenditure on compensatory programs for disadvantaged children and more privatization of public schools. These claims, supported by the Secretary of Education in the Reagan administration, William Bennett, also contained a generous dose of school bashing and teacher bashing. William Bennett, E.D. Hirsh, Allan Bloom,[86] and other ideologues found fault with the idea that curriculum should be relevant, methods engaging, and materials inclusive of writers outside the usual canon. In their opinion, this "watered down" the educational regimen. The ideological slant of these views is evident, as is the politics of *A Nation at Risk* itself. According to conservative educators like Bloom, Bennett, and Hirsh, schools exist to perpetuate the "classics" of European and North American literature and history, which contain white, male, conservative, hegemonic content. They do not want critical, independent thinkers; they want people who think in a certain way, who are willing to obey their "betters," and who are trained to adopt the views of others.

The purpose of education, according to *A Nation at Risk*, is to improve the nation's economy, but the fact is that schools do not control corporate practices that erode the economy. Many forces, like globalization, the elimination of manufacturing jobs, downsizing, and wage cuts in industry are matters controlled by business. As Berliner and Biddle put it, "The claim [that additional government expenditures on public education are not effective] was greeted with dismay by educators and endorsed with enthusiasm by fiscal conservatives and those critical of public education."[87] Unfortunately the claim had a profound political impact, focusing educational reform on testing rather than implementing reforms known to be beneficial, like excellent materials, integrated schools, universal pre-kindergarten, and small classes. In addition, conservatives neglected to acknowledge damage done by the lack of decent housing, adequate nutrition, public transportation, health insurance, a livable wage, and a nontoxic environment. Business often fights regulation of hazardous pollution, as does the lead industry. Environmental toxins contribute to the expense of the services that schools provide.

It is well documented that racial inequity in special education is rampant.[88] Nevertheless, conservatives like Eric Hanushek, Diane Ravitch, and Chester Finn continue to cite the Coleman Report's finding that emphasizes family and student characteristics as the main influences on performance, not school spending. Unfortunately, things that improve education are not free. Even those unequivocally shown to be effective, like small class sizes in the primary grades, are still disputed by conservatives. Criticizing the methodology, size, and scope of Hanushek's review of studies showing that class size makes no difference, Bruce and Berliner defend two substantial field experiments that conclude the opposite: Indiana's Project Prime Time and the Tennessee STAR study, which used large, randomly assigned control and treatment groups observed over a period of years.[89] Both of these experiments showed real, lasting benefits of a pupil-teacher ratio of less than 20:1 in the primary grades.

The standards movement, laudable in many ways, is not a substitute for real reforms that help children. Minority and immigrant children are adversely affected by the practices instituted in the name of reform. Setting children up to fail by requiring them to meet a standard, but not providing the resources they need is at best ineffective. At worst, it is a deliberate policy to keep them in their place—in low-wage service jobs. The provision of No Child Left Behind (NCLB) that children from "failing" schools be allowed to transfer is not workable. Other schools will not have enough places for transfers; transportation will be a problem for poor parents who work; entire schools, like some in New York City where more than 90 percent of the students fail to meet standards, will have to be dismantled, but something must replace them. These are not the schools of middle-class and wealthy white children; they are schools attended by children of color. Already, administration of NCLB has become difficult even before the ultimate sanctions go into effect. Early in 2003, parents in New York brought a class action suit against the city for denying the tutoring services and transfers promised by NCLB. Many other parents did not know that their children were eligible. According to the *New York Post*, "Department of Education statistics show that just 3,670 parents of students in low-performing schools applied for transfers, and 1,507 were granted. Meanwhile, 20,000 students are receiving tutoring services. But . . . nearly 300,000 students in 331 [failing] schools [in New York City] eligible for transfers or tutoring aren't getting it."[90] These services are simply not available; providing them would drain school budgets even more. To add to this, the money required to fund NCLB, not forthcoming from the federal government, is being channeled to Bush family friends; for instance, McGraw Hill is benefiting from a windfall in sales of curriculum and materials geared to required tests.[91] Labeling schools, and the children in them, "failing" is a cruel deceit. It would be better to reform the conditions that cause the failure.

Deborah Meier, the architect of reform in the Central Park East schools, describes successful reforms that transformed a school district in Harlem.[92] She does not believe that the standards movement is a meaningful way to reform.[93] Instead, her teachers formulated their own standards; made structural changes like longer class periods, which integrated subjects; kept student cohorts together for several years; evaluated students by performance rather than tests and grades; and instituted service learning, which linked school and community. Classes and school units were small, set up within larger buildings when necessary. Students were admitted by lottery (with preference given to siblings), so they were there by choice, but not hand-selected from the elite. The schools involved parents in their children's activities. Many children from a segregated community of mostly lower socioeconomic status residents graduated and went on to post-secondary education. In a city where 30 percent of the students overall drop out before graduation, more than 90 percent of Central Park East Secondary School students graduated and went on to post-secondary education. Although small experiments like this are useful, they need to spread to the surrounding neighborhood schools. The charter school movement was initiated to act as a beacon for reforms in the public schools; however, this has not happened in many places where charter schools were established. Instead, they drain resources from already struggling public schools. Furthermore, charter schools often do not provide special education services. A charter school that advertises itself as a "full inclusion" school is, in effect, announcing that it cannot provide services for children whose needs are greater than the classroom teacher can handle. Such children are further concentrated in public schools, which cannot deny them services.

Interestingly, the standards movement actually lowered standards in New York, where the passing grade on Regents exams was "temporarily" lowered to 55 percent during a phase-in period. When the time ran out, the policy was extended. Ironically, the standards movement may lower standards. Rothstein comments that this might not be a bad idea, given the impact on students' life chances if they do not graduate from high school. Other states appear to be lowering standards as well.[94] Predictions that NCLB will contribute to higher dropout rates with a disproportionately higher impact on poor and minority students are confirmed in a 2003 report, "Left Out and Left Behind: NCLB and the American High School," from the Alliance for Excellent Education.[95] In addition, the mandated tests are often flawed, scoring goes awry at the testing companies, or tests do not reflect the content taught or correlate with the state's learning standards. Testing companies, for whom NCLB is a windfall, do not have appropriate materials prepared,[96] but states are required to report implementation of NCLB on time, so they can't wait for valid and reliable tests to be developed. Furthermore, there is a built-in incentive to lower standards. States with higher standards are penalized under NCLB because more schools may be identified as "failing." Students may opt to leave, taking funding with them. Often they do not leave for other public schools, but for private schools, which may be religious schools. This exodus creates even more "failing" in the schools, concentrating students who cannot attend an alternative school because of transportation, lack of parental involvement, or socioeconomic, racial, or immigrant status. Because additional costs often accompany the use of vouchers, poverty is likely to become more concentrated among the children left behind. In the meantime, the rich, who already send their children to private schools, receive a subsidy from vouchers.

Other problems exist with the so-called "excellence movement." For one thing, it matters how excellence is defined. "Excellence" often consists of getting a high score on various state-mandated tests. Students and teachers can adapt to preparing for specific tests, if they know what skills or facts will be tested or, at least, if they can predict them accurately. This kind of guessing game can lead to odd activities, however. One year my student teachers in rural, western New York were mysteriously putting Venn diagrams into almost every lesson plan. I later found out that during the previous year, pupils had not done well on the section of the state eighth-grade language arts examination on "graphic organizers." Venn diagrams seemed to be the vehicle of choice for repairing this fault. The next year, Venn diagrams dropped out of sight. Presumably either students improved in their use of graphic organizers on the test, or Venn diagrams did not appear on the test the previous year. As Walt Haney shows, the "Texas miracle" is less than miraculous; it is more like slight of hand.[97] Omitting students from the test group, retaining students who then drop out, and identifying them for special education so that they are not included in the test group all contributed to the "miracle."

Unfortunately, Alfred North Whitehead's criticisms of external examinations in *The Aims of Education and Other Essays* still go unheeded.[98] Whitehead's idea is still cogent—externally imposed examinations stifle real education, substituting a superficial knowledge of disconnected "facts"—whose origin, use, or connection to the real world are unexplored—for in-depth knowledge that students know how to apply. Berliner and Amrein compared the state test scores of students in eighteen states that have had high-stakes testing to those same cohorts' scores on four external standard measures of achievement, which the researchers chose to ascertain whether state high-stakes tests linked to state standards had indeed improved general learning overall.[99] They found that

> . . . in all but one analysis, student learning is indeterminate, remains at the same level, or actually goes down when high-stakes testing policies are instituted. Because clear evidence for increased student learning is not found, and because there are numerous reports of unintended consequences associated with high stakes testing policies (increased dropout rate, teachers' and schools' cheating on exams, teachers' defection from the profession, all predicted from the uncertainty principle), it is concluded that there is need for debate and transformation of current high-stakes testing policies.[100]

Amrein and Berliner substantiated the operation of the uncertainty principle in social science in their study. Modeled on the Heisenberg Uncertainty Principle in physics, it states that the means of measurement changes the measurement itself. In social science, this becomes "the more important that any quantitative social indicator becomes in social decision-making, the more likely it will be to distort and corrupt the social process it is intended to monitor."[101] The attachment of rewards and punishments to the tests—whether it is not allowing a student to graduate from high school, or depriving "failing" schools of funding, or firing teachers—creates a situation in which abnormal attention must be paid to the test, with a consequent impact on curricular content, teaching strategies, and use of instructional time for trivial activities such as drilling for the tests. Mandating a standard curriculum, often minutely specified, as happened in New York long ago and Ontario recently,[102] assumes that teachers are incapable of self-direction, do not know their subject matter or their students, and lack the discipline to maintain high standards in the absence of supervision. High-stakes testing demands a statewide, mandated curriculum. One result of such policies is that teachers leave a profession which lacks professional autonomy and respect, discounts professional expertise, demands long hours, and is not well paid.[103]

Another result of high-stakes testing is the impact of the tests on minority and immigrant children. Even if proponents of testing are right to believe that the tests are valid, reliable, and appropriate to the curriculum and abilities of each child (an unlikely proposition for externally set examinations), when disadvantaged, minority, and immigrant children routinely do less well than advantaged white children, the tests are clearly biased against them. As Judge DeGrasse held in *CFE* in 2001, if the outcomes of education are substantially worse for poor and minority children (or any group for that matter), the schools are not providing a sound basic education. Moreover, as the National Center for Fair and Open Testing argues, the tests have a cumulative effect, lowering students' self-esteem and creating self-fulfilling prophecies of failure. Second grade teacher Brenda Engle writes:

> Differences in background show up vividly in the early years of schooling: some children arrive in school never having actually handled a book or in some cases seen one close up; others have had books read to them since infancy. These differences tend to diminish in the face of their common school experience. Narrowing the gap between the more and less advantaged students is one of the great potentials of the public school system. Premature testing, however, by highlighting differences, will reinforce them in the minds of children. Young children are not likely to have the kind of perspec-

> tive that allows them to see the possibility of catching up. Since they always know who did well and who did badly children will sort themselves out accordingly. They will be likely to characterize themselves relative to their classmates as good readers (like fast runners) or bad readers (like slow runners). The early identification some poor testers will make of themselves as academic losers will be difficult at the very least to undo later.[104]

This perception can cause students to drop out to avoid the stigma attached to failure. They see little chance of earning rewards, like graduating, getting a scholarship, or finding a job. They may have few role models of educated professionals. Despite the fact that dropouts have been decreasing from the 1970s to the 1990s, the percentages for blacks and Hispanics are still substantially higher than those for whites.[105] In addition, the figures include as "completers" those who received a GED, which carries substantially less academic rigor.[106] According to Richard Rothstein of the *New York Times*, the dropout rate rose from 26 percent nationally in 1990 to 30 percent in 2001.[107] He disagrees with official estimates showing an increase in the "completion rate" since many "completers" obtain a GED. Rothstein admits that dropout rates are "notoriously hard to calculate." However, rates are underestimated rather than overestimated. Students who simply disappear are frequently presumed to have moved to another district. Rothstein blames the increase on standards-driven reform and high-stakes testing. Rothstein predicts that the dropout rate in states imposing higher standards, as New York has done in eliminating the so-called local diploma and requiring five Regents Exams to graduate, will escalate. In New York City, Chancellor Levy confirmed these fears in 2001.[108] The English examination was already causing more students whose native language is not English to drop out in New York.[109] In March 2006, The Silent Epidemic, a report on dropouts nationwide by Bridgeland, DiIulio, and Morrison, listed the graduation rate of the New York's class of 2002 as less than 60 percent.[110] Amrein and Berliner also note the disparate impact of high-stakes testing on minority children and speakers of languages other than English, as do Gerald Bracey and many others.[111] Furthermore, as Peter Schrag of the *Los Angeles Daily Journal* reported, "many who fail exit exams lack equal resources."[112]

Researchers at Johns Hopkins University investigated the "promoting power" of high schools in thirty-five of the largest cities in the United States using National Center for Educational Statistics (NCES) data. "Promoting power" consists of the percentage of seniors who graduate from their ninth- or tenth-grade entering class. They found that the "promoting power" is often less than 50 percent in thirty-five of the largest cities in the United States, although there are variations.[113] The larger the school, and the higher the percentage of minority students, the higher the dropout rate is. Texas is particularly egregious, despite the "Texas miracle" showing improvement on state-mandated test scores statewide.[114] Statistics like these are getting worse,[115] and researchers suspect results from high-stakes testing and no-promotion policies will worsen the situation further.[116] Average dropout rates mask the seriousness of the situation for the most vulnerable school populations, poor, urban, students of color attending large, impersonal urban schools. At North Philadelphia's Strawberry Mansion High School only 147 seniors graduated in spring 2000, about one-third of the entering class.[117] In New York, twelve schools in the list of Schools Under Registration Review are "drastically failing" their students, who fail at rates of more than 90 percent on various criteria.[118] At the secondary level, all students were required to pass the Regents English exam starting in 2000. This policy sharply increased the already high dropout rate among English language learners (ELLs). ELL students comprise 14 percent of the student population, but more than 31 percent of them dropped out in 2001, as compared to 17 percent in 1998.[119] In the meantime, there is a shortage of more than 3,000 bilingual teachers in the city.[120] A substantial number of the cities with the highest dropout rates are in Texas. It is likely that improvement in passing grades on Texas Assessment of Academic Skills (TAAS) tests is due more to students dropping out than to increasing achievement overall. The national graduation rate is said to be 86 percent, but students who receive GEDs are included. The percentage of students who receive regular high school diplomas is more likely to be around 75 percent.[121] According to the report, "Raising Our Sights: No Senior Left Behind," from the Woodrow Wilson Foundation's National Commission on the High School Senior Year, "the more you learn, the more you earn."[122] Their graphic points out that college graduates make much more money than high school dropouts on average, and women make less than comparably educated men, but it neglects to mention the racial gap in dropout rates and wages.[123] However, in cities with 30 to 50 percent dropout rates, the problem begins in the ninth grade (and even earlier), where many students are retained. Retained students frequently do not graduate.[124] The disparate impact of standardized tests on racial and ethnic minorities and children living in regions of concentrated unemployment and poverty is obvious. However, in the United States, unlike some European countries, disparate impact of government policy on women and racial or ethnic minorities must be proven to be intentional for a civil rights claim to stand up in court. *Alexander* v. *Sandoval* made this more difficult in 2001 by disallowing a private right to sue under the implementing regulations of the Civil Rights Act.[125] This needs to be changed. The problems of discrimination, lack of resources, poverty, lead poisoning, prejudice, go unmentioned in the Woodrow Wilson

Report, which calls for more rigor, a more academic curriculum, more requirements, and more Advanced Placement classes, citing the failure of United States education in comparison to schools in other countries, very much as *A Nation at Risk* did.[126] I taught AP English from 1982 to 1994 in Topeka, Kansas, during which time I had two black students and only a handful of working-class students, although the course was, in effect, open enrollment. Minority and working-class youth were neither prepared nor encouraged to participate. Others could not afford the test fee of $75.

Schools or Prisons: Which Side Are You On?

Students in repressive high schools have long compared schools to prisons. Unfortunately the comparison is often justified. There are many similarities. But the comparison is becoming more deadly; many U.S. teenagers actually are in prison. Rates of incarceration have climbed steadily since 1995.[127] According to the Bureau of Justice Statistics publication, *Prisoners in 2001*, 108,965 prisoners were held in juvenile facilities as of October 9, 1999.[128] More chilling still, schooling seems to be channeling certain youths to prison. In 2001, a total of 35,600 prisoners under state or federal jurisdiction were eighteen to nineteen years old. In this age range, 8,900 are white; 17,400 are non-Hispanic black; and 7,000 are Hispanic, despite the lower ratio of blacks and Hispanics in the general population. With prisoners twenty to twenty-four and twenty-five to twenty-nine added to the eighteen- to nineteen-year-olds, the proportion of non-Hispanic blacks to Hispanics and whites becomes staggering. Of prisoners aged eighteen to twenty-nine, in 2001, 138,900 were whites; 246,400 were non-Hispanic blacks; and 89,700 were Hispanic.[129] Many of these are likely to be high school dropouts. Dropout rates have remained relatively constant since 1987, after decreasing from 1972 to 1987. Moreover, blacks and Hispanics have disproportionately high rates—6.9 percent for non-Hispanic whites, 13.1 percent for non-Hispanic Blacks, and 27.8 percent for Hispanics, as compared to an overall dropout rate of 10.9 percent in 2000.[130] Added to this is a distressingly high adult illiteracy rate (testing at Level 1) in the United States of 20.9 percent, making it the third most illiterate nation after Poland and Ireland.[131] According to the National Institute for Literacy (NIFL), 14.2 percent of state prison inmates had only an eighth-grade education; 28.9 percent had some high school; 25.1 percent had a GED; and only 18.5 percent were high school graduates (in 1997).[132] Of prisoners held in state prisons, about 20 percent were aged seventeen to twenty-four in 2000.[133] Prisoners held in adult facilities are rarely provided with educational resources, despite the fact that recidivism is greatly reduced when people receive some education in prison. The education provided to teens in juvenile facilities often consists of GED programs. Some community colleges and universities offer courses for prisoners, yet Congress barred inmates from receiving Pell Grants to pay tuition in 1994, which excludes many of them from the programs.[134] NIFL reports a decline in classes for prisoners since 1991 of about 20 percent.[135] Lack of education may account for much of the 40 percent recidivism rate within three years of release.[136]

The argument that prisoners should not receive a free education for which law-abiding citizens have to pay seems persuasive to many people. However, depriving prisoners of opportunities to become educated redirects the aim of imprisonment from rehabilitation to retribution. Nor does it account for the fact that poor education leads to imprisonment in the first place. Estimates range anywhere from $20,000 to $40,000 to house a prisoner for a year. Four children could receive a Cadillac education for $40,000 a year. Surely it is more humane and more economical to educate children well in the first place. If this has failed, it remains more humane and economical to educate prisoners. A great deal of social damage is done to families of prisoners as well. According to a Web site promoting responsible fatherhood, 85 percent of prisoners come from fatherless homes.[137] According to NIFL, 68.2 percent of prisoners were not high school graduates in 1997.[138] According to the National Adult Literacy Survey, "[a]bout 7 in 10 prisoners perform in Levels 1 and 2 on the prose, document, and quantification scales." Their skills are significantly lower than those of average householders. Prisoners' demographics also differ—65 percent of prisoners are minorities, but 24 percent of householders; 51 percent of prisoners have completed high school, but 76 percent of householders.[139] This lack of skills and educational attainment, combined with an accompanying low sense of self-worth among prisoners, likely renders prisoners less employable. It also provides overwhelming evidence of racial discrimination in the justice and educational systems.

It is a national disgrace that the prison population in the United States topped 2 million on June 30, 2002, making its incarceration rate the highest in the world.[140] Despite crime rates going down throughout the 1990s, the incarceration rate continues to increase at the beginning of the twenty-first century. This is happening despite the fact that violent crime decreased by 34 percent and property crime by 31 percent in large cities during the 1990s, jurisdictions that accounted for 45 percent of crime in 1990.[141] The growth in incarceration is attributed mostly to increasing numbers of inmates in state prisons for violent and drug offenses. At any given time, 1 out of 142 citizens are in prison or jail. According to the Sentencing Project, "The incarceration rate (numbers of prisoners per 100,000 population) rose from 313 in 1991 to 461 in 1998, an increase of

47 percent . . . the black rate of incarceration in state prisons . . . increased from 6.88 times that of whites to 7.66."[142] This means that one in seven African-American men is jail or prison at any given time. Jonathan Kozol reports that one out of four of the children living in Mott Haven, Brooklyn, the neighborhood that he writes about in *Ordinary Resurrections,* has a father in prison.[143] It seems to make sense that if the violent crime rate is down, incarceration should be down, because deterrence should be up, which should reduce arrests. However, to many, the decreasing crime rate means that prison works. But these arguments cut both ways: how can arrests be up, when crime is decreasing? Perhaps more police on the beat means more policing? According to Jenni Gainsborough and Marc Mauer of the Sentencing Project, the increase is largely due to increased arrests for nonviolent drug offenses.[144] In addition, in states where incarceration rose less steeply, crime dropped anyway.[145] A large part of the explanation of the increasing incarceration rate is the politicized nature of "tough on crime" policies. Marc Mauer points out that arresting nonviolent drug offenders does not reduce crime, unless that crime is harm to themselves. Treatment works better, with fewer disruptions to families, especially children. Another part of the explanation may be racial profiling; another, mandatory sentencing that is imposing longer sentences and giving judges less flexibility; another, the disparate penalties assigned to various crimes;[146] and yet another, three-strikes laws that are imposing harsh penalties for minor crimes. Saddest of all, evidence points to much of it being due to the inadequate education afforded to minority youth. In the meantime, expenditures for prisons increase while expenditures for education decrease.[147]

This is bad enough in itself, but felon disenfranchisement laws make it worse. The United States Constitution used language intentionally leaving it up to the states to devise felony disenfranchisement laws at the state level. The record of the constitutional debates makes it clear that this was done so that the Southern states could easily disenfranchise ex-slaves. Crimes more likely to be committed by blacks (robbery) were subject to disenfranchisement whereas crimes committed by whites (murder) were not.[148] States differ in the extent of disenfranchisement; some disenfranchise people only while they are in prison or jail; some disenfranchise people for a specified length of time; but others impose lifetime disenfranchisement. The Sentencing Project reports that 1.4 million African-American men, 13 percent of the black adult male population, are disenfranchised, more than 36 percent of the total disenfranchised population. Ten states disenfranchise more than one in five adult black men. The group's prediction that "[at] current rates of incarceration . . . in states with the most restrictive voting laws, 40 percent of African American men are likely to be permanently disenfranchised" in the near future is certainly far from a democratic ideal.[149] Not surprisingly, Florida permanently disenfranchises ex-felons. In addition to "legitimate" disenfranchisement, Florida hired a "consultant" to compile lists of ex-felons for the 2000 election that were replete with errors. In New York, the Legal Defense Fund of the NAACP protested felon disenfranchisement in *Hayden* v. *Pataki*, but their complaint was denied in federal district court.[150] Kweise Mfume, president and CEO of the NAACP, in reactivating the organization's Prison Project in 2001, cited the states' use of "ex-felony offender disenfranchisement laws as another means of keeping people out of the voting booth whether they are ex-felons or not."[151] Furthermore, incarceration severely reduces the earnings potential of ex-felons, which impacts minorities more than whites, especially young black men, because of the disparate incarceration rates. As Bruce Western and Becky Pettit show, "the unemployment rate fell to its lowest in thirty years—around 4.5% by the summer of 1998 . . . [while] the incarceration rate had risen to the highest level in U.S. history, with more than 1.5 million men, disproportionately minorities, detained in American prisons and jails."[152] Because the unemployment rate does not include prisoners, both black and white unemployment is even higher than it appears to be in official figures, but the disparity is higher for blacks. Pettit and Western continue, "Joblessness among disadvantaged [unskilled] young black men rose even as unemployment dropped to a thirty year low [during the 1990s economic expansion]."[153] White employment comes at the cost of black imprisonment. Not only that, but the effect of a prison record has a lifetime reduction of earnings potential between 10 percent and 30 percent.[154] Three mechanisms contribute: incarceration is stigmatizing, it erodes job skills, and it reduces social contacts.[155]

Finally, as if all the above were not enough, there is another connection, one between juvenile delinquency and lead poisoning. Dr. Herbert Needleman, whose pioneering work on lead poisoning was discussed in chapter 5, has issued a new study that links lead poisoning, suffered mainly by poor, urban, minority children (and poor rural children in lead mining towns), to juvenile delinquency. Previous studies, one as early as 1943, noted that children with a history of lead poisoning were likely to become oppositional, aggressive, or violent, and were learning-disabled.[156] Needleman tested the bone lead levels of 194 adjudicated juvenile delinquents in Allegheny County, Pennsylvania, comparing them with those of a control group of 146 nondelinquent youths from the same high schools and neighborhoods in the city of Pittsburgh. He found that the bone lead levels were four times higher in the adjudicated delinquents than in the controls. The study controlled for race, parent education and occupation, presence of two parental figures in the home, number of children in the home, and neighborhood crime rates.[157] Because of the logistics of recruitment, it proved impossible for Needleman and his colleagues to match controls to subjects within each high school classroom, which they initially proposed doing. To correct for this bias, they checked for the influence of the school by rerunning their analysis for subjects and controls in the same school. They found almost identical differences in bone lead levels.[158] In addition, both white and African-American subjects had lower grades than controls. This is no surprise, because it is known that lead impairs cognitive functioning.

Needleman states that more research is needed. A possibility for some error in the findings resides in the imbalance of the controls. Whites volunteered at a much higher rate than blacks, hence there were fewer African-American controls. However, Needleman's study agrees with two previous ecological studies that showed a positive correlation between homicide in high lead areas and violent crime in counties with high sales of leaded gasoline.[159] Other studies point to the effect of brain lesions and other brain disorders on violent offenders. Other neurotoxins are "acknowledged as facilitators of criminal behavior."[160] Another vast area of research investigates the connections between ecological pollution in children's environments and the harmful effects on the children themselves, linking an unhealthy environment to disorders ranging from learning disabilities and asthma to cancer. Unfortunately, harmful public policies continue to locate toxic waste disposal in poor communities. In the present political climate, environmental protection takes a back seat to corporate profits. This hurts everyone in the long run, although the toll on children of the poor is high and immediate.

Remediable Errors, Sound Public Policies

Although this chapter has dealt with some depressing statistics, the good news is that much of it is remediable. The children who have been harmed by racism will not forget that harm, but children are resilient. They bounce back, given half a chance. As my principal used to say, "Nothing succeeds like success." Give children a chance to succeed, and they will. Furthermore, educators know what works and educational researchers are capable of finding out if other, new ideas work as well. Improvements in education may well pay for themselves though less incarceration, less illness, less poverty and unemployment, less despair and drug use, and less wasted human potential. It certainly seems worth a try.

Overall, equitable funding of education may go a long way toward solving problems of both poverty and racism. This chapter suggests some additional reforms. Desegregate schools and neighborhoods; use affirmative action to assure a diverse society; abandon standardized tests with high stakes attached; reorganize schools into smaller units with smaller classes; hold high expectations of all students; avoid stereotyping; cease privatizing the schools; eliminate stratified school systems in which some schools are holding pens for students before they go to prison while others prepare students for college; rehabilitate prisoners instead of punishing them; make sure that youthful prisoners or otherwise uneducated prisoners have a chance to become educated; abandon long-term felon disenfranchisement; reform the legal system's overt racism; and, overall, be humane in seeking solutions to long-standing, difficult-to-address social problems. Lead poisoning is completely preventable. Poisoned children can be treated, although the damage done in early childhood is permanent. Landlords and owners can be required to clean up lead contamination. Governmental assistance for this purpose can be established. Community education efforts about lead poisoning like that in North Philadelphia can be made a priority. Lead can be banned from exterior paint. Low-income housing can be integrated into suburban communities. Youth employment opportunities can be improved. Drug abusers can be treated, rather than punished. The conditions of life for people at the bottom of the social ladder can be ameliorated. If people have hope, they will make more of their lives. But they must be offered a chance to succeed. Solutions are there for the taking if the political good will to seek and implement them arises. Democracy cannot do less and remain democratic. If public policies, such as felon disenfranchisement, exclude too many people and leave too many social problems unsolved, it becomes difficult to call a government democratic. Fredrick Douglass saw this in 1867; it is high time for the principle of democratic government to be realized.

Chapter 7

Education Funding and Progress

We owe it to these children not to let the doors be closed before they're even old enough to know how many rooms there are, how many other doors there are beyond the one or two that they can see. . . . Most children in poor places do not even get partway into the mansion of their dreams.

Jonathan Kozol
Ordinary Resurrections, 2000
Chapter 22

Citizenship, Racism, and Classism

Schools are perhaps the single most important institution in a democracy. Voting rights, civil rights, civil behavior, democratic participation in government on all levels, and many other rights and responsibilities of citizens depend on widespread, quality education. School funding, a matter of social justice, is often the largest item in the state budget. The Supreme Court affirmed in *Brown* that education is the most important function for any state. The education of children both depends on and determines what kind of a place a state shall be. Resources for education must be adequate, if not abundant, distributed fairly, and used well in programs properly implemented by qualified teachers. When schools are underfunded, buildings dilapidated, teachers underpaid, materials and resources scarce, and pupils undernourished, ill, or living in dire poverty, children suffer. The state suffers indirect harm from the loss of children's potential contribution. The state also incurs direct harm from poorly equipped schools. The workforce may be inadequately prepared, crime may increase, social unrest may disrupt normal operations. The harm done to individuals is perhaps the worst: their development arrested, their potential stunted, and their energy sapped. Such a state, at best, lacks humanity. At worst, it cultivates depravity. Surely this is unjust, especially in a democracy, a state in which every citizen must be prepared to participate in the government.

"Citizen" may, of course, be defined narrowly. At different times, and to different degrees, men under thirty-five, men without property, women, felons, immigrants, free blacks, and slaves have been excluded from the citizenry of the United States. According to Matthew Frye Jacobson, in 1790 immigrants were limited to "free white persons" since only these were deemed worthy of citizenship.[1] In the colonial period, "white persons" did not include Slavs, Celts, Spaniards, Mediterraneans, Russians, French, Germans, and Swedes [!], who were considered "swarthy" (one step above "tawney") and therefore unfit for self-government by none other than Benjamin Franklin (Jacobson, 40). The term "Caucasian" was invented much later in the nineteenth century. Race was (and still is) often confounded with ethnicity. As immigration grew, prejudice against immigrants grew. Many supposedly respectable scholars spoke of the inferiority of "savages" and "barbarians."[2] The eugenics movement flourished. It was generally accepted that certain immigrants were incapable of being improved by rational discourse (Jacobson, 41, and throughout). Jacobson documents a curious illogic in which rationality was linked to skin color, which was confounded by socially constructed categories of race and ethnicity masquerading as legitimate biological determinations. The Immigration Restriction Act of 1924 reflected these biases, basing immigration quotas on the 1890 census to tilt the proportion of the "races" back to what was perceived as the original composition of immigration. In the process, the "white race" was subdivided, and characteristics of inferiority were attributed to Italians, Germans, Jews, Eastern Europeans, and others (68). Chinese and Japanese were excluded altogether (except when needed for cheap labor). Nativists rejected the principle that "all men are created equal" in favor of one that might have stated, "all men of the superior race are created equal." They reserved the right to decide who belonged to the superior race, although they often represented it as God's selection. Hence the popularity of the eugenics movement, which predicated that racial crossing would always result in offspring of the "inferior type." The specter of "race suicide" by whites was raised to heighten popular prejudices (80–81).

A large part of the debate over slavery concerned the future of freed slaves. Before the Civil War, black men were also considered unfit to govern themselves even in the free states of the North. Schemes to "repatriate" freed blacks to Africa dominated the discourse from the 1820s to the 1920s, as illustrated by the efforts of the American Colonization Society. Blacks themselves adopted this solution in the 1920s, led by Marcus Garvey. Enfranchised after the war, blacks were harassed, taxed, intimidated, and murdered by whites for voting. With the passage of the Fifteenth Amendment, Southern states rewrote their constitutions to exclude black voters. Jim Crow Laws, poll taxes, literacy tests, grandfather clauses and other stratagems including physical intimidation and murder effectively deprived blacks of the right to vote. According to the American Civil Liberties Union,

> This display of racist ingenuity was a source of pride to South Carolina's infamous Senator "Pitchfork" Ben Tillman, who led one of the bloodiest campaigns against black enfranchisement. Said Tillman: "We have done our level best. We have scratched our heads to find out how we could eliminate every last one of them. We stuffed ballot boxes. We shot them. We are not ashamed of it."[3]

Historically there were many mechanisms to restrict the franchise. One mechanism that remains is felon disenfranchisement, discussed in chapter 6. The voters who were excluded, often "mistakenly," from voting in the 2000 presidential election in Florida were largely black. Another is defective equipment; the voting machines that malfunctioned, leaving "pregnant chads" and "hanging chads," were largely in minority areas. The refusal of the courts to postpone California's 2003 gubernatorial recall election ignored the disparity created by outdated voting machines in so-called "minority" precincts.[4] A third mechanism for limiting the franchise is politically motivated redistricting like that carried out in Texas by Republicans in 2003. Voting districts can be maneuvered sufficiently that the black vote, or the Democratic vote, or whatever vote is the target, is diluted enough to have little or no effect. These incidents are not coincidental, but symptoms of a dysfunctional democracy.

Making children the targets of discrimination and prejudice that limits their potential might seem even more abominable than depriving adults of the vote, except that adults who vote can protect their children. However, the guarantees of equal protection under the law and the right to due process have not protected children from harm caused by racism and poverty. Children have done nothing to deserve being undereducated, malnourished, lead-poisoned, and then incarcerated or condemned to a life of minimum wage work that scarcely suffices to feed them, let alone their families. However, statistics linking already disadvantaged children to poor instruction, a more rigid curriculum, and fewer qualified teachers, reveal that they systematically receive fewer resources than their more advantaged counterparts.[5] Such children, often relegated to the lower tracks of the educational system in the United States,[6] end up imprisoned and disenfranchised.

Although racial discrimination plays a large role, social class also is a determining factor in the quality of a child's schooling. Martin Luther

King Jr. recognized the harm done by economic discrimination in his speech to the Memphis sanitation workers,[7] noting that both black and white working-class people have suffered economic discrimination. King admonished his own children (and all educated people), ". . . there are millions of God's children who will not and cannot get a good education, and I don't want you feeling that you are better than they are. For you will never be what you ought to be until they are what they ought to be."[8] Democracy requires that all citizens reach their potential, not just some. This is precisely why social justice in the educational systems of democracies is so important.

Theories of Justice and Social Justice

In the *Nichomachean Ethics*, Aristotle distinguished among various kinds of justice. He divided injustice into that of which "the motive is gain [of honor or money or safety]" and that which is "concerned with all the objects with which a good man is concerned."[9] The first kind he calls "particular justice," as opposed to the second, which corresponds to Plato's idea of the virtue, or justice in general. For Aristotle, particular justice is "a species of the proportionate." Distributive justice, then, is a subcategory of particular justice, requiring that money, honors, and other goods, be distributed proportionately, by determining who deserves what (1131^a 29ff, Barnes, 1785). The proportionality depends on the circumstances, the people involved, and a notion of equity. In a certain sense, people get what they deserve. For instance, in the *Politics*, Aristotle says that the best flute player should have the best flute, not the person of aristocratic birth or the wealthiest person.[10] The next form of justice concerns the righting of actions that violated the just proportion—rectificatory justice (*Nicomachean Ethics*, 1131^b 25–32, Barnes, 1786). This "looks only to the distinctive character of the injury" and treats the parties as equal, if one is in the wrong and the other is being wronged, and if one has inflicted injury and the other has received it" (1132^a 5–6, Barnes, 1786). In rectificatory justice, "the judge tries to equalize things, by means of the penalty, taking away from the gains of the assailant" (1132^a 9–10, Barnes, 1786). Rectificatory justice "consists in having an equal amount before and after the transaction," which can be either voluntary or involuntary (1132^b 19–22, Barnes, 1787). Aristotle denies that either distributive justice or rectificatory justice consists of reciprocity, or that reciprocity, unqualified, is justice (1132b 22–1133^a 6, Barnes, 1787–1788). Wounding someone requires an action that somehow rectifies the situation, not wounding someone else in return. Returning evil for evil does not accomplish any good or restore any proportionality. Neither do involuntary acts require the same punishment as voluntary acts. Only voluntary acts can rightly be called just or unjust. The third kind of justice Aristotle distinguishes is political justice, that which is practiced between equals in a state. Some of it is natural, which is the same in any locality; other parts of it are legal, or conventional, such as a fine for some misdeed, and can differ regionally (1133^b 26–35, Barnes, 1790). Aristotle also includes private justice enacted in families as a kind of particular justice. In particular justice, then, Aristotle included distributive justice, rectificatory justice, political justice, and justice in families.

Aristotle's concept of distributive justice is essentially a concept of fairness in the distribution of things pertaining to merit. The problem of distributive justice is, then, to determine who merits what. Simple equality doesn't serve, since people differ in their talents and abilities, as well as their needs. So Aristotle formulated a concept of equity. In a society of equals, then, "unjust action consists of assigning too much to oneself of things good in themselves, and too little of things evil in themselves" (1133^b 34–35, Barnes, 1790). Equity corrects the law when the law covers things as if they were universal, but they are not, since ". . . the equitable is just, but not the legally just but a correction of legal justice," Aristotle says. He continues, ". . . while both [the legally just and the equitable] are good, the equitable is superior" (1137^b 10, Barnes, 1795). In this case, what is equitable would be to restore what was lost to a Rochester child harmed by inequitable school funding which was nevertheless equal, belying the decision in the *Paynter* case. The funding was equal but the results were not. Likewise, equality, not equity, was served in *CFE II*, since New York City could only claim it needed a share of the funds available equal to that other areas of the state received. Equality is better than inequality, but equity is better than equality. Many school children do not even have equality, let alone equity.

Meritocracy as the basis of equity was often a dangerous idea in the political history of the United States because of a false basis for claiming merit. Merit was judged to come from position, wealth, race (itself a falsified concept), and gender, not the excellences of individuals. Furthermore, it is not easy to judge merit. Criteria can be misleading, popular culture may establish derogatory stereotypes that seem nonetheless real, as Jacobson's work shows, and a person's own opinion of his or her merit may create self-fulfilling prophecies formed by such stereotypes. In 1792, Jefferson suggested that Virginia provide three years of elementary school to boys and girls, rich and poor alike, provided they were white. Following that, rather arbitrarily, Jefferson advised that the one best boy [sic] from each of his proposed free, coeducational elementary schools "be raked from the rubbish" and sent to grammar school. Many would be dismissed after the first year. After six years, half of those left would be dismissed, destined to become the teachers in the grammar schools.

The other half would proceed on to university, after which, with luck, some would become leaders of their country. For Jefferson's time, this plan was an improvement. However, despite the remarkable principle he created in the Declaration of Independence, Jefferson was no proponent of equality, let alone equity. The mode of selection of those meriting education was crude—the scholars would be white, boys, and "geniuses."[11] The state of Virginia declined to enact his plan, but for the wrong reasons. It was too advanced for them, even in the first decades of the nineteenth century.

More than a hundred years later, in 1927, pioneer psychometrician Helen Thompson Woolley called the relatively new science of psychometrics "a coarse and clumsy tool."[12] Despite this, she worked on developing and refining psychometrics for most of her life.[13] By the 1950s, Conant and others believed that the Educational Testing Service could accurately identify those who "merited" a higher education.[14] Test bias did not seem to occur to them. In 2001, Amrein and Berliner demonstrated that the "clumsy tool" of testing distorts the data it purports to measure. They pointed to the phenomenon of teaching to the test, which can raise students' performance in a one domain of knowledge, while it lowers their performance in another, perhaps wider, perhaps just different, domain.[15] The measuring device, the test, distorts the data, just as photons distort measurements in the Heisenberg effect in physics.[16] M. Gail Jones, et al. argue that focusing on preparing for tests "narrows the curriculum," impacting negatively on teaching practices, especially in language arts and social studies.[17] "Item" coaching, where students are taught how to answer particular items, may be the worst practice (Jones et al., 66, 70–71), but any teaching to the test is generally limiting and harmful. It discriminates against minority students, deprives teachers of their autonomy, and creates false comparisons among schools and between children.

Agreement on how to identify "merit" remains elusive, at best. At worst, definitions are often self-serving. Without a reliable measure of merit, a system that excludes some on the basis of merit is suspect. When the method of selection is inaccurate, biased, and disproportionately excludes members of racial, ethnic, or gender groups, meritocracy cannot be democratic, by any stretch of the imagination. Moreover, meritocracy itself belies the principle that human beings are equal in human dignity, and therefore deserve equal treatment in the allocation of primary goods. Different talents may require different development, and may result in different destinies, but inequitable treatment based on a false system of difference cannot be just. Nevertheless, merit often appears as an argument supporting inequitable school funding; opponents (whose children are usually safely ensconced in good schools) claim that spending more money on "those children" will not benefit them, an argument encouraged by the Coleman Report, Eric Hanushek, and others. A fair system of distributive justice in Aristotle's sense may be impossible in the absence of a clear criterion of merit. Once there is no distributive justice, it is difficult to rectify maldistribution by rectificatory justice. Something like Marx's criterion of distribution may be required "[f]rom each according to his [sic] ability, to each according to his need."[18] Marx saw no incompatibility between communism and democracy, unlike most conservatives in the United States. Unfortunately, instead of equity rectifying harms done, children who need more resources receive fewer under a false concept of meritocracy. Equitable school funding might correct this, if poor people were not blamed for their poverty but were given the resources to amend it instead. Distributive justice could correct this if a concept of equal human dignity were substituted for meritocracy.

The problem of political justice lies in determining who shall be considered equals. In Aristotle's time, few were so considered. According to Aristotle, the best state would consist mostly of middle-class people, who, because of their similar interests, would be in the best position to establish a stable and enduring state.[19] He realized that this would not always be possible, but also that it could be promoted by public policies, which it was by "one man alone of all who ever ruled in Greece [Solon]" (1196^a 36–38, Barnes 2058). In 1776, the Declaration of Independence stated a lofty ideal—"All men [sic] are created equal"—well, at least all white men over thirty-five who owned property. The principle was in place; however, the reality crept forward at a snail's pace. Blacks were considered three-fifths of a man for purposes of representation in the Constitution drafted in 1790, and no part of a man for purposes of voting. Gradually, the property qualification was reduced, the voting age went down to twenty-one and later eighteen, and black men, and later, women, got the vote. Despite the Voting Rights Act of 1965, felony disenfranchisement still deprives black and minority people of the vote at a higher rate than white people. Notably, the United States Constitution lacks an equal rights amendment. So political justice has not solved the problem of the maldistribution of public goods, not yet.

The problem of rectificatory justice is to determine what harm has been done, by whom, assess the damages, and collect on behalf of the victim. This form of justice is practiced in civil suits. It could provide the rationale for school finance reform—adequate resources to undo previous harm done, if undergirded with a concept of equitable distribution. Disparate impact cases in civil rights law were based on the idea of rectifying a wrong. However, since *Alexander* v. *Sandoval* (2001), individuals are effectively denied the right to sue for violations of civil rights that cannot be proved to be intentional, even though they are certainly negligent. In criminal cases, instead of justice as compensation for losses, justice has become reciprocity, against which Aristotle warned. However, in the United States, rarely is anything restored to the victims of crime; instead, they have the dubious satisfaction of witnessing the criminal punished. Supposedly, this deters others from committing crimes. According to some researchers, the deterrent effect does not exist.[20] Victimless, non-violent crimes are also punished, often quite severely, even if no damages can be assessed. This is not rectification but retribution. Coupled with "three-strikes" laws,[21] mandatory sentencing,[22] and the war on drugs (rather than prevention and treatment), justice as retribution has created a nation of more than 2 million prisoners. In the case of school funding, inequitable and inadequate schools work to harm disadvantaged children already harmed by others, rather than restoring the maldistribution to what is proportionate.

If, indeed, rectificatory justice held sway, freed slaves would have received reparations in 1865. Instead, "The State of the Dream 2004: Enduring Disparities in Black and White," a report from United for a Fair Economy, documents disparities that have scarcely ameliorated, some of which have worsened, since the 1960s. According to the report, at the present rates, it will take 210 years until blacks achieve parity with whites in child poverty, 581 years until blacks achieve parity in income, and 1,664 years to achieve parity in home ownership. In fact, the report notes that the racial gap in some areas has actually widened since the 1960s. For instance, black unemployment is more than double the white rate, 10.8 percent versus 5.2 percent in 2003, a wider gap than in 1972, and black infants are two-and-a-half times as likely as white infants to die before age one, a greater proportion than in 1970. School completion is increasing among blacks, but so is the gap between black and white household wealth. A typical black family has 58 percent of the income of a white family, a 2 percent decrease since 1968. Such statistics are shocking evidence of injustice.[23]

In the *Apology*, Socrates proposed yet another theory of punishment, punishment as rehabilitation. People naturally seek the good, according to Socrates. Aristotle, less sanguine about human character, noted that people could know the good and still fail to behave accordingly, either from weakness, incontinence, or depravity. Socrates, who believed that "no one does evil willingly,"[24] concluded that people who commit crimes do so out of ignorance. Failure to pursue the good indicates that they don't know what the good is. They also may not recognize that evil harms evildoers as well as their victims. According to this theory, people who do evil are owed an education to remedy their ignorance. Even though some people may not agree that all criminal behavior stems from ignorance, it is worth trying to identify and remediate that which does. It is more humane and more effective in the long run, to remedy the ignorance that results in crime than merely to punish the criminal. Furthermore, if crime stems from poor social conditions, it is incumbent on democratic governments to remedy them. Yet little rehabilitation takes place in U.S. prisons while the social conditions that produce criminal behavior persist. As many as 80 percent of prison inmates are high school dropouts, functionally illiterate, unemployed and perhaps unemployable, and lacking a way to make a living by modalities other than crime, at least in their own view. Poorly educated in the first place, such people rarely receive an education worthy of the name in prison; instead, they learn to be better criminals. Rehabilitation is ignored in favor of placing blame on individuals and families, as if individuals were at fault for the conditions that elicit criminal behavior. Poverty, racism, and despair, all fixable, exacerbate criminal behavior. The culture of revenge may even promote criminal behavior by example. The claim by the president that "our cause is just" in attacking Iraq in revenge for the 9/11 attacks on the World Trade Center, in which Iraqis were not involved, portrays a culture of revenge that may well escalate violence in our society. Indeed, as Paul O'Neill's revelations suggest, the war against Saddam Hussein was planned long before the 9/11 attack.[25] Rehabilitation is certainly a better ideal of justice for democracy than vengeance, both on the domestic scene and in foreign policy.

Prevention of crime is an alternative to rehabilitation. Social justice, which may prove a powerful preventive, aims to establish humane conditions for living, which includes such things as health care, education, nutrition, decent living and working conditions, full employment, a livable wage, child care, and direct aid to the needy. At minimum, social justice means not being deprived of a basic standard of living because of conditions that are not the fault of the person so deprived. Work for low-skilled people has been moved to less developed countries that have lower wages and fewer other costs for employers. However, in an affluent society, a higher standard of living is owed to the majority of the people, since their work makes the affluence of others possible. Social justice ameliorates inequities caused by birth, health, education, geographic location, or other accidental or coincidental circumstances. There is much evidence, some of it reviewed in earlier chapters, that a lack of social justice creates serious problems. This confirms Aristotle's idea of justice as proportionality in the distribution of public goods.

Although the source of many problems lies in entirely preventable external causes—lead poisoning, poor education, poverty, unemployment, and discrimination—the connection these and incarceration rates is largely ignored in favor of blaming the individual for his or her condition. Governments could provide correctives—a nontoxic environment, good schools, a livable minimum wage, earned income tax credits, and more. Unfortunately, the rich are becoming richer and fewer while the poor are becoming poorer and more numerous in the United States, a trend the government could choose to end or ameliorate.[26] Inequitable school funding widens such rifts, making it a policy dangerous for democracy. In the short run, many do not see why they should spend money on schools that their own children do not attend, pay for medical care or legal advice for the poor, or provide food for the needy. Able to isolate themselves from the masses, they have not yet considered the problems of living in a society sharply divided between haves and have-nots. In the long run, however, social justice benefits everyone.

Social justice demands that children receive at least equal educational resources, gauged by inputs, no matter where they happen to live, who they or their parents happen to be, or what sort of handicapping conditions they may have experienced. Equitable educational resources, gauged by outcomes, would be better. Such a policy must be accompanied with adequate resources for success, not sanctions for failure. Children need nutrition, health care, a nontoxic environment, and many such goods, to flourish.[27] When provision of these conditions is refused, lack of adequate schools seems even more unfair, because education can improve children's life chances. Both Plato and Aristotle agreed that the best form of society must promote education.[28] Most reasonable people concur. No goal acceptable in a democracy can be pursued by harming children. Investment in their future will pay off not only economically, but also morally, by creating opportunities for human flourishing. Rectificatory justice would advise treatment (rehabilitation) for those already harmed by poverty. But it makes even more sense to remediate the conditions under which the children of the poor continue to be harmed. Although expensive, the price tag of lead abatement, prenatal care, early childhood education, and nutrition programs could scarcely exceed the billions appropriated for preemptive war in Iraq, programs to develop new (and illegal) tactical nuclear weapons, the projected "Star Wars" missile defense system (which has proven unreliable in test after test), and establishing colonies on the moon and on Mars, all programs pursued by George W. Bush at the expense of social programs.

John Rawls suggests that the idea of the "veil of ignorance" will harness self-interest to promote the public good. In Rawls' opinion, people should design institutions in ignorance of the social class they will belong to under the system they set up.[29] Of any proposed system, they must ask whether a person in the least advantaged group would prefer the arrangement. Rawls thinks it would be possible to promote such decision making through the institutions a society establishes. "Ideally the rules should be set up so that men [sic] are led by their predominate interests to act in ways which further socially desirable ends" (Rawls, 57). Rawls suggests that we imagine a situation in which the distribution of primary goods, such as rights and liberties, powers and opportunities, income and wealth, and the resultant self-respect, are equal. His claim: if certain inequalities of power and wealth would make everyone better off, they are acceptable, otherwise not. According to Rawls, then, "injustice is simply inequalities that are not for the benefit of all" (62). Inequitable school funding fits Rawls' definition of injustice perfectly. According to his idea, policy makers would propose a funding system without knowledge of which schools their children would attend. Rawls assumes that social classes will exist and that self-interest will predominate in their motivation. These assumptions should at least be examined.

The problem of social justice is how to obtain "the greatest good for the greatest number," to adopt John Stuart Mill's principle of utilitarianism. Many people in the United States casually equate democracy and capitalism, assuming that social justice results from a combination of political freedom and the free market. Cass Sunstein disputes this assumption in *Free Markets and Social Justice*, claiming that capitalism depends on the rule of law to thrive, which stands in opposition to absolute freedom. The corporate scandals of the last years of the twentieth century affirm his judgment; lack of regulation resulted in numerous abuses. Capitalism depends on regulation of practices such as insider trading and spurious accounting practices. As Sunstein says, "Markets typically reward people on the basis of factors that are irrelevant from the moral point of view."[30] For Sunstein, social justice results from provision of at least "minimally decent opportunities" if not "equal opportunities" for people to form preferences and exercise choices leading to good lives without interference from distorting conditions like extreme deprivation, discrimination, or toxic environments (385).

Martin Luther King acknowledged the importance of social justice in his speech to the Southern Christian Leadership Conference in 1967:

> When the Constitution was written, a strange formula to determine taxes and representation declared that the Negro was sixty percent of a person. Today another curious formula seems to declare that he is fifty percent of a person. Of the good things in life, the Negro has approximately one half those of whites. Of the bad things of life, he has twice those of whites. Thus half of all Negroes live in substandard housing. And Negroes have half the income of whites. When we view the negative experiences of life, the Negro has a double share. There are twice as many unemployed. The rate of infant mortality among Negroes is double that of whites and there are twice as many Negroes dying in Vietnam as whites in proportion to their size in the population.

In other spheres, the figures are equally alarming. In elementary schools, Negroes lag one to three years behind whites, and their segregated schools receive substantially less money per student than the white schools. One-twentieth as many Negroes as whites attend college. Of employed Negroes, seventy-five percent hold menial jobs.[31]

In 1968, King enthusiastically predicted that solutions would be enacted by a coalition of the people who had been oppressed and their supporters. This still seems possible, on behalf of citizens who have less than their share of social goods, but it hasn't happened yet. King recognized the imperative of economic justice in a state.

> Whether the solution be in a guaranteed annual wage, negative income tax, or any other economic device, the direction of Negro demands has to be toward substantive security. . . . Our nation is now [1966] so rich, so productive, that the continuation of persistent poverty is incendiary because the poor cannot rationalize their deprivation.[32]

It is incumbent on a well-functioning democracy to establish social justice. Without social justice, people's efforts to attain economic sufficiency are not rewarded. If their efforts are not rewarded for long enough, people may well stop making them. This sets up yet another barrier to overcome. In 1997 William Junius Wilson asked, in his classic work of sociology, what happens when work goes away?[33] The answer is jobless ghettos, despair, hopelessness, underfunded schools, racial antagonisms, and self-perpetuating economic stagnation for people for whom there is no work. They become outsiders, the truly disadvantaged. They have little stake in continuing arrangements as they are.[34] For Rawls, such conditions would not be accepted by anyone who designs policy under "the veil of ignorance," nor would these inequalities conceivably be of benefit to all. Downsizing has moved large numbers of jobs to countries where low wages are the rule. The removal of low-skilled and manufacturing jobs from the United States has escalated following the North American Free Trade Agreement, which is likely to continue.[35] Manufacturing jobs declined steadily in the United States in the wake of NAFTA.[36] A new Free Trade of the Americas treaty without protections for the workers from subsistence wages, dangerous working conditions, and environmental hazards, will not stem the tide. It will encourage it. As King said in 1963,

> I am cognizant of the interrelatedness of all communities and states. . . . Injustice anywhere is a threat to justice everywhere. We are caught in an inescapable network of mutuality, tied in a single garment of destiny. Whatever affects one directly, affects all indirectly.[37]

Social justice is required for democracy to flourish; a culture of promoting human flourishing must prevail. If children were the priority, and inequitable school funding were considered immoral, substantive school reform could take center stage. Under socially just conditions, the need for special education could decrease tremendously in a generation.[38] Experiments in whole school reform[39] might proceed unhampered by external factors. The achievement gap might begin to close. Then skilled workers from local schools would work in local industries and other projects. A socially just society would make it a priority to find meaningful work for all. Such a change would not be easy to work out in all its complexity, but it should be possible. As Michael Fullan describes complexity theory, systems interact, making solutions difficult and complicated, but not impossible.[40] Nothing in the theory necessitates negative interactions. In a socially just society, systems are more likely to interact positively. This could make school reform a matter of applying research into the nature of teaching and learning, rather than a matter of fighting for basic funding, or penalizing schools for failing to improve their test scores. School reform would undoubtedly still be contentious, but, instead of dealing only with instrumentalities, reform could deal with research into the substantial issues of curriculum, pedagogy, and motivation.

Instead of restoring the balance lost due to poor social policies, justice in the United States relies heavily on incarceration. Under the concept of zero tolerance, students are arrested for things that used to fall in the category of misbehavior in school, incarcerated, deprived of an education, acclimated to the criminal elements they encounter in prison or jail, and returned to society none the better, and often far worse, for their experience. Imprisoned adolescents do not receive much, if any, education, especially those tried as adults. The conditions they are subjected to seem Kafkaesque, even barbaric, considering that many of them have troubled childhoods.[41] In New York, a fifteen-year-old juvenile is tried as an adult. Essayists in Herival and Wright, *Prison nation: The Warehousing of America's Poor*, detail the problems, many of which affect people other than the prisoners.[42] Minority prisoners from urban areas are incarcerated in rural white America, perpetuating racial stereotypes. Harsh drug laws, three-strikes laws, and long sentences for victimless crimes result in generations of young people growing up with relatives in prison. A woman can be imprisoned for twenty years for giving her boyfriend a ride to a place where he made a drug deal entirely unbeknown to her. Absent fathers lose contact with their children. Prisons located in remote areas make visits difficult, if not impossible. Disruption of family ties creates more antisocial behavior, springing from bitterness, isolation, and resentment. For the prisoners, lack of education, which lands them in prison, is perpetuated and increases their lack of education. Rehabilitation is rare. A criminal record reduces future earnings by a huge percentage. Prison jobs at third-world wages reduce jobs for citizens on the outside (133–135). A group advocating privatization of prisons unabashedly states that there is money to be made from cheap prison labor.[43] In their view, the profit motive is not a dangerous political force advocating policies that result in more prisoners being retained longer, but it is. Private prisons must keep their beds full to satisfy their investors. Recidivism is rampant. According to Alan Elsner, "Two-thirds of those released from prison or parole are re-arrested within three years."[44] Rural towns like Susanville, California, vying for prison contracts, soon found out that the economic benefits of prison construction are temporary, while the disadvantages are many and long-lived. Guards are brought in from outside. According to Herival and Wright, local people find themselves surrounded by a culture of violence (73–84). Prison guards are prone to engage in domestic violence as well (80–81).

According to Garrett Albert Duncan, the consequences of incarceration are not "unintended." Duncan argues that the history of white control of schooling for children of color establishes a presumption of intentionality.

> The prison-industrial system is a legacy of 20th century partial solutions to the central problem—the color line or "race relations"—that haunt the 21st century. Far from being novel, today's prison-industrial complex is a variation on past educational and legal measures aimed at subjugating people of color in the U.S. As in earlier times, the prison-industrial complex warehouses outcasts and social dissenters; similar to the prisons and chain gangs of old, it fulfills economic needs in several ways. It meets the ever-increasing profit demands of capitalism and creates a variety of jobs, both "Negro jobs" in the inside and respectable ones on the outside [prison construction workers, guards and officials] that absorb [displaced] white workers. . . . For instance, in Kankakee, Illinois, where the unemployment rate in 2000 [was] nearing 30%, the county's community college is restructuring its curriculum to provide training . . . [to prepare people for 950 jobs in a new women's prison being opened in 2002.][45]

Duncan believes that urban pedagogies are deliberately creating a "superfluous population" through a "watered down, outdated curriculum" that deprives youth of color of access to the signs and symbols they need to claim a role in the new economy beyond low-level service jobs. The rate at which youths of color are channeled to prison is too effective to be accidental. Duncan's theory is reminiscent of Marx's idea of an industrial reserve army consisting of the lumpenproletariat.

In a nation with what Alan Elsner calls a prison habit, democracy is diminished by prisoners' absence from the community as well as their disenfranchisement. Without the vote, there are no built-in safeguards. The lack of distributive and rectificatory justice cannot bode well. Vengeance rarely works to promote good in the long run. Lack of the political will to implement social justice retards school funding reform and, indeed, educational reform itself.

Factors that Retard School Finance Reform

There are many factors that retard school finance reform in addition to the lack of social justice. There is a great deal of inertia in school reform in general.[46] Unfortunately, this inertia targets relatively powerless people: children and people living in poverty. Recognition that education is a fundamental right must take place, the sooner the better. Racial discrimination, which is increasingly polarizing American society, may come back to haunt the white majority when they become the minority, as is happening in many of our cities and some states. From a humanitarian standpoint, this polarization has long been harming everyone. Inequitable school funding is a problem that must and can be solved.

That racism and poverty contribute to inequitable school funding is evident at every turn. Inequitable school funding contributes to the cycle of poverty that traps many of our citizens, as well as depriving our country of the advantage of well-educated, self-supporting citizens whose potential, multicultural contributions to our society are fully realized. The crisis in New York represents the kinds of harms that are being done. Eventually, the will to reform must become political, although it often starts in the judicial arena. Court decisions provide the stimulus in school finance reform, but legislation must implement any court decision for it to become both policy and practice at the state level. Ultimately, teachers, school administrators, citizens, parents, and students must be committed to equity for all children in our schools at the local level for it to become a reality.

The charge of judicial activism also hampers school finance reform because courts are reluctant to intrude on legislative powers, so they do not create a meaningful template by which to judge a constitutional reform. More ambitious goals, such as those expressed by the Kentucky court in *Rose*, set a template that is more inclusive than other state courts have been willing to set, even adding that the goals are not to be construed as preventing the Kentucky General Assembly from establishing a system that accomplishes more.[47] The Kentucky court did not mandate how to accomplish these goals, leaving that to the legislature and local school authorities. Instead, the judges set a template for the legislature to use in judging whether reforms were constitutionally acceptable. It is notable that the Kentucky General Assembly reformed the entire educational system, making significant improvements in a fairly short time. Justice LeLand DeGrasse's more modest template could serve the same purpose in New York, were the legislature willing to use it. Other courts have been unwilling to set any template at all, avoiding any appearance of judicial activism. But courts cannot avoid the task of judging the constitutionality of the laws.

Legislative inaction is another factor that hampers reform of school-funding inequities. In Texas, New Jersey, and New York, school-finance decisions did not go well initially. In New Jersey, a staunch Supreme Court stuck by its decisions, eventually forcing the New Jersey State Legislature to pass a school-finance reform bill that satisfied the court after twenty-five years of litigation in the long-running *Robinson* v. *Cahill* and *Abbott* v. *Burke* cases. The court refused to supply a template, which may have contributed to the time it took to obtain a plan that the courts approved (from 1973 to 1991), but the legislature also refused to comply with a good will. In New York, school-funding cases have dragged on for more than thirty years. *Campaign for Fiscal Equity* finally emerged victorious after two cycles of appeals and counter appeals, but there is no legislation yet. Justice DeGrasse set a template, not as ambitious as Kentucky's, but a template nevertheless. Noting that he was using a "dynamic interpretation" of the New York constitution, paying attention not only to the letter but also to the spirit of the law,[48] DeGrasse was careful to address the issue of separation of powers when he constructed a template for an adequate education. His defense against the charge of judicial activism was, "[a] template is a guide for constructing something, not the thing itself" (*CFE IIa* at *13).

The Appellate Division judges replied that DeGrasse had gone "too far in stating that education must prepare students for employment somewhere between low-level service jobs and the most lucrative careers" and that he had not provided any statistics for his assertion that low-level service jobs "frequently do not pay a living wage."[49] However, the Court of Appeals reversed their ruling in *CFE IIc*, and remanded the case to De-Grasse's court. On the same day, the same court refused to overrule dismissal of charges in *Paynter*, leaving the children in Rochester racially and economically segregated, isolated from mainstream society. This is counter to *Brown I* and *II*, but the ideal of desegregation ordered by *Brown* is fast coming unraveled. Despite the court victory, the New York State Legislature adjourned in 2004 and 2005 without reforming the school funding formulae, despite the Zarb Commission's recommendation. The political will to complete the task is absent.

In addition, the courts are also likely to be largely white and male. The dissenting voices belong to black justices like Thurgood Marshall and LeLand DeGrasse and others who understand the predicament of children of color and children of poverty who attend inequitably funded schools. Marshall's dissent to *Rodriguez*, often quoted as *dicta*, despite being on the losing side in a five-to-four vote, exemplifies the power of what Neal Katyal calls "judges as advice-givers."[50] But it is not enough simply to publish dissenting opinions when the majority sets the precedent. Marshall answered every assertion made in *Rodriguez* with a powerful counter argument, but that did not change the vote.

Another judicial issue is the appropriate level of scrutiny. Five judges concurring in the majority opinion in *Rodriguez* chose to use the lowest level of judicial scrutiny, rational basis scrutiny, ruling that the right to an education is not "fundamental" under the United States Constitution, which does not have an education clause. Furthermore, *Rodriguez* ruled that children who attend property-poor schools are not a "suspect class," since wealthy children might live in property-poor districts and the reverse.[51] The Supreme Court stated that admittedly egregiously inequitable funding in Texas could pass United States constitutional muster because the rational basis (whose rationality I have questioned earlier in this book) that Texas officials offered was local control. The linkage between local control and local funding is assumed. But there is no *prima facie* reason that local control requires local funding, which will continue to be inequitable as long as the tax bases of districts differ and local funding is derived from local property taxes. When the case was returned to the state level, the Texas Supreme Court did not shrink from its duty to interpret the law, nor did the judges allow local control, the basis for San Antonio's claim in *Rodriguez*, to trump the need for equity.

> We have not been unmindful of the magnitude of the principles involved, and the respect due to the popular branch of government. Fortunately, however, for the people, the function of the judiciary in deciding constitutional questions is not one which it is at liberty to decline.[52]

Texas courts decided that "efficient" means "productive" and productivity implies equality.[53] However, many other state courts have chosen to follow the *Rodriguez* court in allowing local control to trump equity, or even equality, in school funding, in spite of the fact that almost all states have education clauses, equal rights clauses, and some have antidiscrimination clauses.

Another factor appears to me to be the overwhelming dominance of "whiteness." Unmasking the "normalcy" of white privilege so that people can recognize its embedded invisibility in our society is a daunting project. As Vicki Carter puts it,

> As whiteness is starting to be examined and as a critical multicultur-
> alism begins to be introduced . . . some forms of whiteness have
> taken up residence in spaces that are less easily critiqued . . . [these]
> are sites of cultural imperialism, recolonization, racism, patriarchy,
> or whiteness.[54]

Although Carter is referring to the virtual reality of electronic
media, there are many places where whiteness is enshrined in education
in the United States; for instance, social studies, literature, athletics, and
extra curricular activities, for starters. Difficult as it may be to overcome
these embedded and hidden prejudices, it should not be impossible.

All the cases in New York involved schools with minority populations higher than 80 percent. In the *Paynter* cases in Rochester, the
minority population is 90 percent. These cases should have been desegregation cases. The desegregation case brought by the National Association for the Advancement of Colored People (NAACP) and the Justice
Department in Yonkers[55] was settled, but not much to the advantage of
the children involved, except it "returned the schools to local control."[56]
Schools are resegregating nationwide.[57] The big question is, what entity
holds the political and judicial power? It does not seem to be educators,
parents, and students, especially those concerned with the education of
children of poverty and children of color. New York State's vice chancellor of schools Adelaide Sanford, a black woman, was defeated in her bid
to become chancellor in March 2002 by a secret twelve to four vote by the
Board of Regents, which is an appointed body. In May 2002, Sanford described the Board of Regents as being dominated by "very well-to-do men
of European ancestry." She stated that the board is run by lobbyists and
other powerful people who represent the providers of educational services, not the consumers; their voices—parents, guardians, and students—go unheard. Sanford charged that the providers are the ones
who "give huge amounts of money" to politicians, making them unwilling to reform educational funding.[58] Sanford's accusations ring true. If
mostly white children had been involved in the school finance and civil
rights cases in New York, something would have been done about it years
ago.[59] Unfortunately, the powers-that-be are intent on maintaining their
own interest.

In *Whiteness Visible: The Meaning of Whiteness in American Culture and
Literature*, Valerie Babb illustrates the historical development of the idea
that white people and white culture (which is perceived by its perpetrators as white, English, Protestant, and largely male) are superior. Babb
draws her evidence from an examination of literature, art, history,
schools, textbooks, etiquette books, the pseudo-science of phrenology,
the eugenics movement, and even the Chicago World's Fair, which fea-

tured a pseudo-scientific exhibit showing whites as the pinnacle of evolution. This may help explain why, after the Warren court's historic decision in *Brown I*, and even after *Brown II*, segregation was *not* outlawed "with all deliberate speed." It might also explain why there is little outrage at the resegregation now underway at an accelerating pace in schools, including those in the South that once achieved some degree of desegregation.[60] Charlotte-Mecklenburg, once a model of voluntary busing to achieve desegregation, was recently awarded unitary status, as many Southern districts have been. That achieved, they are free to resegregate. Superintendent Eric Smith, who shepherded the Charlotte-Mecklenburg district through its successful desegregation plan, resigned in May 2002 in the wake of the undoing of his work.[61] Many northern cities never did achieve desegregation. Consequently, New York has the dubious distinction of having schools that are among the most segregated in the nation and that also have some of the widest gaps in school spending.[62] As Donald S. Yarab commented in 1990, writing about the *Edgewood* cases, the high tax rates and inferior academic programs found in property-poor districts locks them into a cycle of poverty, because the location of new businesses, which would increase their tax base, depends on low taxes and good schools.[63] In many places, an unacknowledged, and perhaps unconscious, racism has retarded school-funding reform.

The issue of local control has retarded school funding reform. The unanimous ruling of the Warren court in *Brown I* had tremendously far-reaching consequences for public schooling, far more than the *Rodriguez* case would have had, if *Rodriguez* judges had decided to rule Texas funding unconstitutional. The *Brown* court was unanimous in condemning segregation in the schools. Yet the *Rodriquez* judges were hesitant to interfere in educational matters on the grounds of local control. Underlying that decision was the fact of segregation. Alamo Heights students were largely white; Edgewood students largely Mexican-American. But segregated school districts are the creation of the state. Despite *Brown's* precedent in declaring education subject to a federal court ruling, the divided *Rodriguez* court did not overrule Texas funding partly because of "the new federalism."[64] As they noted, ". . . the Texas financing system and its counterpart in virtually every other State will not pass muster," *if* they were to apply strict scrutiny (*Rodriguez*, *17). Consequently, they did not, declaring,

> In such circumstances [where there is more than one constitutionally permissible method of solving problems], the judiciary is well advised to refrain from imposing on the states inflexible constitutional restraints that could circumscribe or handicap . . . the research . . . and experimentation . . . vital to finding solutions. (*43)

Unfortunately the court did not rule that equitable school funding was necessary to support education as an implicit right that underlies other explicit rights. Voting also is not a right granted by the Constitution, yet the right to vote receives federal protection. The *Rodriguez* court ignored the precedent set by *Brown* in the name of the "presumption of validity" of state statutes (*17). Following *Rodriguez*, many state courts chose rational basis scrutiny, which allows "local control" to stand as the rational basis states can claim for inequitable school funding. However, states do have education clauses; many states have equal rights clauses and antidiscrimination clauses as well. Nor does the judiciary need to impose a particular solution, or even a template for a solution, as the New Jersey Supreme Court chose not to do. Judges can simply order the funding formulae to be revised, leaving the adequacy of the revision up to the legislature and future court rulings, should the parties bring another suit challenging the remedy.

A brief survey of the court cases that have succeeded and those that have failed indicates that the landmark successes are cases involving mostly rural white children. In Wyoming, Montana, Vermont, Kentucky, and Tennessee, cases involved mostly white children. In Illinois, Ohio, Alabama, Pennsylvania (Philadelphia), cases involving mostly urban black children or cases that occurred in states that have large black populations failed. In New York, the *Paynter* case, which involved urban black children, failed, even though the *CFE* case succeeded. The difference lay in the fact that *CFE* claimed unequal funding, but *Paynter* claimed unequal educational outcomes. The concept of equity would have fixed that, because it implies that resources must be sufficient to equalize outcomes for all children. In New York and New Jersey, cases involving urban black children took thirty years to resolve in the courts, although New York still awaits legislative resolution in the funding of schools.

The question of who holds the political power also determines how school reform issues work out. Poor people are relatively powerless, although, as Aristotle remarked some 2,400 years ago, "But in fact, the rich are few and the poor many."[65] If numbers meant more than the power of money in democracies, the poor would prevail. Paid lobbyists for specialized and corporate interests of many kinds, from the tobacco companies to the National Rifle Association, dominate politics in a democratic country where it takes enormous sums of money to run for public office. Despite this discouraging picture, in some states the political will to work on the problem of school reform seems more evident than in others. The wording of state constitutions also has an impact, although perhaps not as much as would seem reasonable. Although almost all states have an education clause, the clauses are classified into four categories according to the strength of support for education.[66] However, the strength of the education clause does not seem to be highly correlated to the action state courts are willing to take.[67] Connecticut's comparatively weak clause has resulted in two progressive rulings on school funding, *Horton* v. *Meskill*[68] and *Sheff* v. *O'Neill* (1996).[69] However, the situation is more complicated than a simple court ruling; neither of these rulings has led to substantial reform. In New York, with a clause that the state must provide a "sound, basic" education in the same category as the Connecticut clause, engaged in a thirty-year battle, with no statewide legislative solution in sight as of this writing.[70] In addition, where the judicial will is present, the political will may be absent, but it takes both the court and the legislature to effect reform.

Arguments against relying on the courts for reform of state school-finance schemes are numerous. States can reform inequitable school funding before a court orders them to do so, but most require prodding. One of the primary concerns is separation of powers. Courts also argue they are not competent to decide educational policy, although they stand by their duty to rule on the constitutionality of laws. However, funding is not the same thing as policy making. Another is the so-called slippery slope argument—that all social services will have to be regulated by the courts if schools are. Another argument is that the courts will lose their efficacy if they make rulings they are unable to enforce. Although these arguments have some truth, the pitfalls they identify can be avoided. Most courts have been careful to leave the means of a constitutional funding formula up to the legislature. The *Rose* court provided a detailed template defining an adequate education, but refrained from telling the legislature how to fund it and the school authorities how to implement it. The Appellate Division overruled DeGrasse's decision partly on the basis of the earlier formulation that only a "minimally adequate" education was required (*CFE IIb* at *4). Fortunately, the Court of Appeals reversed this in *CFE IIc*. When the legislature failed to meet DeGrasse's deadline, he appointed a three-man panel of Special Referees to devise a solution. Although DeGrasse accepted their solution on February 14, 2005, imposing a 90-day deadline, the legislature must still enact legislation to implement it. In the meantime, the governor appealed Justice DeGrasse's acceptance of the order of the Special Referees. The Appellate Division upheld this appeal on March 23, 2006, which would throw the matter back into the hands of the legislature unless the Court of Appeals overrules it.[71] And so the case drags on. The efficacy argument remains, yet courts cannot refuse to hear legitimate cases, or to rule on issues of constitutionality on the grounds that their rulings might not be enforced.

The level of scrutiny a court chooses to apply in a case also affects its ruling. Rational basis scrutiny allows a "legitimate state purpose" to trump equal protection claims if the right is not declared "fundamental."

At the federal level this makes more sense than in state courts. The rationalization states give for inequitable funding is local control, following *Rodriguez.* Unlike federal courts, state courts cannot refuse to address school funding—schooling is a state concern—but they still choose rational basis scrutiny, which allows other considerations, usually local control, to trump what should be a fundamental right, namely equitable schooling. Even where decisions mandating equitable funding exist, many states only undertake reform reluctantly when their appeals are exhausted. Kentucky's choice to cooperate with the court was an exception. Likewise, in Vermont, the Supreme Court preempted the lower court's function to declare their state's funding unconstitutional and the legislature cooperated in record time. But this is unusual. Rural white children were involved in both cases. Judicial action alone won't solve the school-funding crisis. The legislature, school authorities, and ultimately teachers, students, and parents, must implement reforms that are effective in minimizing the differential educational outcomes between children in property-rich and property-poor districts and children of different racial, ethnic, and economic groups. Equity in funding is necessary as a prelude to discovering reforms that work, although the exploration of effective methods is underway. We have evidence already of things that work, such as small classes in the primary grades, Head Start or pre-K, teaching for meaning, and more. Many of these require money. Even simple basics that no one disagrees on, such as up-to-date textbooks, computers, desks, and science laboratories, require money.

Under rational basis scrutiny, local control has become almost sacrosanct, but it does not grant property-poor districts the ability to obtain sufficient funding for needed reforms. Control of state-funding formulae belongs to states, which create districts and delegate authority to them. In the 1950s and 1960s in the United States and in the 1990s in Canada, states and provinces consolidated districts to save on administrative costs. They did not consult the districts, whose populations often objected vociferously. Local taxing authority is important if schools are to be allowed to exceed the state's allotment, but that authority cannot exceed what is possible, nor does it allow property-poor districts to get blood out of a stone. Flexibility in spending is also important for local control. Both of these are regulated more or less in various states. There is legal disagreement over how independent districts are.[72] Even conservatives admit "in fact, local control has been steadily eroding for some time."[73] Jonathan Kozol agrees in his classic book, *Savage Inequalities.*[74] Despite the fact that it lies at the basis of the *Rodriguez* decision, local control is quite limited. The state controls district boundaries, teacher education and certification, standards, testing, and, in many cases, selection of materials,[75] a mandated curriculum, and even report cards. Districts can hire personnel (if they are certified), determine class sizes (unless the state has regulated that), decide on course offerings beyond what is required by the state (if they can afford any), build new schools or close old ones (unless there are rules covering the utilization of spaces), set tax rates, and run bond issues for capital improvements (subject to the limits of their taxable property, state regulations, and voter approval), design curriculum and choose materials unless regulated (subject to what they can afford), and determine miscellaneous district policies. Curriculum, often regulated by the state, has been usurped in practicality by the necessity to teach to state standards and administer tests to fulfill the requirements of No Child Left Behind (NCLB).[76] Districts have little control over special education, which is mandated by federal law, although they are required to pay for it, a huge new cost that has been accompanied by lower federal aid over the last twenty or so years. According to Richard Rothstein, increases in school budgets are mostly special education costs; the money applied to regular education decreased from 58.5 percent in 1991 to 56.8 percent in 1997.[77] Yet despite the lack of meaningful local control, this issue still trumps other considerations in some school finance litigation. Furthermore, the writers of the No Child Left Behind legislation were not hampered by the idea of local control.

In the big five cities in New York, the districts are so large, and their taxing authority limited by law, that they have even less local control. The mayors of New York City and Rochester assumed control of city schools in spring of 2002. In New York City, the community school boards currently fear dissolution; the chancellor, Harold Levy, was fired in August 2002, replaced by the mayor's appointee, Joel Klein. Among his first acts, Klein rehired three superintendents whom local boards have been trying to fire. The mayor rescinded a law that community school boards must approve such appointments so that his chancellor would be free to make them.[78] This scarcely seems like local control. Yet a plan to subdivide these districts into smaller, more manageable units, which would be less subject to the kind of graft and corruption that thrives in big districts, is not considered. More centralization prevails instead. Yet Appellate Division judges in *CFE IIb* replied that DeGrasse's charge of "inefficient bureaucratic practices and lengthy review and approval processes" hindering repairs of schools had been corrected by testimony of school officials that "all immediately hazardous conditions had been eliminated, and all buildings had been made watertight," a general claim that did not address many of the particulars that Campaign for Fiscal Equity witnesses had established to DeGrasse's satisfaction.[79] Instead, the judges used the concession of the plaintiff's own expert witness, on cross examination, that "'investing in the family' rather than the schools '*might* pay off even more'" (*16) (italics mine). They *might* have noted that the state does not have a constitutional obligation to "invest in the family," nor do they actually propose such an "investment." What they say is ". . . more spending on education is not necessarily the answer . . ." and they suggest that ". . . the cure lies in eliminating the socioeconomic conditions facing certain students" (*16). They did not suggest that the state take up this challenge, not did they see that education might provide the vehicle. The cities where local control is practically nil are precisely the places where the local control argument has been used to deprive children of equitable funding. Although I see no *prima facie* reason why local control cannot be maintained while funding is supplied by the state, or even the federal government, in general it is true that increased demands for accountability often follow increased state funding, as in Vermont and Ontario. In both Ontario and Vermont, where a uniform property tax rate was set provincewide or statewide, state curriculum, state testing, and state-mandated reporting followed state funding. But many states, especially New York, already have such state mandates (and more) without equity in funding or a uniform tax rate. In most states, many districts are losing local control because of the state standards movement and the imposition of unfunded federal mandates. As Marshall pointed out in *Rodriguez*, "At present, then, local control is a myth for many of the local school districts in Texas."[80]

Another problem with obtaining equitable school funding, one that emerges in times of fiscal crisis, is adequacy. A higher state share resolves equity issues, but may make adequate funding more vulnerable to fluctuation, especially if states rely on sales taxes. Formulae will be dependent on the state's commitment to education, how the purpose of schooling is defined, and the type of costing-out studies that are done. Under court orders, states have undertaken "costing out" studies to determine the level of funding necessary to fulfill their constitutional mandate. But there is disagreement on the proper method of "costing out." In addition, costs must be continually updated. In Ontario, costs based on 1996 benchmarks resulted in massive shortfalls by 2002.[81] Inadequate funding resulted from reforms motivated by a desire to cut taxes rather than to improve schooling. In 2002, Ontario Boards in Halton, Toronto, Hamilton-Wentworth, and Ottawa-Carlton claimed that they simply could not submit balanced budgets according to provincial guidelines.[82] Premier Eves chose not to update the benchmarks based on 1996 costs, although his own commission recommended doing so, which cost him reelection.

Ideological reasons also contribute to people's reluctance to institute equity in school funding. With the startling correspondences of the impact of race and class on statistics ranging from infant mortality to family income, it becomes difficult to tell which of the two is the primary cause. Ellen Brantlinger writes revealingly about how middle-class teach-

ers and parents in a largely white, Midwestern town rationalized class
advantage and maneuvered to keep their children isolated from the
working-class children of the town. She interviewed teachers, parents,
and administrators in a town that had a divide between the good schools
located in middle-class neighborhoods and poor schools in working-class
neighborhoods. Brantlinger found that redistricting is not an option politically, since the middle-class and upper-class parents and teachers are
intent on retaining their children's isolation from the children of the
lower socioeconomic classes. Middle-class parents found it easy to ratio-
nalize the advantages their children had. A retired superintendent privately assured Brantlinger that he deplored the economic isolation
promoted by school district lines in "Hillsdale" but saw no possibility of
redistricting. Administrators succumbed to the demands of middle-class
parents for honors and Advanced Placement classes for their "gifted"
children, while they tolerated fewer resources and less well-qualified
teachers for the "others."[83]

The self-interest of Brantlinger's subjects corresponds to the idea
that schools ought to engage in competitive tests and grading practices,
competitive sports, tracking, categorizing, and other exclusionary practices (Brantlinger, 188–199). Practices such as rank-ordering children
and awarding them prizes such as scholarships comparative to their rank
in class are even commended as preparing children for "the real world"
of competitive capitalism. Cooperative learning has become more common in the lower grades in the last three or four decades, but emphasis
on standardized tests may drive this underground. The ideological support for these practices is the belief that human beings are inevitably self-
interested advanced in the *Federalist Papers*, as discussed in chapter 1.
Unfortunately, the devices supposed by the authors of the *Federalist Papers*
to prevent self-interested factions proved ineffective. But the idea that
each person's unfettered pursuit of his or her own interest will result in
what is good for the whole persists. As George Counts pointed out in his
speech to the Progressive Education Association in 1932, such an idea is
outmoded in an industrialized society.[84]

Brantlinger recommends replacing an ideology based on greed and
vanity by an ethics based on "social reciprocity . . . which is based on see-
ing others as being as valuable as self, and in which one's actions towards
others are consistent with the way one wants to be treated" (193). She
feels that, despite widespread acceptance in philosophy and religion, such
an ethic "slips away into obscure shadows when certain people . . . focus almost exclusively on self-gain . . ." (193). Immanuel Kant would agree; in
his view, people succumb to their "inclinations," which overpower their
rational acceptance of the categorical imperative, which commands them
to treat other people as ends in themselves, never as a means to their end.

Since Kant proposes a rational, deontological ethic, he maintains that it can be learned.[85] Aristotle and Dewey both propose that ethics is learned initially by habit, the former promoting "moderation in all things," the latter, habits of open-mindedness, responsiveness to others, and willingness to consider the aims of the group.[86] Such attitudes are learned in school, and could substitute ethical principle for the ideology that self-interest is inevitable and unconditionally acceptable.

If local control is truly important, as it may well be, then money must be available to fund local programs, reduce class size, provide up-to-date textbooks, hire well-qualified teachers, and other items that districts can control. Obviously, money must be spent wisely and the results of reforms researched carefully. Because it is clear that court cases alone don't solve the school-funding crisis, the next necessity is a commitment to the public good, which will allow sufficient funding for all children to maximize their potential to meet high standards. This requires the political will to serve the public good on the part of both constituents and legislators. After that, educators must provide research-based evidence of appropriate pedagogy to maximize potential. Beyond that, it matters what the purpose of schooling is said to be. But, even if the purpose of schooling is defined by a minimal conception of what is adequate, as the New York Appellate Division affirmed in *CFE IIb* in 2002, surely the function of public schools in a democracy concerns the public good, ultimately. The public good could not be better served than by maximizing children's potential, or at least providing an adequate opportunity to function effectively as a citizen, a family member, a worker, and an individual whose potential contributions to society create a livable future for all members of a society.

The question is how to create the political will to implement such a plan. As things stand now, the political will seems to go mostly the other way. Inequitable school funding, low test scores, and segregated schools and housing cannot be merely coincidental; they are too pervasive. Deliberate policies like red-lining neighborhoods so that mortgages are not available, setting an unlivable minimum wage, lack of enforcement of HUD regulations, and an unwillingness to build lead-safe, low-income housing in the suburbs are the results of harmful public policies with known disparate impact on certain groups. They contribute to the increasing income gap, unemployment for the poor and minorities, incarceration rates that are disturbingly discriminatory, and other social ills. Some exclude the poor from voting, others from being in good health, yet others from making a livable wage. Some deliberately poison children. Many are governmental policies that keep the poor poor and maintain racial segregation and prejudice. The gap in school spending nationwide remains relatively intractable, except where it has been addressed by court-ordered, legislatively implemented remedies. Even where there is improvement, as there is in some states, simple equality, let alone equity, often does not exist. New York is among the states with the highest per-pupil spending *on average*. Unfortunately this is not equitably distributed. Other states spend much less. Although equity within states is at least a topic of debate, inequity among states has not even been addressed. Although it is abundantly clear that inequitable school funding hurts everyone, there is a lack of willingness to face up to the harms done. The political will must be found to undo these harms. In search of this, I move on to factors that may help reform.

Factors that Promote School Finance Reform

In some states the legislature cooperated with the courts on school finance reform. In Kentucky, a joint commission of stakeholders worked on the legislation required by the courts, where an effort begun in 1990 continues to refine the Kentucky Educational Reform Act (KERA), provides motivation with the Kentucky Accountability Program (KAP), and measures results with Kentucky Institutional Results Informational System (KIRIS).[87] Although not without controversy, the Kentucky effort began paying off in increased scores about seven years later, shown in data collected by the Commonwealth Accountability Testing System (CATS) from 1998 to 2003.[88] In Vermont, likewise, the legislature cooperated with the state's Supreme Court in *Amanda Brigham* v. *State of Vermont* (1997), passing Act 60 that same year. Again, not without controversy, Vermont's finance reforms of 1997 to 2004 resulted in closing the spending gap, the tax equity gap, and the achievement gap for children in property-poor towns.[89] Even though the "sharing pool" was eliminated for the 2004–2005 school year, there is some hope that the inequities will not increase too drastically, because the state sets the rates and collects property taxes statewide and the state share has increased dramatically. Measures for supplementing the state budget inflows to pay for this consist of sales taxes, although on "unnecessary" items like beer, soda, and restaurant meals. If people forego these items, the supplemental revenue may be in jeopardy. In Hawaii and Delaware there is one district in the state, which promotes equality. There are many such equalizing devices, perhaps the simplest of which is increasing the state share of the education budget. In New York, the share hovers around 45 percent to 50 percent, creating vast inequities.

Another fiscal policy that would help equalize spending would be to fund state and federal mandates fully. Special education spending is responsible for the large increase in education spending overall. Although the Appellate Division in *CFE IIb* criticized the New York schools for inefficiency, suggesting that "the savings created by returning

improperly referred students to the general school population (where
the cost is 50% to 75% less per student than special education) would
amount to hundreds of millions of dollars, if not $1 billion, even after ac-
counting for the cost of redirecting students to the general population,"[90] the judges neglected the fact that special education is tightly
regulated by state and federal law. Although there is certainly room for
reform here, since minority children are often placed in special education inappropriately,[91] this putative savings could not account for all the
deficiencies in the city's schools. But societies could protect children
from debilitating environmental toxins.

Another change that has been taking place nationally, including in
school-finance reform cases, changes the focus in education from inputs
to outputs. Under this conception, the inputs are not adequate until the
outputs are satisfactorily achieved. Good teachers practice this all the
time. If children don't learn, they reflect on their teaching practices to
devise improvements. If teachers blame the children instead, then they
will see no need to improve their teaching. The Appellate Division
judges in *CFE IIb* were looking at input measures. They missed the point
of the new focus on outputs when they said

> However, the proper standard is that the state must offer all children
> the *opportunity* [emphasis in the original] for a sound basic educa-
> tion, not ensure that they actually receive it. Thus the mere fact that
> some students do not achieve a sound basic education does not nec-
> essarily mean that the State has defaulted on its obligation. Notably,
> the standard is a 'sound basic education,' not graduation from high
> school, nor can the State be faulted if students do not avail them-
> selves of the opportunities presented. (*15)

This is a classic case of blaming the victim. Adequacy of funding (at
least by some standard) might be assured if states provided the resources
needed for every child to meet the state standards. In *CFE IIb*, lawyers for
the state defended the racial gap in scores by claiming that the state's
standards are "merely aspirational" (*5). Luckily for the children of New
York City at least, the Court of Appeals overruled this interpretation of a
"sound, basic education." In the court's words,

> That conclusion [there was no evidence quantifying how many
> drop-outs fail to obtain a sound basic education] follows from the
> Appellate Division's premise that a sound basic education is im-
> parted by eighth or ninth grade. *A sound basic education, however,
> means a meaningful high school education.* Under that standard, it may,
> as a practical matter, be presumed that a dropout has not received a
> sound basic education. (*CFE IIc* at *914) (italics mine)

Another beneficial practice for school finance reform is that states could "level up" in their efforts to equalize school financing, as is being done in Vermont, Kentucky, and Texas, with varying degrees of success. "Leveling down," as was done in California, or capping expenses, as was done in Kansas prior to the Supreme Court decision in *Montoy* v. *State*, have serious drawbacks.[92] Some states are working on "costing out" studies that will, reformers hope, insure adequate funding. I fear that this might be disappointing, because state legislators seem to care more about taxes than adequacy. Reformers will do well to recall, from Ontario's experience, that such costing-out procedures require constant updating, since the costs change.

Disaggregating the data on tests by race/ethnicity, economic disadvantage, disability, limited English proficiency, migrant status, and gender, as commanded by No Child Left Behind legislation, can also prove beneficial, if the gaps are addressed in useful ways. Penalizing low-performing schools financially, however, makes no sense whatsoever. This practice will not result in improvement. Moving students to other schools is both costly and impractical, and will have the result of further degrading the so-called failing school. In addition, remedies such as tutoring are funded by the districts, which takes money away from other programs. On top of this, testing has increased to such an extent as to be counterproductive, taking away instructional time and influencing instructional practices and materials. Tests often drive the curriculum, as teachers in New York know all too well. Test bias, unreliability, and invalidity, pose serious problems. As researchers Amrein and Berliner found, students' general knowledge declines because the mandated tests cover a specific, narrow domain of knowledge. Standardized tests discriminate against English Language Learners and poor and minority students whose education has not prepared them well.[93] This excludes them from scholarships and college admissions, although their "fault" lies in poor preparation in underfunded schools, rather than lack of talent. Other possible state reforms include strengthening the education clause by adding a constitutional amendment. In addition, states could target state aid to property-poor districts more effectively; many fail to do so, as reported in the "targeting scores" of *Education Week's* Quality Counts issues starting in 2000.[94]

Although there is dispute about whether court cases result in more and better reforms, it is clear that a big factor in the success of school-finance reform has been the persistence of the reformers in bringing suits, continuing appeals, constructing solutions, and insisting on social justice in federal, state, and district policies. In 1996, R. Craig Wood and David Thompson recommended, among other things, "if cases can develop a nexus between education and resource disparities in terms of educational failure and the impact on individuals, the plaintiffs may prevail."[95] This nexus might be provided by the continuing emphasis on testing, again, if it is reliable and valid, and properly interpreted. Most citizens are shocked by the disparate results and do not assume the inferiority of the children, but rather opt to improve the schools. Information is critical, but so is the political will to do something with that information.

An action useful to school-funding reform (or any reform, for that matter), which teachers can implement in their rooms without asking anyone's permission, is to teach critical literacy through critical pedagogy, since critical literacy will raise a new generation of persistent reformers who will continue to address problems of social justice. An emphasis on social justice in schools of education would help; such issues are often addressed in foundations classes, but sometimes not elsewhere. Plaintiffs must be incredibly persistent in the face of repeated defeats, which takes a determined and perspicacious citizen who feels strongly that what he or she does is important. The *Robinson* and *Abbott* cases in New Jersey went through twenty-five years of appeals; in New York, cases took thirty years. By the time most of these cases are settled, the children involved in the original suits have long since graduated.

It seems possible, although unlikely in the present political climate, that civil rights actions could lead to a federal court decision that would mandate reform nationwide. DeGrasse had the right idea when he suggested reform of the funding formula statewide in *CFE IIa*,[96] rather than just ordering that more money be spent on children in New York City. However, civil rights claims in both recent New York cases were turned down. Nevertheless, inequitable school funding clearly is a state civil rights issue. The NAACP in New York continues to pursue this angle. An amendment to the Civil Rights Act allowing personal suits on the basis of disparate impact would solve the problem raised by *Sandoval*, making cases based on disparate impact possible again.

In addition to factors that promote school finance reform that have been tried in some places, there are others that have not been tried, or not tried very seriously. Although they predict that school finance reform will take place in the judicial arena, Wood and Thompson warn that schoolc finance reform, pursued by itself, may have unintended consequences: for instance, less money for other vital social services (104). Although they maintain that "equity has long been the goal of social and economic reform" (103), I find this increasingly hard to believe, given the notable lack of success in the last quarter of the twentieth century. Wood and Thompson also argued that unless state aid distribution formulas "fully eliminate any wealth-related [disparity in] educational opportunity" (103), plaintiffs could argue that the state violated its own legislative intent, depriving it of the rational basis argument. This strategy failed in New York, where flat grants and save-harmless provisions clearly negated the intended equalizing effect of the formula, but continue unchallenged. Perhaps this will be reformed as a result of *CFE IIc.*

Reform of the economic and social issues that affect children's performance in school would be at the top of my list after court-ordered, legislatively implemented school finance reform. Increasing the minimum wage would help enormously. Providing essential social services (often provided in other developed nations) such as health care, universal pre-K, subsidized day care, nutrition for pregnant women and young children (which is done to some extent through WIC), paid maternity leave, and others would also help. Decent, lead-safe, low-income public housing, integrated into higher-income and/or suburban neighborhoods rather than isolated in inner cities would help. Inexpensive, efficient public transportation would help. A guaranteed minimum income, such as Martin Luther King suggested in his speech to the Memphis sanitation workers the day before he was assassinated, would help. Earned Income Tax Credits do help the working poor and could be expanded.

Taking *Brown* seriously and really integrating schools would help. This would require overturning cases that subsequently made desegregation difficult, if not impossible, as I noted in chapter 1. State courts could use stricter scrutiny measures in examining the right to an education guaranteed in their state constitutions. Intermediate scrutiny would work, because it would require states to demonstrate that their policies did not have unintended effects on other important rights, so that local control would not trump gross and glaring inequities in school funding. State courts could also enforce their own equal protection clauses, pass their own civil rights legislation, and ensure equity for their citizens in many domains. There are other federal reforms that would help as well, such as enforcing fair housing laws, providing tuition help or rebates to certified teachers willing to teach in high-needs districts, and providing funding so that every child eligible for Head Start could receive services. Disallowing felony convictions to permanently disenfranchise voters would also help.

A comprehensive federal equal rights amendment could include the right to an education (see Appendix 7.1). In addition, the United States could ratify the United Nations Universal Declaration of Human Rights, which guarantees the right to an education. Indeed, inequitable education everywhere ought to be addressed if we truly desire a global society with enough equity to grant autonomy to all the world's peoples. If the United States complied with the rights guaranteed by the United Nations Declaration, then education would become a fundamental right. This could be done without ratifying the Declaration, although that seems silly. Either the United States supports human rights or it does not.

That these suggestions would be considered seriously is unlikely, especially in the present political climate where Americans seem willing to support a unilateral, preemptive strike to effect "regime change" in Iraq (that is, depose a foreign leader) contrary to international law, apparently without thinking about the moral, political, or economic cost, although that seems to be changing as the war wears on. There is plenty of work for dedicated reformers to do on the domestic front. Inequitable school funding contributes to the widening gap between rich and poor, which threatens the practice of genuine democracy here and elsewhere. It seems clear to me that the right to an education ought to be considered fundamental. I hope reformers can continue working toward equity in school finance as an important step to ensuring every child an equal opportunity to succeed, even in the face of other detrimental conditions that remain unaddressed. Education does have the power to raise individuals above their circumstances, even if it cannot cure all social ills.

Lessons Learned and Future Strategies

One of the first lessons to be learned is that school finance reform is not likely to arrive all in one piece, all at one time. Lacking instant revolution, small improvements are better than stagnation. Better than that is a plan for incremental improvement, phased in as reformers adapt and expand their goals. Who is responsible for school funding, what the outcomes of policy decisions are, and what is needed to improve the achievement of all children should be clear to the public. Until the causes of problems are apparent, people find it hard to take action. Society needs to develop a sense of the importance of social justice in a democracy. A culture that values diversity, education, intellectual and cultural freedom, discovery, creativity, and active involvement in the world is much more likely to seek and obtain educational reform.

School funding should aim at providing the best education possible, not unlovely goals such as a minimally adequate education, preparation for low-level service jobs, mere functional literacy, or merely being able to subsist. Retreating to the standard of providing an eighth-grade education is not supportable in these times. Such paltry goals do not inspire generosity, support for education, or innovation in teaching and learning. The joyful accomplishments of children and teachers do inspire such support and must be highlighted by the media. School- and teacher-bashing must become a political liability to any candidate for office. Education should be seen as the priority it is—that upon which our future depends. Instead of denigrating the uselessness of "throwing money at the schools," educators and citizens alike can generate excitement over the possibilities of reform: less crime, less unemployment, a higher standard of living, and most important, less waste of human potential.

Determining the cost of an excellent education should be possible. One method, the so-called "excellent schools" method, is to identify a successful school in an area and use it as the model, amending costs as required for inflation, geographical location, labor market factors, and student need. Another, the so-called "costing out" strategy, is to identify and price all the components of an excellent education, which again will vary by a number of factors according to needs and conditions.[97] On the former method, the pitfall is that the excellence so defined may well be below what is achievable. On the latter method, the pitfall is that there will be a tendency to underestimate the potential costs. Any method must be reviewed and adjusted periodically, as the Rozanski Report recommends. As Ontario's experience shows, funding that may have been close to adequate five years ago becomes grossly inadequate in the absence of adjustment. Ontario's experience shows that yearly adjustments are necessary. In New York, both the Zarb Commission and the Special Referees agree costs must be updated, but Ontario's experience indicates that every four or five years is not sufficient.

After assessing the cost, or perhaps before, educators and politicians must be able to link reforms to performance without destroying the reciprocity and spontaneity of good teaching and learning. The public will demand that the link be shown. The goal of transparency, in Ontario's reforms as elsewhere, is necessary to maintain public support. However, national or state test scores should not constitute a single standard for excellence. There are many other ways to provide accountability. Schools could be more open to clients, districts could promote community involvement and become involved themselves in their communities, teachers could plan projects that involve students in community activities, schools could provide day care for young children, after-school care for elementary school children, homework labs for older children, and even hot lunches for elders. Schools could become community centers; many already are.

School-funding reform should be depoliticized, as much as possible. New funding formulae should be transparent, fair, equitable, flexible, and adequate. Formulae should be reviewed frequently. If formulae are based on cost benchmarks, these must be updated in a timely fashion. If school funding remains the states' responsibility, the federal government must function reliably to help poor states provide as good an educational system as rich states. Spending should be adjusted for different needs, localities, costs, and, to some extent, local preferences. Money should be drawn from a large area to ameliorate the effects of geographical differences in communities' wealth; if not by state, perhaps by larger districts, even perhaps federally-funded according to a fair formula but spent under local control. Americans are very docile in paying their income taxes. Maybe schooling should be funded by these and military expenditures by property taxes. Formulae should allow for local control in spending, choice of programs, and setting of priorities, as long as these do not interfere with all children's right to an education. Capital improvement projects such as building and repair must be supported to the extent necessary in each community. Depoliticizing school funding may seem impossible, but people are generally not well informed about who controls spending on education and who sets policy. Having information may well help to correct people's misapprehensions. The president has little power over schooling, which diminishes as the federal share of the school budget shrinks. Imposing unfunded mandates is unpopular with those who can assess their impact properly. Indeed, the state of Vermont contemplated not abiding by the No Child Left Behind Act and foregoing its federal money, a paltry 4 percent to 8 percent, perhaps not even enough to cover the costs of the unfunded federal mandates for testing imposed by the Act. In April, 2005, the National Education Association (NEA) and school district co-plaintiffs in Michigan, Texas, and Vermont sued the government, challenging the additional costs of the No Child Left Behind Act (NCLB) in *Pontiac* v. *Spellings*. The law itself specifies that "nothing in the law mandates a state . . . to spend any funds or incur any costs not paid for under this act." United States district court Judge Bernard Friedman dismissed the charges on November 23, 2005.[98] The NEA plans to appeal.

Until society develops a sense of social justice, individuals will have to continue to seek redress for inequitable school funding in the courts. Post-*Rodriguez*, this means state courts. In New York, post-*Paynter*, this may mean new strategies, especially if the legislature addresses its reforms to New York City alone. If law-makers do this, they will spawn a series of additional lawsuits on behalf of other cities. A state constitutional right to a "meaningful high school education" cannot be limited to one city, as the Alliance for Quality Education rightly points out. Courts may not be the fastest or the best vehicle for school finance reform, but they are the vehicle of last resort. But, if a climate of support for education could arise, discrediting the Coleman Report, *A Nation at Risk*, and other education-bashing instrumentalities in our culture, courts might not need to hear claims that education is inadequate, inequitable, or underfunded, because it would not be so. Heeding the fiscally conservative view that spending money up front on education is cheaper and more reliable than spending more money later on incarceration might establish such a climate of support for public education. Early childhood education, with the gains made supported throughout a child's elementary school career, is significantly cheaper and more beneficial than imprisonment in adolescence or adulthood. Cutting off the school-to-prison pipeline is humane, cost-efficient, and good for society.

According to the Preamble of the Constitution, the federal government's purpose includes "to promote the general welfare." Unfortunately, since the Preamble enumerates no specific duties, legal cases are not brought under this clause. Nevertheless, I would argue that education promotes the general welfare more than any other government expenditure. Beach and Lindahl also suggest that the Ninth Amendment points to the existence of unenumerated rights.[99] The right to vote in federal elections has been construed as being among them; so could education. They also cite instances of official documents that speak of education as a "birthright."[100] Jurists argue that it is more likely that state constitutions could be amended than the federal constitution. Barring a reversal of *Rodriguez*, a federal equal rights amendment, however unlikely, could establish education as a fundamental right. An equal rights amendment (ERA) was introduced every year from 1923 to 1982. In June of 1982, after a long struggle, the ERA was stopped three states short of ratification. In July, it was reintroduced, and has been every year since.[101] The much more inclusive text I suggest seems even less likely to be ratified. Nevertheless, if we were to place justice above expediency, such an amendment would solve not only the funding inequities of the public schools but also other long-standing problems of equity and social justice. (See Appendix 7.1.)

In his dissent to *Rodriguez*, Thurgood Marshall argued that "interests" do not have to be explicitly guaranteed by the constitution to be considered "fundamental . . . [if] they are, to some extent, interrelated with constitutional guarantees."[102] Many rights considered fundamental would be impossible or difficult to guarantee without education. Surely a flourishing democracy would promote these rights as fully as possible through a lively critical literacy, rather than follow a narrow and unlovely ideal of mere functional literacy. Rights admitted to be fundamental include: the right to vote and serve on a jury (which can be abrogated by criminal conviction, but remains fundamental otherwise), the right to engage in interstate commerce (taken broadly, to participate in the economy), the right not to be subjected to involuntary servitude (taken broadly, the right to obtain meaningful work at a fair wage under decent conditions), the right to equal protection of the laws (which requires knowledge of what they are), the right to the privileges and immunities guaranteed to all citizens by states without abridgment (which requires knowledge of what they are and an understanding of when they are being violated), the right to free speech (which requires a good working vocabulary and critical thinking skills to be effective), the right to freedom of religion (which is enhanced if everyone understands the multiplicity of religious views that exist), and various legal protections, such as the right to privacy, the right to a writ of *habeas corpus,* the right not to incriminate oneself, and the rights not to be subjected to double jeopardy or suffer cruel and unusual punishment (which require that people know their rights, or at least recognize whether their lawyer or the court system is protecting them).

When such rights are acknowledged, either in politics or in law, inequitable school funding will become anathema. Until then, inequitable school is a national disgrace that sullies the name and practice of democracy. What is needed is a culture of excitement about education. Aiming for a world-class educational system stands a far better chance of evoking such excitement than aiming for a "minimally adequate" education, even though minimally adequate is better than inadequate. Aiming at the best for all children is an inspiring ideal, much more appealing than aiming to do better on tests than the next district, which could be accomplished by that district doing poorly. Cooperation for widespread improvement is a far better rallying cry than competition for limited rewards. During the civil rights movement, many people were inspired by the lyrics of a simple song, "We shall overcome, some day." Their lofty purpose of affirming that human dignity is the sole basis for respect of all people creates the meaning of the abstract principle, "all men and women are created equal." So too are all boys and girls. If we fail to provide them with the education they need to prosper, history will judge our democracy lacking. If we persist in seeking a divided world where some prosper and others fail, we ourselves shall have failed to achieve the simple principle on which this country was predicated.

According to Michael Fullan's complexity theory, reforms in one arena will undoubtedly have an impact on other areas, many of which will not be anticipated.[103] School-funding reform is undoubtedly complex. Reallocation of state money will affect other state expenditures, impose conditions under which the money is to be spent, and rearrange priorities. Furthermore, school-funding reform is only the beginning of school reform itself. Any money allocated must be used wisely. Which comes first? Do we wait to reform school funding until we know how to use it wisely? Or do we increase school funding and find out how to use it by monitoring the results of programs? Fullan's theory advises that, in any complex situation, people do not arrive at perfection of theory first, but develop approximations to their goals as they experiment with likely strategies, study the results, and refine their strategies in an endless cycle of learning. Careful experimentation of this sort will undoubtedly be necessary in reforming school funding, and even more necessary in the aftermath to achieve whole school reform, the goal of which, for Fullan, is closing the achievement gap. Complexity is not an insuperable problem, but a challenge that must be faced, for the sake of the children. If people wait to increase educational spending until they are sure that they know how to spend it to the best advantage, they will never start.

Equitable school funding? Complex, yes. Expensive, yes. But necessary, for the children's sake.

Appendixes

Appendix 2.1
The New York Constitution, Article XI, Education

Sec. 1.   The legislature shall provide for the maintenance and support of a system of free common schools, wherein all the children of this state may be educated.

Sec. 2.   The corporation created in the year one thousand seven hundred eighty-four, under the name of The Regents of the University of the State of New York, is hereby continued under the name of The University of the State of New York. It shall be governed and its corporate powers, which may be increased, modified or diminished by the legislature, shall be exercised by not less than nine regents.

Sec. 3.   Neither the state nor any subdivision thereof, shall use its property or credit or any public money, or authorize or permit either to be used, directly or indirectly, in aid or maintenance, other than for examination or inspection, of any school or institution of learning wholly or in part under the control or direction of any religious denomination, or in which any denominational tenet or doctrine is taught, but the legislature may provide for the transportation of children to and from any school or institution of learning.

Appendix 2.2
New York School Finance Litigation, 1973 to 2003

Case	Brought	Appealed	Outcome	Date
Levittown Union Free School District v. *Nyquist*	1973	*Levittown* SC (favorable), AD (dismissed), and COA (dismissal upheld; U.S. Supreme Court (refused to hear)	present school funding formula constitutional; no federal jurisdiction	1982
REFIT v. *Cuomo*	1992	*REFIT* SC, AD, COA (dismissed, dismissal upheld twice)	present school funding formula constitutional	1995
City v. *State*	1994	Charges dismissed, combined with *CFE Ia* and *Ib* at SC and AD	all charges dismissed, not reinstated, city cannot sue the state under soverign immunity	1995
CFE v. *State* (first round)	1994	*CFE Ia* SC (part of charges dismissed), *CFE Ib* AD (remaining charges dismissed), *CFE Ic* COA (case allowed to proceed to trial in 1995	some charges dismissed at SC, remaining dismissed at AD, some reinstated at COA, case can proceed to trial (round two), led to second round of CFE cases	1995
CFE v. *State* (second round)	1999	*CFE IIa* SC (favorable), *CFE IIb* AD (overturned); *CFE IIc* COA (remanded to Supreme Court [trial court] for implementation)	upheld at SC, dismissed at AD, upheld and remanded at COA, deadline July 2004; three-judge panel appointed; new deadline of July 2005; panel's findings appealed; appeal upheld, AD 2006	2003

Appendix 2.2
(*continued*)

Case	Brought	Appealed	Outcome	Date
AALDF v. *NY*	1998	all state and federal charges dismissed		1998
Caesar v. *Pataki*	2000	SC, case survived a challenge to dismiss; AD case dismissed	charges dismissed after *Sandoval,* *US SC* ruled that there is no private right to sue under implenting regulations of Civil Rights Act of 1964, appeal planned	2002
NYCLU v. *State*	2002	SC, charges dismissed	SURR list discretionary, minimally adequate facilities are OK (following *CFE IIb* AD)	2002
Paynter v. *State*	1999	SC, charges partly dismissed; AD, remaining charges dismissed; COA appeal denied	charges dismissed at all three levels, no inequitable funding means no remedy, civil rights not violated	2003

SC = Supreme Court (the trial court in NY); AD = Appellate Division; COA = Court of Appeals (the highest court in NY)

Appendix 7.1
A Proposed Equal Rights Amendment

This amendment is pursuant to constitutional guarantees of individual rights to life, liberty, and the pursuit of happiness and the parallel constitutional obligation of legislators to promote the general welfare. The right to life, liberty, and the pursuit of happiness (claimed in the Declaration of Independence and guaranteed by Constitutional Amendments XIV, XV, XIX, and XXVI) includes the implicit right not to be segregated from mainstream society on grounds of race, socioeconomic status, ethnicity, age, or sexual identity. Such segregation produces inherently unequal institutions, among them educational institutions.

Because human beings have an equal right to participate in a meaningful way in running their government and governing their own lives, they have a right to education; health care; child and elder care and maternity/paternity leave; basic necessities such as food, clothing, and shelter; meaningful work; a living wage; equal pay for equal work; decent and safe working conditions, including vacations; access to music, art, and culture; and an environment free of pollution, violence, and deprivation.

Therefore, no person in the United States shall be subject to discrimination in education, employment, housing, medical care, or social services on account of gender, race, ethnicity, religion, language, age, disabilities, health conditions, or sexual identity.

Because the safety of human society depends on these conditions being fully realized, legislators and judges have a double responsibility: (1) to ensure that individual rights are not violated and (2) to ensure that the general welfare of the people is promoted by appropriate acts of legislation and judicial review.

Notes

Preface

1. *Serrano* v. *Priest (Serrano I)*, No. 29820, 1971 Cal. LEXIS 273 at *619 (Cal. August 30, 1971).

2. *Brown* v. *Board of Educ. (Brown I)*, No. 1, 1954 U.S. LEXIS 2094 at *495 (U.S. May 17, 1954).

3. *Pennsylvania Ass'n for Retarded Children (PARC)* v. *Pennsylvania*, No. 71–42, 1972 U.S. Dist. LEXIS 13874 (E.D. Pa. May 5, 1972).

Chapter 1

1. John Locke, *Second Treatise of Government* (Indianapolis: Hackett, 1980, originally published in 1692), 111–112 (Section 222).

2. John Locke, *Some Thoughts on Education* (Hoboken, NJ: Bibliobytes eBook ISBN: 0585049432, originally published, 1692).

3. Mary Wollstonecraft, *A Vindication of the Rights of Women*, ed. Carol H. Poston (New York and London: W.W. Norton, 1975, originally published in 1792).

4. Vivien Jones, "A Bio-Bibliographical Note About Mary Wollstonecraft," http://www.futurenet.co.uk/Penguin/Academic/classics96/britclassisauthor.html (accessed 5/1/03).

5. John Stuart Mill, *On Liberty*, ed. Elizabeth Rappaport (Indianapolis: Hackett, 1978, originally published in 1859), 104–105.

6. The First Amendment contains the establishment clause. "Congress shall make no law respecting an establishment of religion, or prohibiting the free exercise thereof; or abridging the freedom of speech, or of the press; or the right of the people peaceably to assemble, and to petition the Government for a redress of grievances." U.S. Const. amend. I. The Fourteenth Amendment contains the due process and equal protection clauses. "All persons born or naturalized in the United States, and subject to the jurisdiction thereof, are citizens of the United States and of the State wherein they reside. No State shall make or enforce any law which shall abridge the privileges or immunities of citizens of the United States; nor shall any State deprive any person of life, liberty, or property, without due process of law; nor deny to any person within its jurisdiction the equal protection of the laws." U.S.

Const. amend XIV, § 1. Note, however, there is no mention of how, specifically, voting rights in federal elections shall be defined. States did then and still do define who shall be eligible to vote, within the parameters of the Voting Rights Act.

7. *Brown I,* 1954 U.S. LEXIS 2094, mandated desegregation, the cost of which was to be paid mostly by the districts affected. *PARC,* 1972 U.S. Dist. LEXIS 13874, mandated special education in the least restrictive environment, again to be paid for mostly by the states and districts. The Individuals with Disabilities Education Act (IDEA), 20 USCS §1400, *et seq.,* and the recent No Child Left Behind Act of 2001(NCLB), 20 USCS §6301, require states to provide educational services for which they bear much of the cost.

8. *In re Engel* v. *Vitale,* 1959 N.Y. Misc. LEXIS 3126 (N.Y. Sup. Ct. August 24, 1959).

9. Only Hawaii and Delaware have one district statewide.

10. *Brown I,* 1954 U.S. LEXIS 2094, at *494.

11. *Id.* at *495.

12. *Bolling* v. *Sharpe,* No. 8, 1954 U.S. LEXIS 2095 (U.S. May 17, 1954).

13. *Id.* at *499.

14. *Id.* at *498.

15. In *Goss* v. *Lopez,* No. 73-898, 1975 U.S. LEXIS 23 at *574 (U.S. Jan. 22, 1975), the Supreme Court ruled that school officials are required to adhere to minimum due process procedures, as required under the Due Process Clause, before a student is expelled from a public school, since expulsion deprives a student of his or her protected interests in property and liberty. This unfortunately has had little impact on school finance litigation.

16. The due process clause is found in the Fifth as well as the Fourteenth amendments: "No person shall be held to answer for a capital, or otherwise infamous crime, unless on a presentment or indictment of a Grand Jury, except in cases arising in the land or naval forces, or in the Militia, when in actual service in time of War or public danger; nor shall any person be subject for the same offense to be twice put in jeopardy of life or limb; nor shall be compelled in any criminal case to be a witness against himself, nor be deprived of life, liberty, or property, without due process of law; nor shall private property be taken for public use, without just compensation." U.S. Const. amend. The legal definition of what constitutes protected property is pertinent to education law, but *Goss* has, unfortunately, not influenced school funding litigation.

17. *San Antonio Indep. Sch. Dist.* v. *Rodriguez* (*Rodriguez*), 411 U.S. LEXIS 91, 56 (1973) at *38. Unfortunately, the interpretation of education as constitutionally protected "property" in *Goss* was overruled, in effect, by this case. The court concluded, "We have carefully considered each of the arguments supportive of the District Court' s finding that education is a fundamental right or liberty and have found those arguments unpersuasive. In one further respect we find this a particularly inappropriate case in which to subject state action to strict judicial scrutiny."

18. *Serrano I,* 1971 Cal. LEXIS 273.

19. *Id.* at *589.

20. *Rodriguez,* 1973 U.S. LEXIS 91 at *11.

21. Supra at note 18.

22. *Id.* at *28.

23. *Rodriguez,* 1973 U.S. LEXIS 91 at *130 (Marshall, J., dissenting).

24. *Id.* at *90.

25. *Id.* at *90.

26. *Kirby* v. *Edgewood Indep. Sch. Dist.,* No. 3-87-190-CV, 1988 Tex. App. LEXIS 3292 at *862 (Tex. App. December 14, 1988).

27. *Edgewood Indep. Sch. Dist.* v. *Kirby,* No. D-0378, 1991 Tex. LEXIS 21 (Tex. February 25, 1991).

28. Teresa Palomo Acosta, *"Edgewood ISD* v. *Kirby,"* in the Handbook of Texas Online, nd, http://www.tsha.utexas.edu/handbook/online/articles/view/EE/ire2.html (accessed 4/4/03).

29. *Robinson* v. *Cahill,* 1973 N.J. LEXIS 261, at *480 (N.J. April 3, 1973). Supplemental opinion at *Robinson* v. *Cahill,* 63 1973 N.J. LEXIS 173 (1973).

30. *Plessy* v. *Ferguson,* No. 210, 1896 U.S. LEXIS 3390 (U.S. May 18, 1896). The judges in *Plessy* ruled that the Thirteenth Amendment to the U.S. Constitution, abolishing slavery and involuntary servitude, is not violated by a state statute requiring separate accommodations for white and colored persons on railroads [and, by extension, elsewhere] at *551. Since the case concerned separate railway carriages for blacks and whites on an intrastate railway line, the Court ruled that the commerce clause does not forbid the practice, at *547.

31. *Brown* v. *Board of Educ. (Brown II),* No. 1, 1955 U.S. LEXIS 734 (U.S. May 31, 1955).

32. Gary Orfield, Susan Eaton et al., *Dismantling Desegregation: The Quiet Reversal of* Brown v. Board of Education (New York: The New Press, 1996). (Hereafter Orfield and Eaton, *Dismantling Desegregation*).

33. *Milliken* v. *Bradley (Milliken I),* No. 73-434, 1974 U.S. LEXIS 94 (U.S. July 25, 1974).

34. *Milliken* v. *Bradley (Milliken II),* No. 76-447, 1977 U.S. LEXIS 141 (U.S. June 27, 1977).

35. *Brown I,* 1954 U.S. LEXIS 2094, at *494.

36. *Rose* v. *Council for Better Education, Inc.,* No. 88-SC-804-TG, 1989 Ky. LEXIS 55 (Ky. June 8, 1989).

37. *Id.* at *212.

38. *Id.* at *121–213.

39. *Spallone* v. *United States; Longo* v. *United States; Chema* v. *United States; City of Yonkers* v. *United States,* Nos. A-172, A-173, A-174, A-175, 1988 U.S. LEXIS 3284 (U.S. September 1, 1988).

40. *Stone ex rel. Paynter* v. *New York (Paynter)* No. 75, 2003 N.Y. LEXIS 1672 (N.Y. June 26, 2003).

41. *Education Week,* Quality Counts: 2003, http://www.edweek.org/sreports/qc03/REPORTS/equity-t1.cfm (accessed 5/5/03). The table on resource equity lists only ten states: Hawaii, Utah, Delaware, New Mexico, Florida, Nevada, Arkansas, Minnesota, Oklahoma, and Kansas, as having a grade of B− or more for equity in resources.

42. *Board of Educ.* v. *Dowell,* No. 89-1080, 1991 U.S. LEXIS 484 (U.S. January 15, 1991).

43. Jennifer Jellison, "Study finds resegregated neighborhood schools in Oklahoma City fail to meet district promises of achievement and equity" (Harvard Graduate School of Education News, September 16, 1996), http://gseweb.harvard.edu/news/features/oklahomacity091611996.html (accessed 5/4/03). According to Jellison, "There is little evidence to support the claims about the benefit of neighborhood schools that the district set forth in court. The policies that appeared to 'work' reveal inequalities when the numbers are disaggregated between majority-black schools and the rest of the district's elementary schools. And the safeguards installed originally in the [neighborhood schools plan] to ensure [that] equity was maintained for the majority-black districts and that the district remained desegregated have all but disappeared" (np).

44. *Missouri* v. *Jenkins*, No. 93-1823, 1995 U.S. LEXIS 4041 (U.S. June 12, 1995).

45. Erica Frankenberg, Chungmei Lee, and Gary Orfield, "A Multiracial society with segregated schools: Are we losing the dream?" (Harvard Civil Rights Project, January 2003), http://www.civilrightsproject.harvard.edu (accessed 4/2/03). (Hereafter Frankenberg et al., Losing the dream).

46. *Sheff* v. *O'Neill*, No. 15255, 1996 Conn. LEXIS 239 (Conn. July 9, 1996).

47. The settlement reached in the *Sheff* case was threatened by 2003 Connecticut budget cuts. See Campaign for Fiscal Equity, Access, In the news, "Connecticut's *Sheff* v. *O'Neill* settlement in jeopardy," http://www/accessednetwork.org/states/ct/EndangeredSettlement5-2-03.htm (accessed 5/6/03).

48. Dennis R. Parker, "Racial and ethnic isolation post *Sheff* v. *O'Neill*," *Equity and Excellence in Education* 32, no. 2 (1999) 6–7.

49. Frankenberg et al., Losing the dream, 50.

50. James H. Carr, "The complexity of segregation: Why it continues 30 years after the Enactment of the Fair Housing Act," *Cityscape: A Journal of Policy Development and Research*, 4, no. 3 (1999), 140.

51. *Paynter*, History at *19 ff, review of other state rulings at fn.2, and discussion of segregated housing at *14–15.

52. Martin Carnoy, *School Vouchers: Examining the Evidence* (Economic Policy Institute, 2001) especially 12–20 (for new research), but the whole book is pertinent to this question.

53. Katrina Bulkley and Jennifer Fisler, "A Review of the Research on Charter Schools" (Consortium for Policy Review in Education, Philadelphia, June 2002) ERIC, EA 023 580, accessed 02/10/04.

54. Brea Willingham, "Parents go to court to improve kids' schooling; Albany School districts in Albany, New York City named in filing that aims to secure better services," *Albany Times Union*, January 28, 2003, Capital Region, p. 81. LexisNexis news (accessed 5/6/03).

55. Helen Gao, "Willing to stay behind? Students pass on chance to transfer from failing schools," *The Daily News of Los Angeles*, Friday, February 7, 2003, Valley Edition, News, p. 11, LexisNexis news (accessed 5/6/03).

56. Richard D. Kahlenberg, "Mixing classes: Why economic desegregation holds the key to school reform," *Washington Monthly Journal* online, December 2002, http://www.washingtonmonthly.com/features/2000/0012.kahlenberg.html (accessed 5/2/03) 4. See also Martin Carnoy, "Vouchers are no cure-all for short-

changed schools" (Economic Policy Institute, October 6, 2000), http://www. epinet.org/content.cfm/webfeatures_viewpoints_vouchers (accessed 5/6/03). See also Bernadette Medige, "The privatization of public education, Part 1 and Part 2," *Buffalo Report*, April 19 and May 2, 2003, http://buffaloreport.com/articles/ 030419medige.html and http://buffaloreport.com/articles/030502medige.html (accessed 5/2/03).

57. See Jean Anyon, *Ghetto schooling: A Political Economy of Urban Educational Reform* (New York: Teachers College Press, 1997) and Sue Books, "School funding: Justice v. equity" (*Equity & Excellence in Education*, 32:2, December 1999), 53–58.

58. Henry Louis Gates Jr., "America Beyond The Color Line" (PBS documentary, aired February 5–8, 2004).

59. Health and Human Services, "The 2002 Health and Human Services Poverty Guidelines," http://aspe.os.dhhs.gov/poverty/02poverty.htm (accessed 5/8/03).

60. Barbara Ehrenreich and Francis Fox Piven, "Without a Safety Net: Welfare reform was supposed to free poor mothers from dependency and get them into the job market. But what happens when the jobs are gone?" (*Mother Jones*, July/August 2001), http://www.motherjones.com/magazine/MJ02/without_ safety.html (accessed 5/7/03).

61. Kim Phillips-Fein, "The education of Jessica Rivera," *The Nation*, November 25, 2002, 20–24. See also Barbara Ehrenreich and Francis Fox Piven, "Who's Utopian Now?" *The Nation*, February 4, 2002, http://www.thenation. com/doc.mhtml?i=20020204&s=ehrenreich (accessed 5/5/03).

62. Ehrenreich and Piven, "Without a Safety Net."

63. John Jay, James Madison, and Alexander Hamilton, *The Federalist Papers* (New York: New American Library, 1961), 77.

64. Christopher Jencks and Meredith Phillips, "America's next achievement test: Closing the black-white test score gap," *American Prospect*, no. 40 (September–October 1998) Infotrac (accessed 4/2/03) 1–2.

65. Conference: The Supreme Court, racial politics, and the right to vote: *Shaw* v. *Reno* and the future of the Voting Rights Act, *American University Law Review* 44:1 (Fall 1994) LexisNexis legal research (accessed 5/8/03).

66. Kristen Safier, "The Question of a Fundamental Right to a Minimally Adequate Education," *University of Cincinnati Law Review* 69 (Spring 2002), 993–1022. Despite *Rodriguez's* ruling that inequitable funding is not unconstitutional in 1973, in *Plyler* v. *Doe*, 457 United States 202, 45 U.S. 582 (1983), the court ruled that excluding immigrant children from education entirely in Texas "can hardly be considered rational unless it furthers some substantial goal of the State," which the court was convinced it did not. *Plyler* at *223–224.

67. Edmund Burke, *Reflections on the French Revolution* (Harvard Classics, vol. 24, Collier, 1909), 183.

68. David Tyack and Larry Cuban, "Why the Grammar of Schooling Persists," chap. 4, *Tinkering Toward Utopia: A Century of Public School Reform* (Cambridge, Mass.: Harvard University Press, 1995), 85–109.

69. William E. Thro, "Judicial analysis during the third wave of school finance litigation: The Massachusetts decision as a model, *Boston College Law Review* 35 (1994), 597–598 n. 4. The three waves are: 1) equality cases focusing on

the federal equal protection clause (*Serrano I*, 1971, to *Rodriguez*, 1974; 2) equity cases focusing on state equal protection and education clauses (from *Robinson* v. *Cahill*, 1973, to *Rose*, 1989); and 3) equity focusing on education clauses; and 4) adequacy cases (the latter added by Kevin Randall McMillan), which were based on inputs initially, but have lately been based, at least in part, on outcomes (*Campaign for Fiscal Equity* v. *State*, 2003). A fifth wave may be identified as civil rights cases, but these will have to be pursued in state courts, post *Rodriguez*, and have been made difficult, if not impossible, by *Sandoval* v. *Alexander* (2003), see chapter 2.

70. For example, Connecticut (weak clause), good decision, little action, followed by a second case, same result; New York (weak clause), good trial court decisions, overturned on appeal until 2003, court-mandated reform not implemented after thirty years of litigation; New Jersey (strong clause), good court decisions, but much resistance on the part of the legislature over many years, reforms finally implemented after roughly thirty years of litigation.

71. For example, South Dakota, Oregon, Idaho.

72. For example, Kentucky and Vermont, although Vermont made reforms in 1997, changed them in 2000, and changed them again in 2005, before their effectiveness was clear.

73. Kentucky.

74. New Jersey.

75. For instance, Justice DeGrasse's template in *Campaign for Fiscal Equity* at the trial court.

76. Hanushek, E. A., "Throwing Money at the Schools," *Journal of Policy Analysis and Management* 1, 19–41.

77. For instance, in New York in 2003, the state was forced to throw out the results of a flawed math test, which, if retained, would have prevented many students from graduating. Heather Hare, "Testing standards put to a test," *The Rochester Democrat and Chronicle* (June 29, 2003), A, 1, 10.

78. Richard Rothstein, "Where's the money going? Changes in level and composition of education spending, 1991–1996," Washington, D.C., Economic Policy Institute, 1997. 1–2. Rothstein accounts for increased enrollment, increased spending on special education, and inflation using the Net Services Index rather than the Consumer Price Index, since schooling is a labor-intensive, low-productive endeavor. He found that school spending was relatively stable 1991–1996, growing only 0.7%. During that time, the share spent on regular education declined from 58.5% to 56.8%.

79. Thomas Kuhn, *The Structure of Scientific Revolutions* (Chicago: University of Chicago Press, 1970). Kuhn's thesis is that new paradigms in science come from outside the boundaries of "normal" science.

80. Bruce J. Biddle, "Foolishness, dangerous nonsense, and real correlates of state differences in achievement," *Phi Delta Kappan* articles online (September 1997), http://www.pdkintl.org/kappan/kbid9709.htm (accessed 4/2/03).

81. John Dewey, "School and Society" in Archambault, Reginald D., ed., *John Dewey on Education* (Chicago: University of Chicago Press, 1964), 295.

82. These items I compiled from thought and reading, as well as the templates found in the Kentucky decision in *Rose* and in DeGrasse's decision in New

York. See also, Jane Fowler Morse, "The Ends of Education" (*Educational Change*, Spring 1996), 1–26.

83. *Levittown* v. *Nyquist,* 1982 N.Y. LEXIS 3535 (N.Y. June 23, 1982).

84. Defendants-Respondents' [Campaign for Fiscal Equity] Brief to the Court of Appeals, New York, http://www.accessednetwork.org (accessed 5/8/03) 2. Defendants' argument was accepted by the New York Appellate Division, First Department in *Campaign for Fiscal Equity, Inc. (CFE IIb)* v. *New York,* No. 5330, 2002 N.Y. App. Div. LEXIS 7252 (N.Y. App. Div. June 25, 2002). See chapter 2, "The Crisis in New York" for a full history of the New York cases.

85. Beth Reinhardt, "California's cities face staggering problems, but urban schools get little extra help from Sacramento," *Education Week on the Web,* http://www.edweek.org/sreports/qc98/states/ca-n.htm (accessed 7/24/03).

86. Powell v. Ridge, No. 98-1223, 1998 U.S. Dist. LEXIS 22328 at *42 (E.D. Pa. Nov. 18, 1998). Writing for the court, Judge Herbert J. Hutton found that disparate impact did not apply: "The Plaintiffs assert, in substance, that the discriminatory impact arises because the uniformly applied state formula for allocating basic education funds among the 501 school districts does not bring about the same result in Philadelphia as it might in another, more affluent district, because of Philadelphia's special needs. The Plaintiffs' factual allegations, even when assumed to be true for purposes of this motion, do not, as a matter of law, state a disparate-impact claim. The Plaintiffs' Complaint is merely a 'we-need-more-money' allegation of a type that has been held non-actionable." The Court dismissed the complaint on that basis.

87. *Sandoval, individually and ex rel. all others similarly situated* v. *Hagan,* No. 98-6598, 1999 U.S. App. LEXIS 30722 (11th Cir. Nov. 30, 1999),

88. For a full discussion of this issue see the analysis of *Alexander* v. *Sandoval* in chapter 2. *Sandoval* v. *Hagan* became *Sandoval* v. *Alexander* on appeal due to a change in the state's Attorney General.

89. *Alexander* v. *Sandoval, Individually and ex rel. all others similarly situated,* No. 99-1908, 2001 U.S. LEXIS 3367 (U.S. April 24, 2001).

90. *Brown I,* 1954 U.S. LEXIS 2094, at *493, "Such an *opportunity,* where the state has undertaken to provide it, is a right which must be made available to all on *equal* terms" (emphasis added).

91. State Reply Brief in *CFE IIc,* "However, the proper standard is that the state must offer all children the opportunity of a sound, basic education; not *ensure* that they receive it" (emphasis in the original), http://cfequity.org (accessed 5/11/03), 26.

92. *Campaign for Fiscal Equity, Inc., Respondents* v. *State of New York et al., Appellants,* No. 74, The Court of Appeals of New York, 2003, LEXIS N.Y. 1678 (*CFE IIc,* Court of Appeals) at *66–67. For a full account of the Campaign for Fiscal Equity cases, see chapter 2.

93. Michael Heise contends that the combination of the excellence movement (standards and testing) and school funding litigation is dangerous and may have a dampening effect on reform of educational policy on account of the possibility of lawsuits based on students' not reaching high standards. Michael Heise, "Symposium: Children and education: Tensions within the parent-child-state

relationship triad: The courts, educational policy, and unintended consequences," *Cornell Journal of Law and Public Policy* 11 (2002): 633–662.

94. Anemona Hartocollis, "An advantage for seasoned students," *New York Times,* December 20, 2001, Late Edition, Sec. D; p. 3; col. 4, LexisNexis news (accessed 5/12/03). See also Kathleen Kennedy Manzo, "Urban students lag in reading and writing, NAEP scores show," *Education Week* on the Web, July 22, 2003, http://edweek.org (accessed 7/25/03).

95. Helen F. Ladd and Janet S. Hansen, *Making Money Matter: Financing America's Schools* (Washington, DC: National Academy Press, 1999), 12.

96. Peter Schrag, "High stakes are for tomatoes," *Atlantic Monthly,* August 2000, http://www.theatlantic.com/issues/2000/08/schrag.htm (accessed 5/11/03).

97. *Pontiac* v. *Spellings,* Civil Action No. 05-CV-71535-DT, 2005 U.S. Dist. LEXIS 29253 (Nov. 23, 2005) at *12.

98. George D. Strayer and Robert Murray Haig, *The Financing of Education in the State of New York: A Report Reviewed and presented by the Educational Finance Inquiry Commission under the Auspices of the American Council on Education,* Washington, DC (New York: Macmillan, 1923) 176.

99. John E. Coons, William H. Clune III, and Stephen D. Sugarman. *Private Wealth and Public Education* (Cambridge, MA: Harvard University Press, Belknap Press, 1970).

100. I cover this topic more fully in chapter 4, "Executive Reform in Ontario."

101. Peter Van Harten, "Rebel trustees meet to plan battle; But ex-Ottawa board chair denounces deficit-budget scheme as credibility killer," *Hamilton Spectator,* August 14, 2002, A07.

102. Abby Goodnough, "Consensus on City schools: Overview; Mayor wrests control of city schools under tentative deal," *New York Times,* June 7, 2002, A1, LexisNexis news (accessed 5/11/03).

103. I cover this topic fully in chapter 2, "The Crisis in New York."

104. Defendants-Respondents' Reply Brief in *CFE IIb,* 4, http://www.cfequity.org (accessed 5/10/03).

105. *Alexander* v. *Sandoval,* No. 98-1908, 2001 U.S. LEXIS 3367 (U.S. April 24, 2001). *Sandoval* v. *Hagan,* No. 96-D-1875-N, 1998 U.S. Dist. LEXIS 8301 (M.D. Ala. June 3, 1998); *Sandoval* v. *Hagan,* No. 98-6598, 2000 U.S. App. LEXIS 10896 (11th Cir. Nov. 30, 1999).

106. *Brigham* v. *Vermont,* No. 96-502, 1997 Vt. LEXIS 13 (Vt. Feb. 5, 1997).

107. Peter Teachout, "'No simple disposition: The *Brigham* case and the future of local control over school spending in Vermont," *Vermont Law Review,* 22:1 (Fall 1997), 21–24.

108. Lorna Jimerson, "A Reasonably Equal Share: Educational Equity in Vermont" (February 2001) and "Still A Reasonably Equal Share: Update on Educational Equity in Vermont Year 2001–2002," The Rural School and Community Trust, February 21, 2002, www.ruraledu.org/publications.html (accessed 5/12/03).

109. For more detail on school finance litigation in Vermont see chapter three, "Sharing in Vermont."

110. Erik Ness, "Getting the lead out: Students, toxins, and environmental racism," *Rethinking Schools* 18:2 (Winter 2003), 18–21.

111. George Counts, "A call to the teachers of the nation" (New York: John Day Company, 1933). See also David Tyack and Larry Cuban, *Tinkering Toward Utopia: A Century of Public School Reform* (Cambridge: Harvard University Press, 1995) and Sandford W. Reitman, *The Educational Messiah Complex: American Faith in the Culturally Redemptive Power of Schooling* (Sacramento, Calif.: Caddo Gap Press, 1992).

Chapter 2

1. *Campaign for Fiscal Equity, Inc. (CFE IIc), Respondents* v. *State of New York et al., Appellants*, No. 74, The Court of Appeals of New York, 2003, N.Y. LEXIS 1678.

2. *Stone ex rel Paynter (Paynter)* v. *New York*, No. 75, 2003 N.Y. LEXIS 1672 (N.Y. June 26, 2003).

3. Joel S. Berke, Margaret E. Goertz, and Richard J. Coley, *Politicians, Finance, and City Schools: Reforming School Finance in New York* (New York: Russell Sage Foundation,1984) 2–3. (Hereafter Berke, et al., *Politicians*).

4. Strayer, George D., and Robert Murray Haig, *The Financing of Education in the State of New York: A Report Reviewed and Presented by the Educational Finance Inquiry Commission under the auspices of The American Council on Education*, Washington, D.C. (New York: Macmillan, 1923), 176. (Hereafter Strayer and Haig, *Financing*).

5. Austin D. Swanson, "The Effects of Chronic Retrenchment," in Paul R. Mort, ed., Director of Staff Studies, *A New Approach to School Finance: 1961 Review of Fiscal Policy for Public Education in New York State* (New York State Educational Conference Board: New York, September 1, 1961), 3 (Hereafter Mort).

6. John. W. Polley, "Variations in Impact of Municipal Government on Ability to Support Schools" in Mort, 22–34.

7. Swanson, "Effects," in Mort, 16.

8. Clarence H. Tompkins, "Nature of the Burgeoning Municipal Government," in Mort, 35–43.

9. Austin D. Swanson, "The Small School Correction," in Mort, 44–50.

10. George R. Sullivan, "A Proposed Plan for Distribution of State Aid for Education In New York," in Mort, 51–56.

11. Sullivan, "Proposed Plan," in Mort, 55–56.

12. By the 1970s, Coons, Clune, and Sugarman addressed the same problem. Their proposed "power equalizing formula" would tie the tax effort a district is willing to make to the amount of state aid the district was eligible to receive. John E. Coons, William H. Clune III, Stephen D. Sugarman, *Private wealth and public education* (Cambridge, MA: Harvard University Belknap Press, 1970).

13. Berke et al., *Politicians*, 4–5.

14. Karl Widerquist, "Checkerboard II: An Analysis of Tax Effort, Equalization, and Extraordinary Aid," Educational Policies Panel (February 2001), http://www.cdpriorities.org/Pubs/pubs.html (10/24/02) 1.

15. H. Carl McCall, "School Finance Reform, A Discussion Paper," State Comptroller's Office (October 1995), http://www.osc.state.ny.us/reports/schools/1995/10-95.htm (accessed 10/28/02) (no pagination).

16. *Levittown* v. *Nyquist (Levittown)*, 1982 N.Y. LEXIS 3535 at *51–52 (N.Y. June 23, 1982).

17. *Id.* at *52.

18. *Rochester Board of Educ.* v. *Nyquist* and *Levittown Board of Educ.* v. *Nyquist,* No. 82-639; No. 82-655, 1983 U.S. LEXIS 3048 (U.S. Jan. 17, 1983) (Rochester City School District was one of the Intervenor-Plaintiffs in the case.)

19. *Alexander* v. *Sandoval (Sandoval), individually and ex rel. all others similarly situated,* No. 99-1908, 2001 U.S. LEXIS 3367 (U.S. April 24, 2001).

20. *Id.* at *303 (Stevens, J. dissenting).

21. *University of California* v. *Bakke,* No. 76-811, 1978 U.S. LEXIS 5 (U.S. June 28, 1978).

22. *Sandoval,* 2001 U.S. LEXIS 3367 at *286–287. The Court seems to admit that this is a change in strategy, but contends that the strategy of the "ancien regime," of forty years ago had long since been abandoned. Topping this sweeping declaration off with a little joke, the court noted, "Having sworn off the habit of venturing beyond Congress's intent, we will not accept respondents' invitation to have one last drink."

23. The Campaign for Fiscal Equity cases went through the courts twice. The first set is referred to collectively as *Campaign for Fiscal Equity I or CFE I.* These were combined with *City* v. *State* at the trial court and the Appellate Division. In the Court of Appeals, *CFE I* was tried separately and allowed to go to trial, whereas *City* v. *State* was dismissed. This case is referred to as *CFE/1995.* This case allowed *Campaign for Fiscal Equity* to be tried. In New York the trial court is the Supreme Court, next is the Appellate Division, and the highest court is the Court of Appeals. This set of cases collectively is referred to as *CFE II.* In my text, I will designate Supreme Court cases Ia or IIa, Appellate Division cases Ib or IIb, and Court of Appeals cases Ic or IIc.

24. *Campaign for Fiscal Equity (CFE IIb)* v. *New York,* 2002 N.Y. App. Div. LEXIS 7252 at *24 (N.Y. June 25, 2002).

25. "New York has the widest gap between rich and poor – study," *Rochester Democrat and Chronicle,* April 24, 2002, http://www.cbpp.org/1-18-oostfp.htm (accessed 9/01/02).

26. Anemona Hartocollis, "Racial gap in test scores found across New York," *New York Times* on the Web, March 28, 2002, http://www.nytimes.com/2002/03/28/education/28SCOR.html (accessed April 10, 2002). According to the article, in eighth grade English statewide, 55% of whites met standards, compared with 24% of blacks, 26% of Hispanics, and 59% of Asians. In the city, figures were 57% of whites, 24% of blacks, 25% of Hispanics, and 56% of Asians. In eighth-grade math, 52% of whites met standards statewide, 13% of blacks, 16% of Hispanics, and 58% of Asians. In the city, only 45% of whites met standards, 12% of blacks, 14% of Hispanics, and 54% of Asians. These figures are averages that included the schools that did well. In individual low-performing schools, figures were much lower.

27. Kathleen Kennedy Manzo, "Urban students lag in reading and writing NAEP scores show," *Education Week* on the Web, Web Extra, 7/22/03, http://www.edweek.org (accessed 7/25/03).

28. Erica Frankenburg and Chungmei Lee, "Race in American Public Schools: Rapidly Resegregating School Districts," the Harvard Civil Rights Project, August 2002, http://www.law.harvard.edu/groups/civilrights/publications/reseg_districts02/synopsis.html (accessed 9/20/02). Frankenburg and Lee give the following comparisons in various tables: New York was second only to Baltimore in the lowest black exposure to whites at 6.6% in 2000 (p. 19). New York is in sixth place for the lowest exposure of Latinos to whites (p. 21). Between 1988–2000, New York City dropped from 9.8% exposure of blacks to whites to 6.6% with no desegregation plan in place (p. 13).

29. Bruce Lambert, "Study calls L.I. most segregated suburb," *New York Times*, June 5, 2002, B5, LexisNexis News (accessed 9/20/02).

30. In *Education Week's* Quality Counts Issue of 2000, New York had an equity indicator of 56, which gave it a grade of F. Only five other states were worse in that year. One of those, Vermont, reformed its school funding system in 1997 through its Act 60, with greater equity as the result, http://www.edweek.org/sreports/qc00/tables/equity-tl.htm (accessed 10/22/01). By 2001, New York dropped to the next to the last on equity measures, surpassed only by New Hampshire, which is also currently working on the problem. http://edweek.org/sreports/qc01/tables/equity-tlb.htm (accessed 9/12/02). The 2002 Quality Counts issue focused on early childhood; New York got special mention as one of three states that is phasing in universal pre-K regardless of family income.http://edweek.org/sreports/qc02/templates/article.cfm?slug=17exec.h21 (accessed 9/20/02). As laudable as it is, this is not an equalizing measure. For equity measures for any year, see the appropriate Quality Counts issues in the archives, http://www.edweek.org. By the 2004 Quality Counts issue, New York had worked its way up to a C- with an equity indicator of 71.

31. Lynn Olson, "The great divide" (*Education Week* on the Web, Quality Counts 2003), http://www.edweek.org/sreports/qc03 (accessed 7/26/03).

32. Diane Jean Schemo, "Neediest Schools Receive Less Money, Report Finds," *New York Times* on the Web, August 9, 2002. LexisNexis News (accessed 9/10/02).

33. Kevin Carey, The Funding Gap: Many States Still Shortchange Low-income and Minority Students (The Education Trust, 2004) and The Funding Gap, 2005, The Education Trust, Winter 2005, Table 1, page 3, http://www.edtrust2.org (accessed 3/14/06).

34. The Funding Gap, 2005, Table 2, page 5, and Table 3, page 6.

35. Brennan, *The Funding Gap* (The Education Trust, 2002), http://www.2edtrust.org (14 March 2006), 3 and The Funding Gap, 2005.

36. Manzo, Urban students lag.

37. Chuck Collins, Chris Hartman, and Holly Sclar, "Divided Decade: Economic Disparities at the Century's Turn," December 15, 1999, United for a Fair Economy, http://www.faireconomy.org/press/archive/1999/Divided_Decade/divided_decade.html (accessed 9/27/02).

38. United States Census Bureau, *Income, Poverty, and Health Insurance Coverage in the United States: 2003,* http://www.census.gov/hhes/www/income.html (accessed 6/17/05).

39. National Center for Children in Poverty, Data Wizard, http://www.nccp.org/wizard/wizard.cgi (accessed 6/20/05).

40. "Census: Poverty Rises, Income Falls," *New York Times* on the Web, September 25, 2002, http://www.nytimes.com/aponline/national/AP-Poverty.html (accessed 9/25/02). Child poverty is defined as all children under 18 years of age living under the federal poverty guidelines. According to the Department of Health and Human Services's website, poverty guidelines are $18,100 for a family of four, http://aspe.hhs.gov/poverty/02poverty.htm (accessed 9/28/02). For a review of the devastating impact of the increasing income gap nationwide, see Holly Sklar, "Poverty up, income down, except for the top five percent," Knight Ridder/Tribune News Service, September 30, 2002, http://dsausa.org/lowage/lowwage.html (accessed 10/17/02).

41. Paul Scherrer, "One in four US children under six live in poverty" July 22, 1998, World Socialist Web Site, http://www/wsws.org/news/1998/july 1998/pov-jul22.shtml (accessed May 5, 2003).

42. Children's Defense Fund, "Updated children in the states." January 2003, http://www.childrensdefensefund.org/states/all_states.pdf (accessed 7/26/03).

43. Drake Bennett, "Freedom to fail: The false flexibility of the President's welfare plan" (*The American Prospect,* April, 2003) http://www.prospect.org/print/V14/4/bennett-d.html (accessed 7/25/03).

44. Marion Wright Edelman, quoted in "More Black children living in extreme poverty" (Associated Press, May 1, 2003, Washington), http://www.rochersterdandc.com/news/forprint/0501stort4_news.shtml (accessed 7/26/03).

45. National Center for Children in Poverty, "Basic facts about low income children: Birth to age 18," National Center for Children in Poverty Web site, July 2005, http://www.nccp.org (accessed 7/31/05).

46. 104 P.L. 193.

47. Kim Phillips-Fein, "The Education of Jessica Rivera: Trading in their Books for Buckets, Welfare Recipients Learn 'Responsibility'" (*The Nation,* 275:18, November 5, 2002), 20–23.

48. The 2003 reauthorization of TANF funding has been under debate for a year. In 2002, the House passed a version that included the president's desired 40-hour work week, as well as other provisions likely to deprive the program of more funding. The Senate balked, passed its own version requiring 30 hours, to which the House responded with a bill almost identical to their earlier version. The bill is waiting for agreement on provisions as of this writing.

49. Drake Bennett, Freedom to fail, 18.

50. National Center for Children in Poverty, Research Forum on Children, Families, and the New Federalism: Relationships Between Child Welfare and Child Well-Being: A Research and Policy Discussion, October 2001, www.research forum.org., press release available at http://www.nccp.org/pub_ssu02i. html (accessed 7/28/03).

51. Personal Responsibility and Individual Development for Everyone Act (PRIDE), Committee Reports, 108th Congress, 1st Session, Senate Report 108–162, 108 S. Rpt. 162, LexisNexis Congressional (accessed 11/21/03).

52. Jennifer Mezey, Sharon Parrott, Mark Greenberg, and Shawn Fremsadt, "Reversing direction on welfare reform: President's budget cuts childcare for more than 300,000 children," Center on Budget and Policy Priorities, February 10, 2004, http://www.cbpp.org (accessed 2/15/04).

53. United States Department of Health and Human Services. Temporary Assistance for Needy Families, Program Instruction (No. TANF-ACF-PI-2005-01), April 14, 2005, http://www.acf.dhhs.gov/programs/ofa/pi-ofa/pi2005-1.htm (accessed 6/17/05).

54. For information and analysis of the ongoing TANF debate see Center on Budget and Policy Priorities, available at http://www.centeronbudget.org (last accessed 6/17/05).

55. *Board of Educ.* v. *Nyquist,* 1978 N.Y. Misc. LEXIS 2270 (N.Y. Sup. Ct. June 23, 1978).

56. *Board of Educ.* v. *Nyquist,* 1981 N.Y. App. Div. LEXIS 14777 (N.Y. App. Div. Oct. 26, 1981).

57. *Board of Educ.* v. *Nyquist,* 1982 N.Y. LEXIS 3535 (N.Y. June 23, 1982).

58. *Id.* at *44, n. 5.

59. *Reform Educational Financing Inequities Today (REFIT,* Appellate Division*)* v. *Cuomo,* No. 92-08663, 1993 N.Y. App. Div. LEXIS 12346 (N.Y. App. Div. June 15, 1995).

60. *Reform Educational Financing Inequites Today (REFIT,* Court of Appeals) v. *Cuomo,* No. 2, 1995 N.Y. LEXIS 1137 (N.Y. June 15, 1995).

61. *Campaign for Fiscal Equity Inc. (CFE Ia)* v. *New York,* and *City of New York* v. *New York (City* v. *State),* Nos. 111070/93 and 401210/93, 1994 N.Y. Misc. LEXIS 418 (N.Y. Sup. Ct. June 21, 1994).

62. I am not sure why this ruling holds in the face of the city's Title VI claim, especially before *Sandoval.* One of the exceptions is if the state forces the city to do something unconstitutional. Discrimination is unconstitutional, by both the New York and U.S. Constitutions.

63. *CFE/City* v. *State,* 1994 N.Y. Misc. LEXIS 418 at *498.

64. *Campaign for Fiscal Equity, Inc. (CFE Ib)* v. *New York* and *City of New York* v. *New York (City* v. *State,* Appellate Division) Nos. 52842 and 52843, 1994 N.Y. App. Div. LEXIS 11329 (N.Y. App. Div. Nov. 15, 1994).

65. *Campaign for Fiscal Equity (CFE/1995)* v. *New York,* No. 117A, 1995 N.Y. LEXIS 1145 (N.Y. June 15, 1995).

66. *City of New York* v. *New York (City* v. *State)* No. 117B, 1995 N.Y. LEXIS 1144 (N.Y. June 15, 1995).

67. *African Am. Legal Defense Fund ex rel (named) students of the New York City Pub. Sch. System and their Parents (AALDF),* v. *New York State Dep't. of Educ.* No. 95 Civ. 3039 (RO), 1998 U.S. Dist. LEXIS 8496 (S.D. N.Y. June 8, 1998).

68. *Id.* at *334.

69. *Hans* v. *Louisiana,* No. 4, 1890 U.S. LEXIS 1943 (U.S. Mar. 3, 1890).

70. *AALDF* at *335.

71. John Devine, *Maximum Security: The Culture of Violence in Inner-city Schools* (Chicago and London: University of Chicago Press, 1996).

72. *AALDF* at *336.

73. *Ceasar [sic]* v. *Pataki (Caesar* v. *Pataki)*, No, 98 Civ. 8532, 2002 U.S. Dist. LEXIS 5098 (S.D. N.Y. March 25, 2002). [In the Lexis entry, the name Caesar is misspelled as Ceasar.]

74. The NYCLU did not include New York City children in the suit, since a case was already underway on their behalf in *Campaign for Fiscal Equity* v. *State.* New York Civil Liberties Union, Litigation Docket, http://www.nyclu.org/docket.html (accessed 9/23/02).

75. Bruce Lambert, "Study calls L.I. Most Segregated Suburb," *New York Times,* June 5, 2002, B5. See also Tom Walsh, "Harvard Study Points to Segregation in the Suburbs," *Boston Herald,* May 31, 2002, http://www.bostonherald.com/news/local_regional/segr05312002.htm (accessed 9/20/02).

76. *Caesar* v. *Pataki* at *2.

77. *Id.* at *4.

78. *Graus ex rel. Graus, individually and ex rel all others similarly situated* v. *Kaladjian,* 93 Civ. 3743 (JSR), 1998 U.S. Dist. LEXIS 6020 (S.D. N.Y. April 28, 1998). In *Graus,* Judge Jed S. Rakoff ruled that a plaintiff may not challenge the due process procedures of the hearing under 42 U.S.C. § 1983.

79. New York Civil Liberties Union, In the Courts, (NYCLU Web site) available at http://www.nyclu.org/docket.html (accessed 7/3/03).

80. *New York Civil Liberties Union (NYCLU,* Appellate Division) v. *New York,* No. 93834, 2004 N.Y. App. Div. LEXIS 881 at *811 (N.Y. App. Div. Jan. 29, 2004). (Plaintiffs' action for declaratory judgment and injunctive relief denied. Tesesi, J., Albany Co. N.Y. Sup. Ct. July 10, 2002.)

81. American Civil Liberties Union, "N.Y.C.L.U. Announces Plan to Appeal Decision in Important School Reform Case" NYCLU Web site, http://www.aclu.org/news/n120398a.html (accessed 8/28/02) n.p.

82. *"New York Civil Liberties Union* v. *State of New York,* Decision of interest" *New York Law Review* 228 (July 11, 2002) 24, LexisNexis legal research (accessed 10/28/03).

83. Bruce Schneider, Kevin J. Curnin, Jennifer Lallite, and Joseph E. Strauss, *"Caesar* v. *Pataki"* Litigation Docket, NYCLU Web site, http://www.nyclu.org/docket.html (accessed 8/4/03).

84. Campaign for Fiscal Equity, *"CFE* v. *State of New York:* An analytic overview of the Court of Appeals decision," http://www.cfequity.org (accessed 6/8/03).

85. Maria Behncke, Alliance for Quality Education, Personal communication with the author, July 31, 2003.

86. *New York Civil Liberties Union (NYCLU)* v. *New York,* No. 93834, 2004 N.Y. App. Div. LEXIS 881 (N.Y. App. Div. Jan. 29, 2004).

87. *New York Civil Liberties Union (NUCLU)* v. *New York,* No. 3, 2005 N.Y. LEXIS 172 (N.Y. Feb. 15, 2005).

88. Winnie Hu, "Accord Reached in School Bias Suit Against Yonkers," *New York Times* on the Web, January 9, 2002, http://nytimes.com/2002/01/09/education/09YONK.html (accessed 1/10/02).

89. *Campaign for Fiscal Equity, Inc.* v. *New York*, No. 117A, 1995 N.Y. LEXIS 1145 at *312 (N.Y. June 15, 1995). (*CFE/1995*).

90. *Campaign for Fiscal Equity v. State*, No.: 111070/93, 2001 N.Y. Misc. LEXIS 1 (N.Y. Sup. Ct., N.Y. Co., Jan. 9, 2001).

91. "Regents extend 55 passing grade: Regents make sweeping changes teachers wanted in math, physics," *New York Teacher*, October 22, 2003, http://www.nysut.org/newyorkteacher/2003-2004/031022regents02.html (accessed 2/15/04).

92. Scott Joftus and Brenda Maddox-Dolan, "Left out and left behind: NCLB and the American high school," Alliance for Excellent Education Web site, April 2003, http://www.all4rd.org/publications/reports.html (accessed 7/15/05) 9.

93. Marianne Winglee, David Marker, and Allison Henderson, "A recommended approach to providing high school dropout and completion rates at the state level." National Center For Education Statistics, Washington, DC, February 2000, publication 2000–305.

94. Joe Williams and Alison Gendar, "Graduation rate in City just 50% . . . and it's likely to go lower," *New York Daily News*, April 11, 2003, 12, LexisNexis news (accessed 8/9/03).

95. New York State Education Department "Distribution of New York State's Public and Nonpublic High School Graduates by Post-High School Plans and Racial/Ethnic Group, 1990–1991 to 2000–2001," http://www.highered.nysed.gov:80/oris/Graduation_Rates.htm (accessed 8/10/03).

96. According to Williams and Gendar, "Graduation rate in city," the lowest performing high school in New York City in 2003 was William H. Taft High School in the Bronx, which graduated 14.8% of its entering class.

97. Campaign for Fiscal Equity, "Definition of a Sound Basic Education," http://cfequity.org/sbeddef.html (accessed 4/3/02).

98. *CFE IIa*, 2001 N.Y. Misc. LEXIS 1 at *12.

99. Raymond Domanico, "State of NYC Public Schools, 2002," Manhattan Institute website, Civic Report #36, March 2002, http://manhattan-institute.org (accessed 11/25/03), 8, 11. The Manhattan Institute is a conservative think tank.

100. Sometimes conservative analysts seem to contradict themselves on this point. See Abigail Thernstrom's article posted at the Web site of the Manhattan Institute, "Education's division problem: Schools are responsible for the main source of racial inequality today" in which Thernstrom proclaims, "At the minimum, these kids (students of color whose scores are substantially lower than their white peers) should have schools with superb curricular materials and more time "on task"—longer school days, weeks and years." Her conclusion: charter schools will provide this (cited from *Los Angeles Times*, Nov. 13, 2003), http://manhattan-institute.org.html_latimes_division_p.htm (accessed 11/25/03).

101. *CFE Ic,* Court of Appeals at *317.

102. *Campaign for Fiscal Equity, Inc.* (*CFE IIb*). v. *New York,* No. 5330, 2002 N.Y. App. Div. LEXIS 7252 at *22 (N.Y. App. Div. June 25, 2002).

103. *Van Dusartz* v. *Hatfield,* No. 3-71 Civ. 243, 1971 U.S. Dist. LEXIS 11281 (D. Minn. Oct. 12, 1971), quoted in R. Craig Wood and David C. Thompson, *Educational Finance Law,* 2nd edition (National Organization on Legal Problems in Education (NOLPE): Topcka, Kansas, 1996), 59–60.

104. *CFE IIb,* 2002 N.Y. App. Div. LEXIS 7252 at *8.

105. "Uncertified teachers outside NYC get a break," News all the time, August 13, 2003, http://1010wins.com/topstories/winstopstories_story_223161111.html (accessed 8/13/03).

106. Campaign for Fiscal Equity, "School funding ruling leaves Governor Pataki open for criticism" http://www.cfequity.org/June%2025%20Decision Coverage/6-26-02NY1.htm (accessed 7/1/02).

107. "Blaming the victim," *New York Times* on the Web, June 26, 2002 (accessed 7/1/02).

108. Bob Herbert, "The bare minimum," *New York Times* on the Web, June 27, 2002 (accessed 7/1/02).

109. Campaign for Fiscal Equity, "Recent Press Coverage," Campaign for Fiscal Equity's Web site, June 27, 2003, http://cfequity.org/6/25-02press html (accessed 7/1/02).

110. "Fiscal Equity Group to Proceed With Education Funding Case," News in Brief, *New York Law Journal* 228 (December 3, 2002), 1.

111. *Stone ex rel. Paynter and ex rel. All Others Similarly Situated* (*Paynter,* Supreme Court) v. *New York,* No. 98.10280, 2000 N.Y. Misc. LEXIS 569 (N.Y. Sup. Ct. Nov. 14, 2000).

112. *Stone ex rel. Paynter, and ex rel. All Others Similarly Situated* v. *New York,* No. (232), CA 99-724, 2000 N.Y. App. Div. LEXIS 3626, at *820 (N.Y. App. Div. Mar. 29, 2000). This ruling declared that school districts are " a statutory system whereby citizens at the local level, acting as part of school district units containing people with a community of interest and acting together to govern themselves, have made basic decisions on funding and operating their own schools." These were "vested by the State with broad powers" and could not "be consolidated . . . without [their] consent." This ruling affirms local control.

113. *Paynter, Individually and ex rel. All Others Similarly* Situated, No. 98/10280, 2000 N.Y. Misc. LEXIS 569 (N.Y. Sup. Ct. Nov. 14, 2000).

114. Michael Zeigler, "Panel Rejects Suit Over Aid to Schools," *New York Law Journal,* New York Law Publishing Company, December 31, 2001) LexisNexis legal research (accessed 3/25/02).

115. *Alexander* v. *Sandoval,* 2001 U.S. LEXIS 3367.

116. New York State Urban Development Corporation (UDC), section 6265 "repealed . . . the UDC's authority to construct low income housing without the municipality's approval." *Paynter,* Supreme Court at *236.

117. *Stone ex rel. Paynter* (*Paynter,* Appellate Division) *and ex rel. All Others Similarly Situated,* v. *New York,* No. (1288) CA 01-0057, 2001 N.Y. App. Div. LEXIS 12508 (N.Y. App. Div. Dec. 21, 2001).

118. The Civil Rights Act of 1964 (42 USC section 1983, Title VI).

119. *Campaign for Fiscal Equity, Inc. (CFE IIc)* v. *New York*, No. 74, 2003 N.Y. LEXIS 1678 (N.Y. June 26, 2003)

120. *Stone ex rel. Paynter (Paynter*, Court of Appeals*)* v. *New York*, No. 75, 2003 N.Y. LEXIS 1672 (N.Y. June 26, 2003).

121. Samuel Maull, "New York judge accepts panel's school funding report; state vows appeal" (Associated Press State & Local Wire, February 14, 2005, Monday, BC cycle), LexisNexis news (accessed 6/20/05).

122. New York State Assembly, Bill Summary—A08598, http://assembly. state.ny.us/ (accessed 6/21/05).

123. New York State Assembly, Bill Summary—A03179, http://assembly. state.ny.us/ (accessed 6/21/05).

124. See *CFE* lawyers' argument that *Sandoval* does not apply to the *CFE* case in "Brief for Plaintiffs-Respondents," http://cfequity.org/CFEAppealBrief.htm (accessed 4/24/02), 154–157.

125. *CFE IIc*, 2003 N.Y. LEXIS 1678, at*64. "The State need only ascertain the actual cost of providing a sound basic education in New York City. Reforms to the current system of financing school funding and managing schools should address the shortcomings of the current system by ensuring, as a part of that process, that every school in New York City would have the resources necessary for providing the opportunity for a sound basic education" (references omitted).

126. *Id.* at *69.

127. United States Department of Labor, "History of Changes to the Minimum Wage Law," http://www.dol.gov/esa/minwage/coverage.htm (accessed 9/10/02). The federal minimum wage has not changed since 1997, despite many studies showing that it is impossible to live decently on that amount, even without children. See also Jared Bernstein and Jeff Chapman, "Time to Repair the Wage Floor: Raising the Minimum Wage to $6.65 will Prevent Further Erosion of its Value," Economic Policy Institute Brief #180, May 22, 2002, http://www.epinet. org/Issuebriefs/ib180.html (accessed 9/15/02).

128. Al Baker, "Over Pataki Veto, Minimum Wage to Rise to $7.15" (*New York Times*, Section A; Col. 3; pg. 1 (December 7, 2004), LexisNexis news (9/29/05).

129. Barbara Ehrenreich, *Nickel and Dimed: On (Not) Getting By in America* (New York: Henry Holt and Company, 2001).

Chapter 3

1. Thomas B. Parrish, Christine S. Hikido, and William Fowler, *Inequalities in Public School District Revenues (National Center for Educational Statistics*, Statistical Analysis Report, 1998, NCES 98-210), 106.

2. *Brigham* v. *State of Vermont (Brigham* v. *State)*, No. 96–502, 1997 Vt. LEXIS 13 (Vt. February 5, 1997).

3. Parrish et al., *Inequalities*, 107–108.

4. Parrish et al., *Inequalities*, 106.

5. Bruce Biddle and David C. Berliner, "A Research Synthesis: Unequal School funding in the United States" *Educational Leadership* 29:8 (May 2002), http://www.ascd.org/reading room/eled/0205/biddle.html (accessed 9/3/03).

6. Parrish et al., *Inequalities*, 122. The five measures are: 1) the restricted range (the difference between schools in a state at the fifth percentile and the ninety-fifth percentile); 2) the federal range ratio (the restricted range divided by the value for the student at the fifth percentile); 3) the McLoone Index (comparing total revenues for all students below the median with a calculation of what would have to be received to bring them up to the median revenue per student for the state); 4) the coefficient of variation (100 times the standard deviation divided by the mean); and 5) the Gini coefficient (comparing the cumulative proportion of the aggregated revenues per student with the cumulative proportion of students when students are ranked in ascending order of revenues per student).

7. Biddle and Berliner, "A research synthesis," 48.

8. Vermont Department of Education, "Laws and Regulations: Act 60 - The Equal Opportunity Education Act: Fact Sheet, Comparison of tax rates to per pupil spending before and after Act 60," http://www.state.vt.us/educ/new/html/laws/act60_fact_sheet.html (accessed 9/13/03).

9. William Mathis, "Civil Society and School Reform: Vermont's Act 60," http://www.act60.org/mathis_version.htm (accessed 9/4/03). The reader should know that this Web site was supported by opponents of Act 60, who prefaced the article with the following: "A Left-Wing History of Vermont's Act 60, Editor's note: This paper is presented here to illustrate how differently ardent Act 60 proponents perceive and portray everyday events related to Vermont's controversial education funding law. As such, it is intended to be instructive and appears exactly as written by the author. Readers are warned that they may experience intense emotion, high blood pressure, insomnia and other adverse reactions to what they may perceive as utter manure."

10. William Mathis, "Local Control and Act 60," Act 60: Working for Equal Educational Opportunity in Vermont, 1998, Concerned Vermonters for Equal Educational Opportunity (CVEEO), http://www.act60works.org/ (accessed 9/2/03).

11. *Brigham* v. *State,* 1997 Vt. LEXIS 13 at *250.

12. Mathis, "Local Control," 6.

13. *Brigham* v. *State,* 1997 Vt. LEXIS 13 at *266.

14. Peter Teachout, "'No Simple Disposition': The Brigham Case and the Future of Local Control over Spending in Vermont" (*Vermont Law Review* vol. 22:21,1997), 31.

15. Laws and Regulations, Act 60 - The Equal Educational Opportunity Act: Fact Sheet, Overview [apparently written in 2000–2001, described in the document as the "current" school year], Vermont Department of Education Web site, http://www.state.vt.us/educ/new/html/laws/act60_fact_sheet.html (accessed 9/13/03).

16. The state share has ranged from 20% to 37% prior to 1997, 84% in 1999, to 60.7% in 2002. *Education Week,* Quality Counts issues for the cited years,

http://www.edweek.org, archives, (accessed 9/3/03). Changes in Act 60 legislation in 2002 may well have been responsible for the recent decline. Further changes during 2003–2005 affected the proportion differently for different towns. See also William J. Mathis, "Vermont" in *Public School Finance in the United States and Canada: 1998–1999,* National Center for Education Statistics, U.S. Government Department of Education, Office of Educational Research and Improvement, NCES 2001-309, 1.

17. William J. Mathis, "Vermont," NCES 1998, 1.

18. *Stowe Citizens for Responsible Government* v. *Vermont (Stowe),* No. 98-116, 1999 Vt. LEXIS 41 at *559 (Vt. Mar. 3, 1999).

19. Mathis, "Vermont," NCES 1998, 7–8.

20. Mathis, "Civil Society" (Web site owner's comment reported at note 9 supra).

21. Mathis, "Civil society," note 34.

22. Lorna Jimerson, "Still A Reasonably Equal Share": An update on equity in Vermont, 2001–2002," The Rural School and Community Trust Web site, February, 2002, http://www.ruraledu.org (accessed 9/6/03).

23. William J. Mathis, "Is Act 60 Working?" Act 60 Works website, December 2000, http://www.act60works.org/fsmathis1200.html (accessed 9/12/03).

24. Mathis, "Is Act 60 Working?"

25. Mathis, "Vermont," NCES, 3.

26. *Anderson* v. *Vermont,* No. 98-047, 1998 Vt. LEXIS 479 (Vt. Dec. 22, 1998).

27. *Stowe Citizens for Responsible Government (Stowe)* v. *Vermont,* No. 98–116, 1999 Vt. LEXIS 41 (Vt. March 3, 1999), at *599.

28. Robert Tomsho, "Class Struggle: Fund-Raising Drive for Schools Leaves Manchester Disunited—A Vermont Town Replaces Taxes With Donations, But Some Won't Give—It's Greed, Plain and Simple," *Wall Street Journal,* February 6, 2001, Eastern Edition, LexisNexis news (accessed 6/5/01).

29. "Withholding schools want state to release federal funds," Associated Press State and Local Wire, April 8, 1999, PM Cycle, LexisNexis news (accessed 7/3/01). Three towns using this strategy in 1999 were Dover, Whitingham, and Searsburg.

30. "Act 60 Opponents could cost the state $25 million," Associated Press State and Local Wire, February 19, 1999, PM cycle, LexisNexis news (accessed 10/4/01). In February 1999, an Associated Press story set the figure the state could lose in the sharing pool at $25 million.

31. Jim Kenyon, "The loophole not taken," *Valley News* (Barnard, VT), December 2, 2001, B1. http://www.act60works.org (accessed 9/20/03). This story relates how two wealthy Barnard residents refused to pay the "voluntary" levy, contributing their "assessed" share to the sharing pool instead.

32. "Wilmington officials decide not to withhold Act 60 money," Associated Press state and local wire, April 15, 1999, AM Cycle, LexisNexis news (accessed 10/4/01).

33. Christopher Graff, "Governor accuses Lieutenant Governor of being misguided," Associated Press, April 16, 1999, http://www.sover.net~auc/It-gov.htm (accessed 9/12/03).

34. "Freeman Foundation money getting put to use in schools," Associated Press, September 7, 1999, PM cycle, LexisNexis news (accessed 10/4/01).

35. Act 60: What You Should Know, "Another Lesson in Reality for Montpelier: The Freeman Foundation Weighs in on Act 60," February 24, 1998, http://www.act60.org/found.htm (accessed 10/4/01).

36. "Lawmakers try to figure out how to deal with grants to schools," Associated Press State and Local Wire, January 21, 1999, PM cycle, LexisNexis news (accessed 10/4/01).

37. "Freeman Trustees May Keep up Donations," Associated Press State and Local Wire, December 6, 2000, BC Cycle, LexisNexis news (accessed 10/4/01). A mention of this possibility is also seen in "School fund-raisers falling short of goals," Associated Press State and Local Wire, May 29, 2001, Tuesday, BC Cycle, LexisNexis news (accessed 10/4/01).

38. Associated Press, December 6, 2000, Wednesday, BC cycle, LexisNexis news (accessed 10/4/01).

39. *Burlington Free Press*, December 12, 2000.

40. Jeffery Pascoe, "Vermont's next education funding mechanism," Act 60: What You Should Know, 7/22/00, http://www/act60.orgnextmech.htm (accessed 9/4/03).

41. Pascoe, "Vermont's next" (np).

42. J. Peter Gratiot, "Factors Controlling Foundation Spending in Vermont," *Journal of Education Finance* 26 (Fall 2000), 200. This seems like a weak argument to me, given that NCES figures show a gross disparity.

43. Gratiot's other independent variables are, in order of decreasing importance, according to his calculations: 1) ADM, Average Daily Membership (number of pupils); 2) ETR, Effective Tax Rate (which used to be set by voters each year under the old system); 3) ROR, Resident Ownership Ratio (indicates the proportion of residents who vote for school budgets to nonresidents who do not); 4) EGL, Equalized Grand List (a measure of the taxable real property in a district per pupil); 5) RTBI, Resident School Tax Burden (does not include nonresidents); 6) AGI, Adjusted Gross Income per pupil [Gratiot also runs his regression analysis with other measures of income]; 7) AID (State aid to schools per pupil); 8) NRSTx (nonresident tax). Gratiot, pp. 228–231.

44. Gratiot, 237.

45. John E. Coons, William H. Clune, and Stephen D. Sugarman, *Private Wealth and Public Education* (Cambridge Mass.: Harvard University Belknap Press, 1970).

46. Act 60: What you should know, http://www.act60.org. See also a companion web site supporting Act 60 at http://www.act60works.org.

47. State of Vermont, Office of the Governor Web site, September 12, 2002, http://www.gov.state.vt.us/biography.php3 (accessed 9/13/03).

48. Jim Douglas, "Budget Address," January 2003, Vermont Office of the Governor Web site, http://www.gov.state.vt.us/budget_message.php3 (accessed 9/12/03).

49. Ross Snyed, "Dean outlines vision of education funding law," Associated Press state and local wire, January 14, 1999, LexisNexis news (accessed 9/12/03).

50. Vermont Bill Tracking System. H. 480, An Act relating to Education Funding, http://www.leg.state.vt.us/docs/legdoc.cfm?URL=/docs/2004/bills/passed/H-480.htm (accessed 7/10/03).

51. Howard Weiss-Tisman, "School funding grab irks Vt. Towns," *Brattleboro Reformer,* March 5, 2005, Saturday, MediaNews Group, Inc. and the New England Newspaper Group, Inc., LexisNexis news (accessed 7/15/05).

52. "Governor enacts amendment to Act 68 into law," Associated Press and Local Wire, Montpelier, Vermont, February 17, 2004, Tuesday, BC cycle, LexisNexis news (accessed 3/2/04).

53. Greg Kocher, "State providing less than it's required to, group says," *Lexington Herald Leader,* Friday, June 7, 2003, http://www.kentucky.com/mld/heraldleader/6181950.htm (accessed 3/2/04).

54. Lorna Jimerson, *A Reasonably Equal Share: Educational Equity in Vermont, A Status Report—Year 2000–2001,* The Rural School and Community Trust Policy Program, February 2001, http://www/ruraledu.org/docs/vtequity/vt_appendices.html (accessed 7/31/05), 3–4.

55. See also Peter T. Kilborn, "Vermont Spending Plan Seems to Help Schools," *New York Times* on the Web, January 31, 2001, http:/www.nytimes.com/ (accessed 10/4/01).

56. David S. Wolk, Commissioner of Education, Vermont Department of Education, *The Equal Educational Opportunity Act: Measuring Equity,* April 17, 2001, State Board of Education, 120 State Street, Montpelier, Vermont 05620, 2001, http://www.state.vt.us/educ.act60/EEO_Report_05_01.pdf (accessed 10/1/01), 1.

57. Lorna Jimerson, "Still "A Reasonably Equal Share": Update on Educational Equity in Vermont: Year 2001–2002," The Rural School and Community Trust, February 2002, http://www.ruraledu.org/docs/vtequity/vt_rep02_72ppi.pdf (accessed 2/3/04).

58. Rachel Thompkins, "Vermont's Act 60 Continues to Improve Equity for State's Students," *Rural Policy Matters* 4, no. 3 (March 2002) http://www.ruraledu.org/rpm/rpm403b.htm (accessed 9/12/03).

59. Jimerson, 2002, 11.

60. Wolk, 15–20.

61. Wolk. 15. See also, Peter T. Kilborn. "Vermont Spending Plan Seems to Help Schools." *New York Times,* January 31, 2001, LexisNexis news (accessed 9/2/03).

62. Wenglinsky, H. "Finance Equalization and Within-school Equity: The Relationship between Education Spending and the Social Distribution of Achievement" (*Educational Researcher* vol. 20, no. 4, 1998), 269–283.

63. Vermont Department of Education, School Data & Reports, "Per pupil spending by school type 2002 and 2003," http://www.state.vt.us/educ/new/html/data/perpupil.html (accessed 9/2/03).

64. Mathis, "Local Control," 15.

65. David Gram, "Ambitious agenda mostly met," Associated Press and Local Wire, May 30, 2003, LexisNexis news (accessed 9/8/03).

66. Pascoe, "Vermont's next education funding mechanism."

67. Vermont State Department, Legislative Summary for 2003, "Significant Education Bills that passed in 2003," http://www/state.vt.us/educ/new/html/mainlaws.html#summary (accessed 9/9/03).

68. Mathis, "Vermont," 2. See also Overview of Vermont's Education Funding System Under Act 68 & Act 130, Vermont Department of Education, November 2005, http://state.vt.us/educ/new/html/pgm_finance_data/school_funding_info. html (accessed 3/14/06) 3. This document sets of 2006 state share at 83%, page 3.

69. Vermont Department of Motor Vehicles, "Effective October 1, 2003 Vermont's Sales Tax rate increases from 5% to 6%," http://www.aot.state.vt.us/dmv/HOME/news/MiscellaneousOTHERNews/SalesTaxIncrease.htm (accessed 3/2/04).

70. Bess Keller, "Vermont: Tax shifts help buoy education spending," *Education Week,* July 1, 2003, http://edweek.org (1 October 2003).

71. Keller, Vermont: Tax shifts, n.p.

72. *Stowe,* 1999 Vt. LEXIS 41 at *559.

73. "Douglas signs school funding bill," Associated Press and local wire, June 18, 2003, BC Cycle, Montpelier, Vermont, LexisNexis news (accessed 9/20/03).

74. Lisa Stansky, "Tax turf war; States, companies clash on 'loophole'," *National Law Journal* 26; No. 21 (January 26, 2004): 1. LexisNexis legal research (accessed 5/31/04).

75. Campaign for Fiscal Equity, "Vermont school funding bill provides a lesson for New York," June 2, 2003, http://www.cfequity.org/06-02-03 Vermont.htm (accessed 8/6/03).

76. "Roundup! What went on is state legislatures this year/Vermont." *Rural Policy Matters: A Newsletter of Rural School and Community Action* 5, no. 7 (July 2003), http://www.rural edu.org/rpm/rpm507c.htmvt (accessed 9/6/03).

77. Howard Weiss-Tisman, "School funding grab irks Vt. Towns," *Brattleboro Reformer,* Saturday, March 5, 2005, LexisNexis news (accessed 7/15/05).

78. Ross Snyed, "House revised education funding, turns aside bid to repeal tax," Associated Press state and local wire, April 14, 2005, Thursday, BC Cycle, LexisNexis news (retrieved 7/15/05).

79. Vermont Legislative Bill Tracking System, Vermont Bill #H.1, http://www.leg.state.vt.us/database/search/resultsresults.cmf (accessed 7/15/05 and 3/14/06).

80. Julia Levy, "Blame for 'Teacher Crisis' is laid at feet of Bloomberg" *New York Sun,* May 7, 2004 Friday, New York Section, LexisNexis news (accessed 5/31/04).

Chapter 4

1. Some of this information came from an audiotaped interview with Nancy Nailer, Peter Stokes, and Russ Riddle of the Ontario Ministry of Education and Training on January 19, 2000. (Hereafter Ministry interview.) In addition, I

consulted many Ontario Ministry of Education Web sites and articles, Ontario Secondary School Teachers' Federation Web sites, and news sources.

2. Arthur Drache, "Reading, writing, and religion: uproar over private subsidies overlooks old law," *National Post Canada*, December 19, 2001, Lexis-Nexis news (accessed 11/11/03).

3. "Ontario 55th out of 63 in North American Education Spending," Ontario Secondary School Teachers' Federation Web site, http://osstf.on.ca/www/issues/edfi/survey.html (accessed Oct. 19, 2000) 1–2.

4. Stephen B. Lawton, *The Price of Quality: The Public Finance of Elementary and Secondary Education in Canada* (Toronto: Canadian Education/Association Canadienne Association d'Education, 1987).

5. "Underfunding of Public Education," Ontario Secondary School Teachers' Federation, http://osstf.on.ca/www/issues/edfi/underfunding.html (accessed Oct. 19, 2000) 1–2. The U.S. average is $7,254 per-pupil expenditure; the Canadian average, $4,934 per-pupil expenditure (both in U.S. dollars).

6. Chris Malkiewich, Ontario Secondary School Teachers' Federation executive assistant, audiotaped personal interview, January 22, 2000.

7. George Martell, *A New Education Politics: Bob Rae's Legacy and the Ontario Secondary School Teachers' Federation* (Toronto: James Lorimer, 1995) 233–239.

8. Ontario Universities Application Centre, News and stats, "Impressive number of students apply for fall 2003 admission," January 17, 2003, http://www.ouac.on.ca/news/dblcohort/ni-jan17press.html (accessed 11/13/03).

9. Ministry interview, January 20, 2000.

10. Ontario Ministry of Education and Training, *Excellence in Education: Student-Focused Funding for Ontario, A Guide Book* 1999–2000, http://www.edu.gov.on.ca.eng/document/brochure/excelfue.html (accessed 9/20/99) 5. (Guidebook 1999–2000). This number was reduced from 34 types of grants under the old system.

11. Guidebook 1999–2000, p. 5–8.

12. A Local Priorities Grant and a Declining Enrolment Grant were added in 2002–2003, plus additional flexibility in spending the money in some other grants. Ontario, Ministry of Education, "Student-Focused Funding: Technical Paper 2002–03," http://www.search2.gov.on.ca:8008/compass?ui=sr&scope=student%20focused%20funding%202002&page=2&view-template=simple1 (accessed 11/15/03).

13. Gordon W. Nore, "Strike Notes: green ribbons, politics, and patronage [Bill 160]," *Canadian Business and Current Affairs, Our Times, Ltd.* 17, no.1 (January/February 1998) 11.

14. Michael Pereira, "A 'crisis' in government: Bill 160 and the Ontario Teachers Strike," personal Web site, nd, http://mike-pereira.com (accessed 6/5/04).

15. Ontario Secondary School Teachers' Federation, OSSTF issues, (nd), www.osstf.on.ca/www/issues/teacherl/160rulin.html (accessed 6/4/04).

16. The Ontario Public School Boards' Association, *Fast Reports: Weekly Information for Decision-makers in Education* 10, no. 30 (November 20, 1998), http://www.opsba.org/pubs/fast/arch/1998/98-11-20.htm (accessed 6/4/04).

17. Ontario Secondary Schools Federation, "The education funding model impact on students' education" (OSSTF Web site) http://www.osstf.on.ca/issues/issmonth/fndconcn.html (accessed 10/26/03).

18. Ministry interview, January 19, 2000.

19. The material that follows comes from the OSSTF interview, January 22, 2000, unless otherwise indicated by the text or footnote.

20. Even so, in January 2000, a court case concerning the right to tax, which is constitutionally vouchsafed to separate boards, claimed that public boards should have a corresponding right. OSSTF interview, January 22, 2000.

21. Michele Landsberg, "Tory Policies Slowly Poison Public Education," *Toronto Star,* June 18, 2000, Edition 1, LexisNexis news (accessed 8/3/00).

22. David C. Berliner and Bruce J. Biddle, *The Manufactured Crisis: Myths, Fraud, and the Attack on America's Public Schools* (Reading, MA: Addison-Wesley, 1995).

23. Anne Jones, "Ban on teachers' strikes the latest affront," *Hamilton Spectator* (Ontario, Canada), Monday, June 2, 2003, LexisNexis news (accessed 11/15/03).

24. "Education partners launch campaign to recruit Ontario teachers; Data shows shortage in areas of math and science," Canada Newswire, Ltd., Toronto, Monday, March 24, 2003, LexisNexis News (accessed 3/9/04).

25. OSSTF interview, January 22, 2000.

26. Personal audiotaped interviews with four Ontario boards of education in the Toronto and surrounding area, January 20–22, 2000. I have not identified the individual boards; one was separate, one urban, one rural, and one suburban.

27. George Martell, *A New Education Politics: Bob Rae's Legacy and the Response of the Ontario Secondary School Teachers' Federation* (Toronto: James Lorimer, 1995).

28. OSSTF interview, January 22, 2000.

29. Ontario Regulation 275/01, made under the Education Act, July 4, 2001, http://www.e-laws.gov.on.ca/DBLaws/Source/Regs/English/2001/R01275_e.htm (accessed 11/28/03).

30. OSSTF interview, January 22, 2000.

31. For publications concerning the yearly student-focused funding plans see Ontario Ministry of Education and Training Web site, http://www.edu.gov.on.ca/eng/funding/index.html.

32. Fact Sheet: Special Education Grant, Ontario Ministry of Education and Training, March 2000, http://www.edu.gov.on.ca/eng/document/nr/00.03/fs2.htm (accessed 10/6/00).

33. "An Examination of the Relationship between Higher Standards and Students Dropping Out: Flash Research Report #5," New York City Board of Education. Division of Assessment and Accountability, 110 Livingston Street, Room 728, Brooklyn, NY 11201: March 1, 2001 (ERIC Document 451 317) 7, 8.

34. Educational Improvement Commission, home page, http://eic.edu. gov.on.ca/eicroot/english/home/default.asp (accessed 12/20/99).

35. Deborah Meier, *The Power of Their Ideas: Lessons for America from a Small School in Harlem* (Boston: Beacon Press, 1995).

36. Jones, M. Gail, Brett D. Jones, and Tracy Y. Hargrove. *The Unintended Consequences of High Stakes Testing* (Oxford: Rowman and Littlefield, 2003).

37. Such additional funds, denied to *Nyquist's* "intervener districts" became the subject of *Campaign for Fiscal Equity* v. *State of New York*. These expenses have been recognized in the creation of New Jersey's "special needs districts" in response to the six *Robinson* and six *Abbott* cases, although effective remedies may still be lacking, twenty-five years after *Abbott I*.

38. Fact Sheet: Early Learning Grant, Ontario Ministry of Education and Training, March 2000, http://www.gov.on.ca/eng/document/nr/00.03/fs4. html (accessed 10/06/00).

39. Landsberg, "Tory Policies."

40. I used figures on total enrollments and total per pupil expenditures from the 1999–2000 and the 2000–2001 Parents' Guide to Student-Focused Funding to calculate this figure.

41. Fact Sheet: Special Education Grant, March 2000, Ontario Ministry of Education and Training Web site, http://www.edu.gov.on.ca/eng/document/nr/00.03/fs2.html (accessed Oct. 6, 2000).

42. Backgrounder: Standards on Instructional Time, Ontario Ministry of Education and Training, March 9, 2000, http://www.edu.gov.on.ca/eng/document/nr/00.03/bg2.html (accessed 10/6/00).

43. Backgrounder: Investments in Quality for 2000–2001, Ontario Ministry of Education and Training, March 9, 2000, http://www.edu.gov.on.ca/eng/document/nr/00.03.bg1.html (accessed 10/6/00).

44. News Release: Ontario's investment in education grows by $190 million, Ontario Ministry of Education and Training, http://www.gov.on.ca/eng/document/nr/00.03/funding.html (accessed 10/6/00).

45. Parents' Guide to Student-focused Funding 2001–2002, Ministry of Education and Training, Ontario, March 2001, http://www.edu.gov.on.ca/eng/funding/fund0102.html#financial (accessed 11/16/03) 1. (Hereafter Parents' Guide, 2001–2002)

46. Anne Bayefsky, "We Must Fund All schools Equally," *Toronto Star*, January 18, 2000, LexisNexis news (accessed October 28, 2000).

47. Landsberg, "Tory Policies."

48. Heather Sokoloff, "Rise in Private School Tax Credit Put Off: Credit Remains $700 in One-year Delay of Increase," *National Post*, Ontario edition, June 18, 2002, LexisNexis news (accessed 11/13/03).

49. Ed Morgan, "The Case for Religious Education," *Toronto Star*, June 27, 2003, A21, LexisNexis news (accessed 11/11/03).

50. Christina Blizzard, "School tax credit a 'half-baked scheme,'" *London Free Press* (London, Ontario), December 24, 2001, LexisNexis news (accessed 11/13/03)

51. Parent's Guide 2001–2002, 3.

52. Ontario Universities Application Centre, Impressive number (note 8 supra).

53. Pat Comley and Penny Hopkins, "How to beat the double cohort blues," Ontario School Counselors' Association, nd, http://www/osca.ca/Beat-cohort.htm (accessed 11/13/03). This extraordinary document advises students to "take responsibility for your own post-secondary planning" by "start[ing] as early as possible—elementary school is best" and "concentrat[ing] on the journey, not the destination" as if tuition increases, fewer scholarships, and fewer university places could be overcome by "marketing yourself." Parents are similarly advised to encourage "your child to pursue a dream" but "encourage alternative goals if initial goals are unobtainable."

54. David Corson, "Ontario students as a means to the government's ends," Ontario Centre for Policy Alternatives, http:www.policyalternatives.ca/on (accessed 10/26/03).

55. Karla Scoon Reid, "Ontario Grapples With School Funding," *Education Week*, February 5, 2003, http://edweek.org (accessed 11/12/03).

56. Mordecai Rozanski, Chair, *Investing in Public Education: Advancing the Goal of Continuous Improvement in Student Learning and Achievement: Report of the Education Equality Task Force, 2002*, Ministry of Education and Ministry of Training, December 2002, http://mettowas21.edu.gov.on.ca/eng/document/reports/task02/report.html (accessed 10/10/03). (Rozanski Report)

57. Hugh McKenzie, "Magna Budget Aftermath: The Sweet Revenge of Erik Peters," The Canadian Centre for Policy Alternatives, *Behind the Numbers* 5, no. 1 (November 5, 2003), www.policyalternnatives.ca (accessed 11/24/03), 1.

58. Erik White, "Education report ignored vital issues: Union leaders" *The Standard* (St. Catharine's, Ontario), December 19, 2002, final edition, LexisNexis news (accessed 11/15/03).

59. Hugh McKenzie, " The manager myth (or how Ernie Eves balanced Ontario's budget one year in a row)," *Behind the scenes: Ontario 2003*, Canadian Centre for Policy Alternatives, http://www.policyalternatives.ca (accessed 11/23/03).

60. McKenzie, Magna Budget aftermath, 1.

61. The Editorial Board, "The betrayal of the Ontario teachers' strike: The lessons for all workers," World Socialist Web site, November 17, 1997, http://www.wsws.org/workers/1997/nov1997/ont-n17.shtml (accessed 3/9/04).

62. Canadian Centre for Policy Alternatives, *Behind the Issues: Ontario 2003*, http://www.policyalternatives.ca (accessed 10/25/03).

63. Hugh McKenzie, "Telling tales out of school: How the Ontario government is(n't) funding education," Ontario Alternative Budget 2003, technical paper #5, http://www.policyalternatives.ca/on/oab2003-education-hilights.html (accessed 10/26/03).

64. Jeff Harder, "Strike by teachers looming, school board officials warn," Sun Media Corp, *London Free Press*, Ontario, Canada March 18, 2000, LexisNexis news (accessed 6/9/04).

65. David Lewis Stein, "905 schools face funding crunch, too" (*Toronto Star*, August 27, 2002, Ontario Edition p. A21), LexisNexis news (accessed 9/13/02).

66. Mitchell Beer, "In the eye of the storm: Ottawa pushes back against school board takeovers," The Canadian Center for Policy Alternatives Web site, http://www.policyalternatives.ca/eduproj/ososottawa.html (accessed 10/26/03).

67. Robert Benzie, "Eves Seizes Toronto School Board; Budget deficits left 'no other option,' Wittmer says; Liberals, NDP say Voters will Punish Tories; Parents threaten lawsuits over expected cuts," (*National Post*, August 28, 2002, Toronto edition), LexisNexis news (accessed 9/13/02). See also "Tories Stoop to New Low by Firing Ottawa Carlton School Trustees," Ontario Secondary Schools Teachers' Federation, http://www.osstf.on.ca/www/pub/pressrel/sept01aug17-202.html (accessed 9/13/02).

68. Gail Stuart, Vice-Chair of Our Schools, Our Communities, presentation to a hearing on education issues held in Ottawa on January 30, 2003, by the provincial Liberal Opposition, http://www.ourschools-ottawa.ca/ (accessed 11/26/03).

69. Beer, In the eye of the storm.

70. "McGuinty to McGuinty: What are you going to sell?" Canada Newswire Ltd., National Political News, Toronto, September 25, 2003, LexisNexis news (accessed 11/15/03).

71. Editorial, "Getting elected was the easy part," Sun Media Corporation, *Stratford Beacon* (Herald, Ontario) October 4, 2003, LexisNexis news (accessed 10/09/03).

72. Andrea Baille, " Sweeping majority for McGuinty Liberals," Sun Media Corporation, *Brockville Recorder & Times* (Brockville, Ontario), October 3, 2003, LexisNexis news (accessed 10/9/03).

73. Howard Hampton, "The 1.5 billion solution," *Toronto Star*, Ontario edition, Opinion, September 23, 2002, LexisNexis news (accessed 11/15/03).

74. New Democratic Party Platform, "Why McGuinty is evasive on school funding," September 16, 2003, http://www.publicpower.ca/issues-news/article_342.shtml (accessed 11/15/03).

75. Colin Perkel, "More money, kinder approach but Tories struggle to win over education critics," *Canadian Business and Current Affairs*, Canadian Press Newswire, September 3, 2003, section S, LexisNexis news (accessed 11/15/03).

76. "McGuinty government restores local voice to Toronto's public school students: Elected trustees resume control of their local schools," Ontario Ministry of Education and Training, What's New, February 18, 2004, http://www.edu.gov.on.ca/eng/new/new.html (accessed 3/9/04).

77. "McGuinty government keeps promise to invest in education: Delivers urgent learning boost for students," Ontario Ministry of Education and Training, What's New, December 3, 2003. http://www.edu.gov.on.ca/eng/new/new.html (accessed 3/9/04).

78. "McGuinty government taking action to help kids succeed," Ontario Ministry of Education and Training, What's New, March 5, 2004, http://www.edu.gov.on.ca/eng/new/new.html (accessed 3/9/04).

79. "Delivering Excellence for all Ontario students," Ontario Ministry of Education and Training, http://www.edu.gov.on.ca/eng/document/reports/excellence/index.html#change (accessed 7/20/05).

80. "CTF studies critical of Ministry Cost of Education document," Ontario Secondary Schools Teachers' Federation, http://www.osstf.on.ca/ (accessed 3/9/04).

81. Berliner and Biddle, *The Manufactured Crisis.*

82. Clifton Joseph and Paul Webster, "Teacher testing," CBC's *The National,* April 2000, Indepth: Education, http://www.cbc.ca/national/magazine/testing/ (accessed 11/26/03). "It's a long running battle which started at a strategy meeting when former Education Minister, John Snobolen was taped presenting a decidedly contentious approach to education reform. 'Creating a useful crisis is what part of this will be about . . . if you don't bankrupt it, well, you'll improve it to death,' he said."

83. Jennifer Quinn, "When all is said and done, it's about leadership," *Toronto Star,* September 27, 2003, National Report, B01, LexisNexis news (accessed 10/07/03).

84. Hugh McKenzie, "Ontario's tax cuts since 1995: The real tally," The Canadian Centre for Policy Alternatives, Behind the issues: Ontario 2003, http://www.policyalternatives.ca (accessed 10/26/03).

85. Mohammed Adam, "A Province wide 'Affliction': Ontario School Boards have cut services, slashed jobs and raided reserves to provide children with a uniformly high-quality education. But still, many of the boards lack the money to do the job properly," *Ottawa Citizen,* March 26, 2002, D1, LexisNexis news (accessed 9/13/02). Many Philadelphia schools were seized by the state and given to the Edison Company to run in 2002. Philadelphia involves 220,000 students, Toronto 200,000. For Philadelphia story, see Jacques Steinberg, "In largest schools takeover, state will run Philadelphia's," *New York Times,* December 22, 2001, Late Edition, Section A1, LexisNexis news (accessed 10/17/02).

86. Robert Balfantz and Nettie Legters, "How many central city high schools have a severe dropout problem, where are they located, and who attends them? Initial estimates using the common core of data," Harvard Civil Rights Project Conference: Dropouts in America: How severe is the problem? What do we know about intervention and prevention? Cambridge, MA, January 13, 2001, http://www.gse.harvard.edu/news/features/conf01132001.html (accessed 11/14/03). In 2001, the dropout problem in the U.S. was concentrated in 200 to 300 schools in the 35 largest cities in the U.S. The cities are Indianapolis, Detroit, Cleveland, San Antonio, Baltimore, Fort Worth, Dallas, Houston, Chicago, Philadelphia, New York City, Austin, Columbus, Milwaukee, Denver, Kansas City, Nashville, Memphis, El Paso, Oklahoma City, Portland, Los Angeles, San Francisco, Boston, San Diego, Washington, DC, Long Beach, Phoenix, San Jose, Seattle, Tucson, Virginia Beach, New Orleans, Jacksonville, and Charlotte.

87. Mike Kennedy, "The ASU 100," *The American School and University Magazine,* September 1, 2003, http://asumag.com/ar/university_asu_2/index.htm (accessed 11/15/03).

88. Peter Simon, "In 5 new charter schools, an education revolution; but long term implications are uncertain," *Buffalo News,* May 3, 2003, LexisNexis news (accessed 11/15/03), 1. See also "Board schedules meetings on building usage:

Budget forces closing of more schools," Buffalo Public Schools Web site, http://buffalo.k12.ny.us/news/newsstory.asp?newsid=285 (accessed 11/15/03).

89. Kate McCann, "Dean says he would have turned down No Child Left Behind Money," Associated Press, November 30, 2003, LexisNexis news (accessed 9/26/05).

90. Peter Schrag, "Getting the blues" (*The Nation,* July 17, 2003). http://www.thenation.com/doc.mhtml?i=20030804&c=3&s=schrag (accessed 3/9/04).

91. "Details of the No Child Left Behind Act lawsuit, *Pontiac* v. *Spellings,* filed Wednesday," Associated Press, April 20, 2005, BC cycle, LexisNexis news (accessed 7/26/05). Also see National Education Association, "Stand Up for Children: *Pontiac* v. *Spellings*" n.d., http://www.nea.org/lawsuit/index.html (accessed 3/14/06).

92. The News Hour, "Connecticut sues over NCLB" August 24, 2005, http://www.pbs.org/newshour/bb/education/july-dec05/nclb2_8-24.html (accessed 9/23/05).

93. *Rodriguez,* 1973 U.S. LEXIS 91 at *128. In his dissent to *Rodriguez,* Marshall agreed with the District Court's assessment that "the [defendants] fail to establish a reasonable basis for these classifications [of school districts for the purpose of taxation]" and concluded by saying, "If Texas had a system truly dedicated to local fiscal control, one would expect the quality of the educational opportunity provided in each district to vary with the decision of the voters in that district as to the level of sacrifice they wish to make for public education. In fact, the Texas scheme produces precisely the opposite effect."

Chapter 5

1. Alfred North Whitehead, *The Aims of Education and Other Essays* (New York: New American Library, 1929).

2. Jean Bethke Elshtain, *The Jane Addams Reader* (New York: Basic Books, 2002), 191.

3. Helen Thompson Woolley. *An Experimental Study of Children at Work and in School Between the Ages of Fourteen and Eighteen Years* (New York: Macmillan, 1929) 742–743. See also Jane Fowler Morse, "Ignored but not forgotten: The work of Helen Branford Thompson Woolley," *NWSA Journal* 14:2 (2002), 131–132.

4. Katharine S. Milar, "'A coarse and clumsy tool': Helen Thompson Woolley and the Cincinnati Vocation Bureau" (*History of Psychology* 2:3, 1999), 219–235.

5. James Conant, *Education and Liberty* (Cambridge, MA: Harvard University Press, 1958), 62.

6. Theda Skocpol, "Delivering for young families: The resonance of the GI Bill," *The American Prospect* 27, no. 8 (September–October, 1996) http://www.prospect.org/print/V7/28/skocpolt.html (accessed 2/15/03).

7. *Plessy,* 1896 U.S. LEXIS 3390 at *541.

8. Walter G. Stephen and Joe R. Feagan, eds., *School Desegregation: Past, Present, and Future* (Plenum Press, 1980), 32.

9. *Brown II,* 1955 U.S. LEXIS 734 at *301.

10. Stephen and Feagan, eds., *School Desegregation,* 17.

11. *Green* v. *County Sch. Bd. Of New Kent County,* No. 695, 1968 U.S. LEXIS (U.S. May 27, 1968).

12. *Swann* v. *Charlotte-Mecklenberg Bd. of Education,* No. 281, 1971 U.S. LEXIS 52 (U.S. Apr. 20, 1971).

13. *Keyes* v. *Sch. Dist. #1,* No. 71-507, 1973 U.S. LEXIS 43 (U.S. June 21, 1973).

14. Gary Orfield and Susan Eaton et al., *Dismantling Desegregation: The Quiet Reversal of Brown* v. *Board of Education,* New York: The New Press, 1996) 7.

15. *Freeman* v. *Pitts,* No. 89-1290, 1992 U.S. LEXIS 2114 (U.S. Mar. 31, 1992).

16. *Bd. of Educ.* v. *Dowell,* No. 89-1080, 1991 U.S. LEXIS 484 (U.S. Jan. 15, 1991).

17. Orfield and Eaton, *Dismantling Desegregation,* 6–9.

18. James S. Coleman et al., *Equality of Educational Opportunity* (U.S. Department of Health, Education, and Welfare, U.S. Government Printing Office, 1966), 302.

19. Coleman, quoted in Berliner and Biddle, *Manufactured Crisis,* 71.

20. Gerald Grant, "Shaping social policy: The politics of the Coleman Report," *Teachers College Record* 75, no. 1 (1973), http://www.tcrecord.org/Content. asp?ContentID=1484 (accessed 3/9/04), 17–54. (Hereafter Grant).

21. David Seeley, Seeley-Coleman memos, 1966, http://www.library.csi. cuny.edu/dept/edu/COLESE.HTM (accessed 1/6/03) 2.

22. Seely-Coleman memos, 2.

23. I did not see as direct an accusation as Seeley reports, although Grant comes close to it. He also implies that Seeley's criticism could have been sour grapes. Seeley had been assigned the project initially, and it was later taken away from him. Grant reports that his superiors thought that Seeley's efforts at a section 402 survey "too small." Grant, 21–23.

24. Berliner and Biddle, *Manufactured Crisis,* 71–73.

25. Frederick Mosteller and Daniel P. Moynihan, *On Equality of Educational Opportunity* (New York: Random House, 1972), 25–26.

26. Harold Berlak, "Academic achievement, race, and reform: A short guide to understanding assessment policy, standardized achievement tests, and anti-racist alternatives," http://www.edjustice.org (accessed 1/9/02).

27. Mosteller and Moynihan. See also Bruce J. Biddle and David C. Berliner, "What research says about unequal funding for schools in America," *Education Policy Reports,* Arizona State University (Winter 2002) http://edpolicy reports.org (accessed 1/20/03). See especially the section entitled "Third— Flawed Studies" (np). See also Berliner and Biddle, *The Manufactured Crisis.*

28. *CFE IIb,* 2002 N.Y. App. Div. LEXIS 7252 at *8.

29. Lyndon B. Johnson, Special Message to Congress, March 16, 1964, http://www.fordham.edu/halsall/mod/1964johnson-warpoverty.html (accessed 1/13/03).

30. Chuck Collins, Chris Hartman, and Holly Sklar, "Divided Decade: Economic Disparity at the Century's Turn," December 15, 1999, United for a Fair Economy Web site, http://www.faireconomy.org/press/archive/1999/Divided_Decade/divided_decade.html (accessed Feb. 4, 2000).

31. L. J. Schweinhart and D. P. Weikart, *Young Children Grow Up: The Effects of the Perry Preschool Program on Youths Through Age 15* (Ypsilanti, MI: High/Scope Press, 1980), 75–87. See also Valora Washington and Ura Jean Oyemade Bailey, *Project Head Start: Models and Strategies for the Twenty-first Century* (New York and London: Garland, 1995), 125–135.

32. Rebecca M. Blank, *It Takes a Nation: A New Agenda for Fighting Poverty* (New York and Princeton: Russell Sage Foundation and Princeton University Press, 1997), 99–103.

33. Jared Bernstein, Heather Boushey, Elizabeth McNichol, and Robert Zahradnik, "Pulling Apart: A State-by-State Analysis of Income Trends," Economic Policy Institute, Center on Budget and Policy Priorities, April 2002, http://www/epinet.org (accessed 5/12/02).

34. Blank, 220–221.

35. Sharon Parrott and Jennifer Mezey, "Bush Administration projects that the number of children receiving child care subsidies will fall by 200,000 during the next five years," April 12, 2002; Rachel Schumacher, "Increasing the ability to transfer TANF to CCDF (Child Care and Development Fund) is not the answer to unmet child care needs," February 5, 2003, both documents at Center for Law and Social Policy Web site, http://www.clasp.org/Pubs (accessed 2/11/03).

36. Shawn Fremstad, "Recent Welfare Reform Research Findings: Implications for TANF reauthorization and State TANF policies," Center for Budget and Policy Priorities, January 30, 2004, http://www.cbpp.org/1-30-04wel.pdf (accessed 3/10/04).

37. "Welfare Reform program reauthorized; Healthy Marriage Act, Fatherhood Initiative approved; Work requirement strengthened." PR Newswire US, February 8, 2006, LexisNexis news (accessed 3/15/06).

38. House Education and Workforce Committee passes harmful welfare reauthorization, HT MediaLtd., October 21, 2005, available at LexisNexis news (accessed 3/15/06).

39. "Census: Poverty Rises, Income Falls," *New York Times* on the Web, September 25, 2002.

40. Barbara Ehrenreich, *Nickel and Dimed: On (Not) Getting by in America* (New York: Metropolitan Books, 2001).

41. The Northwest Federation of Community Organizations, "Building a Livable Wage Movement," http://www.nwfco.org/ (accessed 2/13/03).

42. Rachel Schumacher, "Increasing the ability to transfer TANF to CCDF is not the answer to unmet child care needs" (Center for Law and Social Policy, April 12, 2002) http://www.clasp.org (accessed 4/12/02).

43. Sheryl Gay Stolberg, "Democrats Who Backed Tax Cut in '01 Balk Now," *New York Times* on the Web, January 8, 2002.

44. Blank, 108. See also Robin Toner and Cheryl Gay Stolberg, et al., "Decade After Health Care Crisis, Soaring Costs Bring New Strains," *New York Times*, August 11, 2002, Section 1, 1.

45. Jared Bernstein, "Slowing Economy May Revive Inequality," Press Release from the Economic Policy Institute, March 26, 2001, http://epinet.org (accessed 2/6/03).

46. Jan Ondrich, Alex Striker, and John Binger. "Do real estate brokers choose to discriminate? Evidence from the 1989 housing discrimination study," *Southern Economic Journal* 64, no. 4 (April 1998). Infotrac Onefile (accessed 2/8/03).

47. "Justice Gary Stein's concurring and dissenting opinion in *Toll Brothers, Inc.* v. *Township of West Windsor* points out a key fact that reveals two truths about the implementation of the *Mt. Laurel* doctrine in this state. The fact is that since *Mt. Laurel II* was decided in 1983, only 26,000 units of low- and moderate-income housing have been built in New Jersey, out of a total of 480,000 housing units. . . . The second truth is the economic limits of the *Mt. Laurel* doctrine and the builder's remedy. Although the two *Mt. Laurel* decisions proclaim the goal of an economically and racially integrated suburbia, the constitutional duty they create is essentially passive. *Mt. Laurel I* and *II* declare only that the planning and zoning power conferred by New Jersey's constitution may not be used to obstruct the building of low- and moderate-income housing. In *Mt. Laurel I*, the court disclaims either the power to compel that such housing be constructed or to provide the resources to build it. *Burlington County NAACP* v. *Township of Mt. Laurel (Mt. Laurel I)*, 1975 N.J. LEXIS 181 (N.J. March 24, 1975). The result the court foresaw from *Mt. Laurel II* was only that "a builder in New Jersey who finds it economically feasible to provide decent housing for lower income groups will no longer find it governmentally impossible." (*Southern*) *Burlington Co. NAACP* v. *Township of Mt. Laurel (Mt. Laurel II)*, 1983 N.J. LEXIS 2344 (N.J. Jan. 20, 1983). [The Mt. Laurel cases required developers to develop specified amount of low-income housing per units of exclusive, high-income housing. Unfortunately, they did not require the low-income housing to be located near the high-income housing, creating enclaves and ghettos once again.] Opinion, *New Jersey Law Review*, August 19, 2002, Lexis-Nexis (accessed 2/17/03).

48. Jean Anyon, *Ghetto Schooling: A Political Economy of Urban Renewal Projects* (New York: Teachers College Press, 1997), 62–64.

49. Reynold F. Nesiba, "Insurance Redlining: Disinvestment, Reinvestment, and the Evolving Role of Financial Institutions," (book review) *Journal of Economic Issues* 32, no. 3 (September 1998) 901–905, Infotrac onefile (accessed 2/17/03) 901.

50. Anyon, 79–81.

51. Ondrich et al.

52. William Junius Wilson, cited in Fred R. Harris and Lynn A. Curtis et al., *The Millennium Breach: The American Dilemma, Richer and Poorer*, Milton S. Eisenhower Foundation, March 1, 1998, http://www.eisenhowerfoundation.org/frames/main_frameMB.html (accessed 5/22/03), Appendix One.

53. Fred R. Harris, *The Kerner Report: The 1968 report of the National Advisory Commission on Civil Disorders* (New York: Pantheon, 1988) (originally issued in 1968).

54. Fred R. Harris and Lynn A. Curtis, *The Millennium Breach*, Chapter 1, "Thirty Years Later."

55. *Millenium Breach*, Executive Summary, "A National Policy Based on What Works," 3–6.

56. *Millennium Breach*, chapter 6, including tables 6–5 to 6–9.

57. *Millennium Breach*, 124.

58. Fred R. Harris and Lynn A. Curtis, eds., *Locked in the Poorhouse: Cities, Race, and Poverty in the United States.* Milton S. Eisenhower Foundation, 1999. See also James B. Stewart, "Locked in the Poorhouse: Cities, Race, and Poverty in the United States" (book review). *The Review of Black Political Economy* 28, no. 1 (Summer 2000), 67.

59. Pauline Lipman, "Bush's Education Plan, Globalization, and the Politics of Race," *Cultural Logic* 4, no. 1 (Fall 2000), http://eserver.org/clogic/4-1/lipman.html (accessed 3/9/02).

60. Richard Rothstein, "Where's the money going: Changes in the level and composition of educational spending 1991–1996," The Economic Policy Institute, 1997, http://www.epinet.org (accessed 1/7 03).

61. Collins, Hartman, and Sklar, "Divided Decade."

62. 8 U.S.C. 1601 §§ 1601 *et seq.* (2005).

63. G. Sandefur, M. Martin, and T. Wells, "Poverty as a public health issue: Poverty since the Kerner Commission Report of 1968," Institute for Research on Poverty, Discussion paper no. 1158–1198, March 1998, http://econpapers.hhs.se/paper/wopwispod/1158-98.htm (accessed 2/11/03).

64. Sandefur, Martin, and Wells, 26–27.

65. William J. Clinton, The President's Economic Report to the Nation, 1996. http://www.gpoaccess.gov/eop/search.html (accessed 6/15/04), 4.

66. "Census: Poverty Rises, Income Falls," *New York Times* on the Web, September 25, 2002 (accessed 9/25/02).

67. Heather Boushey, Chauna Brocht, Bethney Gundersen, and Jared Bernstein, *Hardships in America: The Real Story of Working Families,* Economic Policy Institute, July 2001, publication # 200107, http://www.epinet.org (accessed 1/5/03), 2.

68. Jared Bernstein et al., "Pulling Apart."

69. Bruce Lambert, "Study Calls L. I. Most Segregated Suburb" *New York Times* on the Web, June 5, 2002 Section B, p. 5, col. 4.

70. Education Week, Quality Counts 2003, http://www.edweek.org/sreports/qc03/templates/state.cfm?slug=17qcny.h22 (accessed 1/8/03). New York gets an A for adequacy of resources, but a D+ for equity.

71. Blank, 5.

72. See also graph and analysis by the Economic Policy Institute, Economic Policy Snapshots, 1998, "The Trade Deficit and Falling Wages," http://www.epinet.org/webfeatures/snapshots/archive/062399/snapshots062399.html (accessed 3/12/03).

73. Dean Baker, "Nine Myths about Social Security," *Atlantic Monthly* (July 1998) (digital edition), http://www.theatlantic.com/issues/98jul/socsec.htm (accessed 3/23/04).

74. A misnomer, since the old Federalist Party advocated more federal power, not less, as does the New Federalism.

75. Bureau of Child and Maternal Heath, Child Health, USA "School Dropouts," 2002, http://mchb.hrsa.gov/chusa02/main_pages/page_13.htm (accessed 3/23/04).

76. Boushey, et al., *Hardships in America.* 5.

77. Jamie Hickner, "Poor children in U.S. Increase to Six Million" (*Columbia University Record* 20, no. 15 (February 3, 1995), http://columbia.edu/cu/record/archives.vol20_iss15/records2015.20.html (accessed 2/12/03). This is a 1998 report based on 1996 figures.

78. "One in four US Children under six live in poverty," World Socialist Web site, http://www.wsws.org/news/1998.july1998/poc-j22.shtml (accessed 2/12/03).

79. Hickner, "Poor children in U.S. Increase to Six Million" (np).

80. Hickner, "Poor children in U.S. Increase to Six Million" (np).

81. "Improving children's economic security: Research findings about increasing family income through employment," National Center for Children in Poverty Web site, Policy Briefs, August 19, 2002, http://www.nccp.org/improving_security_series.html (accessed 2/12/03).

82. Sue Books, "Playing with Numbers, playing with need: schooling and the federal poverty line, *Educational Foundations* 14, no. 2 (Spring 2000): 5–20.

83. J. Lawrence Aber, Director of the National Center for Children in Poverty, "Poor Children in U.S. Increase to Six Million" (interview), (*Columbia University Record* 20, no. 15, February 3, 1995) http://www.columbia.edu/cu/record/archives/vol20/vol20_iss15/record2015.20html (accessed 2/12/03).

84. "Children In Poverty," Child Health USA, Department of Health and Human Services, Maternal and Child Health Bureau, Resource Information Center, 2002, http://www.mchirc.net/HTML/CHUSA-02/main_pages/page_12.htm (accessed 1/14/2003).

85. "Income Stable, Poverty Up, Numbers of Americans With and Without Health Insurance Rise, Census Bureau Reports," US Census Bureau Newsroom, Thursday, August 26, 2004, http://www.census.gov/Press-Release/www/releases/archives/income_wealth/002484.html (accessed 7/6/05).

86. Bruce J. Lanphear, Kim Deitrich, Peggy Auinger, and Christopher Cox, "Cognitive deficits associated with blood lead concentrations <10 micrograms per deciliter in US children and adults," *Public Health Reports,* U.S. Department of Health and Human Services, 2000; 115): 521–529. See also Idit Trope, Dolores Lopez-Villegas, Kim M. Cecil, and Robert E. Lenkinski, "Exposure to lead appears to selectively alter metabolism of cortical gray matter," *Pediatrics* 2001, 107 (June 2001) 1437–1443.

87. "Lead exposure and Behavior," *Pediatrics for Parents* 19, no. 12 (February 2, 2003) 1.

88. See evidence cited above and Mark E. Moss, Bruce P. Lanphear, Peggy Auinger "Association of Dental caries and Blood Lead Levels," *Journal of the American Medical Association* 281, issue 24 (June 23, 1999): 2294. See also A. Roberto Frisancho and Alan S. Ryan, "Decreased stature associated with moderate blood lead concentrations in Mexican-American children" (*American Journal of Clinical Nutrition* 54, no. 3 (September 1991) 516–519. See also Work Group of the Advisory Committee on Childhood Lead Poisoning Prevention, A Review of Health Effects of Blood Lead Levels <10mg/dL (Centers for Disease Control, February 23, 2004).

89. S. G. Selevan, D. C. Rice, K. A. Hogan, S. Y. Euling, A. Pfahles-Hutchens, and J. Bethel, "Blood lead concentration and delayed puberty in girls," *New England Journal of Medicine* 348 no.16 (April 17, 2003) 1527–1536, http://www.ncbi.nlm.nih.gov/entrez/query.fcgi?cmd=Retrieve&db=PubMed&list_uids=12700372&dopt=Abstract (accessed 3/23/04).

90. Larry Aber and Julian Palmer, "Poverty and Brain Development in Young Children," in Mary Jensen and Mary Anne Hannibal, eds., *Issues, Advocacy and Leadership in Early Education* (Boston, London, Toronto, Sydney, Tokyo, and Singapore: Allyn and Bacon, 2000), 63–65.

91. Lanphear et al., "Cognitive deficits.", See also D. C. Bellinger, K. M. Stiles, and H. L. Needleman, "Low-level lead exposure, intelligence and academic achievement: A long term follow-up study," *Pediatrics* 90, (1992) 855–861. See also D. C. Bellinger, J. Sloman, A. Leviton, M. Rabinowitz, H. L. Needleman, and C. Waternaux, "Low-level lead exposure and children's cognitive function in the preschool years," *Pediatrics* 87 (February 1, 1991) 219–227.

92. Committee on Environmental Health, American Academy of Pediatrics, "Screening for Elevated Blood Lead Levels," *Pediatrics* 101, no. 6 (June 1998) 1072–1078, http://www.aap.org/policy/rc9815.html (accessed 1/15/03).

93. Xianchen Liu, Kim N. Deitrich, Jerilyn Radcliffe, N. Beth Ragan, George E. Rhoads, and Walter Rogan, "Do Children with Falling Blood Lead Levels have Improved Cognition?" *Pediatrics* 110, iss. 4 (October 2002) 787–792. Although other studies have shown mixed results, these researchers found that blood lead levels reduced by chelation or succimer did not improve cognition, although reduction of environmental exposure and stimulation by concerned parents may have resulted in the improvement they found in the placebo treated children. These researchers conclude, "We believe that, because of that inconsistency, the data do not indicate that lead-induced cognition defects are reversible. Primary prevention and preventing additional increases . . . remain the only effective means of dealing with lead poisoning." 791.

94. J. Julian Chisolm Jr. "The Road to primary prevention of lead toxicity in children" *Pediatrics* 107 (2001) 581–593. Dr. Chisolm notes that prevention is, in the long run, less expensive than treatment and more permanently beneficial to the population at large. I would add, to the society.

95. Richard Rabin, "Re: Paint Industry did not stop selling lead paint in 1950" (June 7, 2002, electronic letter published by the *American Journal of Public Health*, in response to Nancy L. Rothman, Rita J. Lourie, and John Gaughan, "Lead Awareness: North Philly Style," *American Journal of Public Health* 92, issue 5

[May 2002] 739-741) http://www.ajph.org/cgi/content/abstract/92/5/739 (accessed 2/9/03).

96. Jim Memmott, "Childhood lead poisoning has later toll, expert says," *Rochester Democrat and Chronicle*, Saturday, March 23, 2002, B5.

97. The Sentencing Project, "Facts about prisons and prisoners," August 2002, http://www.SentencingProject.org (accessed 2/12/03). The Sentencing Project reports that "[n]early one in seven (13.4%) black males aged 25–29 were in prison or jail in 2001, as were 1 in 24 (4.1%) Hispanic males and 1 in 55 (1.8%) white males in the same age group."

98. *Hayden* v. *Pataki*, No. 00 Civ. 8586, 2004 U.S. Dist. LEXIS 10863 (S.D.N.Y. June 14, 2004).

99. "Department of Legal Counsel: Voting Rights: Felon disenfranchisement," Community Service Society: Fighting Poverty, Strengthening New York. http://www.cssny.org/legal/voting.html (accessed 3/23/04) (CSS).

100. CSS, "Statements."

101. Committee on Environmental Health, American Academy of Pediatrics, "Screening for Elevated Blood Lead Levels," *Pediatrics* 101, no. 6 (June 1998) 1072–1078, http://www.aap.org/policy/re9815.html (accessed 1/15/03).

102. Anita Weinberg and Maria Woltjen, "Lead Poisoning Persists Despite Laws, City Codes," *Chicago Daily Law Bulletin*, Law Bulletin Publishing Company, October 28, 2002, LexisNexis legal research (accessed 1/6/03).

103. Jim Memmott, "Childhood lead poisoning."

104. Bruce Lanphear outlines the history of so-called allowable levels. In 1960, 60 micrograms per deciliter was considered "safe" (since it did not cause death). In 1971, the government lowered that to 40, in 1978 to 30, in 1985 to 25, and in 1991 to 10. Despite convincing evidence, the government has refused to lower it further. Lanphear et al., Cognitive deficits.

105. Bill Moyers, PBS: Now, May 10, 2002, http://www.pbs.org/now/transcript/transcript117_full.html (accessed 1/15/03).

106. "Lowdown on Lead Poisoning," *Essence Magazine* 21, no. 9 (January 1991) 80.

107. Richard Rabin, "Warnings Unheeded: A History of Childhood Lead Poisoning," *American Journal of Public Health* 29, no. 12 (December 1989) 1673.

108. Gardiner Harris, "Low lead levels could pose risk; government likely to overhaul guidelines on how much is safe for kids," *Wall Street Journal*, September 11, 2002, D1, LexisNexis news (accessed 2/10/03).

109. Committee on Environmental Health, Screening for Elevated Blood Lead Levels.

110. Amhed Gomaa, Howard Hu, David Bellinger, Joel Schwartz, Shirng-Wern Tsaih, Teresa Gonzalez-Cossio, Lourdes Schnaas, Karen Peterson, Antonio Aro, and Mauricio Herndandez-Avila, "Maternal Bone Lead as an independent risk factor for fetal neurotoxicity: A prospective study," *Pediatrics* 110 (July 2002) 110–118.

111. Leonard J. Paulozzi, Joanne Shapp, Robert E. Drawbaugh, and Jan K. Carney. "Prevalence of lead poisoning among two-year-old children in Vermont," *Pediatrics* 96, no. 1 (July 1995) 78, Infotrac (accessed 1/14/03).

112. Bill Moyers, *Now,* May 10, 2002.

113. Author's personal experience, early 1990s.

114. Matthew P. Dumont, "Lead, Mental Health, and Social Action: A View from the Bridge," *Public Health Report 2000,* 115: 505–510, U.S. department of Health and Human Services, LexisNexis legal research, 2/15/03.

115. Julie Ganon Shoop, "HUD Rules Don't Protect Kids from Lead Hazards," *Trial* 30, no. 9 (September 1, 1994) 106.

116. J. Julian Chisolm, "The road to primary prevention of lead toxicity in children," *Pediatrics* 2001, 107: 581–583.

117. James Goodman, "$2 million to fight lead paint in county," *Rochester Democrat and Chronicle,* January 14, 2003, http://www.rochesterdandc.com/news/0114story5_news.shtml (accessed January 14, 2003).

118. "Lead: A toxic legacy" (a three part series), *Rochester Democrat and Chronicle,* Sunday, June 25–Tuesday, June 27, 2006, 1A–10A, 1A–8A, IA–8A. See also Brian Sharp, "City zeros in on lead," *Rochester Democrat and Chronicle,* Friday, June 30, 2006, 1A–11A.

119. Katrina Smith Korfmacher, Ph.D., Outreach Coordinator, Environmental Health Sciences Center, September 2, 2003, "Analysis of dust wipe sampling in 1998–2001 Monroe County HUD grant," http://www.leadsafeby2010.org/Articles (accessed 7/6/05).

120. Carl Weiser, "Critics claim federal panels tilting to right: Cincinnati doctor at center of flap over his appointment," *Cincinnati Enquirer,* Tuesday, November 5, 2002, http://www.enquirer.com/editions/2002/11/05/loc_oh-lead05.html (accessed 1/5/03).

121. Raja Mishra, "Rhode Island wins lead paint suit," *Boston Globe,* February 23, 2006, available at LexisNexis News (accessed 3/25/06). See also, "Paint industry eyes state pact to limit future lead contamination suits," Superfund Report, March 13, 2006, available at LexisNexis News (accessed 3/15/06).

122. Bill Moyers, PBS: Now, May 10, 2002.

123. Bill Moyers, PBS: Now, May 10, 2002.

124. Rabin, "Warnings Unheeded . . ." 1668.

125. Weisner, "Critics claim."

126. Nancy L. Rothman, Rita Lourie, John Gaughan, and Neva White, "A Community-developed, community-based lead poisoning prevention program: Lead awareness: North Philly style," *Holistic Nursing Practice* 14, iss. 1 (October) 47–55. See the follow-up, also by the same authors, "Lead awareness: North Philly style," *American Journal of Public Health* 92, iss. 5 (May 2002) 739–741. The researchers found that blood lead levels in children under six were reduced in the experimental tracts more than in the control tracts. At the end of the three years of intervention there were no children with blood lead levels over 29 micrograms per deciliter in the experimental tracts, resulting from a 5% greater reduction in children with levels greater than 29 micrograms per deciliter in the experimental tracts than in the control tracts (740). Although this is not a "cure," it does illustrate that intensive community-based awareness programs can help.

127. Vernalia R. Randall, Course Syllabus, University of Dayton Law School, "Race, health care, and the law," http:academic.udayton.edu/health/racist.htm (ND) and "Reparations for Slavery are due, but healing isn't about the money, says health care expert" (July 31, 2002), http://www.udayton.edu/news/nr/073102.html (both documents accessed 1/27/03).

128. Centers for Disease Control, Fact Book, 2000/2001, September 2000, http://www.cdc.gov/maso/factbook/main.htm (accessed 1/15/03). (CDC Fact Book 2000/2001).

129. Leslie Casimir, "Maternal death Rate for blacks troubles U.S.," *Seattle Times*, June 9, 2001, http://seattletimes.newsource.com (accessed 1/16/03).

130. Robert A. Lynch, Lorraine Galinka Malcoe, Valerie J. Skaggs, and Michelle C. Kegler, "The relationship between residential lead exposures and elevated blood lead levels in a rural mining community," *Journal of Environmental Health* 63, iss. 3 (October–September, 2000) 43–49.

131. Testimony of Adam Sharpe, Associate Administrator, Office of Prevention, Pesticides, and Toxic Substances, Environmental Protection Agency, before the Senate Subcommittee on Housing and Transportation, http://www/epa.gov/ocir/hearings/tes (accessed 2/14/03).

132. Sharpe, 48.

133. World Health Organization, "Global Estimates of Maternal Mortality for 1995: Results of an in-depth review, analysis, and estimation strategy," http://www.who.int/reproductive-health/publications/RHR_01_9_maternal_mortality_estimates/statement_on_maternal_mortality_estimates.en.html (accessed 1/16/03) table 1.

134. Casimir, Maternal death rate.

135. R. O. Wright, S. W. Tsiah, J. Schwartz, R. J. Wright, and H. Hu, "Association between iron deficiency and blood lead level in a longitudinal analysis of children followed in an urban primary care clinic," *Journal of Pediatrics* 142, no. 1 (January 2003) 9–14.

136. Sue Books, "Environmentally induced damage to children: a call for broadening the critical agenda," (2002) ED 420 399. Books' article points out that related illnesses, such as tuberculosis, asthma, allergies, respiratory disease, depression, and violent anger are increasing, particularly in the inner cities. These illnesses, considered an affliction of the poor, are, in reality, the results of environmentally induced damage that affects children's performance in school.

137. Centers for Disease Control, Asthma Page, http://www.cdc.gov/asthma/children.htm (accessed 8/3/05).

138. Gary Sandefur, Molly Martin, and Thomas Wells, March 1998. "Poverty as a Public health Issue: Poverty since the Kerner Commission Report of 1968" (University of Wisconsin Institute for Research on Poverty), http://econpapers.hhs.se/paper/wopwispod/1158-98.htm (accessed 2/11/03).

139. Jonathan Kozol, *Savage Inequalities* (New York: Crown Publishers, 1991) 175.

140. An executive summary, description, and text of the No Child Left Behind Act of 2001 is available at http://www.ed.gov/offices/OESE/esea/.

Chapter 6

1. Jay R. Campbell, Catherine M. Hombo, and John Mazzeo, "NAEP 1999 Trends in Academic Progress: Three Decades of Student Performance," August 2000, The Nation's Report Card, National Assessment of Educational Progress, 1999,   http://nces.ed.gov/nationsreportcard/pubs/main1999/2000469.asp (accessed 3/23/04).

2. "Unemployment rate by age, race, and sex, 2001, 2002, U.S.," http://www.infoplease.com/ipa/A0104716.html (accessed 3/23/04). See also "Unemployment rates by race, December 2002–2003," State Health Facts online, Henry J. Kaiser Family Foundation, http://www.sces.org/lmi/data/trends/charts/Chartroom/sld022.htm (accessed 3/23/04).

3. State Rates of Incarceration by Race, the Sentencing Project, 2004, http://www.sentencingproject.org/pdfs/racialdisparity.pdf (accessed 3/23/04).

4. See Table 5.2 supra.

5. "Closing the Achievement Gaps in Urban Schools: A Survey of Academic Progress and Promising Practices in the Great City Schools," October 1999, Council of the Great City Schools Web site, http://www.cgcs.org/reports/achievement_gaps.html (accessed 3/23/04).

6. *Brown I*, 1954 U.S. LEXIS 2094 at *495.

7. Coleman Report, "Indirect evidence suggests that school factors make more difference in achievement for minority groups than for whites; for Negroes, this is especially true in the South . . . it is children who come the least prepared to school for whom the characteristics of a school make the most difference." 297. This remark is largely ignored in the report's conclusion. In addition, the report's bar graphs showing children's exposure to other racial groups are the most extreme for whites, although blacks are also segregated. Consequently, the one thing that the report might have recommended to improve things for black children—desegregation—receives little notice. The report does not seem to consider this information important enough to revise their conclusion that school factors do not affect achievement as much as "quality of peers" and the socioeconomic circumstances of the child.

8. Coleman Report, 29.

9. Christopher Jencks and Meredith Phillips, "America's next achievement test: closing the black-white test score gap," *The American Prospect* 40, (September–October 1998) 7.

10. Erica Frankenberg, Chungmei Lee, and Gary Orfield, "A multiracial society with segregated schools, Are we losing the dream?" Harvard Civil Rights Project Web site, Harvard University, January 2003, http://www.civilrights project.harvard.edu (accessed 3/10/04).

11. *Brigham*, 1997 Vt. LEXIS 13, at *267.

12. William D. Duncome and John F. Yinger, "Performance Standards and Educational Cost Indexes: You can't have one without the other" in Helen F. Ladd, Rosemary Chalk, and Janet S. Hansen, eds. *Equity and Adequacy in Educational Finance: Issues and Perspectives* (Washington, DC: National Academy Press, 1999) 260–297.

13. The judges agreed with the appellants that "The term 'function effectively' does imply employment," but they limited this to "the ability to get a job, and support oneself, and thereby not be a charge on the public fisc." They explicitly excluded any consideration of how a person could support him or herself on the minimum wage, declaring instead "Society needs workers in all levels of jobs, the majority of which may well be at the low level." Nor did they consider the decline in employment opportunities in inner cities. Their unspoken conclusion is easy to supply. Those children who have "minimally adequate" schooling can become the low level workers which society needs. *CFE IIb*, 2002 N.Y. App. Div. LEXIS 7252, at *8.

14. Shannon P. Duffy, "Judge throws out Philly's school district race case," *Legal Intelligencer* (November 23, 1988): 1, LexisNexis legal research (accessed 5/26/03).

15. ". . . the skills required to enable a person to obtain employment, vote, and serve on a jury, are imparted between grades eight and nine . . . ," *CFE IIb*, 2002 N.Y. App. Div. LEXIS 7252 at *8.

16. *Rose* template, Chapter 1, 8–9; DeGrasse's template, Chapter 2, 56.

17. *Horton* v. *Meskill*, Nos. 12499, 12501, 12501, 1985 Conn. LEXIS 665 (Conn. Jan. 15, 1985), the *Sheff* cases in Connecticut, and the *Paynter* and *CFE* cases in New York.

18. James E. Ryan, "The influence of race in school finance reform," *Michigan Law Review* 98 (November 1999): 480 and n. 246.

19. For Virginia, see "Testing Our Schools," the Merrow Report, *Frontline*, March 28, 2002, http://www.pbs.org/wgbh/pages/frontline/shows/schools/testing/theme.html (accessed 4/26/03). For Philadelphia see, "Rescue Mission," News Hour, December 11, 2002, http://www.pbs.org/newshour/bb/education/july-dec02/rescue_mission_12-11-1.html (accessed 4/26/03).

20. Valerie E. Lee and David T. Burkam, *Inequality at the Starting Gate: Social Differences in Achievement as Children Begin School* (Washington, DC: Economic Policy Institute, 2002), 84.

21. Gary Orfield, Susan Eaton, and the Harvard Project on School Desegregation, *Dismantling Desegregation: The Quiet Reversal of* Brown v. Board of Education (New York: The New Press, 1996), 1–22.

22. James E. Rosenbaum, "Changing the geography of opportunity by expanding residential choice: Lessons from the Gautreaux Program," *Housing Policy Debate* 6, issue 1 (1995) 231–269. See also "Latest Decision on *Gautreaux* v. *Chicago Housing Authority*," National Housing Law Project, *Housing Law Bulletin* 27 (October 1997), http://www.nhlp.org/html/hlb/1097/1097gautreaux.htm (accessed 3/23/03): np.

23. Helen Ferris, " New Loan Program Inspires Affordable Housing," *New Jersey Law Journal*, May 2, 2005, LexisNexis legal research (accessed 8/5/05). The Mt. Laurel cases held that suburban municipalities have an obligation to plan and provide for their fair share of the unmet regional need for safe, decent housing affordable to low- and moderate-income households. Unfortunately, there was no provision to have the low-income housing integrated into other, higher income developments. The Balanced Housing Program, administered under the state's Fair Housing Act, resulted from the Mt. Laurel cases in New Jersey.

24. Martin Carnoy, *School Vouchers: Examining the Evidence*, 2001, Economic Policy Institute Web site, http://www.epinet.org (accessed 3/25/03).

25. John Devine, *Maximum Security: The culture of violence in inner-city schools* (Chicago: University of Chicago Press, 1996). Jonathan Kozol, *Ordinary Resurrections: Children in the years of hope* (New York: Crown Publishing, 2000).

26. Jacques Steinberg, "Private Groups get 42 schools in Philadelphia" *New York Times*, national desk, April 18, 2002, A1, LexisNexis news (accessed 8/20/02).

27. Jack Jennings, "The challenges of NCLB," Center on Educational Policy, March 2, 2003, http://www.cep-dc.org/pubs/speakingoutmarch2003/speakingoutmarch2003.htm (accessed 3/25/03).

28. Gerald W. Bracey, "No Child Left Behind: Where does the money go?" Educational Policy Studies Laboratory, Arizona State University, June 2005, http://www.edpolicylab.org (accessed 6/30/05).

29. David Roediger, *Towards The Abolition of Whiteness* (London and New York: Verso, 1994), 184 ff.

30. Roediger, *Towards the Abolition*, 186.

31. Roediger, *Towards the Abolition*, 184. See also Matthew Frye Jacobson, *Whiteness of Different Color: European Immigrants and the Alchemy of Race* (Cambridge, MA: Harvard University Press, 1998).

32. Roediger, *Towards the Abolition*, 127–187.

33. The editors of *Ebony*, *Pictorial History of Black America* (originally published by Johnson Publishing Company, Inc., Chicago, 1971) http://www.callandpost.com/blackhistory/p241.htm (accessed 3/25/03).

34. Jacobson, *Whiteness*, 140–142.

35. Valerie Babb, *Whiteness Visible: The Meaning of Whiteness in American Literature and Culture* (New York: New York University Press, 1998.)

36. Kincheloe, Joe L. "The Struggle to Define and Reinvent Whiteness: A Pedagogical Analysis." *College Literature*. 26:3 (1999) 162–195. ProQuest, document ID: 45683503 (accessed 4/5/04).

37. Jacobson, *Whiteness*, 117.

38. Henry A. Giroux, "Rewriting the discourse of racial identity: Towards a pedagogy and politics of whiteness," *Harvard Educational Review* 67:2 (Summer 1997): np, http://home.gwu.edu/~pryder/English11_S01/giroux_racial%20identity.htm (accessed 4/5/04).

39. *Grutter* v. *Bollinger*, No. 02-241, 2003 U.S. LEXIS 4800, at *365 (U.S. June 23, 2003).

40. *Gratz* v. *Bollinger*, No. 02-516, 2003 U.S. LEXIS 4801 (U.S. June 30, 2003).

41. *Grutter*, 2003 U.S. LEXIS 4800 at *365

42. Valerie Babb, *Whiteness Visible*, 45.

43. Dr. Craig Venter, president and chief scientific officer, Celera Genomics Corporation, speaking at the White House celebration of the completion of the sequencing of the human genome on June 26, 2002, http://www.genome.gov/page.cfm?pageID=10001356 (accessed March 24, 2003).

44. The Rural School and Community Trust, "Rural schools score major victory in Arkansas Supreme Court," November 2002, http://www.ruraledu. org/issues/finance/ar_victory.htm (accessed 3/23/03).

45. *Tennessee Small Sch. Systems* v. *McWherter (McWherter II)*, S.C. No. 01-S01-9209-CH-0010, 1993 Tenn. LEXIS 114 (Tenn. March 22, 1993).

46. *Tennessee Small Sch. Systems* v. *McWherter (McWherter I)*, 1992 Tenn. App. LEXIS 486 (Tenn. Ct. App. June 5, 1992).

47. James E. Ryan, "The influence of race in school finance reform," 453.

48. Ryan, "The influence of race in school finance reform," 454.

49. *Horton* v. *Meskill*, Nos. 12499, 12501, 12501, 1985 Conn. LEXIS 665 (Conn. Jan. 15, 1985).

50. "Third Annual ACCESS Conference focuses on achieving education reform in difficult times," Campaign for Fiscal Equity, Access Web site, http://www.accessednetwork.org/conference03.htm (accessed 3/23/03).

51. United States Department of Justice: Civil Rights Division, Educational Opportunities Section, "Overview," April 24, 2002, http://www.usdoj.gov/crt/edo/overview.htm (accessed 4/8/03).

52. Gerald Grant, "Shaping Social Policy: The Politics of the Coleman Report," *Teachers College Record* 75, no. 1 (September 1973) 47–50.

53. "Settlement reached in *Sheff* v. *O'Neill*: Pact calls for three-pronged approach," *Connecticut Law Tribune* 29 no. 3 (January 27, 2003) 1.

54. "Court says Charlotte can stop busing plan" *Holland Sentinel* (Holland, Michigan), Saturday, September 22, 2001, http://www.hollandsentinel.com/stories/092201/new_0922010030.shtml (accessed 6/5/03).

55. Bureau of Justice Statistics, "Prisoners in 2001," NCJ 195189, July 2002, http://www.ojp.usdoj.gov/bjs/abstract/p01.htm (accessed 6/3/03).

56. Karl O. Haigler, Caroline Harlow, Patricia O'Connor, and Anne Campbell, "Executive Summary of Literacy Behind Prison Walls: Profiles of the Prison Population from the National Adult Literacy Survey," National Assessment of Adult Literacy, National Center for Education Statistics, http://nces.ed.gov/naal/resources/execsummprison.asp (accessed 6/5/03). This study is based on data from the 1992 National Assessment of Adult Literacy. A link to the entire study is available at this site.

57. Bureau of Justice Statistics, "Juvenile Felony Defendants in Criminal Courts: Survey of 40 Counties, 1998," NCJ 197961, May 2003, http://www.ojp.usdoj.gov/bjs/abstract/jfdcc98.htm (accessed 6/6/03).

58. John Devine, *Maximum Security*, 201.

59. For instance, compulsory attendance, higher school leaving ages (resulting from child labor laws), sex education, desegregation (now being undone), more widespread early childhood education (but not enough Head Start placements), vocational education (when it is not decades behind current technological advances, as it often is), bilingual education (now under attack), English as a Second Language, multicultural education (when it is done pluralistically, without marginalizing diverse cultures), special education (but minorities are more likely to be identified) and its latest manifestation, inclusion (when it is not done simply as a cost-cutting measure), and more.

60. The School-to-Prison Pipeline Conference, sponsored by the Harvard Civil Rights Project and Northeastern University's Institute on Race and Justice, May 15–16, 2003, Cambridge, Massachusetts. For program and mission see: http://www.civilrightsproject.harvard.edu/convenings/schooltoprison/synopsis.php (accessed 4/5/04). See also John Devine, *Maximum Security*.

61. Diane J. English and Cathy Spatz Widom, "Childhood victimization and delinquency, adult criminality, and violent criminal behavior: A replication and extension," A Report to the United States Justice Department, February 1, 2002, http://www.ncjrs.org/pdffiles1/nij/grants/192291.pdf (accessed 6/4/03). Paper presented at the 2000 American Society of Criminology Conference, November 14–18, 2000.

62. Edith Rasell and Lawrence Mishel, "Shortchanging Education: How United States Spending on Grades K–12 Lags Behind Other Industrial Nations," Economic Policy Institute, 1990, http://www.lights.com/epi/virlib/Briefing Papers/1990/shortchanginge.PDF (accessed 3/25/03) 1.

63. Richard Rothstein, "Where's the money going?: Changes in the level and composition of education spending, 1991–1996," Economic Policy Institute, 1997, http://www.epinet.org/content.cfm/books_wheremoneyes (accessed 3/23/03).

64. *Lau* v. *Nichols*, No. 72-6520, 1974 U.S. LEXIS 151 (U.S. Jan. 21, 1974).

65. "Kansas court rules school funding system unconstitutional," *The Rural School Funding* 2, iss. 20 (December 5, 2003), The Rural School and Community Trust Web site, http://www.ruraledu.org/issues/finance/news220.htm (accessed 4/7/04).

66. John Milburn, "Kansas Supreme Court rules spending bill meets requirement for more education dollars," Associated Press, July 8, 2005, Friday BC cycle, Topeka, Kansas, LexisNexis News (accessed 7/9/05).

67. Rothstein, "Where's the money going?" 3.

68. Daniel J. Losen and Gary Orfield. "Racial inequity in special education," Harvard Civil Rights Project, June 2002, http://www.civilrightsproject.harvard.edu/research/specialed/IDEA_paper02.php (accessed 4/7/04).

69. Wade Biddix, Allison Garrison, William Marrow, and Kristina Miller, "Social Equity in Special Education," www.people.vcu.edu/~bwooldri/_pdf_docs/social_equity_pdf/sep_spec_ed.pdf (retrieved 4/7/04), 7–8.

70. Howard Berlak, "Academic Achievement, Race and Reform," Educational Justice website, May 2001, http://www.edjustice.org/ (accessed 3/31/03).

71. "Study: only "50-50" chance of high school graduation for U.S. minority students, Weak accountability rules found," Harvard Civil Rights Project Web site, February 25, 2004, http://www.civilrightsproject.harvard.edu/news/press releases.php/record_id=45/ (accessed 4/7/04).

72. Tim Wise, "Not-so-little white lies: Education and the myth of black anti-intellectualism," *Znet*, *Z Magazine*, 11/6/02, http://www.zmag.org/sustainers/content/2002-11/26wise.cfm (accessed 3/23/03).

73. Wise, "Lies," np.

74. Martin Carnoy and Richard Rothstein, "Hard lessons in California: Minority pay gap widens despite more schooling higher scores," Economic Policy Institute, 1996, http://www.epinet.org (accessed 5/6/03).

75. Wise, "Lies," np.

76. Carl L. Bankston III and Stephen J. Caldas, "The American school dilemma: race and scholastic performance," *Sociological Quarterly* 38, no. 3, 423–430 (np in Internet version, author's introduction).

77. Bankston and Caldas, introduction.

78. Vincent J. Roscigno. "Race and reproduction of educational disadvantage," *Social Forces* 76, no. 3 (March 1998).

79. Ronald F. Ferguson, "Teachers' perceptions and expectations and the black-white test score gap," *Urban Education* 38, no. 4 (July 2003) 460–495.

80. Robert I. Lerman, *Improving career outcomes for youth: Lessons from the US and OECD Experience* (US Department of Labor, July 2000, Research and Evaluation Series 01-D), 8.

81. Ryan A. Smith, "Racial differences in access to hierarchical authority: An analysis of change over time, 1972–1994," *Sociological Quarterly* 40 issue 3 (Summer 1999), http://caliber.ucpress.net/loi/tsq (accessed 4/3/04).

82. Chuck Collins, Betsy Leondar-Wright, and Holly Sklar, *Shifting Fortunes: The Perils of the Growing American Wealth Gap*, United for a Fair Economy Web site, http://ufenet.org/press/archive/1999/shifting_fortunes_press.html (accessed 3/31/03).

83. The National Commission on Excellence in Education (NCEE), "Introduction," in *A Nation at Risk*, Government Printing Office, Washington, DC 1983, http://www.ed.gov/pubs/NatAtRisk/index.html (accessed 4/3/03). [In subsequent references, I use section titles to direct the reader to quotes, since the document has no page numbers in the Internet version.]

84. Christopher Edley Jr. and Johanna Wald, "The grade retention fallacy," Harvard Civil Rights Project staff, *Boston Globe*, opinion/editorial, December 16, 2002, http://www.civilrightsproject.harvard.edu/research/articles/retention_edley.php (accessed 2/15/03).

85. Berliner and Biddle, *The Manufactured Crisis*. See also chapter 5, supra.

86. Allan Bloom, *The Closing of the American Mind* (New York: Simon and Schuster, 1987); William Bennett, ed., *The Book of the Virtues: A Treasury Great Moral Stories* (New York: Simon and Schuster, 1993); E. D. Hirsh, *Cultural Literacy: What Every American Ought to Know* (New York: Random House, 1987).

87. David C. Berliner and Bruce J. Biddle, "What research says about small classes and their effects," Arizona State University Education Policy Reports Project (Winter 2002), http://www.asu.edu/educ/epsl/EPRP/Reports/EPRP-0202-101/EPRP-0202-101.htm, (accessed 2/15/03) "Surveys and econometric studies," paragraph 4, np.

88. Daniel J. Losen and Gary Orfield, eds., *Racial Inequity in Special Education* (Cambridge, MA: Harvard University Press and the Harvard Civil Rights Project, 2002), http://civilrightsdproject.harvard.edu.

89. Berliner and Biddle, "What research says," "Trial Programs and Large Field Experiments," np.

90. Stefan C. Friedman and Carl Campanile, "Tutor tempest: Moms sue Klein for ed rights" *New York Post*, January 28, 2003, all editions, 017. LexisNexis news (accessed 4/9/03).

91. Gerald W. Bracey, "No Child Left Behind: Where Does the Money Go?" Educational Policy Studies Laboratory, Arizona State University, June 2005, www.asu.edu/educ/epsl/EPRU/ documents/EPSL-0506-114-EPRU-exec.pdf (accessed 7/22/05).

92. Deborah Meier, *The Power of Their Ideas: Lessons for America from a Small School in Harlem.* (Boston: Beacon Press, 1995).

93. Deborah Meier, *Will Standards Save Public Education?* (Boston: Beacon Press, 2000).

94. David J. Hoff, "States revise the meaning of 'proficient'," *Education Week* on the Web, October 9, 2002, http://www.edweek.org (accessed 3/25/03). See also, Schools Not Jails Newswire, "California v. Leave No Child Behind Act," http://www.SchoolsNotJails.com/article.php?sid=106 (accessed 4/25/03).

95. Scott Joftus, policy director, and Brenda Maddox-Dolan, "Left out and left behind: NCLB and the American High School," Alliance for Excellent Education Web site, April 2003, http://www.all4ed.org/publications/NCLB/index.html (accessed 7/10/05).

96. David B. Caruso, "Firms see potential windfall in education reforms," Associated Press, Philadelphia, December 1, 2002, Association for Supervision and Curriculum Development Web site, http://www.ascd.org/cms/index.cfm?TheViewID=1573 (accessed 4/8/04).

97. Walt Haney, "The Myth of the Texas Miracle in Education," *Educational Policy Analysis Archives* 8, no. 41 (August 19, 2000), http://www.epaa.asu.edu (accessed 7/10/05).

98. Alfred North Whitehead, *The Aims of Education and Other Essays* (New York; New American Library, 1949 c. 1929.)

99. Audrey L. Amrein and David C. Berliner, "High-stakes testing, uncertainty, and student learning," *Education Policy Analysis Archives* 10, no. 18 (March 28, 2002), http://epaa.asu.edu/epaa/v10n18/ (accessed 4/10/04).

100. Amrein and Berliner, "High stakes testing, uncertainty, and student learning," "Abstract," (np).

101. Amrein and Berliner, "High stakes testing, uncertainty, and student learning," "The Heisenberg Uncertainty Principle applied to social science," (np).

102. For example, see the curricula for grades 11 and 12 in Ontario at the Ministry of Education, http://www.edu.gov.on.ca/eng/document/curricul/curric1112.html (accessed 4/31/03). Grades 11 and 12 were the last to be revised and implemented provincewide in the educational reform process started by the Harris government.

103. Gregory Cizek, "High-stakes testing must pass the integrity test," *The Commercial Appeal*, Memphis, TN, September 21, 2003, Sunday final edition; B5, LexisNexis news (accessed 4/10/04). See also Gail M. Jones, Brett D. Jones, and Tracy Y. Hargrove, *The Unintended Consequences of High-stakes Testing* (Lanham, MD: Rowman & Littlefield, 2003).

104. Brenda S. Engle, "Second grade testing: a position paper," Fairtest Web site, http://www.fairtest.org/arn/2gradeny.html (accessed 3/31/03).

105. National Center for Education Statistics quick tables, Public High School Dropouts from the School Year 2000–2001, Table 3 by race/ethnicity and state, http://nces.ed.gov/pubs 2004/dropout00-01/table_3.asp (accessed 4/14/04).

106. The Center on Education Policy, "Did you know? Fewer Students are dropping out of school," www.ctredpol.org (accessed 2/12/03). In 1972, 12% of whites, 21% of blacks, and 34% of Hispanics ages sixteen to twenty-four were not enrolled in school, had not completed high school or a GED. In 1996, the figures were 7%, 13%, and 29%. Although there is evidence of some improvement, in more than twenty years the gaps are still extreme.

107. Richard Rothstein, "Lessons: Dropout rate is climbing and likely to go higher," *New York Times,* October 9, 2002, Wednesday, Late Edition, B8, LexisNexis News (accessed 4/15/04). The National Center for Education Statistics reports figures for 2000–2001 at http://nces.ed.gov/quicktables/result.asp? SrchKeyword=dropout&topic=1-Elementary%2FSecondary&Year=200 (accessed 4/15/04).

108. Anemona Hartocollis, "High school dropout rate rises, and Levy fears new test will bring huge surge," *New York Times,* February 28, 2001, B6. But see also, "Not-so-simple reasons for dropout rate; students deny being scared off by Regents tests, as officials say," *New York Times,* March 22, 2001, B6, both at LexisNexis news (accessed 3/12/03).

109. Jennifer Medina, "Critics say Regents English tests push immigrants to drop out," *New York Times* on the Web, June 23, 2002, http://www.nytimes. com/2002/06/23STUD.html (accessed 7/2/02).

110. John M. Bridgeland, John J. DiIulio Jr., and Karen Burke Morrison, The Silent Epidemic: Perspectives of High School Dropouts: A Report by Civil Enterprises in association with Peter D. Hart Research Associates for the Bill and Melinda Gates Foundation, March 2006. http://www.civicenterprises.net/pdfs/ thesilentepidemic3-06.pdf (accessed 3/13/06).

111. Amrein and Berliner, "High stakes testing, uncertainty and student learning;" Gerald W. Bracey, "High stakes testing," Center for Education Research, Analysis, and Innovation, School of Education, University of Wisconsin-Milwaukee, December 5, 2000, http://www.asu.edu/educ/epsl/EPRU/documents/cerai-00-32.htm (accessed 4/14/04); Irma Guadarrama, "Language Minority Students: Finders or Losers of the American Dream?" *Discovering Our Experience: Studies in Bilingual/ESL Education* (Fall 1993) www.ncela.gwu.edu/miscpubs/twu/ discovering/ lmstudents.htm (accessed 3/23/04).

112. Peter Schrag, "Many who fail exit exams lack equal resources," *Los Angeles Daily Journal* 115, iss. 200 (October 15, 2003): 6, LexisNexis news (accessed 4/4/04).

113. Robert Balfanz and Nettie Legters, "How Many Central City High Schools Have a Severe Dropout Problem, Where Are They Located, and Who Attends Them? Initial Estimates Using the Common Core of Data." Paper presented at the Harvard Civil Rights Project Conference on Dropouts," January 13, 2001, cited in testimony of Christopher Edley Jr., "Keeping the Promise of No Child Left Behind": Success or Failure Depends Largely on Implementation by the United States Department of Education," U.S. House of Representatives,

Committee on Education and the Workforce, Oversight Hearing on the Implementation of the No Child Left Behind Act, July 24, 2002, 3.

114. Walt Haney, "Revisiting the Myth of the Texas Miracle in Education: Lessons about Dropout Research and Dropout Prevention," http://www.civilrightsproject.harvard.edu/research/dropouts/haney.pdf (accessed 4/7/03).

115. Nat Hentoff, "The High Stakes Testing Trap," *Village Voice,* New York, November 5, 2002, LexisNexis news (accessed 3/31/03). See also Michael A. Fletcher, "Progress on dropout rate stalls; Critics say test drive could worsen problem," *Washington Post,* March 3, 2001, LexisNexis news (accessed 4/6/03).

116. Fletcher, "Progress on dropout rate stalls."

117. Hentoff, "The high stakes testing trap," np.

118. Hentoff, "The high stakes testing trap," np. According to Hentoff, "In the October 14 *New York Post,* Carl Campanile and Leah Haines report on 12 drastically failing schools on the State Education Department's ominous list of Schools Under Registration Review. Among them: Junior High School 258 in Bedford-Stuyvesant: 'a staggering 99 percent of eighth-graders flunked the math exam and 92 percent flunked the English test.' And PS 92 in Harlem: '92 percent of the students failed to meet math standards.'"

119. Medina, "Critics say."

120. Medina, "Critics say."

121. Rothstein, "Lessons."

122. Raising Our Sights: No Senior Left Behind, Final Report of the Woodrow Wilson National Commission on the High School Senior Year, Woodrow Wilson Foundation, October 2001, http://www.woodrow.org (accessed 4/4/03).

123. Raising Our Sights, 8.

124. Jones, Jones, and Hargrave, *Unintended Consequences,* 129–130.

125. See chapter 2 above.

126. Raising Our Sights, 11.

127. Paige M. Harrison and Allen J. Beck, Prisoners in 2001, *Bureau of Justice Statistics Bulletin,* July 2002, NCJ 195189 Washington, DC, http://www.ojp.usdoj.gov/bjs/ (accessed 4/25/03).

128. "Prisoners in 2001," 4.

129. "Prisoners in 2001," 11.

130. Phillip Kaufman, Martha Naomi Alt, and MPR Associates, "Dropout Rates in the United States: 2000," National Center for Education Statistics, NCES 2002-114, iii, http://nces.ed.gov/pubs2002/droppub_2001/ (accessed 4/15/04).

131. National Institute for Literacy (NIFL), "International Adult Literacy Survey," http://www.nifl.gov/nifl/facts/IALS.html (accessed 4/30/03).

132. National Institute for Literacy (NIFL), "Correctional Education Facts," http://www.nifl.gov/nifl/facts/correctional.html#correctional (accessed 4/10/03).

133. NIFL, "Correctional Education Facts."

134. Gary Boulard, "Unchained remedy; Are community colleges the answer to educating thousands of America's prisoners and turning them into productive members of society?" *Community College Week* 14, no. 26, (August 5, 2002): 6–9, available through LexisNexis News (accessed 4/10/03).

135. Boulard, "Unchained remedy."

136. Boulard, "Unchained remedy."

137. "Fatherless Homes breed violence." http://www.fathermag.com/news/2778-stats.shtml (accessed 4/29/03).

138. NIFL, "Correctional Education Facts," 1.

139. Karl O. Haigler, Caroline Harlow, Patricia O'Connor, and Anne Campbell, "Literacy behind prison walls: Profiles of the prison population from the National Adult Literacy Survey," Executive Summary, National Assessment of Adult Literacy, 1992, NCES, Washington, DC, http://nces.ed.gov/naal/resources/exec summmprison.asp#litskills (accessed 4/4/03).

140. Bureau of Justice Statistics Press Release, "Nation's prison and jail population exceeds 2 million for the first time," (Bureau of Justice Statistics, Washington, DC, April 6, 2003, http://www.ojp.usdoj.gov/bsj/pub/press/pjim02pr.htm (accessed 4/8/03).

141. Bureau of Justice Statistics Press Release, "Education and training requirements for big city police officers increase, starting salaries remain flat," Bureau of Justice Statistics, 202/307-0784, Washington, DC, May 12, 2002, http://www.ojp.usdoj.gov/bjs/pub/press/pdlc00pr.htm (accessed 4/8/03).

142. Jenni Gainsborough and Mark Mauer, "Diminishing returns: Crime and incarceration in the 1990s," The Sentencing Project, September 2000, http://www.sentencingproject.org (accessed 4/14/03) 3.

143. Jonathan Kozol, "Persistent Inequalities: The challenges of leadership in education," Speech given at SUNY Geneseo, NY, April 23, 2003. Kozol describes this community in detail in *Ordinary Resurrections* (New York: Crown Publishers, 2000).

144. Jenni Gainsborough and Marc Mauer, Americans Behind Bars: United States and International Rates of Incarceration, The Sentencing Project, September 2000, http://www.sentencingproject.org (accessed 4/3/03), 6.

145. Vince Beiser, "How We Got to Two Million: How did the Land of the Free become the World's Leading Jailer?" *Mother Jones* Special Report, July 10, 2001, http://www.motherjones.com/prisons/print_overview.html (accessed 4/7/03), 2.

146. For instance, crack cocaine carries a much higher sentence than powder cocaine, despite the known fact that the effects of these two forms of the drug are not different. The difference is that blacks use the less expensive crack but whites use powder cocaine.

147. Beiser, "How we got," 3.

148. Adina Fowler Morse, Unpublished Paper, "Felon Disenfranchisement," Seton Hall Law School, 2000.

149. The Sentencing Project, *Losing the Vote*, Overview and Summary, http://www.hrw.org/reports98/vote/usvot98o.htm#P466_16849 (accessed 4/30/03).

150. Judge McKenna ruled against the plaintiffs in the United States District Court, *Hayden* v. *Pataki*, No. 00 Civ. 8586, 2004 U.S. Dist. LEXIS 10863 (S.D.N.Y. June 14, 2004).

151. National Association for the Advancement of Colored People, "NAACP reactivates Prison Project," NAACP News, March 4, 2002, http://www.naacp.org/news/releases/prisonproj03402.shtml (accessed 4/30/03).

152. Bruce Western and Becky Pettit, "Incarceration and racial inequality in men's employment," *Industrial & Labor Relations Review* 54, iss. 1 (October 2000) 1.

153. Western and Pettit, "Incarceration and racial inequality," 7.

154. Bruce Western, "The impact of incarceration on wage mobility and inequality" (*American Sociological Review*, vol. 67, iss. 4 (August 2002). As Western points out, unemployment rates may lead people to commit crimes, but "intensifying the punishment of drug and violent offenders, and recidivists" caused more young black men to have prison records, 527.

155. Western, "Impact," 528.

156. Herbert L. Needleman, Christine McFarland, Roberta B. Ness, Stephen E. Ficnberg, and Michael J. Tobin, "Bone lead levels in adjudicated delinquents: A case control study" (*Neurotoxicology and Teratology* 24 (2002), p. 711.

157. Needleman, "Bone lead levels," 711.

158. Needleman, "Bone lead levels," 714.

159. Needleman, "Bone lead levels," 715.

160. Needleman, "Bone lead levels," 715.

Chapter 7

1. Matthew Frye Jacobson, *Whiteness of a Different Color: European Immigrants and the Alchemy of Race* (Cambridge: Harvard University Press, 1998), 22.

2. For instance, John Stuart Mill, who ought to have known better, wrote in *On Liberty* that "barbarians and savages" were not included in his arguments, since they were incapable of benefiting from rational discourse.

3. "Reaffirmation or Requiem for the Voting Rights Act? The Court will decide," A Public Policy Alert from the American Civil Liberties Union, May 1995, ACLU online archives, http://www.aclu.org/ (accessed 11/30/03).

4. David Kravets, "Appeals court rehears postponement of California recall election," Associated Press, September 22, 2003, available at LexisNexis news (accessed 1/6/03).

5. Valerie E. Lee and David T. Burkam, *Inequality at the starting gate: Social background differences in achievement as children start school*, chapter 4, "Social disadvantage and school quality" (Economic Policy Institute, 2002), 63–77.

6. Daniel J. Losen and Gary Orfield, "Racial inequality in special education: Executive summary for federal policy makers," Harvard Civil Rights Project Web site, http://www.civilrightsproject.harvard.edu/research.php (accessed 1/3/03).

7. Martin Luther King Jr. "I've been to the mountaintop," speech given to the Memphis sanitation workers, April 3, 1968, http://www.stanford.edu/group/King/popular_requests/ (accessed 1/4/03).

8. Martin Luther King Jr., Quotes on education, January 7, 1968, http://www.stanford.edu/group/King/popular_requests/ (accessed 1/4/03).

9. Aristotle, *NE*, 1130^b 1–5, Barnes, 1784.

10. Aristotle, *Politics*, 1282^b 35–1283^a 4, Barnes, 2037.

11. Thomas Jefferson, *Notes on Virginia,* "A Bill on Education in the revised codes of Virginia," Washington ed., viii, 388, Ford ed., iii, 251, 1782, available at http://etext.virginia.edu/jefferson/ (accessed 11/30/03).

12. Katharine S. Milar, "'A coarse and clumsy tool:' Helen Thompson Woolley and the Cincinnati Vocation Bureau," *History of Psychology* 2, no. 3 (1999) 219–235.

13. Jane Fowler Morse, "Gone, but not forgotten: The work of Helen Thompson Woolley" *National Women's Studies Association Journal* 14, no. 2, 121–147.

14. James Bryant Conant, *Education and Liberty: The Role of Schools in a Modern Democracy* (Cambridge, MA: Harvard University Press, 1958) 56–58.

15. M. Gail Jones, Brett D. Jones, and Tracy Y. Hargrove, eds., *The Unintended Consequences of High-stakes Testing* (Lanham: Rowland and Littlefield, 2003, see especially chapter 4, "Truth or consequences: preparing for the tests," 61–77.

16. Amrein and Berliner, see chapter 6, note 95.

17. Jones et al., *Unintended Consequences,* 54–56. Research indicates that some teachers believe that their teaching methods improved after high-stakes testing was implemented, but this effect appears to be most common in subjects that are easily assessed objectively such as mathematics. In high-poverty districts where scores are low to begin with, drill-and-skill techniques increase test scores more often than in schools that get good test scores already.

18. Karl Marx, *Critique of the Gotha Program,* Part I, np, http://www.marxists.org/archive/marx/works/1875/gotha/ (accessed 8/15/05).

19. Aristotle, *Politics,* Book IV, Chapter 11, 1295^b 35–1296^a 21, Barnes, 2057–2058.

20. Death Penalty Information Center, "Facts about the death penalty and deterrence," http://www.deathpenaltyinfo.org/article.php?scid=12&did=167#STUDIES (accessed 1/4/03). A study that shows that the murder rate is highest in the South, where the murder rate is increasing with more rapidly than in other regions with fewer executions. The murder rate in the South, which accounts for 82% of the executions, increased by 2.1%, while the murder rate in the Northeast, which accounts for less than 1% of the executions, decreased by 5%.

21. Janet Gilmore, "Three strikes can't take credit for state's [California's] drop in crime," Inner City Struggle Web site, March 21, 2001, http://innercitystruggle.org/story.php?story=30 (accessed 1/18/04). Gilmore reports on a study by Franklin Zimring, a law professor at University of California, Berkeley, which shows that three-strikes laws passed in California in 1994 "had no measurable impact on crime in California" (np). But they did increase the number of people incarcerated at any one time by imposing longer sentences.

22. Supreme Court Justice Steven Breyer, "Mandatory sentencing should be abolished," speech at the University of Nebraska, November 20, 1998, Common Sense for Drug Policy Web site, http://www.csdp.org/ (accessed 1/26/04).

23. Dedrick Muhammad, Attieno Davis, Meizhu Lui, and Betsy Leondar-Wright, "The State of the Dream 2004: Enduring Disparities in Black and White," United for a Fair Economy, January 15, 2004, http://www.ufenet.org/press/2004/StateoftheDream2004_pr.html (accessed 1/19/04).

24. Socrates, *Apology,* in Edith Hamilton and Huntington Cairns, *The Collected Works of Plato* (Bollingen Series LXXI, Pantheon Books, 1961), 12, Stephanos 26a.

25. CBS News, *60 Minutes*, January 11, 2004. "Bush sought 'way' to invade Iraq?" http://www.cbsnews.com/stories/2004/01/09/60minutes/main592330.shtml (accessed 1/19/04).

26. Chuck Collins, Chris Hartman, and Holly Sklar, "Divided Decade: Economic Disparity at the Century's Turn," December 15, 1999, United for a Fair Economy Web site http://www.ufenet.org/press/archive/1999/Divided_Decade/divided_decade.html (accessed 1/10/02).

27. G. Keith Warriner, Kathleen McSpurren, and Alice Nabalamda, "Social Justice and Environmental Equity: Distributing Environmental Quality," *Environments* 29, iss. 1 (August 2001) 85, InfoTrac (accessed 1/22/03).

28. Aristotle, *Politics*, Book VIII, 1337^a 10–17, Barnes, 2121; Plato, *Republic*, in Hamilton and Cairns, entire, but see especially Book VII, 747–772.

29. John Rawls, *A Theory of Justice* (Cambridge, Mass.: Harvard University Belknap Press, 1971), 40.

30. Cass Sunstein, *Free Markets and Social Justice* (Oxford: Oxford University Press, 1997), 384–385.

31. Martin Luther King Jr., "Where do we go from here?" Southern Christina Leadership Conference, Presidential Address, August 16, 1967, http://www.hartford-hwp.com/archives/45a/062.html (accessed 11/30/03).

32. Martin Luther King Jr., "The last steep ascent," *The Nation*, March 14, 1966, reprinted in Victor Navasky, ed., *Perspectives from the Pages of* The Nation, *1865- 2000*, The Nation Press, NY, 2000, 96.

33. William Junius Wilson, *When Work Disappears: The World of the New Urban Poor* (New York: Vintage Books, 1997.)

34. William Junius Wilson, *The Truly Disadvantaged: The Inner City, the Underclass, and Public Policy* (Chicago: University of Chicago Press, 1987).

35. Bernie Sanders, "The View from Mexico," *The Nation*, 13 (2 February 2004), http://www.thenation.com/docprem. mhtml?i=20040202&s=sanders (accessed 2/11/04).

36. Jesse Rothstein and Robert Scott, "NAFTA and the states: Job destruction is widespread," Economic Policy Institute, Issue Brief #119, September 19, 1997, http://www.epinet.org/content.cfm/issuebriefs_ib119 (accessed 1/19/04).

37. Martin Luther King Jr., "Letter from a Birmingham Jail," April 16, 1963, http://almaz.com/nobel/peace/MLK-jail.html (accessed 1/19/04).

38. Richard Rothstein and Karen Hawley Mills, "Where's the Money Gone? Changes in the level and composition of Education spending," Economic Policy Institute, 1995, available at http://www.epinet.org/content.cfm/books_where-moneygone (accessed 1/19/04), and Richard Rothstein, "Where's the Money Going? Changes in the level and composition of education spending, 1991–1996," Economic Policy Institute, 1997, http://www.epinet.org/cgi-bin/shop/shop.cgi (accessed 1/19/04).

39. Jim McChesney, "Whole school reform" (ERIC Digest, No. 124, 1998) ED427388.

40. Michael Fullan, *Change Forces with a Vengeance* (London and New York: Routledge/Falmer, 2003).

41. Steve Liss, *No Place for Children: Voices from Juvenile Detention* (Austin: University of Texas Press, 2005).

42. Tara Herival and Paul Wright, *Prison Nation: The Warehousing of America's Poor* (New York: Routledge, 2003.)

43. *Crime and Punishment in America: 1997 Update,* "Bringing Down Costs through Privatization," The National Center for Policy Analysis Web site, http://www.ncpa.org/studies/s209/s209g.html (accessed 1/26/04). The article recommends that prison labor be expanded as a boon for capitalists and private prison developers. It makes four recommendations: 1) repeal or liberalize the various state and federal laws that restrict trade in prison-made goods; 2) repeal the laws that compel government agencies to buy prison-made goods in favor of competitive bidding for government purchases; 3) create prison-enterprise marketing offices within prison and jail systems; and 4) allow private prison operators to profit from the gainful employment of convict labor.

44. Alan Elsner, "America's prison habit" (*The Washington Post,* 1/24/04) available at http://justicepolicy.org, newsroom (accessed 2/4/04). See also Alan Elsner, *Gates of Injustice: America's Prison Crisis* (Upper Saddle River, NJ: Prentice Hall, 2004.

45. Garrett Albert Duncan, "Urban Pedagogies and the Celling of Adolescents of Color," revised from a paper delivered at Critical Resistance: Beyond the prison-industrial complex, a conference held at University of California at Berkeley, September 25, 1998, http://www.infotrac.galegroup.com (accessed 4/16/03).

46. See Richard A. Gibboney, *The Stone Trumpet: A Story of Practical School Reform 1960–1990* (Albany: State University of New York Press, 1994) and David Tyack and Larry Cuban, *Tinkering Toward Utopia: A Century of Public School Reform* (Cambridge: Harvard University Press, 1995).

47. See Chapter 1, pages 8–9, for the text of the Kentucky template in *Rose.*

48. *CFE IIa* at*16.

49. *CFE IIb* at *8.

50. Neal Kumar Katyal, "Judges as Advice Givers," *Stanford Law Review 50* (1998) 1709–1824.

51. *Rodriguez,* 1973 U.S. LEXIS 91, *28.

52. *Edgewood Independent School District, et al.* (*Edgewood II*) v. *William Kirby,* et al. 777S.W.2d 391; 1989 Tex. LEXIS 129; 33 Tex Sup. J. 12, Oct 2, 1989 at *394.

53. *Id.* *396.

54. Vicki K. Carter, "Virtual Shades of Pale: Educational Technologies and the Electronic 'Other,'" in Nelson Rodriguez and Leila E. Villaverde, eds., *Dismantling White Privilege: Pedagogy, Politics, and Whiteness* (New York: Peter Lang, 2000) 25–40.

55. *United States* v. *Yonkers Board of Educ.,* No. 93-6342, 1994 U.S. LEXIS 16681 (partially decided 2d Cir. July 5, 1994).

56. Winnie Hu, "Accord reached in School Bias Suit Against Yonkers," *New York Times* on the web, January 9, 2002 (accessed 1/10/02) 2.

57. Erika Frankenberg and Chungmei Lee, "Race in American public schools: Rapidly resegregating school districts," August 8, 2002, http://www.civilrightsproject.harvard.edu/research/deseg/reseg_schools02.php (accessed 9/30/02).

58. Michael Gormley, "Legislature won't reform schools, Regents can't," Associated Press and Local Wire, May 6, 2002, LexisNexis news (accessed 9/23/02).

59. James E. Ryan, "Schools, race, and money," *Yale Law Journal* 109 (November 1999), 249ff.

60. Frankenberg et al., "Losing the dream."

61. Frye G

aillard, "Race and Schools: Once Again, Charlotte is poised at a Crossroads," http://www.cln.com/archives/charlotte/newsstand/c041799/cover. htm (accessed 09/25/02); "Supreme Court declines to hear appeals," PR Newswire, April 15, 2002, LexisNexis news (accessed 9/25/02); "Charlotte-Mecklenburg Schools Chief Resigns," Associated Press and Local Wire, May 24, 2002, LexisNexis news (accessed 9/25/02).

62. Kevin Carey, The Funding Gap: Many States Still Shortchange Low-Income and Minority Students, The Education Trust, Fall 2004, http://www2. edtrust.org/EdTrust/Product+Catalog/browse2.htm#funding (accessed 8/15/05) Chart 1, page 2 and Chart 3, page 5.

63. Donald S. Yarab, "Case Comment: *Edgewood Independent School District* v. *Kirby*: An education in school finance reform," *Case Western Reserve Law Journal* 40 (1990): 889–898, LexisNexis legal research (accessed 9/19/02).

64. Donald M. Linhorst, "Federalism and social justice: implications for social work" (*Social Work* 47 issue 3 (July 2002): 201, n. 8, Proquest document ID 147290751 (accessed 10/28/02). Linhorst is of the opinion that the federal government is in the best position to promote social justice, even though the attitude of presidents and other officials differs on this question in different historical periods. He quotes a 1979 study by Magill (Magill, R. S. 1979). *Community decision making for social welfare: Federalism, city government, and the poor.* (New York: Human Services Press.) According to Linhorst, Magill "concluded that social justice is not promoted when giving local communities substantial control over decision making for social policies. He suggested that federal oversight or control is needed to ensure that local communities meet the social justice needs of all their citizens." (no pagination given in this ProQuest document). In this, Linhorst and Magill agree with Rebecca M. Blank that the federal government should be responsible for social programs that apply nationally.

65. Aristotle, *Politics*, Book III, chapter 8, 1280a 4–6, Barnes, 2031.

66. William E. Thro. "To Render Them Safe The Analysis of State Constitutional Provisions in Public School Finance Reform Litigation," *Virginia Law Review* 75 (1989), 1639–1679.

67. Paula J. Lundberg, "State Courts and School Funding, A Fifty State Analysis, *Albany Law Review* 63 (2000), 1101–1146.

68. *Horton*, 1985 Conn. LEXIS 665.

69. "Settlement reached in *Sheff* v. *O'Neill*: Pact calls for three-pronged approach," *Connecticut Law Tribune* 29, no. 4 (January 27, 2003) 1.

70. For a review of these categories, see Joseph S. Pratt, "Note: School Finance Battles: Survey Says? It's All Just a Change in Attitudes," *Harvard Civil Rights-Civil Liberties Law Review* 34 (Summer 1999), 547, 551–553.

71. *Campaign for Fiscal Equity, Respondents* v. *State of New York, Appellants,* No. 6915, 2006 N.Y. App. Div. LEXIS 3598 (N.Y. App. Div. March 23, 2006).

72. In *Paynter,* where it was convenient, districts were conceived as independent entities, which might be harmed by a ruling requiring desegregation; in *New York Performance Standards Consortium* v. *New York State Department of Education,* 293 A.D.2d 113; 714 N.Y.S.2d 349; 2002 N.Y. App. Div. LEXIS 4790, the ruling did not allow a coalition of twenty-seven independent schools to retain their variance from required state testing. This case is also under appeal.

73. Hanushek et al., *Making Schools Work* (Washington, DC: The Brookings Institution, 1994), 139.

74. Jonathan Kozol, *Savage Inequalities.*

75. Ironically, textbook selection is statewide in Texas, where *Rodriguez* allowed local control to trump disparities in funding. Amrein and Berliner document the fact that Texas children, although improving their scores on the TAAS in the so-called Texas miracle have declined on independent measures of learning (as have children in other states with high stakes testing). For a summary of their findings on Texas, see Amrein and Berliner, "High Stakes Testing," 14–17.

76. Interestingly, in New York, local control over curriculum and testing was recently denied to a group of schools belonging to the New York Performance Standards Coalition. See Legal Section at their Web site, http://performance assessment.org/legal.php (accessed 9/10/02).

77. Rothstein, "Where's the Money Going?"

78. Abby Goodnough, "Klein Bypasses Local Boards and names 3 School Chiefs," *New York Times,* September 11, 2002, Wednesday, late edition, B3, Lexis-Nexis news (accessed 10/28/02).

79. *CFE IIb,* 2002 N.Y. App. Div. LEXIS 7252, at *10.

80. In his dissent to *Rodriguez,* Marshall agrees with the District Court's assessment that "the [defendants] fail to establish a reasonable basis for these classifications [of school districts for the purpose of taxation]" and concludes by saying, "If Texas had a system truly dedicated to local fiscal control, one would expect the quality of the educational opportunity provided in each district to vary with the decision of the voters in that district as to the level of sacrifice they wish to make for public education. In fact, the Texas scheme produces precisely the opposite effect." Marshall, dissenting in *Rodriguez,* 1973 U.S. LEXIS 91 at *129–130.

81. Mohammed Adam, "A Province wide 'Affliction': Ontario School Boards have cut services, slashed jobs and raided reserves to provide children with a uniformly high-quality education. But still, many of the boards lack the money to do the job properly," *Ottawa Citizen,* March 26, 2002, p. D1, LexisNexis news (accessed 9/13/02). Philadelphia schools were also seized, and given to the Edison Company to run in 2002. Philadelphia involves 220,000 students, Toronto 200,000. For the Philadelphia story, see Jacques Steinberg, "In largest schools takeover, state will run Philadelphia's," *New York Times,* December 22, 2001, late edition, A1, LexisNexis news (accessed 10/17/02).

82. Robert Benzie, "Eves Seizes Toronto School Board; Budget deficits left 'no other option,' Wittmer says; Liberals, NDP say Voters will Punish To-

ries; Parents threaten lawsuits over expected cuts," *National Post,* August 28, 2002, Toronto Edition. LexisNexis news (accessed 9/13/02). See also "Tories Stoop to New Low by firing Ottawa Carlton School Trustees: OSSTF Web site, http://www.osstf.on.ca/www/pub/pressrel/sept01aug17-202.html (accessed 9/13/02).

83. Ellen Brantlinger, *Dividing Classes: How the Middle Class Negotiates and Rationalizes School Advantage* (New York: Routledge/Falmer, 2003), 154–155.

84. George Counts, "A Call to the teachers of the nation" (New York: John Day Company, 1933).

85. Jane Fowler Morse, "Fostering Autonomy," *Educational Theory* 47, no. 1 (Winter 1997) 31–50.

86. Aristotle, *Nichomachean Ethics,* Book II, chapter 9, 1109[a] 20–1109[b]26 Barnes, 1751–1752. John Dewey, "The ethical principles underlying education," in John Dewey, *The Early Works, 1882–1898,* vol. 5: 1895–1898 (Carbondale and Edwardsville: Southern Illinois University Press, 1972), 54–83.

87. "Kentucky School Reform Efforts Bear Fruit," Wisconsin Center for Education Research archives, July 6, 1998, http://www.wcer.wisc.edu/archives/feature/jul98a.asp (accessed 9/27/02).

88. Kentucky Department of Education, Progress in the Commonwealth Accountability System (CATS), http://www.education.ky.gov/ (accessed 2/9/04).

89. Lorna Jimerson, "Still 'A Reasonable Equal Share': An Update on Educational Equity on Vermont" February, 2002, Rural Education and Community Trust Web site, http://www.ruraledu.org/keep_learning.cfm?record_no=137 (accessed 9/26/02). See also Jane Fowler Morse, "Equitable School Funding: Lessons from Vermont, New York, and Ontario," unpublished paper presented at AESA in November 2001.

90. *Campaign for Fiscal Equity (CFE IIb)* v. *New York,* 2002 N.Y. App. Div. LEXIS 7252, at *17.

91. Greg Toppo, "Harvard Report says blacks three times as likely to be special ed students." March 2, 2001, LexisNexis news (accessed 10/30/02).

92. *Montoy* v. *State,* No. 92,032, Supreme Court of Kansas, 278 Kan. 769; 102 P.3d 1160; 2005 Kan. LEXIS 2, January 3, 2005, Opinion Filed, Judgment entered by *Montoy* v. *State,* 112 P.3d 923, 2005 Kan. LEXIS 347 (Kan., 2005)

93. Amrein and Berliner, "High stakes testing," 1–16.

94. See *Education Week,* "Comparing Equity Indicators," http://www.edweek.org/reports/qc00/tables/equity-t1.htm (accessed 10/21/01).

95. R. Craig Wood and David Thompson, *Educational Finance Law: Constitutional Challenges to State Aid Plans—An Analysis of Strategies* (Topeka, KS: National Organization on Legal Problems in Education, 1996) 107.

96. *CFE IIa,* 2001 N.Y. Misc. LEXIS 1 at *115.

97. William F. Duncombe and Anna Lukemeyer, "Estimating the cost of educational adequacy: A comparison of approaches," paper presented March 2002 American Education Finance Association 2002 Annual Conference, Albuquerque, NM, http://cpr.maxwell.syr.edu/efap (accessed 8/21/05). The Educational Finance and Accountability Program of the Maxwell School at the University of Syracuse has many additional analyses of issues in school finance reform.

98. "Details of the No Child Left Behind Act Lawsuit, *Pontiac* v. *Spellings*, filed Wednesday," Associated Press, April 20, 2005, BC Cycle, Washington, D.C., LexisNexis news (accessed 7/12/05). See also National Education Association, "Stand up for children: *Pontiac* v. *Spellings*," http://www.nea.org/lawsuit/index. html (accessed 3/14/06). *Pontiac* v. *Spellings*, Civil Action No. 05-CV-71535-DT, 2005 U.S. Dist. LEXIS 29253 (U.S. November 23, 2005).

99. Amendment IX, " The enumeration in the Constitution, of certain rights, shall not be construed to deny or disparage others retained by the people." The corollary that the non-enumeration of certain rights in the Constitution (such as voting in a federal election) should not be taken to disparage those rights could be extended to cover the right to an education.

100. Beach and Lindahl, "Can There Be A Right," 5, 9.

101. National Organization of Women, Chronology of the Equal Rights Amendment 1923–1996, http://www.now.org/issues/economic/cea/history. html (accessed Oct. 3, 2000).

102. Marshall's dissent to *Rodriguez* at *103.

103. Michael Fullan, *Change Forces*.

Bibliography

Aber, J. Lawrence. Director of the National Center for Children in Poverty. "Poor children in U.S. increase to six million." *Columbia University Record* 20, no. 15 (3 February 1995). Interview, http://www.columbia.edu/cu/record/archives/vol20/vol20_iss15/record2015.20.html (12 February 2003).

Aber, Larry, and Julian Palmer. "Poverty and brain development in young children." In Mary Jensen and Mary Anne Hannibal, *Issues, Advocacy and Leadership in Early Education.* Boston, London, Toronto, Sydney, Tokyo, Singapore: Allyn and Bacon, 2000.

Act 60: What You Should Know. "Another lesson in reality for Montpelier: The Freeman Foundation weighs in on Act 60." (24 February 1998), http://www.act60.org/found.htm (4 October 2001).

Addams, Jane. "The Public school and the immigrant child." In Jean Bethke Elshtain, *The Jane Addams Reader.* New York: Basic Books, 2002.

Alliance for Quality Education. News and Proposed New York Education Funding Bill, "Schools for New York's Future Act," http://ourkidscantwait.org (1 October 2005).

American Civil Liberties Union. "N.Y.C.L.U. announces plan to appeal decision in important school reform case." *NYCLU,* http://www.aclu.org/news/n120398a.html (28 August 2002).

American Civil Liberties Union. "Reaffirmation or Requiem for the Voting Rights Act? The Court will decide." A Public Policy Alert, May 1995, http://www.aclu.org (30 November 2003).

Amrein, Audrey L., and David C. Berliner. "High-stakes testing, uncertainty, and student learning." *Education Policy Analysis Archives* 10, no. 18 (28 March 2002), http://epaa.asu.edu/epaa/v10n18 (10 April 2004).

Anthony, Susan B. "Letter to Dr. Sarah R. Dolley," in Ida Husted Harper. *The Life and Work of Susan B. Anthony,* vol. 3. Indianapolis: Hollenbeck Press, 1908, 1204.

Anyon, Jean. *Ghetto Schooling: A Political Economy of Urban Educational Reform.* New York: Teacher's College Press, 1997.

Aristotle. *Nichomachean Ethics*, in Jonathan Barnes, ed. *The Complete Works of Aristotle*. Princeton University Press, 1984.

Aristotle. *Politics*, in Jonathan Barnes, ed. *The Complete Works of Aristotle*. Princeton University Press, 1984.

Association for Career and Technical Education. "Welfare: Current Status." (1 March 2004), http://www.acteonline.org/policy/legislative_issues/welfare_status.cfm (10 March 2004).

Babb, Valerie. *Whiteness Visible: The Meaning of Whiteness in American Literature and Culture*. New York: New York University Press,1998.

Baker, Dean. "Nine myths about social security." (digital ed.). *Atlantic Monthly*. July 1998, http://www.theatlantic.com/issues/98jul/socsec.htm (23 March 2004).

Baldas, Teresa. "New ammo for funding actions: Fresh legal arguments from unlikely source: No Child Left Behind Act." *National Law Journal* 26:5 (February 14, 2005) 11ff.

Balfantz, Robert, and Nettie Legters. "How many central city high schools have a severe dropout problem, where are they located, and who attends them? Initial estimates using the common core of data." Quoted by permission of the Harvard Civil Rights Project, 13 January 2001.

Balkin, Jack M., ed. *What Brown Should Have Said*. New York: New York University Press, 2001.

Bankston III, Carl L., and Stephen J. Caldas. "The American school dilemma: Race and scholastic performance." *The Sociological Quarterly* 38, no. 3: 423–430.

Beach, Robert H., and Ronald A. Lindahl. "Can there be a right to education in the United States?" *Equity & Excellence in Education* 33, no. 2 (September 2000): 5–12. ERIC document Accession No: EJ614018 3.

Beer, Mitchell. "In the eye of the storm: Ottawa pushes back against school board takeovers." The Canadian Centre for Policy Alternatives, http://www.policyalternatives.ca/eduproj/ososottawa.html (26 October 2003).

Behncke, Maria. The Alliance for Quality Education. Personal communication (31 July 2003).

Beiser, Vince. "How we got to two million: How did the Land of the Free become the world's leading jailer?" *Mother Jones* Special Report, 10 July 2001, http://www.motherjones.com/prisons/p;rint_overview.html (7 April 2003).

Bellinger, D. C., K. M. Stiles, A. Leviton, M. Rabinowitz, H. L. Needleman, and C. Waternaux. "Low-level lead exposure and children's cognitive function in the preschool years." *Pediatrics* 87 (1 February 1991) 219–227.

Bellinger, D. C., K. M. Stiles, and H. L. Needleman. "Low-level lead exposure, intelligence and academic achievement: A long term follow-up study." *Pediatrics* 90 (1992) 855–861.

Bennett, Drake. "Freedom to fail: The false flexibility of the president's welfare plan." *The American Prospect*, April 2003, http://www.prospect.org/print/V14/4/bennett-d.html (25 July 2003).

Bennett, William, ed. *The Book of Virtues: A Great Treasury of Moral Stories*. New York: Simon and Schuster, 1993.

Berke, Joel S., Margaret E. Goertz, and Richard J. Coley. *Politicians, Finance, and City Schools: Reforming School Finance in New York*. New York: Russell Sage Foundation, 1984.

Berlak, Harold. "Academic achievement, race, and reform: A short guide to understanding assessment policy, standardized achievement tests and anti-racist alternatives" (19 May 2001), http://www.edjustice.org (9 January 2002).

Berliner, David C., and Bruce J. Biddle. *The Manufactured Crisis: Myths, Fraud, and the Attack on America's Public Schools.* New York: Longman, 1995.

Berliner, David C., and Bruce J. Biddle, "What research says about small classes and their effects." Education Policy Studies Laboratory, Arizona State University (Winter 2002), http://www.asu.edu/educ/epsl/EPRP/Reports/EPRP-0202-101.htm (15 February 2003).

Bernstein, Jared. "Slowing economy may revive inequality." Economic Policy Institute, March 26, 2001, http://epinet.org (6 February 2003).

Bernstein, Jared et al. "Pulling apart: A state-by-state analysis of income trends." Economic Policy Institute, Center on Budget and Policy Priorities. April 2002, http://www/epinet.org (12 May 2002).

Bernstein, Jared, and Jeff Chapman. "Time to repair the wage floor: Raising the minimum wage to $6.65 will prevent further erosion of its value." *Economic Policy Institute Brief* 180 (22 May 2002), http://www.epinet.org/Issue briefs/ib180.html (15 September 2002).

Biddix, Wade, et al. "Social equity in special education," www.people.vcu.edu/~bwooldri/_pdf_docs/social_equity_pdf/sep_spec_ed.pdf (7 April 2004).

Biddle, Bruce J. "Foolishness, dangerous nonsense, and real correlates of state differences in achievement. *Phi Delta Kappan online,* http://www.pdkintl.org/kappan/kbid9709.htm (2 April 2003).

Biddle, Bruce J., and David C. Berliner. "A research synthesis: Unequal school funding in the United States." *Educational Leadership* 29:8 (May 2002) 48–59, http://www.ascd.org/readingroom/eled/0205/biddle.html (3 September 2003).

Biddle, Bruce J., and David C. Berliner. "What research says about unequal funding for schools in America" *Education Policy Reports,* Arizona State University (Winter 2002), EPSL-0602-102-EPRP, http://www.asu.edu/educ/epsl/eprp.htm (20 January 2003).

Blank, Rebecca M. *It Takes a Nation: A New Agenda for Fighting Poverty.* New York and Princeton: The Russell Sage Foundation and Princeton University Press, 1997.

Bloom, Allan. *The Closing of the American Mind.* New York: Simon and Schuster, 1987.

Books, Sue. "Environmentally induced damage to children: A call for broadening the critical agenda." ERIC, ED420399.

Books, Sue. "Playing with numbers, playing with need: Schooling and the federal poverty line." *Educational Foundations,* 14, no. 2 (Spring 2000): 5–20.

Books, Sue. "School funding: Justice v. equity." *Equity & Excellence in Education* 32:2 (December 1999) 53–58.

Boulard, Gary. "Unchained remedy: Are community colleges the answer to educating thousands of America's prisoners and turning them into productive members of society?" *Community College Week* 14, no. 26 (5 August 2002) 6–9. LexisNexis news (10 April 2003).

Boushey, Heather, Chauna Brocht, Bethney Gundersen, and Jared Bernstein. *Hardships in America: The real story of working families.* Washington, DC: Economic Policy Institute, 2001, http://www.epinet.org (5 January 2003).

Bracey, Gerald W. "No Child Left Behind: Where does the money go?" Educational Policy Studies Laboratory, Arizona State University, June 2005, http://www.edpolicylab.org (30 June 2005).

Bracey, Gerald W. "High Stakes Testing." Center for Education Research, Analysis, and Innovation, School of Education, University of Wisconsin-Milwaukee, December 5, 2000, http://www.asu.edu/educ/epsl/EPRU/documents/cerai-00-32.htm (14 April 2004).

Brantlinger, Ellen. *Dividing Classes: How the Middle Class Negotiates and Rationalizes School Advantage.* New York: Routledge/Falmer, 2003.

Brennan, Jeanne, ed. *The Funding Gap.* Washington DC: The Education Trust, 2002, http://www/edtrust.org (29 September 2002).

Breyer, Steven (Supreme Court Justice). "Mandatory sentencing should be abolished." Speech, University of Nebraska, 20 November 1998. Common Sense for Drug Policy Web site, http://www.csdp.org (26 January 2004).

Bridgeland, John M., John J. DiIulio Jr., and Karen Burke Morrison. The Silent Epidemic: Perspectives of High School Dropouts: A Report by Civic Enterprises in association with Peter D. Hart Research Associates for the Bill and Melinda Gates Foundation, March 2006. http://www.civicenterprises.net/pdfs/thesilentepidemic3-06.pdf (14 March 2006).

Buffalo Public Schools, "Board schedules meetings on building usage: Budget forces closing of more schools." Buffalo Public Schools Web site, http://buffalo.k12.ny.us/news/newsstory.asp?newsid=285 (15 November 2003).

Bulkley, Katrina, and Jennifer Fisler. "A review of the research on charter schools." *Consortium for Policy Review in Education.* Philadelphia, June 2002. ERIC, EA 023 580. (10 February 2004).

Bureau of Child and Maternal Health. "School Dropouts." Child Health USA, 2002. http://mchb.hrsa.gov/chusa02/main_pages/page_13.htm (23 March 2004).

Bureau of Justice Statistics, Press Release. "Education and training requirements for big city police officers increase, salaries remain flat." Washington, DC, 12 May 2002, http://www.ojp.usdoj.gov/bjs/pub/press/pdlc00pr.htm (8 April 2003).

Bureau of Justice Statistics. "Juvenile felony defendants in criminal courts: Survey of 40 counties, 1998." (NCJ 197961, May 2003), http://www.ojp.usdoj.gov/bjs/abstract/jfdcc98.htm (6 June 2003).

Bureau of Justice Statistics. "Nation's prison and jail population exceeds 2 million for the first time." Press Release. Washington, DC, 6 April 2003, http://www.ojp.usdoj.gov/bsj/pub/press/pjim02pr.htm (8 April 2003).

Bureau of Justice Statistics. "Prisoners in 2001." (NCJ 195189, July 2002). http://www.ojp.usdoj.gov/bjs/abstract/p01.htm (3 June 2003).

Burke, Edmund. *Reflections on the French Revolution.* Harvard Classics, vol. 24. Collier, 1909.

"California v. Leave No Child Behind Act." Not Jails Newswire, http://www. SchoolsNotJails.com/article.php?sid=106 (25 April 2003).

Campaign for Fiscal Equity. "Costing out primer." Campaign for Fiscal Equity Web site, http://accessednetwork.org/resources/costing-out.htm (26 September 2002).

Campaign for Fiscal Equity. Defendants-Respondents' Brief to the Court of Appeals. New York, http://www.accessednetwork.org (8 May 2003).

Campaign for Fiscal Equity, Public Engagement. "Definition of a sound basic education," http://cfequity.org/sbeddef.html (3 April 2002).

Campaign for Fiscal Equity. "Vermont school funding bill provides a lesson for New York." 2 June 2003, http://cfequity.org/06-02-03Vermont.htm (6 August 2003).

Campaign for Fiscal Equity. "School funding ruling leaves Governor Pataki open for criticism." http://www.cfequity.org/June%2025%20DecisionCoverage/6-26-02NY1.htm (1 July 2002).

Campaign for Fiscal Equity. "Third Annual ACCESS Conference focuses on achieving education reform in difficult times," http://www.accessed network.org/conference03.htm (23 March 2003).

Campaign for Fiscal Equity. "State Reply Brief in *CFE IIc*," http://cfequity.org (11 May 2003).

Campaign for Fiscal Equity. "*CFE* v. *State of New York*: An analytic overview of the Court of Appeals decision," http://www.cfequity.org (8 June 2003).

Campbell, Jay R., Catherine M. Hombo, and John Mazzeo. "NAEP 1999 trends in academic progress: Three decades of student performance," August 2000. (The Nation's Report Card, National Assessment of Educational Progress, 1999), http://nces.ed.gov/nationsreportcard/pubs/main1999/2000469. asp (23 March 2004).

Canadian Centre for Policy Alternatives, Web site reports. "Behind the Issues: Ontario 2003," http://www.policyalternatives.ca.on (25 October 2003).

Carey, Kevin. The Funding Gap: Many States Still Shortchange Low-Income and Minority Students, The Education Trust, Fall 2004, http://www2.edtrust. org (15 August 2005).

Carnoy, Martin. *School Vouchers: Examining the Evidence.* Economic Policy Institute, 2001, http://www.lights.com/cgi-bin/epi/shop/shop.cgi?command= listitems&pos=0&type=group&group=28 (25 March 2003).

Carnoy, Martin. "Vouchers are no cure-all for short-changed schools." Economic Policy Institute, 6 October 2000, http://www.epinet.org/content.cfm/ webfeatures_viewpoints_vouchers (6 May 2003).

Carnoy, Martin, and Richard Rothstein. "Hard lessons in California: Minority pay gap widens despite more schooling higher scores." Economic Policy Institute, 1996, http://www.epinet.org (6 May 2005).

Carr, James H. "The complexity of segregation: Why it continues 30 years after the enactment of the Fair Housing Act." *Cityscape: A Journal of Policy Development and Research* 4, no. 3 (1999): 139–146. Washington, DC: U.S. Department of Housing and Urban Development.

Carter, Vicki K. "Virtual shades of pale: Educational technologies and the electronic 'Other'," in Nelson Rodriguez and Leila E. Villaverde, eds., *Dismantling White Privilege: Pedagogy, Politics, and Whiteness.* New York: Peter Lang, 2000.

Casimir, Leslie. "Maternal mortality—United States 1982–1996," *CDC, MMWR Weekly* 47(34) (4 September 1998): 705–707, http://www.cdc.gov/epo/mmwr/preview/mmwrhtml/00054602.htm (13 January 2003).

CBS. 60 Minutes. "Bush sought 'way' to invade Iraq?" (January 11, 2004), http://www.cbsnews.com/stories/2004/01/09/60minutes/main592330.s html (19 January 2004).

Center on Education Policy. "Did you know? Fewer students are dropping out of school," http://www.ctredpol.org (12 February 2003).

Centers for Disease Control. Asthma Page, http://www.cdc.gov/nceh/air pollution/asthma/children.htm (15 January 2003).

Centers for Disease Control. Fact Book, 2000/2001, September 2000. http://www.cdc.gov/maso/factbook/main.htm (15 January 2003).

Centers for Disease Control. "Vaccines for children." http://www.cdc.gov/programs/immun9.htm (21 January 2003).

Centers for Disease Control. "Maternal Mortality—United States 1982–1996." *MMWR Weekly,* 47(34) (September 4, 1998) 705–707, http://www.cdc.gov/epo/mmwr/preview/mmwrhtml/00054602.htm (13 January 2003).

Children's Defense Fund. "Updated children in the states." (January 2003), http://www.childrensdefensefund.org/states/all_states.pdf (26 July 2003).

"Children in poverty." Child Health USA, Department of Health and Human Services, Maternal and Child Health Bureau, Resource Information Center, 2002, http://www.mchirc.net/HTML/CHUSA-02/main_pages/page_ 12.htm (14 January 2003).

Chisolm Jr., J. Julian. "The road to primary prevention of lead toxicity in children." *Pediatrics* 107 (2001) 581–593.

Chronology of the Equal Rights Amendment 1923–1996. National Organization of Women, http://www.now.org/issues/economic/cea/history.html (3 October 2000).

Clinton, William J. The President's Economic Report to the Nation, 1996, p. 4, http://www.gpoaccess.gov/eop/search.html (15 June 2004).

Coleman, James S. et al. *Equality of Educational Opportunity.* U.S. Department of Health, Education, and Welfare, U.S. Government Printing Office, 1966.

Collins, Chuck, Betsy Leondar-Wright, and Holly Sklar. *Shifting Fortunes: The Perils of the Growing American Wealth Gap,* http://ufenet.org/press/archive/1999/shifting_fortunes_press.html (31 March 2003).

Collins, Chuck, Chris Hartman, and Holly Sklar. "Divided decade: Economic disparity at the century's turn," United for a Fair Economy, December 15, 1999, http://www.faireconomy.org/press/archive/1999/Divided_ Decade/divided_decade.html (4 February 2000).

Comley, Pat, and Penny Hopkins." How to beat the double cohort blues." Ontario School Counselors' Association, http://www/osca.ca/Beatcohort. htm (13 November 2003).

Community Service Society: Fighting Poverty, Strengthening New York. "Department of Legal Counsel: Voting rights: Felon disenfranchisement," http:// www.cssny.org/legal/voting.html (23 March 2004).

"Comparing equity indicators." *Education Week*, http://www.edweek.org/
reports/qc00/tables/equity-tl.htm (21 October 2001).

Conant, James. *Education and Liberty*. Cambridge, MA: Harvard University Press,
1958.

Conference: The Supreme Court, racial politics, and the right to vote: *Shaw* v. *Reno*
and the future of the voting rights act. *The American University Law Review* 44,
no. 1 (Fall 1994). Available at LexisNexis legal research (8 May 2003).

Coons, John E., William H. Clune III, and Stephen D. Sugarman. *Private Wealth and
Public Education*. Cambridge, MA: Harvard University Belknap Press, 1970.

Corson, David. "Ontario students as a means to the government's ends," *Ontario
Centre for Policy Alternatives*, http://www.policyalternatives.ca/on (26 October 2003).

Council of the Great City Schools, "Closing the achievement gaps in urban schools:
A survey of academic progress and promising practices in the great city
schools." Council of the Great City Schools website, October 1999,
http://www.cgcs.org/reports/achievement_gaps.html (23 March 2004).

Counts, George. "A Call to the teachers of the nation." New York: The John Day
Company, 1933.

Death Penalty Information Center. "Facts about the death penalty and deterrence," http://www.deathpenaltyinfo.org/article.php?scid=12&did=167#
STUDIES (4 January 2003).

Department of Health and Human Services, Centers for Disease Control, Fact
Book, 2000/2001, September 2000, http://www.cdc.gov/maso/factbook/
main.htm (15 January 2003).

Department of Health and Human Services. "The 2002 HHS Poverty Guidelines," http://aspe.hhs.gov/poverty/02poverty.htm (28 September 2002).

Devine, John. *Maximum Security: The Culture of Violence in Inner-city Schools*.
Chicago: University of Chicago Press, 1996.

Dewey, John. *The Early Works, 1882–1898*, Vol. 5; 1895–1898. Carbondale and Edwardsville: Southern Illinois University Press, 1972.

Dewey, John. *The Moral Principles Underlying Education*. Carbondale, IL: Southern
Illinois University Press, 1975.

Dewey, John. "School and Society," in Archambault, Reginald D., *John Dewey on
Education*. Chicago: University of Chicago Press, 1964.

Domanico, Raymond. "State of NYC public schools, 2002." Manhattan Institute
Web site, *Civic Report*, no. 36 (March 2002) 8, 11. (25 November 2003).

Douglas, Jim. "Budget Address." Vermont Office of the Governor Web site (January 2003. http://www.gov.state.vt.us/budget_message.php3 (12 September 2003).

DuBois, W.E.B. "Of Mr. Booker T. Washington and others," in Chapter 3 in *The
Souls of Black Folk* (originally published in 1903), http://etext.lib.virginia.
edu/toc/modeng/public/DubSoul.html (14 February 2003).

DuBois, W.E.B. *The Souls of Black Folk*. New York: Penguin Books, 1903.

Duffy, Shannon P. "Judge throws out Philly's school district race case." *The Legal
Intelligencer* 1 (23 November 1988). Available at LexisNexis Legal News (26
May 2003).

Dumont, Matthew P. "Lead, mental health, and social action: A view from the
bridge." U.S. department of Health and Human Services, *Public Health*

Report 2000, 115: 505–510. Available at LexisNexis legal research. (15 February 2003).

Duncan, Garrett Albert. "Urban pedagogies and the celling of adolescents of color." Revised from a paper delivered at Critical Resistance: Beyond the prison-industrial complex. University of California at Berkeley, 25 September 1998. Available at infotrac.galegroup.com (16 April 2003).

Duncombe, William F., and John F. Yinger. "Performance standards and educational cost indexes: You can't have one without the other," in Helen F. Ladd, Rosemary Chalk, and Janet S. Hansen, eds., *Equity and Adequacy in Educational Finance: Issues and Perspectives.* Washington, DC: National Academy Press, 1999.

Duncombe, William F. and Anna Lukemeyer. "Estimating the cost of educational adequacy: A comparison of approaches," paper presented March 2002 American Education Finance Association Annual Conference, Albuquerque, NM, http://cpr.maxwell.syr.edu/efap (21 August 2005).

Ebony, Pictorial History of Black America. Chicago: Johnson Publishing, 1971, http://www.callandpost.com/blackhistory/p241.htm (25 March 2003).

The Economic Policy Institute. "The Trade Deficit and Falling Wages." Economic Policy Snapshots, 1998, http://www.epinet.org/webfeatures/snapshots/archive/062399/snapshots062399.html (12 March 2003).

Educational Improvement Commission home page (Ontario). http://eic.edu.gov.on.ca/eicroot/english/home/default.asp (20 December 1999).

The Education Trust. "The Funding Gap 2005: Low-income and Minority Students Shortchanged by Most States." Washington, DC. Winter 2005, http://www2.edtrust.org/edtrust (14 March 2006).

Ehrenreich, Barbara. *Nickel and Dimed: On (Not) Getting by in America.* New York: Metropolitan Books, 2001.

Ehrenreich, Barbara, and Francis Fox Piven. "Who's utopian now? *The Nation,* 4 (February 2002), http://www.thenation.com/doc.mhtml?i=20020204&s=ehrenreich (5 May 2003).

Ehrenreich, Barbara, and Francis Fox Piven. "Without a safety net: Welfare reform was supposed to free poor mothers from dependency and get them into the job market. But what happens when the jobs are gone?" *Mother Jones* (July/August 2001), http://www.motherjones.com/magazine/MJ02/without_safety.html (7 May 2003).

Elshtain, Jean Bethke. *Jane Addams and the Dream of American Democracy.* New York: Basic Books, 2002.

Elshtain, Jean Bethke, ed. *The Jane Addams Reader.* New York: Basic Books, 2002.

Elsner Alan. *Gates of Injustice: America's Prison Crisis* (Upper Saddle River, NJ: Prentice Hall, 2004.

Engle, Brenda S. "Second grade testing: A position paper," http://www.fairtest.org/2gradeny.html (31 March 2003).

English, Diane J., and Cathy Spatz Widom. "Childhood victimization and delinquency, adult criminality, and violent criminal behavior: A replication and extension" (A report to the United States Justice Department, February 1,

2002). Paper presented at the 2000 American Society of Criminology Conference, November 14–18, 2000, http://www.ncjrs.org/pdffiles1/nij/grants/192291.pdf (4 June 2003).

Falk, Gene. Abstract: "TANF reauthorization: Side-by-side comparison of current law, S. 667, and H.R. 240 (TANF provisions)" Penny Hill Press, No. RL32834, March 29, 2005, http://www.pennyhill.com/index.php?lastcat=73&catname=Welfare&viewdoc=RL32834 (17 June 2005).

"Fatherless Homes breed violence," http://www.fathermag.com/news/2778-stats.shtml (29 July 2003).

Ferguson, Ronald F. "Teachers' perceptions and expectations and the black-white test score gap." *Urban Education* 38, no. 4 (July 2003) 460–495.

Ferris, Helen. "New Loan Program inspires affordable housing." *New Jersey Law Journal*, May 2, 2005. Lexisnexis legal research (6 June 2005).

Frankenberg, Erica, Chungmei Lee, and Gary Orfield. "A multiracial society with segregated schools: Are we losing the dream?" Harvard Civil Rights Project, 2003, http://www.civilrightsproject.harvard.edu/research/reseg03/resegregation03.php (7 February 2004).

Frankenberg, Erica, and Chungmei Lee. "Race in American public schools: Rapidly re-segregating school districts." The Harvard Civil Rights Project (August 2002) http://www.law.harvard.edu/groups/civilrights/publications/reseg_districts02/synopsis.html (20 September 2002).

Fremstad, Shawn. "Recent welfare reform research findings: Implications for TANF reauthorization and State TANF policies." Center for Budget and Policy Priorities, January 30, 2004, http://www.cbpp.org/1-30-04wel.pdf (10 March 2004).

Frisancho, A. Roberto, and Alan S. Ryan, "Decreased stature associated with moderate blood lead concentrations in Mexican-American children." *American Journal of Clinical Nutrition* 54, no. 3 (September 1991) 516—519.

Fullan, Michael. *Change Forces with a Vengeance.* London and New York: Routledge Farmer, 2003.

The Funding Gap 2005: Low Income and Minority Students Still Shortchanged by Most States. The Education Trust, 2005 http://www2.edtrust.org (14 March 2006).

Gaillard, Frye. "Race and schools: Once again, Charlotte is poised at a crossroads," http://www.cln.com/archives/charlotte/newsstand/c41799/cover.htm (25 September 2002).

Gainsborough, Jenni, and Marc Mauer. Americans Behind Bars: United States and International Rates of Incarceration. The Sentencing Project, September 2000, http://www.sentencingproject.org (3 April 2003).

Gainsborough, Jenni, and Mark Mauer. "Diminishing returns: Crime and incarceration in the 1990s." The Sentencing Project, September 2000, http://www.sentencingproject.org (14 April 2003).

Gates Jr., Henry Louis. America Beyond The Color Line. PBS documentary, aired 5–8 February 2004.

Gibboney, Richard A. *The Stone Trumpet: A Story of Practical School Reform 1960–1990.* Albany: State University of New York Press, 1994.

Gilmore, Janet. "Three strikes can't take credit for state's [California's] drop in crime." Inner City Struggle Web site, 21 April 2001, http://innercitystruggle. org/story.php?story=30 (18 January 2004).

Giroux, Henry A. "Rewriting the discourse of racial identity: Towards a pedagogy and politics of whiteness." *Harvard Educational Review* 67, no. 2 (Summer 1997) 285–320.

Gomaa, Amhed, Howard Hu, David Bellinger, Joel Schwartz, Schirng-Wern Tsaih, Teresa Gonzalez-Cossio, Lourdes Schnaas, Karen Peterson, Antonio Aro, and Mauricio Hernandez-Avila. "Maternal bone lead as an independent risk factor for fetal neurotoxicity: A prospective study." *Pediatrics* 110, (July 2002) 110–118.

Grant, Gerald. "Shaping social policy: The politics of the Coleman Report." *Teachers College Record* 75, no. 1, (1973) 17–54.

Gratiot, J. Peter. "Factors controlling foundation spending in Vermont." *Journal of Education Finance* 26 (Fall 2000) 219–248.

Greider, William. "Crime in the suites." *The Nation.* 17 January 2002, http://www. thenation.com/doc.mhtml?I=20020204&s=greider&c=1 (29 September 2002).

Guadarrama, Irma. "Language minority students: Finders or losers of the American dream?" *Discovering Our Experience: Studies in Bilingual/ESL Education* (Fall 2003), http://www.ncela.gwu.edu/miscpubs/twu/discovering/ lmstudents.htm (23 March 2004).

Haigler, Karl O., Caroline Wolf Harlow, Patricia E. O'Connor, and Anne Campbell. Literacy behind prison walls: Profiles of the prison population from the National Adult Literacy Survey. Washington, DC: Assessment of Adult Literacy, NCES, 1992, http://nces.ed.gov/naal/resources/execsumm prison.asp#litskills (4 April 2003).

Haney, Walt. "The myth of the Texas miracle in education." *Educational Policy Analysis Archives*, vol. 8, no. 41 (August 19, 2000), http://www.epaa.asu. edu (accessed 7/10/05).

Haney, Walt. "Revisiting the myth of the Texas miracle in education: Lessons about dropout research and dropout prevention," http://www.civilrghts project.harvard.edu/research/dropouts/haney.pdf (7 April 2003).

Hanushek, Eric A., with Charles S. Benson, Richard B. Freeman, Dean T. Jamison, Henry M. Levin, Rebecca A. Maynard, Richard J. Murnane, Steven G. Rivkin, Richard H. Sabot, Lewis C. Solmon, Anita A. Summers, Finis Welch, and Barbara L. Wolfe. *Making Schools Work: Improving Performance and Controlling Costs*. Washington, DC: The Brookings Institution, 1994.

Hanushek, Eric A., "Throwing money at the schools," *Journal of Policy Analysis and Management* 1: 19–41.

Harris, Fred R. *The Kerner Report: The 1968 Report of the National Advisory Commission on Civil Disorders.* New York: Pantheon, 1988.

Harris, Fred R. and Lynn A. Curtis et al. *The Millennium Breach: The American Dilemma, Richer and Poorer*. The Milton S. Eisenhower Foundation, 1998. http://www.eisenhowerfoundation.org (22 May 2003).

Harris, Fred R., and Lynn A. Curtis, eds. *Locked in the Poorhouse: Cities, Race, and Poverty in the United States*. Milton S. Eisenhower Foundation, 1999.

Harrison, Paige M., and Allen J. Beck. Prisoners in 2001. *Bureau of Justice Statistics Bulletin,* July 2002, NCJ 195189, 11, http://www.ojp.usdoj.gov/bjs/abstract/p01.htm.

Harvard Civil Rights Project. "Dropouts in America: How severe is the problem? What do we know about intervention and prevention?" (13 January 2001). Cambridge, MA, http://www.gse.harvard.edu/news/features/conf 01132001.html (14 November 2003).

Harvard Civil Rights Project. "Race in American Public Schools: Rapidly Resegregating School Districts." 8 August 2002, http://www.law.harvard.edu/groups/civilrights/publications/reseg_districts02/synopsis.html (30 September 2002).

Harvard Civil Rights Project. "Study: Only "50-50" chance of high school graduation for U.S. minority students, Weak accountability rules found." (February 25, 2004), http://www.civilrightsproject.harvard.edu/news/pressre leases.php/record_id=45/ (7 April 2004).

Heise, Michael. "Symposium: Children and education: Tensions within the parent-child-state relationship triad: The courts, educational policy, and unintended consequences." *Cornell Journal of Law and Public Policy* 11 (2002) 633–662.

Hentoff, Nat. "The high stakes testing trap." *The Village Voice,* 5 November 2002, Nation Section, p. 32. LexisNexis news (31 March 2003).

The Henry J. Kaiser Family Foundation. "Unemployment rates by race, December 2002–2003." State Health facts on line, http://www.sces.org/lmi/data/trends/charts/Chartroom/sld022.htm (23 February 2003).

Herival, Tara, and Paul Wright. *Prison Nation: The Warehousing of America's Poor.* New York: Routledge, 2003.

Hickner, Jamie. " Poor Children in U.S. Increase to Six Million." Columbia University Record 20, no. 15 (February 3, 1995), http://columbia.edu/cu/record/archives.vol20_iss15/records2015.20.html (12 February 2003).

Hoff, David J. "States revise the meaning of 'proficient'." *Education Week* on the Web (9 October 2002), http://www.edweek.org (25 March 2003).

Hirsh, E. D. *Cultural Literacy: What Every American Needs to Know.* New York: Vintage Books, 1988.

Human Rights Watch. *Losing the Vote.* Overview and Summary. The Sentencing Project, http://www.hrw.org/reports98/vote/usvot98o.htm#P466_16849 (30 April 2003).

Infoplease online almanac. "Unemployment rate by age, race, and sex, 2001, 2002," http://www.infoplease.com/ipa/A0104716.html (23 March 2004).

Jacobson, Matthew Frye. *Whiteness of a Different Color: European Immigrants and the Alchemy of Race.* Cambridge, MA: Harvard University Press, 1998.

Jay, John, James Madison, and Alexander Hamilton. *The Federalist Papers.* New York: New American Library, 1961.

Jefferson, Thomas. *Notes on Virginia.* "A Bill on Education in the revised codes of Virginia." (Washington ed., vii, 388; Ford ed., iii, 251, 1782), http://etextvirginia.edu/jefferson/ (30 November 2003).

Jellison, Jennifer. "Study finds resegregated neighborhood schools in Oklahoma City failed to meet district promises of achievement and equity." Harvard Graduate School of Education News (16 September 1996), http://gseweb.harvard.edu/news/features/oklahomacity091611996.html (5 April 2003).

Jencks, Christopher, and Meredith Phillips. "America's next achievement test: Closing the black-white test score gap." *The American Prospect* no. 40 (September–October 1998) 1–2, 44–54. Available at Infotrac. (2 April 2003).

Jennings, Jack. "The challenges of NCLB." Center on Educational Policy (2 March 2003), http://www.cep-dc.org/pubs/speakingoutmarch2003/speakingoutmarch2003.htm (25 March 2003).

Jimerson, Lorna. "A reasonably equal share: Educational equity in Vermont." The Rural School and Community Trust. February 2001, www.ruraledu.org/publications.html (12 May 2003).

Jimerson, Lorna. "Still a reasonably equal share: Update on educational equity in Vermont year 2001–2002." The Rural School and Community Trust. 21 February 2002, www.ruraledu.org/publications.html (12 May 2003).

Joftus, Scott, and Brenda Maddox-Dolan. "Left out and left behind: NCLB and the American high school." Alliance for Excellent Education, April 2003, http://www.all4rd.org/publications/reports.html (15 July 2005).

Johnson, Lyndon B. Special Message to Congress (16 March 1964), http://www.fordham.edu/halsall/mod/1964johnson-warpoverty.html (13 January 2003).

Jones, M. Gail, Brett D. Jones, and Tracy Y. Hargrove. *The Unintended Consequences of High-Stakes testing.* Lanham: Rowman and Littlefield, 2003.

Jones, Vivien. "A bio-bibliographical note about Mary Wollstonecraft," http://www.futurenet.co.uk/Penguin/Academic/classics96/britclassics author.html (1 May 2003).

Joseph, Clifton, and Paul Webster. "Teacher testing." CBC's The National In-depth: Education, April 2000, http://www.cbc.ca/national/magazine/testing/(26 November 2003).

Kahlenberg, Richard D. "Mixing classes: Why economic desegregation holds the key to school reform." *The Washington Monthly Journal* online (December 2002), http://www.washingtonmonthly.com/features/2000/0012.kahlenberg.html (2 May 2003).

Katyal, Neal Kumar. "Judges as Advice Givers." *Stanford Law Review* 50 (1998) 1709–1824.

Kaufman, Phillip, Martha Naomi Alt et al. "Dropout rates in the United States: 2000." National Center for Education Statistics, NCES2002-114, iii, http://nces.ed.gov/pubs2002/droppub_2001 (15 April 2004).

Keller, Bess. "Vermont: Tax shifts help buoy education spending." *Education Week* (1 July 2003), http://www.edweek.org.

Kennedy, Mike. "The ASU 100." *The American School and University Magazine*, 1 September 2003, http://asumag.com/aruniversity_asu_2/index.htm (15 November 2003).

Kentucky Department of Education. Progress in the Commonwealth Accountability System (CATS), http://www.education.ky.gov/ (9 February 2004).

"Kentucky school reform efforts bear fruit." Wisconsin Center for Education Research archives. 6 July 1998, http://www.wcer.wisc.edu/archives/feature/jul98a.asp (27 September 2002).

Kincheloe, Joe L. "The struggle to define and reinvent whiteness: A pedagogical Analysis." *College Literature* 26, no. 3 (1999), 162–195. ProQuest document ID: 45683503 (5 April 2004).

King Jr., Martin Luther. Quotes on education. 7 January 1968, http://www.stanford.edu/group/King/popular_requests/ (4 January 2003).

King Jr., Martin Luther. "I've been to the mountaintop." Speech given to the Memphis Sanitation workers, April 3, 1968, http://www.stanford.edu/group/King/popular_requests/ (4 January 2003).

King Jr., Martin Luther. "The last steep ascent." *The Nation*, 14 March 1966, reprinted in Victor Navasky, ed. *Perspectives from the Pages of* The Nation *1865–2000*. New York: The Nation Press, 2000.

King Jr., Martin Luther. Letter from a Birmingham jail. 16 April 1963. http://almaz.com/nobel/peace/MLK-jail.html (19 January 2004).

King Jr., Martin Luther "Where do we go from here?" SCLC Presidential Address, 16 August 1967, http://www.hartford-hwp.com/archives/45a/062.html (30 November 2003).

Korfmacher, Katrina Smith. "Analysis of dust wipe sampling in 1998–2001 Monroe County HUD grant." 2 September 2003, http://www.leadsafeby2010.org/Articles (6 July 2005).

Kozol, Jonathan. *Ordinary Resurrections: Children in the Years of Hope*. New York: Crown Publishing, 2000.

Kozol, Jonathan. "Persistent inequalities: The challenges of leadership in education." Speech given at State University of New York at Geneseo, NY, 23 April 2003.

Kozol, Jonathan. *Savage Inequalities*. New York: Crown Publishers, 1991.

Kuhn, Thomas. *The Structure of Scientific Revolutions*. Chicago: University of Chicago Press, 1970.

Ladd, Helen F., and Janet S. Hansen. *Making Money Matter: Financing America's Schools*. Washington, DC: National Academy Press, 1999.

Lanphear, Bruce J., Kim Deitrich, Peggy Auinger, and Christopher Cox. "Cognitive deficits associated with blood lead concentrations: 10 micrograms per deciliter in US children and adults." U.S. Department of Health and Human Services, *Public Health Reports* 115 (2000) 521–529.

Lawton, Stephen B. *The Price of Quality : The Public Finance of Elementary and Secondary Education in Canada*. Toronto: Canadian Education/Association Canadienne d'Education, 1987.

"Lead exposure and behavior." *Pediatrics for Parents* 19, no. 12, http://www.pedsforparents.com (2 February 2003).

Lee, Valerie E., and David T. Burkam. *Inequality at the Starting Gate: Social Background Differences in Achievement as Children Begin School*. Washington, DC: Economic Policy Institute, 2002, http://www.epinet.org.

Lerman, Robert I. *Improving career outcomes for youth: Lessons from the US and OECD Experience* (U.S. Department of Labor, July 2000, Research and Evaluation Series 01-D) 8.

Linhorst, Donald M. "Federalism and social justice: Implications for social work." *Social Work* 47, iss. 3 (July 2002) 201–209.

Lipman, Pauline. "Bush's education plan, globalization, and the politics of race." *Cultural Logic* 4, no. 1, http://eserver.org/clogic/4-1/lipman.html (9 March 2002).

Liss, Steve. *No Place for Children: Voices from Juvenile Detention.* Austin: University of Texas Press, 2005.

Liu, Xianchen, Kim N. Dietrich, Jerilynn Radcliffe, N. Beth Ragan, George G. Rhoads, and Walter J. Rogan. "Do children with falling blood lead levels have improved cognition?" *Pediatrics* 110, no. 4 (October 2002) 787–792.

Locke, John. *Second Treatise of Government.* Indianapolis: Hackett, 1980.

Locke, John. *Some Thoughts on Education.* Hoboken, NJ: Bibliobytes, 1692.

Losen, Daniel J., and Gary Orfield. Racial Inequality in Special Education. Harvard Civil Rights Project, http://www.civilrightsproject.harvard.edu/research.php (3 January 2003).

"Lowdown on lead poisoning." *Essence* 21, no. 9 (January 1991) 80.

Lundberg, Paula J. "State courts and school funding, a fifty state analysis." *Albany Law Review* 63 (2000): 1101–1146.

Lynch, Robert A., Lorraine Halinka Malcoe, Valerie J. Skaggs, and Michelle C. Kegler. "The relationship between residential lead exposures and elevated blood lead levels in a rural mining community." *Journal of Environmental Health* 63, no. 3 (October–September 2000) 43–49.

Magill, R. S. *Community Decision Making for Social Welfare: Federalism, City Government, and the Poor.* New York: Human Services Press, 1979.

Malkiewich, Chris. Personal audiotaped interview with Ontario Secondary School Teachers' Federation Executive Assistant, 22 January 2000.

Manzo, Kathleen Kennedy. "Urban students lag in reading and writing, NAEP scores Show." *Education Week* on the Web (22 July 2003), http://edweek.org (25 July 2003).

Martell, George. *A New Education Politics: Bob Rae's Legacy and the Ontario Secondary School Teachers' Federation.* Toronto: James Lorimer and Company, 1995.

Marx, Karl. *Critique of the Gotha Program.* In Lewis S. Feuer, ed. *Basic Writings on Politics and Philosophy: Karl Marx and Friedrich Engels.* New York: Doubleday, 1959.

Mathis, William J. "Civil society and school reform: Vermont's act 60," http://www.act60.org/mathis_version.htm (4 September 2003).

Mathis, William J. "Local Control and Act 60." Act 60: Working for Equal Educational Opportunity in Vermont, http://www.act60works.org/ (2 September 2003).

Mathis, William J. "Is Act 60 Working?" In "From the Board Room," posted on the Act 60 Works Web site, December 2000, http://www.act60works.org/fsmathis1200.html (12 September 2003).

Mathis, William J. "Vermont" in *Public School Finance in the United States and Canada: 1998–1999.* National Center for Education Statistics, U.S. Government Department of Education, Office of Educational Research and Improvement, CD ROM, NCES 2001-309.

McCall, H. Carl. "School finance reform, a discussion paper." State Comptroller's Office, October 1995. http://www.osc.state.ny.us/reports/schools/1995/10-95.htm (28 October 2002).

McChesney, Jim. "Whole school reform." ERIC Digest, no. 124, 1998, ED427388.

McKenzie, Hugh. "Magna Budget aftermath: The sweet revenge of Erik Peters." The Canadian Centre for Policy Alternatives, *Behind the Numbers* 5, no. 1 (5 November 2003), http://www.policyalternnatives.ca/on (24 November 2003).

McKenzie, Hugh. " The manager myth (or how Ernie Eves balanced Ontario's budget one year in a row)." The Canadian Centre for Policy Alternatives, *Behind the Scenes: Ontario 2003*, http://www.policyalternatives.ca/on (23 November 2003).

McKenzie, Hugh. "Ontario's tax cuts since 1995: The real tally." The Canadian Centre for Policy Alternatives, *Behind the Issues: Ontario 2003*, http://www.policyalternatives.ca/on (26 October 2003).

McKenzie, Hugh. "Telling tales out of school: How the Ontario government is(n't) funding education." *Ontario Alternative Budget*, technical paper #5. (2003), http://www.policyalternatives.ca/on/oab2003-education-hilights.html (26 October 2003).

McMillan, Kevin Randall. "Note: The Turning Tide: The Emerging Fourth Wave of School Finance Reform Litigation and the Courts' Lingering Institutional Concerns." *Ohio State Law Journal* (1998), 1867–1903.

Medige, Bernadette. "The privatization of public education, part 1 and part 2." *Buffalo Report* 19 (April and 2 May 2003), http://buffaloreport.com/articles/030419medige.html and http://buffaloreport.com/articles/030502medige.html (2 May 2003).

Meier, Deborah. *The Power of Their Ideas: Lessons for America from a Small School in Harlem.* Boston: Beacon Press, 1995.

Meier, Deborah. *Will Standards Save Public Education?* Boston: Beacon Press, 2000.

Mezcy, Jennifer, Sharon Parrott, Mark Greenberg, and Shawn Fremstadt "Reversing direction on welfare reform: President's budget cuts child care for more than 300,000 children." Center on Budget and Policy Priorities, 10 February 2004, http://www.cbpp.org (15 February 2004).

Milar, Katharine S. "'A coarse and clumsy tool': Helen Thompson Woolley and the Cincinnati Vocation Bureau." *History of Psychology* 2, no. 3 (1999) 219–235.

Mill, John Stuart. *On Liberty.* Edited by Elizabeth Rappaport. Indianapolis: Hackett, 1978.

Morse, Adina. "Felon disenfranchisement" (unpublished paper). Seton Law School, 2000.

Morse, Jane Fowler. "The ends of education." *Educational Change* (Spring 1996) 1–26.

Morse, Jane Fowler. "Equitable school funding: Lessons from Vermont, New York, and Ontario." (unpublished paper presented at the American Educational Studies Association), 2001.

Morse, Jane Fowler. "Fostering Autonomy." *Educational Theory* 47, no. 1 (Winter 1997) 31–50.

Morse, Jane Fowler. "Gone, but not forgotten: The work of Helen Thompson Woolley." *NWSA Journal* 14, no. 2 (2002) 121–147.

Mort, Paul R. ed., Director of Staff Studies, *A New Approach to School Finance: 1961 Review of Fiscal Policy for Public Education in New York State.* New York State Educational Conference Board: New York, September 1, 1961.

Moss, Mark E., Bruce P. Lanphear, and Peggy Auinger. "Association of dental caries and blood lead levels." *Journal of the American Medical Association* 281, no. 24 (June 23, 1999) 2294.

Moss, Mark E., Bruce P. Lanphear, and Peggy Auinger. "Effects of blood lead level on growth." *Nutrition Research Newsletter* 10, no. 9 (September 1991) 88.

Mosteller, Frederick, and Daniel P. Moynihan. *On Equality of Educational Opportunity.* New York: Random House, 1972.

Moyers, Bill. PBS: Now. (May 10, 2002), http://www.pbs.org/now/transcript/transcript117_full.html (15 January 2003).

Muhammad, Dedrick, Attieno Davis, Meizhu Lui, and Betsy Leondar-Wright. "The State of the dream 2004: Enduring disparities in black and white." United for a Fair Economy Web site, 15 January 2004: http://www.ufenet.org/press/2004/StateoftheDream2004_pr.html (19 January 2004).

National Association for the Advancement of Colored People. "NAACP reactivates Prison Project." *NAACP News*, 4 March 2002, http://www.naacp.,org/news/releases/prisonproj03402.shtml (30 April 2003).

National Association for the Advancement of Colored People. Information on the *Haydn* v. *Pataki* case at the Web site of the NAACP Legal Defense Fund, http://www.naacpldf.org/ (18 April 2004).

National Center for Children in Poverty. "Improving children's economic security: Research findings about increasing family income through employment." Policy Briefs, August 19, 2002, http://www.nccp.org/improving_security_series.html (12 February 2003).

National Center for Children in Poverty. "Research forum on children, families, and the new federalism: Relationships between child welfare and child well-being: A research and policy discussion." 2001. www.research forum.org., (press release available at http://www.nccp.org/pub_ssu02i.html) (28 July 2003).

National Center for Children in Poverty. "Basic facts about low income children: Birth to age 18." July 2005, http://www.nccp.org (31 July 2005).

National Center for Education Statistics, quick tables, Public High School Dropouts from the school year 2000–2001, http://nces.ed.gov/pubs2004/dropout 00-01/table_3.asp (14 April 2004).

National Center for Education Statistics. *Inequalities in Public Education: Statistical Analysis Report.* U.S. Department of Education, Office of Educational Research and Improvement, July 1998. NCES 98-210.

National Center for Education Statistics. Public School Finance Programs of the United States and Canada: 1998–99. U.S. Department of Education, Office of Educational Research and Improvement. April 2001. CD ROM. NCES 2001-309

National Center for Policy Analysis. "The Economic impact of prison labor." http://www.ncpa.org/studies/s209/s209g.html (26 January 2004).

National Center for Policy Analysis. *Crime and Punishment in America: 1997 Update,* "Bringing Down Costs through Privatization," http://www.ncpa.org/studies/s209/s209g.html (26 January 2004).

National Commission on Excellence in Education. *A Nation at Risk.* Washington, DC: Government Printing Office, 1983, http://www.ed.gov/pubs/Nat AtRisk/index.html (3 April 2003).

National Housing Law Project: Housing Law Bulletin. "Latest decision on *Gautreaux* v. *Chicago Housing Authority,*" http://www.nhlp.org/html/hlb/ 1097/1097gautreaux.htm (23 March 2003).

National Institute for Literacy. Correctional Education Facts. 2000, 2001, http://www.nifl.gov/nifl/facts/correctional.html (10 April 2003).

National Institute for Literacy. International Adult Literacy Survey, http://www. nifl.gov/nifl/facts/IALS.html (30 April 2003).

Needleman, Herbert L., Christine McFarland, Roberta B. Ness, Stephen E. Fienberg, and Michael J. Tobin. "Bone lead levels in adjudicated delinquents: A case control story." *Neurotoxicology and Teratology* 24 (2002) 711–719.

Nesiba, Reynold F. "Insurance redlining: Disinvestment, reinvestment, and the evolving role of financial institutions." Book reviews, *Journal of Economic Issues* 32, no. 3 (September 1998) 901–905.

Ness, Erik. "Getting the lead out: Students, toxins, and environmental racism." *Rethinking Schools* 18, no. 2 (Winter 2003) 18–21.

New Democratic Party Platform. "Why McGuinty is evasive on school funding." (16 September 2003) http://www.publicpower.ca/issues-news/article_ 342.shtml (15 November 2003).

New Jersey Law Review, August 19, 2002. (Editorial). "Decisions." LexisNexis legal research (17 February 2003).

New York City Board of Education. Division of Assessment and Accountability. "An examination of the relationship between higher standards and students dropping out: Flash Research Report #5." (1 March 2001) 7, 8, ERIC Document 451 317.

New York Civil Liberties Union. In the courts, http://www.nyclu.org/ docket.html (3 July 2003).

New York Civil Liberties Union. Litigation docket, http://www.nyclu.org/ docket.html (23 September 2002).

"New York Civil Liberties Union v. *State of New York:* Decision of interest." *New York Law Review* 228 (11 July 2002) 24, LexisNexis legal research (28 October 2003).

New York Law Journal, "Fiscal equity group to proceed with education funding case." News in Brief, 228 col. 1 (3 December 2002) 1.

New York State Constitution, Article XI, Education. Section 1, http://www. findlaw.com (15 August 2003).

New York State Education Department. "Distribution of New York State's public and non-public high school graduates by post-high school plans and racial/ethnic group, 1990–1991 to 2000–2001." Office of Research and Information Systems, http://www.highered.nysed.gov:80/oris/Graduation_Rates.htm (10 August 2003).

The News Hours with Jim Lehrer, "Rescue Mission." December 11, 2002, http://www.pbs.org/newshour/bb/education/july-dec02/rescue_ mission_12-11-1.html (6 January 2003).

The News Hour with Jim Lehrer, "Connecticut sues over NCLB," August 24, 2005, http://www.pbs.org/newshour/bb/education/july-dec05/nclb2_8-24.html (23 September 2005).

The Northwest Federation of Community Organizations. Building a Livable Wage Movement, http://www.seanet.com/~nwfco/Nwfco/building.htm#Minimum%20Wage%20Campaign%20Leaders%20Analyze%20Statewide%20Efforts (13 February 2003).

Nore, Gordon W. "Strike Notes: Green ribbons, politics, and patronage." *Canadian Business and Current Affairs, Our Times, Ltd.*, 17, n. 1 (January/February 1998)11.

Olson, Lynn. "The great divide." *Education Week* on the Web, Quality Counts 2003, http://www.edweek.org/sreports/qc03/templates/article.cfm?slug=17divide.h22&keywords=New%20York (26 July 2003).

Ondrich, Jan, Alex Striker, and John Binger. "Do real estate brokers choose to discriminate? Evidence from the 1989 housing discrimination study." *Southern Economic Journal* 64, no. 4 (April 1998) 88–102.

Ontario Ministry of Education and Training. Backgrounder: Investments in Quality for 2000–2001. (9 March 2000), http://www.edu.gov.on.ca/eng/document/nr/00.03.bg1.html (6 October 2000).

Ontario Ministry of Education and Training. Backgrounder: Standards on Instructional Time, (9 March 2000), http://www.edu.gov.on.ca/eng/document/nr/00.03/bg2.html (6 October 2000).

Ontario Ministry of Education and Training. *Excellence in Education: Student-Focused Funding for Ontario: A Guide Book 1999–2000.* (1997), http://www.edu.gov.on.ca/eng/funding/9900/fund2.html (20 September 1999).

Ontario Ministry of Education and Training. Fact Sheet: Early Learning Grant. (March 2000), http://www.gov.on.ca/eng/document/nr/00.03/fs4.html (6 October 2000).

Ontario Ministry of Education and Training. Fact Sheet: Special Education Grant. (March 2000), http://www.edu.gov.on.ca/eng/document/nr/00.03/fs2.html (6 October 2000).

Ontario Ministry of Education and Training. "McGuinty government keeps promise to invest in education: Delivers urgent learning boost for students." (What's New, 3 December 2003), http://www.edu.gov.on.ca/eng/new/new.html (9 March 2004).

Ontario Ministry of Education and Training. "McGuinty government restores local voice to Toronto's public school students: Elected trustees resume control of their local schools." (What's New, 18 February 2004), http://www.edu.gov.on.ca/eng/new/new.html (9 March 2004).

Ontario Ministry of Education and Training. "McGuinty government taking action to help kids succeed." (What's New, 5 March 2004), http://www.edu.gov.on.ca/eng/new/new.html (9 March 2004).

Ontario Ministry of Education and Training. "News release: Ontario's investment in education grows by $190 million," http://www.gov.on.ca/eng/document/nr/00.03/funding.html (6 October 2000).

Ontario Ministry of Education and Training. Official Biographies, http://www.edu.gov.on.ca/eng/general/biography/bio.html (6 October 2000).

Ontario Ministry of Education and Training. *Parents' Guide to Student-focused Funding 1999–2000*, http://www.edu.gov.on.ca/eng/funding/fund0102.html# financial (6 October 2000).

Ontario Ministry of Education and Training. *Parents' Guide to Student-focused Funding 2001–2002*. (March 2001), http://www.edu.gov.on.ca/eng/funding/ fund0102.html#financial (16 November 2003).

Ontario Ministry of Education and Training. Grades 11 and 12 curricula, http://www.edu.gov.on.ca/eng/document/curricul/curric1112.html (31 March 2003).

Ontario Ministry of Education and Training. "Student-focused funding: Technical paper 2002-03." (2002), http://www.edu.gov.on.ca/eng/funding/ e0203tech.pdf (15 November 2003).

Ontario Ministry of Education and Training. "Delivering excellence for all Ontario students," http://www.edu.gov.on.ca/eng/document/reports/ excellence/index.html#change (20 July 2005).

Ontario Public School Boards' Association. *Fast Reports: Weekly Information for Decision Makers in Education* 10, no. 30 (November 20, 1998), http:// www.opsba.org/pubs/fast/arch/1998/98-11-20.htm (April 6, 2004).

Ontario Regulation 275/01, made under the Education Act, 4 July 2001, http://www.e-laws.gov.on.ca/DBLaws/Source/Regs/English/2001/ R01275_e.htm (28 November 2003).

Ontario Secondary School Teachers' Federation. "Ontario 55th out of 63 in North American education spending," http://osstf.on.ca/www/issues/ edfi/survey.html (19 October 2000).

Ontario Secondary School Teachers' Federation. "The education funding model impact on students' education," http://www.osstf.on.ca/issues/issmonth/ fndconcn.html (26 October 2003).

Ontario Secondary School Teachers' Federation. "CTF studies critical of Ministry Cost of Education document," http://www.osstf.on.ca/ (9 March 2004).

Ontario Secondary School Teachers' Federation. "Tories stoop to new low by firing Ottawa Carlton school trustees," http://www.osstf.on.ca/www/pub/ pressrel/sept01aug17-202.html (13 September 2002).

Ontario Secondary School Teachers' Federation. "Underfunding of Public Education," http://osstf.on.ca/www/issues/edfi/underfunding.html (19 October 2000).

Ontario Universities Application Centre. "Impressive number of students apply for fall 2003 admission," (News and stats, 17 January 2003). http://www.ouac.on.ca/news/dblcohort/ni-jan17press.html (13 November 2003).

Orfield, Gary, Susan Eaton et al. *Dismantling Desegregation: The Quiet Reversal of Brown v. Board of Education*. New York: The New Press, 1996.

Parker, Dennis R. "Racial and ethnic isolation post *Sheff* v. *O'Neill.*" *Equity and Excellence in Education* 32, no. 2 (September 1999) 5–11.

Parrish, Thomas, Christine S. Hikido, and William Fowler. *Inequalities in Public School District Revenues*. National Center for Education Statistics, Statistical Analysis Report, NCES 98-210, July 1998.

Parrott, Sharon, and Jennifer Mezey. "Bush administration projects that the number of children receiving child care subsidies will fall by 200,000 during the next five years," (12 April 2002), http://www.clasp.org/Pubs (11 February 2003).

Parrott, Sharon, and Jennifer Mezey. "Increasing the ability to transfer TANF to CCDF (Child Care and Development Fund) is not the answer to unmet child care needs," (5 February 2003), http://www.clasp.org/Pubs/Pubs_ChildCare?pub_topic=004&year:int=2002&first_year:int=1996 (11 February 2003).

Pascoe, Jeffery. "Vermont's next education funding mechanism." Act 60 - What You Should Know web site (22 July 2000), http://www/act60.orgnext mech.htm (4 September 2003).

Paulozzi, Leonard J., Joanne Sharpe, Robert E. Drawbaugh, and Jan K. Carney. "Prevalence of lead poisoning among two-year-old children in Vermont." *Pediatrics* 96, no. 1, (July 1995) 78. Available at Infotrac onefile (14 January 2003).

Peckover, Lydia. "The History of the GI Bill." Utah Valley State University. *The American Prospect* 27, iss. 8 (September–October 1996). http://www.prospect.org/print/V7/28/skocpolt.html (15 February 2003).

Pereira, Michael. "A 'crisis' in government: Bill 160 and the Ontario teachers' strike." Personal Web site, nd, http://mike-pereira.com (5 June 2004).

Perkel, Colin. "More money, kinder approach but Tories struggle to win over education critics." Canadian Business and Current Affairs, *Canadian Press Newswire*, 3 September 2003, sec. S. Available at LexisNexis news (15 November 2003).

Phillips-Fein, Kim. "The education of Jessica Rivera: Trading in their books for buckets, welfare recipients learn 'responsibility.'" *The Nation*, 275:18 (5 November 2002) 20–23.

Pratt, Joseph S. "Note: School finance battles: Survey says? It's all just a change in attitudes." *Harvard Civil Rights-Civil Liberties Law Review* 34 (Summer 1999) 547, 551–533.

Quality Counts. *Education Week*, 2000. http://www.edweek.org/sreports/qc00.

Quality Counts. *Education Week*, 2001. http://www.edweek.org/sreports/qc01.

Quality Counts. *Education Week*, 2002. http://www.edweek.org/sreports/qc02.

Quality Counts. *Education Week*, 2003. http://www.edweek.org/sreports/qc03.

Quality Counts. *Education Week*, 2004. http://www.edweek.org/sreports/qc04.

Rabin, Richard. "Warnings unheeded: A history of childhood lead poisoning." *American Journal of Public Health* 29, no. 12, (December 1989) 1668–1674.

Rabin, Richard. "Re: Paint Industry did not stop selling lead paint in 1950." (electronic letter published by *The American Journal of Public Health*, in response to Nancy L. Rothman, Rita J. Lourie, and John Gaughan, "Lead Awareness: North Philly Style," *The American Journal of Public Health* 92, no. 5, (June 7, 2002) 739–741, http://ajph.org/cgi/eleters/92/5/739#43 (9 February 2003).

Randall, Vernalia R. "Race, health care, and the law." (31 July 2002), http://www.udayton.edu/health/racist.htm (27 January 2003).

Randall, Vernalia R. "Reparations for slavery are due, but healing isn't about the money, says health care expert." (31 July 2002), http://www.udayton.edu/news/nr/073102.html (27 January 2003).

Rasell, Edith, and Lawrence Mishel. "Shortchanging education: How United States spending on grades K–12 lags behind other industrial nations." Economic Policy Institute,1990, http://www.lights.com/epi/virlib/Briefing Papers/1990/shortchanginge.PDF (25 March 2003).

Rawls, John. *A Theory of Justice*. Cambridge, MA: Belknap Press of Harvard University, 1971.

"Regents extend 55 passing grade: Regents make sweeping changes teachers wanted in math, physics." *New York Teacher*, 22 October 2003, http://www.nysut.org/newyorkteacher/2003-2004/031022regents02.html (15 February 2004).

Reid, Karla Scoon. "Ontario grapples with school funding." *Education Week* (5 February 2003). Reprinted on the Web site of Our Schools, Our Communities, an Ottawa Education Advocacy Group. http://www.ourschools-ottawa.ca/article.php3?story_id=60 (12 November 2003).

Reinhardt, Beth. "California's cities face staggering problems, but urban schools get little extra help from Sacramento." *Education Week*, http://www.edweek.org/sreports/qc98/states/ca-n.htm (24 July 2003).

Reitman, Sandford W. *The Educational Messiah Complex: American Faith in the Culturally Redemptive Power of Schooling*. Sacramento, CA: Caddo Gap Press, 1992.

Rodriguez, Nelson, and Leila E. Villaverde, eds. *Dismanteling White Privilege: Pedagogy, Politics and Whiteness*. New York: Peter Lang, 2000.

Roediger, David. *Towards The Abolition of Whiteness*. London and New York: Verso, 1994.

Roscigno, Vincent J. "Race and reproduction of educational disadvantage." *Social Forces* 76, no. 3 (March 1998) 1033–1061.

Rosenbaum, James E. "Changing the geography of opportunity by expanding residential choice: Lessons from the Gautreaux Program." *Housing Policy Debate* 6, no. 1 (1995) 231–269.

Rothman, Nancy L., Rita J. Lourie, and John Gaughan. "Lead awareness: North Philly style." *American Journal of Public Health*, 92, iss. 5 (May 2002) 739–741.

Rothman, Nancy L., Rita J. Lourie, and John Gaughan. "A community-developed, community-based lead poisoning prevention program: Lead awareness: North Philly style." *Holistic Nursing Practice* 14, no. 1 (October 1999) 47–55.

Rothstein, Jesse, and Robert Scott. "NAFTA and the states: Job destruction is widespread." Economic Policy Institute, Issue Brief #119, 19 September 1997. http://www.epinet.org/content.cfm/issuebriefs_ib119 (19 January 2004).

Rothstein, Richard. "Lessons: Dropout rate is climbing and likely to go higher." *New York Times*, 9 October 2002, Late Edition, Sec. B, col. 1, p. 8. Available at LexisNexis news (15 April 2004).

Rothstein, Richard. "Where's the money going: Changes in the level and composition of educational spending 1991–1996." The Economic Policy Institute, 1997, http://www.epinet.org (7 January 2003).

Rothstein, Richard, and Karen Hawley Mills. "Where's the Money Gone? Changes in the level and composition of education spending." Economic Policy Institute, 1995, http://www.epinet.org/content.cfm/books_where moneygone (19 January 2004).

Rozanski, Mordecai. *Investing in public education: Advancing the goal of continuous improvement in student learning and achievement: Report of the Education Equality Task Force, 2002.* (December 2002), http://mettowas21.edu.gov.on. ca/eng/document/reports/task02/report.html (10 October 2003).

The Rural School and Community Trust. "Vermont's Act 60 continues to improve equity for state's students." *Rural Policy Matters* 4, no. 3 (March 2002), http://www.ruraledu.org/rpm/rpm403b.htm (12 September 2003).

The Rural School and Community Trust. "Roundup! What went on in state legislatures this year/Vermont." *Rural Policy Matters: A Newsletter of Rural School and Community Action* 5, no. 7 (July 2003), http://www.rural.edu.org/ rpm/rpm507c.html (6 September 2003).

The Rural School and Community Trust. "Kansas court rules school funding system unconstitutional." *The Rural School Funding Report* 2, no. 20 (5 December 2003), http://www.ruraledu.org/issues/finance/news220.htm (7 April 2004).

The Rural School and Community Trust. "Rural schools score major victory in Arkansas Supreme Court." *The Rural School and Community Trust.* 2002, http://www.ruraledu.org/keep_learning.cfm?record_no=634 (23 March 2003).

Ryan, James E. "The influence of race in school finance reform." *Michigan Law Review* 98 (November 1999) 432–480.

Ryan, James E. "Schools, race, and money." *Yale Law Journal* 109 (November 1999) 249.

Safier, Kristen. "The Question of a fundamental right to a minimally adequate education." *University of Cincinnati Law Review* 69 (Spring 2002) 993–1022.

Sandefur, Gary D., Molly Martin, and Thomas Wells. "Poverty as a public health issue: Poverty since the Kerner Commission Report of 1968." Institute for Research on Poverty, Discussion Paper No. 1158-98, March 1998, http://econ-papers.hhs.se/paper/wopwispod/1158-98.htm (11 February 2003).

Sanders, Bernie. "The view from Mexico." *The Nation* 13 (2 February 2004), http://thenation.com/docprem.mhtml?i=20040202d&=sanders (11 February 2004).

Schemo, Diane Jean. "Neediest schools receive less money, report finds." *New York Times,* 9 August 2002. Available at LexisNexis news (10 September 2002).

Scherrer, Paul. "One in four US children under six live in poverty." World Socialist Web site (22 July 1998), http://www.wsws.org/news/1998/july_1998/ pov-jul22.shtml (5 May 2003).

Schneider, Bruce, Kevin J. Curnin, Jennifer Lallite, and Joseph E. Strauss. N.Y.C.L.U. Web site, Litigation Docket, "Caesar v. Pataki," http://www. nyclu.org/docket.html (4 August 2003).

The School-to-Prison Pipeline Conference, sponsored by the Harvard Civil Rights Project and Northeastern University's Institute on Race and Justice, Cambridge, MA, May 15–16, 2003, http://www.civilrightsproject.harvard. edu/convenings/schooltoprison/synopsis.php (5 April 2004).

Schrag, Peter. "Getting the blues." *The Nation* (17 July 2003), http://www.the nation.com/doc.mhtml?i=20030804&c=3&s=schrag (9 March 2004).

Schrag, Peter. "High stakes are for tomatoes." *Atlantic Monthly* (August 2000), http://www.theatlantic.com/issues/2000/08/schrag.htm (11 May 2003).

Schrag, Peter. "Many who fail exit exams lack equal resources." *Los Angeles Daily Journal*, 15 October 2003, vol. 115, iss. 200, p. 6, col. 5. Available at Lexis-Nexis news (4 April 2004).

Schulman, Beth. "Yes, union." *The American Prospect* 1, no. 29 (November/December 1996) http://www.prospect.org, (8 May 2003).

Schumacher, Rachel. "Increasing the ability to transfer TANF to CCDF is not the answer to unmet child care needs." Center for Law and Social Policy, (April 12, 2002), http://www.clasp.org (7 February 2003).

Schweinhart, L. J., and D. P. Weikart. *Young Children Grow Up: The Effects of the Perry Preschool Program on Youths Through Age 15*. Ypsilanti, MI: The High/Scope Press, 1980.

"Screening for Elevated Blood Lead Levels." *Pediatrics* 101, no. 6, (June 1998): 1972–1978. Committee on Environmental Health, American Academy of Pediatrics, http://www.aap.org/policy/re9815.html (15 January 2003).

Seeley, David. Seeley-Coleman Memos, 1966, http://www.library.csi.cuny.edu/dept/edu/COLESE.HTM (6 January 2003).

Selevan, Sherry G., Deborah C. Rice, Karen A. Hogan, Susan Y. Euling, Andrea Pfahles-Hutchens, and James Bethel. "Blood lead concentration and delayed puberty in girls." *New England Journal of Medicine*, 16 (April 17, 2003) 1527–1536.

The Sentencing Project. "Facts about prisons and prisoners," August 2002, http://www.SentencingProject.org (12 February 2003).

The Sentencing Project. *Losing the Vote*, Overview and Summary, http://www.hrw.org/reports98/vote/usvot98o.htm#P466_16849 (30 April 2003).

The Sentencing Project. "State rates of incarceration by race," www.sentencing-project.org/pdfs/racialdisparity.pdf (23 March 2004).

The Sentencing Project. "Summary of *Hayden v. Pataki*," Civil Action No. 00-8586, http://www.SentencingProject.org (10 February 2003).

"Settlement reached in *Sheff* v. *O'Neill*: Pact calls for three-pronged approach." *The Connecticut Law Tribune*, 29, no. 4 (27 January 2003) 1.

Sharpe, Adam. Associate Administrator, Office of Prevention, Pesticides, and Toxic Substances, Environmental Protection Agency. Testimony before the Senate Subcommittee on Housing and Transportation, http://www/epa.gov/ocir/hearings/test (14 February 2003).

Shoop, Julie Ganon. "HUD rules don't protect kids from lead hazards." *Trial* 30, no. 9 (September 2004) 106.

Skocpol, Theda. "Delivering for young families: The resonance of the GI Bill," *The American Prospect* 27, iss. 8, (September–October 1996). http://www.prospect.org/print/V7/28/skocpolt.html (15 February 2003).

Smith, Ryan A. "Racial differences in access to hierarchical authority: An analysis of change over time, 1972–1994." *The Sociological Quarterly*, 40, iss. 3 (Summer 1999) 367–396.

Socrates. "Apology," in Edith Hamilton and Huntington Cairns, *The Collected Works of Plato*. Bollingen Series LXXI. Pantheon Books, 1961.

Stansky, Lisa. "Tax turf war: States companies clash on 'loop hole'." *National Law Journal* 26, no. 21 (January 26, 2004) 1.

Stephen, Walter G., and Joe R. Feagan, eds. *School Desegregation: Past, Present, and Future.* Plenum Press, 1980.

Stewart, James B. "Locked in the Poorhouse: Cities, Race, and Poverty in the United States." (Review). *The Review of Black Political Economy* 28, no. 1, (Summer 2000) 67.

Strayer, George D., and Robert Murray Haig. *The Financing of Education in the State of New York: A Report Reviewed and Presented by the Educational Finance Inquiry Commission under the Auspices of the American Council on Education, Washington, D.C.* New York: Macmillan, 1923.

Stuart, Gail. Vice-Chair of Our Schools, Our Communities. Presentation to a hearing on education issues held in Ottawa on January 30 by the provincial Liberal Opposition, http://www.ourschools-ottawa.ca (26 November 2003).

Sunstein, Cass. *Free Markets and Social Justice.* Oxford: Oxford University Press, 1997.

Swanson, Austin D. "The Effects of chronic retrenchment," in Paul R. Mort, ed., Director of Staff Studies, *A New Approach to School Finance: 1961 Review of Fiscal Policy for Public Education in New York State.* New York: New York State Educational Conference Board, 1 September 1961.

Teachout, Peter. "No simple disposition: The Brigham case and the future of local control over school spending in Vermont." *Vermont Law Review* 22, no. 1 (Fall 1997) 21–82.

"Testing our schools." The Merrow Report, Frontline, 28 March 2002 (PBS), http://www.pbs.org/wgbh/pages/frontline/shows/schools/testing/theme.html (26 April 2003).

Thernstrom, Abigail. "Education's division problem: Schools are responsible for the main source of racial inequality today." http://manhattan-institute.org.html_latimes_division_p.htm (25 November 2003).

Thompkins, Rachel. "Vermont's Act 60 continues to improve equity for state's students. *Rural Policy Matters* 4, no. 3, (March 2002), http://www.rural edu.org/rpm/rpm403b.htm (12 September 2003).

Thornton Commission Report. Maryland (January, 2002), http://mlis.state.md.us/other/education (22 September 2002).

Thro, William E. "Judicial analysis during the third wave of school finance litigation: The Massachusetts decision as a model." *Boston College Law Review* 35, no. 4. (1994) 597–615.

Thro, William E. "To render them safe the analysis of state constitutional provisions in public school finance reform litigation." *Virginia Law Review* 75 (1989): 1639–1679.

Trope, Idit, Dolores Lopez-Villegas, Kim M. Cecil, and Robert E. Lenkinski. "Exposure to lead appears to selectively alter metabolism of cortical gray matter." *Pediatrics* 107 (2001) 1437–1443.

Tyack, David, and Larry Cuban. *Tinkering Toward Utopia: A Century of Public School Reform.* Cambridge, MA: Harvard University Press, 1995.

United States Census Bureau. *Income, Poverty, and Health Insurance Coverage in the United States: 2003,* http://www.census.gov/hhes/www/income.html (17 June 2005).

United States Census Bureau. "Income Stable, Poverty Up, Numbers of Americans With and Without Health Insurance Rise, Census Bureau Reports." New room, Thursday, Aug. 26, 2004, http://www.census.gov/Press-Release/www/releases/archives/income_wealh/002484.html (6 July 2005).

United States Department of Education. No Child Left Behind informational Web site, http://www.ed.gov/nclb/landing.jhtml (30 September 2005).

United States Department of Health and Human Services, "Temporary Assistance for Needy Families, Program Instruction" (No. TANF-ACF-PI-2005-01), 14 April 2005, posted at Administration for Children and Families, available at http://www.acf.dhhs.gov/programs/ofa/pi-ofa/pi2005-1.htm (17 June 2005).

United States Department of Health and Human Services. The HHS 2002 Poverty Guidelines, http://aspe.hhs.gov/poverty/02poverty.htm (28 September 2002).

United States Department of Justice: Civil Rights Division, Educational Opportunities Section. "Overview," http://www.usdoj.gov/crt/edo/overview.htm (8 April 2003).

United States Department of Labor. "History of Changes to the Minimum Wage Law." Department of Labor, http://www.dol.gov/esa/minwage/coverage.htm (10 September 2002).

"U.S. Unemployment rates by race, December 2002–2003." State Health Facts online, the Henry J. Kaiser Family Foundation, http://www.sces.org/lmi/data/trends/charts/Chartroom/sld022.htm (23 March 2004).

Venter, Craig (Dr.) President and Chief Scientific Officer, Celera Genomics Corporation. Speaking at the White House celebration of the completion of the sequencing of the human genome on 26 June 2002, http://www.genome.gov/page.cfm?pageID=10001356 (4 March 2003).

Vermont Bill Tracking. H. 480, An Act relating to Education Funding, http://www.leg.state.vt.us/docs/legdoc.cfm?URL=/docs/2004/bills/passed/H-480.HTM (15 July 2005).

Vermont Bill Tracking. H.1, available at http://www.leg.state.vt.us/database/search/resultsresults.cmf (15 July 2005 and 13 March 2006).

Vermont, Office of the Governor website. Biography of Jim Douglas. 12 September 2002, http://www.gov.state.vt.us/biography.php3 (13 September 2003).

Vermont Department of Education. Laws and Regulations: Act 60 - The Equal Opportunity Education Act: Fact Sheet. Vermont State Department of Education, http://www.state.vt.us/educ/new/html/laws/act60_fact_sheet.html (13 September 2003).

Vermont Department of Education. School Data & Reports. "Per pupil spending by school type for 2002 and 2003," http://www.state.vt.us/educ/new/html/data/perpupil.html (2 September 2003).

Vermont Department of Education. "Overview of Vermont's Education Funding System Under Act 68 & Act 130." Vermont Department of Education. November 2005, http://state.vt.us/educ/new/html/pgm_finance_data/school_funding_info.html (14 March 2006).

Vermont Department of Motor Vehicles. "Effective October 1, 2003 Vermont's sales tax rate increases from 5% to 6%." Vermont Department of Motor Vehicles, http://www.aot.state.vt.us/dmv/HOME/news/Miscellaneous OTHERNews/SalesTaxIncrease.htm (2 March 2004).

Vermont State Department. "Significant Education Bills that passed in 2003." Legislative Summary for 2003. Vermont State Department, http://www/state.vt.us/educ/new/html/mainlaws.html#summary (9 September 2003).

Warriner, G. Keith, Kathleen McSpurren, and Alice Nabalamda. "Social justice and environmental equity: Distributing environmental quality." *Environments* 29, iss. 1 (August 2001) 85–99. Available at InfoTrac OneFile Plus. (22 January 2003).

Washington, Booker T. "Atlanta Exposition Address," http://www.ashbrook.org/library/19/btwashington/atlantaaddress.html (6 January 2003).

Washington, Valora, and Ura Jean Oyemade Bailey. *Project Head Start: Models and Strategies for the Twenty-first Century.* New York and London: Garland Publishing Company, 1995.

Weinberg, Anita, and Maria Woltjen. "Lead poisoning persists despite laws, city codes." *Chicago Daily Law Bulletin.* Law Bulletin Publishing Company, 28 October 2002. Available at LexisNexis Academic (6 January 2003).

Wenglinsky, H. "Finance equalization and within-school equity: The relationship between education spending and the social distribution of achievement." *Educational Researcher* 20, no. 4 (1998) 269–283.

Western, Bruce. "The impact of incarceration on wage mobility and inequality." *American Sociological Review* 67, Iss. 4 (August 2002) 526–546.

Western, Bruce, and Becky Pettit. "Incarceration and racial inequality in men's employment." *Industrial and Labor Relations Review* 54, Iss. 1 (October 2000) 3–16.

Whitehead, Alfred North. *The Aims of Education and Other Essays.* New York: New American Library, 1929.

Widerquist, Karl. "Checkerboard II: An analysis of tax effort, equalization, and extraordinary aid." Educational Policies Panel, February 2001. http://www.edpriorities.org/Pubs/pubs.html (24 October 2002).

Wilson, William Junius. *The Truly Disadvantaged: The Inner City, the Underclass, and Public Policy.* Chicago: The University of Chicago Press, 1987.

Wilson, William Junius. *When Work Disappears: The World of the New Urban Poor.* New York: Vintage Books, 1997.

Winglee, Marianne, David Marker, Allison Henderson, Beth Aronstamm Young, and Lee Hoffman. "A recommended approach to providing high school dropout and completion rates at the state level." *Education Statistics Quarterly* 2, iss. 1 (n.d.), http://nces.ed.gov/programs/quarterly/vol_2/2_1index.asp#top (1 July 2006).

Wise, Arthur. *Rich Schools Poor Schools.* Chicago: University of Chicago Press, 1968.

Wise, Tim. "Not-so-little white lies: Education and the myth of black anti-intellectualism." Znet, *Z Magazine,* 6 November 2002, http://www.zmag.org/sustainers/content/2002-11/26wise.cfm (23 March 2003).

Wolk, David S. *The Equal Educational Opportunity Act: Measuring Equity.* (17 April 2001), http://www.state.vt.us/educ.act60/EEO_Report_05_01.pdf (1 October 2001).

Wollstonecraft, Mary. *A Vindication of the Rights of Women.* Edited by Carol H. Poston. New York and London: W.W. Norton, 1975.

Wood, R. Craig, and David Thompson. *Educational Finance Law: Constitutional Challenges to State Aid Plans—An Analysis of Strategies.* Topeka, KS: National Organization on Legal Problems in Education, 1996.

Woodrow Wilson Foundation. Raising Our Sights: No Senior Left Behind. Final Report of the National Commission on the High School Senior Year. Woodrow Wilson Foundation, October 2001, http://www.woodrow.org (4 April 2003).

Woolley, Helen Thompson. *An Experimental Study of Children at Work and in School Between the Ages of Fourteen and Eighteen Years.* New York: Macmillan, 1929.

Work Group of the Advisory Committee on Childhood Lead Poisoning Prevention. A Review of Health Effects of Blood Levels <10mg/dL. Centers for Disease Control, 23 February 2004, http://www.cdc.gov/nceh/lead/ACCLPP/meetingMinutes/lessThan10MtgMAR04.pdf (7 July 2006).

World Health Organization Web site. "Global estimates of maternal mortality for 1995: Results of an in-depth review, analysis and estimation strategy," http://www.who.int/reproductivehealth/publications/RHR_01_9_maternal_mortality_estimates/statement_on_maternal_mortality_estimates.en.html (16 January 2003).

World Socialist Web site. "One in four US children under six live in poverty," http://www.wsws.org/news/1998.july1998/poc-j22.shtml (12 February 2003).

World Socialist Web site. "The betrayal of the Ontario teachers' strike: The lessons for all workers." The Editorial Board. (17 November 1997), http://www.wsws.org/workers/1997/nov1997/ont-n17.shtml (9 March 2004).

Wright, R. O., S. W. Tsiah, J. Schwartz, R. J. Wright, and H. Hu. "Association between iron deficiency and blood lead level in a longitudinal analysis of children followed in an urban primary care clinic." *Journal of Pediatrics* 142, no. 1 (January 2003) 9–14.

Yarab, Donald S. "Case Comment: *Edgewood Independent School District* v. *Kirby:* An Education in School Finance Reform." *Case Western Reserve Law Journal* 40 (1990), available at LexisNexis legal research (19 September 2002) 889–898.

Zeigler, Michael. "Panel rejects suit over aid to schools" *New York Law Journal* (December 31, 2001). Available at LexisNexis legal research (25 March 2002).

Authorities

Cases

Abbott v. *Burke*, No. M-245, 2005 N.J. LEXIS 1624 (N.J. December 19, 2005). [The last of the *Abbott* v. *Burke* cases in New Jersey as of this writing.]

African Am. Legal Defense Fund ex rel (named) students of the New York City Pub. Sch. System and their Parents v. *New York State Dep't. of Educ. (AALDF)*, No. 95 Civ. 3039 (RO), 1998 U.S. Dist. LEXIS 8496 (S.D. N.Y. June 8, 1998).

Alexander v. *Sandoval (Sandoval), Individually and ex rel all others similarly situated*, No. 99-1908, 2001 U.S. LEXIS 3367 (U.S. April 24, 2001).

Anderson v. *Vermont*, No. 98-047, 1998 Vt. LEXIS 479 (Vt. December 22, 1998).

Board of Educ. of Oklahoma City Public Schools v. *Dowell*, No. 89-1080, 1991 U.S. LEXIS 484 (U.S. January 15, 1991).

Board of Educ. Levittown Union Free Sch. Dist. v. *Nyquist*, 1978 N.Y. Misc. LEXIS 2270 (N.Y. Sup. Ct. June 23, 1978).

Board of Educ. Levittown Union Free Sch. Dist. v. *Nyquist*, 1981 N.Y. App. Div. LEXIS 14777 (N.Y. App. Div. October 26, 1981).

Board of Educ. Levittown Union Free Sch. Dist. v. *Nyquist*, 1982 N.Y. LEXIS 3535 (N.Y. June 23, 1982).

Bolling v. *Sharpe*, No. 8, 1954 U.S. LEXIS 2095 (U.S. May 17, 1954).

Brigham v. *State of Vermont (Brigham v. State)*, No. 96-502, 1997 Vt. LEXIS 13 (Vt. February 5, 1997).

Brown v. *Board of Educ. (Brown I)*, No. 1, 1954 U.S. LEXIS 2094 (U.S. May 17, 1954).

Brown v. *Board of Educ. (Brown II)*, No. 1, 1955 U.S. LEXIS 734 (U.S. May 31, 1955).

Burlington County NAACP v. *Township of Mt. Laurel (Mt. Laurel I)*, 1975 N.J. LEXIS 181 (N.J. March 24, 1975).

(Southern) Burlington Co. NAACP v. *Township of Mt. Laurel (Mt. Laurel II)*, 1983 N.J. LEXIS 2344 (N.J. January 20, 1983).

Campaign for Fiscal Equity Inc. v. *New York (CFE Ia)*, and *City of New York* v. *New York (City v. State* trial court), Nos. 111070/93 and 401210/93, 1994 N.Y. Misc. LEXIS 418 (N.Y. Sup. Ct. June 21, 1994).

Campaign for Fiscal Equity, Inc., v. *New York (CFE Ib)* and *City of New York* v. *New York (City v. State* Appellate Division). Nos. 52842 and 52843, 1994 N.Y. App. Div. LEXIS 11329 (N.Y. App. Div. November 15, 1994).

315

Campaign for Fiscal Equity v. *New York (CFE/1995* or *CFE Ic)*, No. 117A, 1995 N.Y. LEXIS 1145 (N.Y. June 15, 1995).

Campaign for Fiscal Equity (CFI IIa) v. *State*, No. 111070/93, 2001 N.Y. Misc. LEXIS 1 (N.Y. Sup. Ct., N.Y. Co., January 9, 2001).

Campaign for Fiscal Equity, Inc. (CFE IIb) v. *New York*, No. 5330, 2002 N.Y. App. Div. LEXIS 7252, (N.Y. App. Div. June 25, 2002).

Campaign for Fiscal Equity, Inc. (CFE IIc), Respondents v. *State of New York et al., Appellants*, No. 74, the Court of Appeals of New York, 2003, LEXIS N.Y. 1678.

Campaign for Fiscal Equity, Respondents v. *State of New York, Appellants*, No. 6915, 2006 N.Y. App. Div. LEXIS 3598 (N.Y. App. Div. March 23, 2006).

Ceasar [sic] v. *Pataki (Caesar* v. *Pataki)*, No, 98 Civ. 8532, 2002 U.S. Dist. LEXIS 5098 (S.D. N.Y. March 25, 2002).

City of New York v. *New York (City* v. *State)*, No. 117B, 1995 N.Y. LEXIS 1144 (N.Y. June 15, 1995).

Edgewood Indep. Sch. Dist. (Edgewood I) v. *Kirby*, 1989 Tex. LEXIS 129 (Tex. October 2, 1989).

Edgewood Indep. Sch. Dist. (Edgewood II) v. *Kirby*, No. D-0378, 1991 Tex. LEXIS 21 (Tex. February 25, 1991).

(In re) Engel v. *Vitale*, 1959 N.Y. Misc. LEXIS 3126, (N.Y. Sup. Ct. August 24, 1959).

Engel v. *Vitale*, No. 468, 1962 U.S. LEXIS 487 (U.S. April 3, 1962).

Freeman v. *Pitts*, No. 89-1290, 1992 U.S. LEXIS 2114 (U.S. March 31, 1992).

Goss v. *Lopez*, No. 73-898, 1975 U.S. LEXIS 2095 (U.S. May 17, 1954).

Gratz v. *Bollinger*, No. 02-516, 2003 U.S. LEXIS 4801 (U.S. June 30, 2003).

Graus ex rel Graus, individually and ex rel all others similarly situated v. *Kaladjian*, 93 Civ. 3743 (JSR), 1998 U.S. Dist. LEXIS 6020 (S.D. N.Y. April 28, 1998).

Green (Green) v. *County Sch. Bd. Of New Kent County*, No. 695, 1968 U.S. LEXIS (U.S. May 27, 1968).

Grutter v. *Bollinger*, No. 02-241, 2003 U.S. LEXIS 4800 (U.S. June 23, 2003).

Hans v. *Louisiana*, No. 4, 1890 U.S. LEXIS 1943 (U.S. March 3, 1890).

Hayden v. *Pataki*, No. 00 Civ. 8586, 2004 U.S. Dist. LEXIS 10863 (S.D.N.Y. June 14, 2004).

Horton v. *Meskill*, Nos. 12499, 12501, 12501, 1985 Conn. LEXIS 665 (Conn. January 15, 1985).

Keyes v. *Sch. Dist. #1*, No. 71-507, 1973 U.S. LEXIS 43 (U.S. June 21, 1973).

Kirby v. *Edgewood Indep. Sch. Dist.*, No. 3-87-190-CV, 1988 Tex. App. LEXIS 3292 (Tex. App. December 14, 1988).

Lake View Sch. Dist. #25 v. *Huckabee*, No. 01-836; 91 S.W.3d 472; 2002 Ark. LEXIS 603; November 21, 2002.

Lau v. *Nichols*, No. 72-6520, 1974 U.S. LEXIS 151 (U.S. January 21, 1974).

Milliken v. *Bradley (Milliken I)*, No. 73-434, 1974 U.S. LEXIS 94 (U.S. July 25, 1974).

Milliken v. *Bradley (Milliken II)*, No. 76-447, 1977 U.S. LEXIS 141 (U.S. June 27, 1977).

Missouri v. *Jenkins*, No. 93-1823, 1995 U.S. LEXIS 4041 (U.S. June 12, 1995).

Montoy v. *State*, No. 92,032, 2005 Kan. LEXIS 2 (Kan. January 3, 2005).

New York Civil Liberties Union v. *New York (NYCLU,* NY Appellate Division), No. 93834, 2004 N.Y. App. Div. LEXIS 881 (N.Y. App. Div. January 29, 2004).

New York Civil Liberties Union (NYCLU, NY Court of Appeals) v. *New York,* No. 3, 2005 N.Y. LEXIS 172 (N.Y. February 15, 2005).

New York Performance Standards Consortium v. *New York State Department of Education,* 293 A.D.2d 113; 714 N.Y.S.2d 349; 2002 N.Y. App. Div. LEXIS 4790.

(Stone ex rel) Paynter (Paynter, Appellate Division*), and ex re All Others Similarly Situated* v. *New York,* No. (232), CA 99-724, 2000 N.Y. App. Div. LEXIS 3626, at *820 (N.Y. App. Div. March 29, 2000).

Paynter, Individually and ex rel All Others Similarly Situated, No. 98/10280, 2000 N.Y. Misc. LEXIS 569 (N.Y. Sup. Ct. November 14, 2000).

(Stone ex rel.) Paynter (Paynter, Court of Appeals) v. *New York,* No. 75, 2003 N.Y. LEXIS 1672 (N.Y. June 26, 2003).

Pennsylvania Ass'n for Retarded Children (PARC) v. *Pennsylvania,* No. 71-42, 1972 U.S. Dist. LEXIS 13874 (E.D. Pa. May 5, 1972).

Plessy v. *Ferguson,* No. 210, 1896 U.S. LEXIS 3390, (U.S. May 18, 1896).

Pontiac v. *Spellings,* Civil Action No. 05-CV-71535-DT, 2005 U.S. Dist. LEXIS 29253 (November 23, 2005).

Powell v. *Ridge,* No. 98-1223, 1998 U.S. Dist. LEXIS 22328 (E.D. Pa. November 18, 1998).

Plyler v. *Doe,* 457 United States 202, 45 U.S. 582 (1982).

Reform Educational Financing Inequities Today v. *Cuomo (REFIT),* NY Appellate Division, No. 92-08663, 1993 N.Y. App. Div. LEXIS 12346 (N.Y. App. Div. June 15, 1995).

Reform Educational Financing Inequities Today v. *Cuomo (REFIT),* NY Court of Appeals), No. 2, 1995 N.Y. LEXIS 1137 (N.Y. June 15, 1995).

Rhode Island v. *Lead Industries Association, inc.,* No. 99-5226, 2005 R.I. Super. LEXIS 79 (May 18, 2005).

Robinson v. *Cahill,* [No number in original], 1972 N.J. LEXIS 388 (N.J. Super. Ct. January 19, 1972). [The first of the *Robinson* v. *Cahill* cases which became the *Abbott* v. *Burke* cases in New Jersey.]

Rochester Board of Educ. v. *Nyquist* and *Levittown Board of Educ.* v. *Nyquist,* No. 82-639; No. 82-655, 1983 U.S. LEXIS 3048 (U.S. January 17, 1983).

Rose (Rose) v. *Council for Better Education, Inc.,* No. 88-SC-804-TG, 1989 Ky. LEXIS 55 (Ky. June 8, 1989).

San Antonio Indep. Sch. Dist. v. *Rodriguez (Rodriguez),* 411 U.S. 1, 56 (1973).

Sandoval v. *Hagan,* No. 96-D-1875-N, 1998 U.S. Dist. LEXIS 8301 (M.D. Ala. June 3 1998).

Sandoval, individually and ex rel all others similarly situated v. *Hagan,* No. 98-6598, 1999 U.S. App. LEXIS 30722 (11th Cir. November 30, 1999).

Serrano v. *Priest (Serrano I),* No. 29820, 1971 Cal. LEXIS 273, (Cal. August 30, 1971).

Serrano v. *Priest (Serrano II),* No. 30398, 1976 Cal. LEXIS 380 (Cal. December 30, 1976).

Sheff v. *O'Neill,* No. 15255, 1996 Conn. LEXIS 239 (Conn. July 9, 1996).

Spallone v. *United States; Longo* v. *United States; Chema* v. *United States; City of Yonkers*
     (Yonkers) v. *United States,* Nos. A-172, A-173, A-174, A-175, 1988 U.S. LEXIS
     3284 (U.S. September 1, 1988).
Stowe (Stowe) Citizens for Responsible Government v. *Vermont,* No. 98-116, 1999 Vt.
     Lexis 41 (Vt. March 3, 1999).
Swann (Swann) v. *Charlotte-Mecklenberg Bd. of Education,* No. 281, 1971 U.S. LEXIS
     52 (U.S. April 20, 1971).
Tennessee Small Sch. Systems v. *McWherter (McWherter I),* 1992 Tenn. App. LEXIS 486
     (Tenn. Ct. App. June 5, 1992).
Tennessee Small Sch. Systems v. *McWherter (McWherter II),* S.C. No. 01-S01-9209-CH-
     0010, 1993 Tenn. LEXIS 114 (Tenn. March 22, 1993).
United States v. *Yonkers Board of Educ.,* No. 93-6342, 1994 U.S. LEXIS 16681,
     (partially decided 2d Cir. July 5, 1994).
University of California v. *Bakke (Bakke),* No. 76-811, 1978 U.S. LEXIS 5 (U.S. June
     28, 1978).
Van Dusartz v. *Hatfield,* No. 3-71 Civ. 243, 1971 U.S. Dist. LEXIS 11281 (D. Minn.
     October 12, 1971).

Statutes

The Civil Rights Act of 1964, 42 U.S.C. 2000e *et seq.*
The Individuals with Disabilities Education Act (IDEA), 20 USCS §1400, *et seq.*
No Child Left Behind Act of 2001(NCLB), 20 USCS §6301, *et seq.*
Personal Responsibility and Work Opportunity Reconciliation Act (PRWORA)
     of 1996, 8 U.S.C. 1601 §§ 1601 *et seq.* (2005).
Personal Responsibility and Individual Development for Everyone Act (PRIDE),
     Committee Reports, 108th Congress, 1st Session, Senate Report 108-162,
     108 S. Rpt. 162, LexisNexis Congressional (accessed 11/21/03).

Index